Publications on Russia and Eastern Europe
of the Institute for Comparative
and Foreign Area Studies
Number 8

Petr Tkachev, the Critic as Jacobin

DEBORAH HARDY

University of Washington Press

Seattle and London

This book is sponsored by the Russian and East European Program of the Institute for Comparative and Foreign Area Studies, University of Washington, Seattle.

Library of Congress Cataloging in Publication Data
Hardy, Deborah, 1927-
    Petr Tkachev, the critic as Jacobin.

    (Publications on Russia and Eastern Europe of the Institute for Comparative and Foreign Area Studies; no. 8)
    Bibliography: p.
    Includes index.
    1. Tkachev, Petr Nikitich, 1844-1886. 2. Revolutionists—Russia—Biography. I. Series: Washington (State). University. Institute for Comparative and Foreign Area Studies. Publications on Russia and Eastern Europe; no. 8.
HX312.T55H37   322.4'2'0924 [B]   76-49170
ISBN 0-295-95547-3

To Scott, John, and Bridget
with gratitude for their
encouragement and support

Contents

Preface

This work attempts to present a complete biography of Petr Nikitich Tkachev, 1844-86, encompassing not only the genesis, development, and vicissitudes of this young revolutionary's thought but also those associations, experiences, and activities that aided in conditioning his ideas.

Tkachev's biographer has no easy task. The atmosphere of St. Petersburg where this young radical first tried his journalistic wings was clouded by police, censors, and occasional other hindrances. Perhaps these conditions caused Tkachev's early developed penchant for secrecy —even, his enemies said, for mystification—to the extent that he probably himself destroyed many early written fragments of value. He never kept a diary. He seems seldom to have entered into correspondence; if he did he must have urged the recipients of his letters to destroy them at once, for only three such documents have ever been unearthed. He was rather shy and not given to expressing his own emotions in conversation, or at least so his acquaintances report. He had few close friends who knew him well outside of his common-law wife, who never wrote about him. Once he had emigrated to Western Europe he took pains to cover his tracks against police investigation so that his activities there must be deduced from a smattering of anecdotes remembered by the people he met. Even police records in places where he lived provide little or no information, for whether or not it was true, he evidently thought of himself as constantly on the run. Consequently, his ideas, hopes, and idiosyncrasies must be extracted from his published works, from those few unpublished remnants that were confiscated and preserved by the history-fostering Russian police, and from the scattered reports of friends and enemies.

Tkachev's mind was conditioned by his readings and his experiences. About the first we can make only a fair guess. He was an inveterate citer of sources in his articles, and it is possible to compile lists of his prolific readings from references and occasional name dropping. But those were books that were legal in Russia and could be cited in the press. On another level the problem will never be solved, for Tkachev himself refused to tell. Although they were never mentioned (not even in his long articles on influential writings in the Russian revolutionary movement) he may have known such items as the leaflet "Young Russia," which appeared in the St. Petersburg underground in 1862; he may have even been influenced by it. He may have read a smuggled copy of Buonarotti and carefully refrained from saying so. Even free from censorship in Geneva, he never cited these works, so his biographer is left without definite proof. Educated guesses are prevalent in this manuscript and often stand at variance with the equally conjectural assertions of other scholars. It would be more of a sin to omit them than to risk being wrong.

In terms of environmental influences Tkachev emerges as particularly vulnerable. He was a quiet man who lived in an exciting time, and he knew it. Although he was always somewhat of a loner, he absorbed the spirit of his youth in St. Petersburg and later wrote of it at considerable length. He knew, albeit casually, journalists and lawyers, schoolteachers and students. Young women romantically involved in the women's rights movement sought him out. He was concerned with, though not a leader in, the student radical set, supporting its drive for privileges long after he dropped out of the university without finishing his degree. Without becoming active in such revolutionary circles as we can trace he absorbed the atmosphere of his city, and some of it (the tensions, the polemicizing, the conspiracy, the threatening violence) became part of his personality and his thinking for the rest of his life. He never changed, not even when the younger generation did. To a great degree he remained a "man of the sixties" when others moved on to a new decade; the most perceptive of his contemporaries saw it themselves. The environment of his youth was a crucial determining factor in the thinking of his lifetime, and for this reason the present writer feels compelled to include it.

In the sixties, when he was not yet thirty, Tkachev built his foundations. In Russia in the legal press he wrote more fluidly, thoughtfully, productively, and perhaps even more honestly than ever again. His later revolutionary writings (barely one-sixth of the page space in his collected works) represent a culmination of sorts, the narrowing and focusing of things he had already thought about, the driving of his ideas into a pointed spire, from whose teetering heights, at least for Tkachev in 1876, there was no place to turn. To understand this radical who died young, one must know his earliest work. This biography attempts to describe Tkachev's ideas from the beginning, to investigate his thinking about worlds remote from revolutionary plans, and to relate these early ideas to what was to come.

Insofar as sources permit I propose to present Tkachev as a child of his times, greatly molded by the atmosphere and experiences of his youth, writing as a literary critic and radical, philosopher and revolutionary, women's liberationist and populist, man of the sixties long past their close, and finally that dreaded, infamous Jacobin conspirator whom contemporary Russian radicals came to despise so violently.

Acknowledgments

No person writes a book alone. The individuals and institutions that have contributed to this one are many, and to all of them I express my deep gratitude. In particular, I would mention the several readers of this manuscript—some whose identity is known to me and others who remain unknown—whose suggestions enormously contributed to whatever it has finally become. The American Council of Learned Societies sponsored my research trip to Western European archives in search of Tkachev. Margery Lang and her colleagues at the Institute for Comparative and Foreign Area Studies have not only been of invaluable assistance but have been a great pleasure to work with.

Material in this manuscript, always in greatly different form, has appeared in print in the *Slavic Review, Russian Review*, and *Canadian Slavic Studies*.

A special paragraph must be reserved to Professor Donald W. Treadgold, who not only started me on Tkachev but has seen me through this and other projects and remains my respected academic advisor and personal friend.

Without my parents, who helped me through many difficult years, this book could never have been written.

Petr Tkachev, the Critic as Jacobin

1

The New Generation

In 1859 Alexander Herzen, the most respected of the older Russian radicals, launched a surprise attack against contemporary Russian criticism, an attack that was at once recognized as directed primarily against N. G. Chernyshevskii and his colleagues.[1] Herzen was living in London where, in collaboration with his long-time friend and companion N. P. Ogarev, he edited *Kolokol* (The Bell), the most successful Russian-language émigré journal in history. Chernyshevskii, with his colleague N. A. Dobroliubov, worked for and determined the policies of *Sovremennik* (Contemporary), the leading St. Petersburg radical journal of its day.[2] Although one Soviet scholar has speculated that Herzen's attack might have been directed at several Russian periodicals, it was taken by Chernyshevskii, Dobroliubov, and the *Contemporary*'s editor, the poet N. A. Nekrasov, to be an insult meant entirely for

1. Herzen's article, entitled (in English) "Very Dangerous!!!" has been reprinted from *Kolokol*, June 1, 1859, in his collected works. See Alexander Herzen (A. I. Gertsen), *Sobranie sochinenii v tridtsati tomakh*, 14: 116-21. Many accounts of the episode described in this chapter have appeared in the Soviet press. Perhaps the most balanced was written by the historian B. P. Kozmin, "Vystuplenie Gertsena protiv 'Sovremennika' v 1859 godu," included in the collection of Kozmin's articles, *Iz istorii revoliutsionnoi mysli v Rossii*. Kozmin's account remains authoritative in spite of some scholarly disputes that have arisen over minor points. Much of the material here presented is drawn from Kozmin.

2. *Sovremennik* was actually edited by N. A. Nekrasov, but policy remained mostly in the hands of Chernyshevskii, the journal's strongest contributor, whose name has long been associated with this periodical.

them.[3] Indeed Herzen had told a friend in London that he planned to give the *Contemporary* a "dressing-down."[4]

The magnitude of the illegal *Bell*'s readership in Russia—Herzen was certain the tsar himself read it[5]—made the attack into a cause célèbre among Russian journalists and their readers. The rumor flew that Herzen's bitterness arose in response to Dobroliubov's long article on "Literary Trifles of the Past Year," in which the young critic had not been easy on the men of the older generation.[6] By coincidence, Dobroliubov's review of the novel *Oblomov* by Ivan Goncharov was in press at the same time as Herzen's attack.[7] Its appearance solidified St. Petersburg opinion as to the nature of the rift in the radical press, for here Dobroliubov was even less sympathetic toward the men of Herzen's generation as Goncharov had portrayed them.

Herzen's article, entitled "Very Dangerous!!!" accused the new generation of Russian critics of lashing out unfairly against its predecessors, of making fun of the genuine sufferings of the gentry of the forties—the "superfluous men," Turgenev had dubbed them[8]—and thus of playing into the hands of the reactionary camp. Herzen did not admire the witty and sharp-tongued polemics of the *Contemporary* and the St. Petersburg press. Accusing them of misusing satire, he came perilously close to calling the new critics heartless. He suggested that the effects of their bitter humor were comparable to the aims sought by that paid corps of despised journalists who once surrounded Nicholas I —that is, the defeat and division of the Russian radical movement. "Very Dangerous!!!" urged the new generation to cease and desist.

---

3. See T. I. Usakina, "Statia Gertsena 'Very Dangerous!!!' i polemika vokrug 'oblichitelnoi literatury' v zhurnalistike 1857-1859 gg.," in *Revoliutsionnaia situatsiia v Rossii v 1859-1861 gg.*, pp. 260-61, 265-66. Cf. Kozmin, *Iz istorii*, p. 607. Usakina believes Herzen may also have been polemicizing against *Otechestvennye zapiski* and *Biblioteka dlia chteniia*.

4. Usakina, p. 265.

5. He made this statement in his memoirs (Alexander Herzen, *My Past and Thoughts*, 3: 1299).

6. Usakina, p. 265; A. E. Koshovenko, "K voprosu o londonskoi vstreche N. G. Chernyshevskogo s A. I. Gertsenom v 1859 g. i formule 'Kavelin v kvadrate,'" in *Revoliutsionnaia situatsiia v Rossii v 1859-1861 gg.*, p. 278.

7. Usakina, p. 257. Goncharov's *Oblomov* was published in 1859 in the usual serialized form in *Otechestvennye zapiski*, another St. Petersburg journal. One of Dobroliubov's most famous critical writings, this review is included in his *Selected Philosophical Essays*, pp. 174-218. Herzen was probably also offended by the sarcastic tone of Dobroliubov's new column *Svistok* appearing regularly in *Sovremennik*.

8. The term was first coined by Turgenev in 1850. It was accepted by Herzen who frequently used it himself (Herzen, *Sobranie sochinenii*, 14: 572).

The astonishing attack seemed, as Franco Venturi suggests,[9] to have allied Herzen temporarily with the liberals against the radicals although even certain liberal critics might have fallen into the company Herzen accused. Chernyshevskii himself took a similar position, and he later called Herzen a "Kavelin squared" after one of the leaders of Russian liberalism.[10] Dobroliubov was so disturbed as to suggest the possibility of a duel.[11] Within a few weeks of the bitter exchange Chernyshevskii, regaining his temper, took the bull by the horns and made a special pilgrimage to London in June 1859 to meet with the grand old man in person.

The actual meeting of these two giants of contemporary Russian radicalism did little to resolve the issues. The men were not persuaded to each others' views. Luckily a young Russian named G. E. Blagosvetlov, who later made his name editing another radical journal, was visiting Herzen at the time. He reported the antagonists' impressions of each other: Herzen of Chernyshevskii, "An astonishingly intelligent man. His presumption of it is only the more surprising. He believes that *Contemporary* is the navel of Russia. We others, sinners—these people have buried us"; and Chernyshevskii of Herzen, "What a brain! But how backward! When one looks from close up, what there is inside is still a Muscovite *barin*!"[12] Neither Chernyshevskii nor Herzen recorded their conversations in writing; the former described them in a letter to Dobroliubov as "boring."[13] He told another colleague that he suggested that Herzen end his sniping and instead propose a constructive system for either revolution or reform.[14] Still elsewhere he referred to Herzen as "an interesting fossilized bone"[15] and described part of their conversation to M. A. Antonovich of the *Contemporary:*

When I finished Herzen looked at me with an Olympian stare and in a cold, dis-

9. Franco Venturi, *Roots of Revolution*, p. 158.

10. Herzen, *Sobranie sochinenii*, 14: 495. This phrase has been subject to interpretation and reinterpretation among Soviet scholars, many of whom seem reluctant to believe that Chernyshevskii could so identify Herzen with the liberals. Koshovenko's interpretation is that Chernyshevskii was comparing Herzen's "aristocratic" life style with that of Kavelin rather than equating their political positions (p. 273). On K. D. Kavelin see Daniel Field, "Kavelin and Russian Liberalism," *Slavic Review* 32, no. 1 (March 1973): 59-78.

11. Venturi, p. 158.

12. Armand Coquart, *Dmitri Pisarev, 1840-1868, et l'idéologie du nihilisme russe*, p. 71, note 1.

13. Koshovenko, p. 272.

14. Venturi, p. 158; Herzen, *Sobranie sochinenii*, 14: 495.

15. Quoted in Evgenii Lampert, *Studies in Rebellion*, p. 255.

respectful tone pronounced this decision: "Yes, from your narrow partisan view-point this is understandable and can be justified, but from a general logical point of view, this merits strict condemnation and cannot be justified."[16]

After four days of talks Chernyshevskii returned to St. Petersburg, the situation still unremedied.

The hostility of the two journals did not immediately disappear. Although Herzen explained publicly that he had no personalities in mind when he wrote his "Very Dangerous!!!" article, he nevertheless subtly continued his barbs in subsequent issues of the *Bell*. A year later he was still attacking the younger generation. His article "The Super-fluous Men and the Bilious Ones" was written with particular reference to Chernyshevskii, Dobroliubov, and Antonovich, all of whom were sons of priests.

All of them were hypochondriacs and physically ill, did not drink wine, and were afraid of open windows; all looked with studied despair at the present and re-minded one of monks who from love of their neighbor came to hurting all human-ity and cursed everything in the world from desire to bless something.[17]

In March 1860 the *Bell* printed an anonymous letter, identified simply as "from a Russian," decrying Herzen's lack of actionism and his loss of faith in revolution as a solution to Russia's woes: "Our situation is frightful, intolerable. The axe alone can deliver us from it, and nothing will do it except the axe. . . . Change your tone! Let your bell no longer ring for prayer, but strike the tocsin. Call Russia to take up the axe."[18] Russian radical society buzzed with the rumor that Chernyshevskii had written the letter himself. Soviet scholars have demonstrated convincingly that he did not.[19] The writer remains anonymous, but the barb hit its mark.

The entire episode is indicative of the generation gap that separated the "men of the forties," of whom Herzen remained the prime example, from the "men of the sixties," whom Chernyshevskii may be said to have anticipated. Both designations, somewhat chronologically inac-curate, have gone down in history. In 1859 Chernyshevskii was thirty-one years old and Herzen forty-seven; the age gap seems hardly insur-mountable. Yet there is no doubt that to a great extent the younger man represented the new outlook prevalent among Russian youth following the drastic defeats of the Crimean War. The confrontation of

16. Quoted in Usakina, p. 267.

17. Quoted in Lampert, *Studies in Rebellion*, pp. 254-55.

18. Quoted in Coquart, p. 18; cf. Lampert, *Studies in Rebellion*, p. 253.

19. See B. P. Kozmin's article on the subject in *Literaturnoe nasledstvo*, nos. 25-26 (1936), pp. 544-75; there is an interesting account in William F. Woehrlin, *Chernyshevskii*, pp. 252-56.

Chernyshevskii and Herzen in London in 1859 may indeed be regarded as the symbolic meeting of two generations, whose points of view merged in certain respects but differed greatly in others.

Twenty years had seen many changes in Russia, and the half-decade following 1860 was to see even more. To recapitulate the history of the entire period is beyond the scope of this work. Nevertheless, the reader cannot comprehend the Russian radical son of 1860 and the differences between him and his father of 1845 without some idea of the social and intellectual mutations that had occurred and were impending.

The old generation, particularly in the minds of the new, had been distinguished by a special social, educational, intellectual, and psychological pattern. Socially most of the men of the forties in the articulate Russian radical group were born into the comfortable gentry, Russia's well-to-do landowning class. These intellectual leaders of Russia owed their leisure to the institution of serfdom that they themselves, to their credit, often deplored. Many of them never had to work for a living, or if they did they assumed semihonorary positions in the civil service. Education was expected of them: education first by governesses, then by travel, then through a few years at a German university. During the long reign of Nicholas I (1825-55) higher education in Russia came close to being their particular prerogative; Count S. S. Uvarov, minister of education, felt strongly that no one should be educated above his station in life, and entry into the Russian universities was restricted accordingly. Intellectually these young men inherited from the past generation, at home and abroad, the outlook and principles of a romantic age.[20] Excitedly they absorbed the plays of Schiller, the philosophy of Schelling and Hegel, the utopianism of Fourier.[21] They fought duels like Pushkin and swore blood oaths like Herzen. Their backgrounds lent them a penchant for speculation and philosophy. Their intellectual enthusiasms lay in impractical realms, remote from the immediate problems around them, or so the younger generation claimed.

To their sons these men of the forties seemed psychologically unfit for the deeds they sometimes contemplated: they were capable only of dreams, hopes, and disappointments. Even those who understood what Russia needed were unable to force themselves to action.

---

20. Early Russian romanticism and its relationship to the literary currents of Western Europe has recently been explored by Peter K. Christoff in *The Third Heart*.

21. Martin Malia in his excellent biography of the young Herzen entitled *Alexander Herzen and the Birth of Russian Socialism* finds in Herzen's intellectual interests a recapitulation of the commitments of many other Russian radical thinkers.

They felt guilty and inadequate; they wrote in their diaries about it. But they did not know what to do. If this picture painted by the younger generation admitted of many exceptions—the critic Vissarion Belinskii was the son of a naval doctor, the grandson of a priest, and not wealthy at all; Nikolai Gogol was a civil servant—it contained enough half-truths so the exceptions could be ignored. To the men of the sixties, the men of the forties often seemed foolish, maudlin, and hopelessly old-fashioned.

Herzen provided an outstanding example.[22] He was par excellence a "repentant nobleman," to use the phrase Turgenev applied to those men of the gentry whose consciences led them to despise serfdom yet whose way of life depended upon it. These men felt superfluous because they were left outside the dynamics of their society, and many of them, isolated on remote provincial estates, had little inclination or opportunity to make socially constructive contributions. Born (illegitimately) to a wealthy father, raised on estates redolent of the gentry way of life, Herzen was in youth a man of leisure with time for contemplation, speculation, education, and romantic flights of fancy. Circumstances left him few other outlets. The government of Nicholas I did not encourage radical journalism, so Herzen's youthful hopes were recorded in a diary rather than in the periodical press. He did not have to earn a living, and what positions he held he accepted more out of his own interest than out of financial need. He led a life rich in spirit, culture, contemplation, and ideals. It is to his great credit that he recognized the unfairness of the system in which he grew up. Perhaps, however, Herzen never completely outgrew a feeling of nostalgia for his childhood and youth. Years later, as the Soviet historian B. P. Kozmin points out in his perceptive study of the Herzen-Chernyshevskii polemic, Herzen identified with and understood his generation. He felt only pity for the lost nobleman who was isolated and had found no constructive position in the world. He saw the Onegins and the Pechorins, as he himself termed them, as truthful, positive forces for their time.[23] Goncharov's Oblomov was not a typical representative of the superfluous man but a *reductio ad absurdum*; nevertheless Herzen understood him and resented the patronizing treatment accorded him in the new Russian press. Constantly denying any superior rights to his own class, Herzen was nevertheless unwilling to admit its uselessness and negativeness. It is on this basis that Kozmin analyzes Herzen's 1859

---

22. Malia's biography of Herzen's early years will probably remain a classic. Herzen's own delightful autobiography, *My Past and Thoughts*, has long been one.

23. Kozmin, *Iz istorii*, pp. 613-16; Herzen, *Sobranie sochinenii*, 14: 118. Onegin was the romantic hero of one of Pushkin's greatest poems; Pechorin is Lermontov's *Hero of Our Times*.

attack on *Contemporary*, the journal in which Dobroliubov had been sarcastic and harsh with Herzen's generation.[24]

After the death of Nicholas I Russia was ripe for change. In describing formation of the new radical intelligentsia, Soviet historians may exaggerate the role of the *raznochintsy*, who were drawn from many ranks and classes: the sons of civil servants, of priests, of shopkeepers, of Russia's smattering of professional men. Yet surely in the years after 1855 rivers of change were eroding the rigid Russian class system. Universities became melting pots. If their students still consisted for the most part of "repentant" and other young noblemen, men of many other classes now joined them to spice the old fare, to add new vigor to the old brew. Some of the newcomers were city-bred; many of them were only one generation removed from the land. Some of them had been born directly of the nobility. They nonetheless rejected their families and the gentry way of life in more violent terms than Herzen had ever considered. They became in a broad sense—and indeed this is one variant definition of the term *intelligentsia* as it was originally used—déclassés, men of no class at all, men who had abandoned their origins because their tastes, thoughts, and inclinations led them to join each other in a new social group. Thus the radical intelligentsia forming in Russian universities was composed of men who put class origins behind them. Their time in the sun arrived after the disastrous and humiliating defeat their country suffered in the Crimean War.

In 1855 the situation in Russia was explosive. The troops of the martinet tsar who had expended his greatest efforts in training his soldiers were no match for the Western allies at Sevastopol. After his father's death Alexander himself realized that something had to be done. He relaxed the controls upon which Nicholas had leaned. Temporarily at least he abandoned Uvarov's principle of restricting enrollment in Russian universities to the landowning elite. Consequently enrollment at St. Petersburg rose from around 375 in 1854 to 1500 a decade later.[25] More startling than their numbers was the new outlook of the

---

24. Kozmin, *Iz istorii*, p. 613.

25. The statistics are from Michael T. Florinsky, *Russia* 2: 804. Enrollment in Russian universities experienced a decline during Nicholas's last years, particularly after his crackdown following the revolutions of 1848. A similar drop in enrollment occurred in the mid-sixties after the year-long closing of the universities (1861-62) and again after Karakozov's attempt on the tsar's life in 1866. The *raznochintsy* probably comprised about one-third of the universities' enrolled students during all of these years; their actual numbers increased as enrollment went up. An excellent and intimate protrayal of university life in the 1860s may be found in S. Svatikov's "Studencheskoe dvizhenie 1869 goda (Bakunin i Nechaev)," from the collection *Nasha strana*.

young university men (women were not yet admitted) of 1860. They had grown up, many of them—even many of those who belonged to the gentry—in poor circumstances. They remained poor as students, barely maintaining themselves on scanty food and in cramped lodgings. Gone was the gentleman-student's valet of Herzen's times. Unlike the middle and wealthy gentry of the past generation, most of the new young men planned to work for a living either because of family impoverishment or because of their own rejection of the land as an aristocratic source of wealth. They were determined to be self-sufficient, practical, and realistic. S. Svatikov in an article published in 1907 has suggested it was their social insecurity that led the new intelligentsia to seek changes. The wealthy gentry was a long-established class; it had economic roots in the land and maintained its clear social status. For the new young men—the *raznochintsy*, the déclassés—nothing was certain. Above all they needed a mobile society that would enable them to move beyond the old class structure. Svatikov viewed their demands for social, intellectual, and political freedom as based on their need for economic security, for jobs, and for the freedom to earn a living.[26] The new intelligentsia sought a place for itself. On a minute scale its appearance in 1860 shook the traditional Russian class structure as the rise of the middle class upset early modern Europe.

The demands of the new generation oriented it toward practicality and action. Most of all the young man of 1860 was interested in getting things done. He seldom worked out abstract philosophical systems; he was too impatient for action. The excitement with which Herzen, Ogarev, and their contemporaries had absorbed German idealism was almost entirely missing in the new generation's attitude toward what it called metaphysics. Young people continued their interest in Western rationalism, but it was directed at science, sociology, socialism, and practical political plans. No longer did young men record their emotions in secret diaries; rather they turned their energies towards demonstrations and illegal manifestoes distributed in the capital city at night. The radical student of the 1860s had little time for what Herzen would have called culture. He avoided overemotional reactions; the sufferings of the old nobility were the object not of his pity but of his scorn. No wonder that to the old generation the young were crass, vulgar, and unappreciative. Evgenii Lampert has written a good description of the

---

26. Svatikov, p. 165. The *raznochintsy* writers of the 1860s and 1870s were aware of the "tragic" position of this "class" and felt a certain solidarity. They often bemoaned their fate and the need to write for a living instead of for their own consciences. There is a delightful description in Vladimir Vladimirovich Bush, *Ocherki literaturnogo narodnichestva 70-80 gg.*, pp. 15-20.

generation gap. Herzen would have agreed that the men of the younger generation were

sterner, harsher, stiffer and more prosaic. Their manner was obtuse and matter-of-fact. They had an element of what Herzen called Arakcheevian ruthlessness, "a passionate rigidity and an eagerness to despatch their victims. . . ." They were plebeian by origin and in outlook, immune from the artistic and aesthetic culture, from the subtleties and sophistications of the educated gentry, or even of the *raznochintsy* of Belinskii's generation. Many of their leading spokesmen . . . were sons of priests, trained in theological seminaries, and they kept much of the confined moral and intellectual atmosphere in which they were brought up but against which they had revolted.[27]

To these young people, Chernyshevskii became the prime hero. They did not completely reject Herzen, and until its last days the *Bell* retained its influence and circulation. But it was Chernyshevskii who bridged the gap to the new generation and showed it the way from the old. He was an unusual person, not always clear headed but always determined, not always sensitive but always critical, not always right but always explorative and interested in new ideas.[28] For a few years as a young man he had been an enthusiastic Hegelian. Later he read the Young Hegelians and turned to Feuerbach's man-centered anthropological system, which he studied and enthusiastically espoused. Chernyshevskii never bothered to work out a clear philosophical outlook; even his materialism remained unrefined and was never carefully argued. His empirical approach he shared with the positivists, whom he read with interest. He speculated in social philosophy, not epistemology, in propaganda, not poetry. Chernyshevskii's view of art and social realism followed the path set down by the earlier radical critic Belinskii. His socialism he may have inherited from Herzen. Yet his early interest in Fourier, whose ideals left their imprint on his work, was replaced by fascination with the more practical experiments of Robert Owen at New Lanark, involving not a select group of chosen disciples but the miserable workers of a Scottish textile mill. The turn away from speculative philosophy in the direction of practical politics, away from romantic idealism to their self-defined realistic materialism, was a hallmark of the new radical generation.

A great many factors aided the men of 1860 in piecing together their new world view. One of them was the policy of the Russian government. It was clear to all thinking members of society that the

27. Lampert, *Studies in Rebellion*, p. 254.
28. A recent biography of Chernyshevskii has been written by Woehrlin (*Chernyshevskii*). See also Francis B. Randall's short guide *N. G. Chernyshevskii* and the rich material presented by Evgenii Lampert, *Sons against Fathers*.

government itself was working out a new vision of Russia. Great changes were in the air, and the excitement they generated was irresistible. Shortly after the Crimean War the new tsar had made it clear that he was going to take the greatest stride of all and emancipate the Russian serf from his three-hundred-year bondage. Soon thereafter rumors of other reforms began to circulate: the reordering of the judicial system, the establishment of new forms of local self-government. Simultaneously with its hints of other changes the government threw much of Nicholas's caution to the winds. It slackened its censorship and even encouraged Russia's journals to debate the new course. It set up commissions (mostly from among the gentry) to plan programs, and relaxed its strict laws on assembly and freedom of speech. The result was that all Russian educated society, from high noble to petty tradesman, buzzed with the excitement of changes to come and the unheard of liberty to think about them.

The key area was that of the press. The first decade of Alexander's reign saw the blossoming of Russian journalism to a degree it was not to experience again until 1905. Censorship by no means disappeared, and many subjects were still taboo. Nevertheless, the press flourished and was relatively free. Journals of all hues and shades sprang up. Polemics raged and insults flew. The reading public delighted in the feuds between Chernyshevskii and M. N. Katkov, a moderate who was to become increasingly nationalistic following the Polish rebellion, or between the Dostoevskii brothers and the nihilist press. Conservatives and liberals, radicals and reactionaries joined the arguments, which evolved around every conceivable legitimate topic. Attacks were thinly disguised, and few readers could doubt identities. M. E. Saltykov-Shchedrin, a satirist who often wrote for *Contemporary*, composed a fable of seven swallows arguing over editorial policy, identifying one swallow as "a despondent novelist," surely Fedor Dostoevskii. Dostoevskii answered in a short story about the *Opportunist*, a title achieved in Russian by scrambling a couple of letters in the word for "contemporary."[29] Other journalists noted the polemic and joined in. Although Herzen disapproved of the sarcasm, no young radical living in Russia's major cities could help but become stimulated and intrigued by the witty exchanges of the periodical press.

A similar ferment took place in the universities, particularly those

---

29. The Russian word for contemporary is *sovremennik;* that for opportunist, *svoevremennik*. This delightful example of a journalistic polemic is published by Ralph E. Matlaw in his collection of Dostoevskii's *Notes from Underground and the Grand Inquisitor with Relevant Works by Chernyshevskii, Shchedrin, and Dostoevsky*, pp. 199-229.

of Moscow, St. Petersburg, and Kiev. Although the statute worked out by Uvarov in 1835 remained in effect, it was tacitly overlooked by university authorities and government alike. Students published collections of their own journalism; in St. Petersburg, they founded a journal called *Kolokolchik* (Little Bell).[30] They held meetings, established funds to help the needy, and set up coffee houses and libraries. Professors became bold and encouraged them. The government henchmen assigned to watch over the universities lapsed into nervous impotence. The appointment of E. P. Kovalevskii, a liberal reformer, as minister of education encouraged the students' hopes. The excitement of the times penetrated the walls of hitherto isolated classrooms.

Abroad, Herzen himself was caught up in it. He and his colleague Ogarev were recovering some of the optimism they had so bitterly lost with the defeat of the European revolutions of 1848. Herzen had been in Paris then, and he had watched firsthand while the socialists and republicans squabbled away their victory into the hands of Louis Napoleon Bonaparte. Deeply discouraged, Herzen had for a time abandoned hope for a new order in his native land. By 1859 he had regained his equilibrium and even more than many of his radical contemporaries came to believe that reforms from above might mend the ills of Russian society. In the months before the emancipation Herzen encouraged the tsar in a series of open letters in the *Bell*, letters that may have been read in that illegal publication by Alexander himself. Chernyshevskii had long since taken the opposite view. As early as 1859 he realized that no tsarist grant of emancipation to the serfs would be enough to satisfy Russia's deep-rooted needs.[31]

These divergent attitudes towards government-instituted reform were a key factor in the clash between Herzen and Chernyshevskii in 1859. His convictions about the vital importance of public opinion at a crucial moment in Russian history determined Herzen's demand that journalism concentrate its forces and end its sarcastic polemicizing; Chernyshevskii could not agree. Political disagreement was re-enforced by different life styles and different views of philosophy, the nature of man, and the human personality. The new generation, Herzen thought, judged men only by their contribution toward some preconceived goal; Herzen's view that ideal man was an end in himself seemed romantic speculation to Chernyshevskii and his friends.[32]

Immediately it was politics that crystallized the hostility. The

30. Coquart, pp. 36-37.
31. See Kozmin, *Iz istorii*, pp. 608-9.
32. Usakina, pp. 258-60; Alfred Kuhn, "Dobroliubov's Critique of *Oblomov:* Polemics and Psychology," *Slavic Review* 30, no. 1 (March 1971): 103.

mutual mistrust of the two men came to a head in regard to a man named Poerio, a Neapolitan who fled to London after his release from imprisonment by Ferdinand II. Poerio had gone to prison for his futile efforts to reform the reactionary Neapolitan government from within. In 1859 Herzen and many other Londoners received him into exile with praise and enthusiasm. Chernyshevskii, on the other hand, made it clear in *Contemporary* that he thought Poerio was a fool. He should have known from the start that the kings of Naples could never be real reformers, nor could, by strong inference, the tsars of Russia.[33] Chernyshevskii was at best dubious about the Great Reforms. Herzen, a man of more impulsive commitments, had hopes—illusions, the *Contemporary* would have said—that came to be dashed. Indeed Herzen's joyful response to Alexander on the occasion of the emancipation ("Thou has conquered, O Galilean!," the dying words of Julian the Apostate) was rapidly replaced by discouragement when the details of the tsar's plan became known.

The disagreement between Herzen and Chernyshevskii on the possible effects of reform heralded what Armand Coquart, a biographer of the Russian nihilist D. I. Pisarev, has called the birth of Russian radicalism.[34] The reforms divided progressive Russian society into liberals and radicals, the former willing to follow Alexander, to work and hope for the extension of the tsar's hesitant program, the latter rejecting all compromise and insisting that only a thoroughgoing revolution could tip the scales toward justice. A great many young people eventually chose the liberal direction, but a sharply vocal group followed Chernyshevskii's radical lead. Their relationship was distinguished by hostility. Few of the radical group were converted to liberalism as the reforms progressed. Little if any space in the radical press was devoted to implementing the Great Reforms. To the radicals it was as if they hardly existed.

Born of a new class dedicated to action and living in a time when action finally seemed possible, the young radicals of the 1860s developed their new world views. In their outlooks the predominant role was reserved to Western intellectual trends. Throughout her modern history Russia had been closer to the West than many staunch patriots were willing to acknowledge. The middle years of the nineteenth century bound the ties even more tightly. New currents in Western thought had a strong impact on Russia's young people.

By 1860 Chernyshevskii and not Herzen lighted their way. It was Chernyshevskii who introduced the young generation to John Stuart

33. Kozmin, *Iz istorii*, pp. 608-9; Usakina, p. 259.
34. Coquart, p. 19.

Mill and utilitarianism, of which he himself was a great exponent. Through him young radicals almost universally adopted the utilitarian ethic, regarding man's happiness as the greatest possible good. Chernyshevskii studied the positivists and passed them on to his readers—August Comte perhaps less then H. T. Buckle, whose *History of England* came to be widely read and admired. Chernyshevskii was interested in science; he and Dobroliubov wrote a number of articles on new scientific trends, adopting the current mechanistic views of the German popularizers, admiring the universally sought scientific and objective methods, asserting the overwhelming influence of physiology on human behavior. Chernyshevskii published John Stuart Mill's *Principles of Political Economy* in translation and described the teachings of Adam Smith, convincing his readers that man's actions were dominated by egotism and self-interest. He reinforced their interest in the world around them, replacing the older generation's explorations into metaphysics with the new scientistic materialism. He was an admirer of the English, and his readers expanded their sights from Continental to English guidance in their studies. The *Contemporary* was a journal of Western ideas whether or not they could be integrated into the Russian experience. In London the exiled *Bell* remained a kind of old-fashioned political potpourri.

Fascinated by the ideas of the West—by its ethics, its science, its sociology, and its history—Chernyshevskii and his radical following nevertheless remained Russian at heart. In a peculiar juxtaposition they rejected Western society as they embraced Western ideas. However intelligent they found John Stuart Mill, they could not condone the government he was describing. Democracy was a sham; even the conservative Dostoevskii thought so.[35] Whatever respect they had for Western intellectuals, they had nothing but scorn for the Western bourgeoisie. Capitalism was crass; Russia must find a better, a more just and civilized system. The men of 1860 lived in two worlds: the intellectual world of the modern industrial West and the sociopolitical world of the backward agrarian East. The dichotomy was irreconcilable in many ways, and its consequences haunted Russian thought for generations. Perhaps young Russia's admiration for Chernyshevskii stemmed in part from his loyalty to Russia, where he remained and whose fate he shared, spending many of his years in exile, ultimately losing his health and his life. Herzen had fled abroad, losing his perspectives on Russia and going over to the other world.

---

35. See the excerpts from "Winter Notes on Summer Impressions" in Dostoevskii's *Notes from Underground*, pp. 181-87. This mistrust of Western socioeconomic forms was common to radical socialists and conservative Slavophiles in Russia.

Too much can be read into a comparison of supposedly typical individuals such as Herzen and Chernyshevskii, each representing his own generation. In the first place, neither of them was really typical; each of them had too much individuality to be the epitome of his times. In the second place, changing times acted on the older man just as they shaped the younger, and Herzen himself was different in 1860 from what he had been in 1848. If the two generations clashed, they had also grown together. Not only had Chernyshevskii shared in Herzen's experiences, as he would readily have admitted, but Herzen had been reshaped by the same influences that directed the younger man.[36] To a certain extent, then, the forties and the sixties merged together in a single flowing current of history.

Yet the men of 1860 used a different approach, and Herzen felt it most keenly of all. Born of a background different from that of Herzen and his contemporaries, the new generation prided itself on its scientific method, admired detached reasoning and practical proposals, scorned sentimentality, and eagerly sought an arena where it might get immediate results. Yet these young people maintained a strong humanitarianism, a devotion to truth, and in some instances (as exemplified by Chernyshevskii's famous novel, *What Is to Be Done?*) an almost puritanical sense of self-sacrifice and of lofty moral ideals. It was a generation, on the whole, no more confused than most.

Into this Russian world, eminently a child of his times, Petr Nikitich Tkachev was born.

----

36. Usakina points out that Herzen became more and more discouraged with the tsarist reforms, thereby moving closer to Chernyshevskii's position (Usakina, p. 270). Although Chernyshevskii may never have grown to respect his older rival, Herzen at one time actually offered to republish *Contemporary* in London at his own expense (*My Past and Thoughts*, 3: 1325).

2

St. Petersburg Beginnings

Petr Nikitich Tkachev was plunged into the atmosphere of Russia's capital city of St. Petersburg during the most violent, tense, and turbulent decade the country had known for nearly half a century. His early years were not untypical of those of any radical student as he attended school, prepared for a career, and occasionally felt the harsh hand of government disapproval. St. Petersburg was Tkachev's city—the headquarters of the government he despised, the city where most of Russia's leading radical journals were published, the seat of her most distinguished university, and most of all the Petrine city that historically was the symbol of Russia's contact with the West, the center for Western thought, and the spiritual home for the West's Russian admirers.

Petr had been born on June 29, 1844, on family estates at a little village named Sivtsov, not far from the town of Velikie Luki in Pskov guberniia.[1] His father died shortly after his birth. Petr was the youngest

---

1. Reliable dates and statistics about Tkachev's life may be found in *Deiateli revoliutsionnogo dvizheniia v Rossii*, vol. 2, col. 1713. Several brief biographical sketches are also helpful; chief among them is the essay "P. N. Tkachev" in the *Russkii biograficheskii slovar*, 20: 597-600. Two émigré Russian journals published obituaries at the time of Tkachev's death: they were *Vestnik Narodnoi voli* (Geneva), 5 (1886), pt. 2: 172-75; and *Obshchee delo* (Geneva), nos. 81, 83 (1886), the latter being of especial interest and available as reprinted in *Byloe*, no. 8 (1907), pp. 156-72. There is a sketch written by Tkachev's cousin and brother-in-law N. F. Annenskii in the *Entsiklopedicheskii slovar* (1901 ed.), 33, pt. 1: 366-67. Venturi, in his *Roots of Revolution*, gives many biographical details in chapter 16. B. P. Kozmin has written a little book on Tkachev in Russia, entitled *P. N. Tkachev i revo-*

17

of four children left in his mother's care; he had an older brother whose fate is unknown and a sister Sofia who was active in the radical movement and died young in 1875.[2] In childhood and young manhood Petr was closest to his other sister Alexandra, who married their first cousin.[3] For periods of time throughout his sojourn in his native land Petr lived with this sister and her husband N. F. Annenskii, who later became famous as a statistician, economist, and one of the editors of *Russkoe Bogatstvo* (Russian Wealth), an influential populist journal. Annenskaia herself made somewhat of a name as a writer of children's books in later years.[4]

The Tkachev family is described in most sources as belonging to the impoverished nobility—a description that might well accord with the situation of most gentry from Pskov, a poor agricultural district. Nevertheless the family was far from destitute by contemporary standards. Tkachev's mother had two brothers who had retired and were living in St. Petersburg by 1862; following the tradition of the less wealthy nobility, one of them had been in provincial government service.[5] She herself lived for the most part in the capital city, making trips to the "village," as Petr called it, during the summer and over long holidays when the children were not in school. Alexandra described her married life in St. Petersburg as fairly comfortable by the standards of the day.[6] Although Tkachev's leading Soviet biographer, the historian B. P. Kozmin, portrays him as fighting to keep the wolf from the door, Petr had

---

liutsionnoe dvizhenie 1860-kh godov (hereafter cited as Kozmin, *Tkachev*). Albert L. Weeks, *The First Bolshevik*, is the first full-length work on Tkachev published in English.

2. Sofia Nikitichna Tkacheva became a teacher in a school sponsored by a group of young radicals, specializing in running its sewing workshop. Such schools were not uncommon in the protest movement of the sixties. Sofia later married a fellow teacher named A. A. Kril, active in the revolutionary movement of the 1870s. See E. S. Vilenskaia, *Revoliutsionnoe podpole v Rossii, 60-e gody, XIX v.*, pp. 341-42. Sofia's death has been recorded by Tkachev's older sister, although she never mentions the mysterious brother and his fate (A. N. Annenskaia, "Iz proshlykh let: Vospominaniia o N. F. Annenskom," *Russkoe bogatstvo*, no. 1 [January 1913], p. 71).

3. Tkachev was one of the witnesses at their wedding in 1866; it took place out of town because not only his family but many priests refused to sanction the marriage of first cousins (Annenskaia, p. 58; see also the biographical sketch of Annenskii in *Novyi entsiklopedicheskii slovar*, 2: 922-23).

4. There is a brief sketch in *Novyi entsiklopedicheskii slovar*, 2: 922.

5. According to Tkachev's own deposition to the police in 1862 at the time of his second arrest (M. Lemke, "K biografii P. N. Tkacheva, " *Byloe*, no 8 [1907], p. 152; see also Annenskaia, p. 53).

6. Annenskaia, p. 58 ff.

money to lend to the less fortunate for important causes.[7] The actual picture is not that of a wealthy family but of people moderately comfortable and able to get along.

Petr never talked about his childhood; he probably regarded it with displeasure. He disliked Sivtsov and once referred to Velikie Luki as an "out-of-the-way and God-forsaken little town."[8] After his father's death responsibility for running the estate (such as it was) fell not only on his mother but on his brother and sisters. Petr was too young to be included. He must have been left a great deal on his own. Deprived of the advantages that wealth had brought young Herzen in terms of governesses and travel, Petr lacked as well Herzen's outgoing friendliness and easy gift for communication. He was small, shy, and uncommunicative. Absorbed in his books and a prolific reader by his midteens, he never seems to have mingled with the people of the village or made particular friends with serfs on the estate. He had a keen mind, but he was a lifelong loner. He may well have been introspective and unhappy like many lonely children.

History has not recorded the details of Petr's early life and training. As a child he may have educated himself or been taught by his sisters. The nature of his education is unknown, but it must have included the study of religion and religious writings: his later works are scattered with Biblical quotations and references. He entered a gymnasium in St. Petersburg at an unknown date. His own writings make it clear that he hated it. His dislike may well have been conditioned by his shyness, his inability to socialize easily, his unwillingness to defy rigid regulations or break out of the mold they imposed. He later compared the gymnasium's atmosphere with that of the very strict theological schools during the reign of Nicholas I: ". . . the same crude despotism, ignorance, slow-witted teachers, the same endless vices, the same thoughtless beatings, and the arbitrary stifling domination of the old pupils over the young ones,"[9] phrases that suggest not only bitterness but fear.

Yet his matriculation at the gymnasium marked the beginning of a long association with St. Petersburg, an association broken only by summers and holidays on the remote family estates. These early years in the capital city were deeply influential in Petr's young life. Now he was probably first exposed to radical thought, a brew that was bubbling

---

7. Kozmin, *Tkachev*, p. 45; in 1869 Tkachev had two hundred rubles to lend his common-law wife toward the purchase of a printing press.

8. P. N. Tkachev, *Izbrannye sochineniia na sotsialno-politicheskie temy*, 3: 53 (hereafter cited as Tkachev, with volume and page).

9. Ibid., 2: 277.

and exploding across the city he loved. One can imagine the eager young pupil drinking in the stimulant. Chernyshevskii's *Contemporary* was the most widely read radical journal in St. Petersburg, and Herzen's illegally imported *Bell* was passed from hand to hand. "Herzen, Chernyshevskii, and Dobroliubov at this time were sovereign in the thoughts of the young generation," wrote A. A. Kornilov; their articles were "taken as revelation."[10] Formal schooling with its strict studies and rigid discipline took second place for the young generation to the exciting, illicit world the radical press evoked. Kozmin has written:

> The character and the world outlook of a Russian youth at this time were created not under the aegis of a school but under the influence of life itself beginning to burst forth. He spent his time not so much on lessons as on the *Contemporary* and the *Bell*. He listened little to the voice of his gymnasium teacher. In his thoughts Herzen, Chernyshevskii, and Dobroliubov reigned supreme. Tkachev was no exception in the ranks of his contemporaries. For him as for them books and journals replaced school.[11]

Although Kozmin may have exaggerated youth's single-mindedness, Tkachev surely knew illegal radical literature as a gymnasium pupil. He later told police that certain satirical poems found in his possession during a search in 1862 dated from these earlier years. By the time he was eighteen he had acquired and read one of Ogarev's most famous and inflammatory proclamations.[12] He was much influenced by Chernyshevskii as his early works demonstrate, and he gave this Russian critic full credit for the leadership of radical youth. Chernyshevskii, Tkachev wrote later, was the "true father and founder of the socialist revolutionary party in Russia."[13] As such he had had more influence on young men of Tkachev's time than any other contemporary. Forced into extremes of submissiveness and obedience at school, young Petr must have enjoyed the intellectual escape the *Contemporary* offered. In class he studied ancient philosophy and languages; he read French, German, and English fluently before he was eighteen. On his own he became acquainted through St. Petersburg journals with the leading European thinkers of his day, from Feuerbach to John Stuart Mill, Jeremy Bentham to Robert Owen.

In 1861 Petr Tkachev, aged almost seventeen, finished his courses.

---

10. A. A. Kornilov, *Obshchestvennoe dvizhenie pri Aleksandr II (1855-1881)*, p. 98.

11. Kozmin, *Tkachev*, pp. 14-15.

12. Lemke, "K biografii," p. 154.

13. In a forward to his French translation of Chernyshevskii's *Chto Delat*, never fully published, in *Ni dieu, ni maître* (Paris), November 21, 1880, reprinted in Tkachev, 4: 413.

With what must have been considerable relief he turned his back on the hated gymnasium. Interested in law and government, he may already have read writers like Jeremy Bentham whose works he cited at length in an early article.[14] His plan was to enroll in the law school of the University of St. Petersburg in the fall.

As fate would have it, young Tkachev prepared to immerse himself in university studies at precisely the time when student disorders reached a peak.[15] St. Petersburg University had seen good years since the accession of Alexander II. The restrictive statute of 1835, which still governed all Russian universities, came to be ignored by students, faculty, and administrators alike as the educated, politically alert stratum of society was caught up in the excitement preceding the Great Reforms. Nicholas II's restrictions on enrollment were no longer rigidly applied. Eager students expanded their classroom activities to establish their own corporate organization, set up loan funds, libraries, and coffee houses. Professors encouraged the publication of student journals and newspapers. Although the innovations clearly violated the letter and spirit of the Uvarov statute, the authorities were in a tolerant mood and looked the other way.

Still the statute was resented by many students who hoped for its amendment. As the writer of an anonymous letter reported to Herzen's *Bell*, the old university regulation "kept the students on the level of gymnasium pupils, gave huge power over them to a police official—the inspector—and systematically separated the professors from the students and from participation in university affairs."[16] Rumors spread that Alexander planned to revise the university statute in the spirit of the other Great Reforms.

In the spring of 1861 the situation changed—unfortunately for the students, in a direction opposite to their hopes. Alexander had apparently found cause for uneasiness. Student meetings had increased in noise and size following the disappointment over emancipation plans (announced in February 1861). Students were observing and espousing

---

14. P. N. Tkachev, "O mirovykh sudiakh," *Vremia*, no. 7 (July 1862), p. 85.

15. Venturi, chap. 8, gives a good brief account of the student movement based in large measure on materials in Kornilov, pp. 98 ff. An excellent account is to be found in Svatikov, pp. 165-82. One of the most detailed articles, including tales of administrators, faculty, and their actions in 1861, is in an anonymous letter printed originally in *Kolokol*, reprinted under the title "Zapiska o peterburgskikh universitetskikh bezporiadkakh" by Mikhail Lemke in *Ocherki osvoboditelnogo dvizheniia "shestidesiatykh godov,"* appendix 4, pp. 468-79. Coquart, as usual, has a fine account on pp. 150 ff. The story of the student movement related herein is based on materials presented in all of the above.

16. Lemke, *Ocherki osvoboditelnogo dvizheniia*, p. 468.

the cause underlying the riots in Poland. A series of petty outbreaks occurred, during one of which a professor was unable to make himself heard over the din of the disrespectful student crowd. Tkachev probably learned about it through the thick walls of his St. Petersburg gymnasium. Late in the spring Alexander appointed Admiral Count E. V. Putiatin, known as a disciplinarian, to replace the minister of education who had served in the position since 1858. Supposedly with his sovereign's approval Putiatin immediately cracked down. His first move was directed against student meetings; regulations published in May provided that all such gatherings on university grounds could be held only with advance permission from the administration. A few weeks later all large meetings were completely banned. At the same time the new minister took a major step towards curtailing what had been free education for the poor. Prior to 1861 any student or auditor was admitted to university classes without the usual fifty-ruble fee upon his demonstration of inability to pay. By Putiatin's new ruling the official definition of poverty was revised downward to the point where the poverty exemption was seldom granted. The admiral-count followed with even more stringent regulations. The students were to give up their uniforms and insignia, the symbols of their newly won corporate organization. Flunking a single examination meant expulsion from the university, a rule that ended the tradition of permitting a failing student to repeat a course. Putiatin submitted to the university faculties a plan whereby students managing student funds and facilities would have to be appointed by the administration and whereby all money awards made from these funds would be subject to confirmation by the rector or the hated government inspector. The faculty council at St. Petersburg protested in alarm and suggested a number of measures to make the new rulings more palatable—particularly their introduction gradually rather than all at once. Putiatin was not to be swayed, however, and the regulations were put into effect. The rector of St. Petersburg University resigned and was replaced by General G. I. Filipson, a man more to Admiral Putiatin's taste. Students and faculty alike were disturbed.

A lack of communication among ministry, faculty, administration, and students characterized the reopening of St. Petersburg University in the autumn of 1861 when Petr Tkachev first presented himself as a student. "It is known," the anonymous letter writer reported in the *Bell*,

what an impression the new rules produced in the whole of Russia. In them, [people] saw a return to the idea of limiting the number of students and of making the universities unavailable again for the majority of the public when in recent times they had been open to anyone who wished [to attend]. The majority of young people, to whom a university diploma meant a position in service and society and a crust of bread, are deprived of the possibility of attending university classes. The poor gentry and civil servants who had prepared their sons for the university were indignant, and indignant too were all to whom education, which exists so little in Russia and comprises such an urgent need, seems dear. Among the students and auditors of the universities the reaction to these measures was even more drastic.[17]

Although the reporter may have exaggerated society's response, there is no doubt the students were upset. Returning students who had heard only indirectly of the new rules found themselves faced with a fifty-ruble admission fee, a blow even more to the heart than the new administrative regulation of their libraries and funds. Tkachev and his colleagues were required to purchase matriculation tickets before they could enter classroom doors. University authorities do not seem to have explained the exact provisions of the Putiatin regulations, and rumors of excesses circulated freely. Disturbances of such magnitude broke out that officials closed the university's doors on September 23. Two days later the St. Petersburg students—Tkachev probably among them—met in protest and paraded through the city to the home of Rector Filipson, escorting him ignominiously back to the university and demanding an explanation of the new rules. A handful of suspected ringleaders were arrested the next day. On October 2 thirty-five other students were arrested after another forbidden meeting, but Petr was apparently not there.

The university nervously reopened for business on October 11. Guards stationed at entrances checked for matriculation tickets. The next day a crowd gathered at the gates. It rapidly grew to nearly three hundred persons. Some of the matriculants tore up their tickets voluntarily; others were barred from the grounds by the protesters who attacked them as strikebreakers. Authorities called the police. In the resulting fracas a few students were injured, some when they attempted to show their solidarity with their friends. Demonstrators were soon arrested en masse. Swept up with the crowd, Tkachev was taken to prison too.

Tkachev's part in the demonstration and his own position in regard to student rights should not be exaggerated. He may have felt strongly about the needs of the student, but the rioting in 1861, like the more serious disturbances eight years later, should not be regarded as a broad social protest movement in which Petr came to be involved. The battle was fought purely and simply against the cutback of student freedoms and the increase in fees; it had no particular political overtones. Moreover, there is no question of Tkachev's being a leader of the student protesters. He was so new to the university that he had probably not even attended class. Not now or later did he show himself to be an incisive

---

17. Ibid., p. 42.

leader in action. This first arrest resulted simply from his being swept up with the crowd, not from any individual insubordinate behavior.

It is impossible to estimate the effect of his first stretch in a Russian prison on young Tkachev, the sheltered student of the gymnasium, the quiet child from the country. He was taken to Kronstadt because the notorious Peter-Paul fortress was filled with the arrested students, and the overflow had to be sent elsewhere. Tales of horror exist about life in Russian prisons; people died there although an astonishing number survived. In 1861 the new St. Petersburg Governor-General Alexander Suvorov was a reasonable man and lenient, if not actually sympathetic, to his young prisoners. The students were permitted visits from relatives who brought extra food and reading materials. Opportunities existed for communication between the cells in which they lived in groups. There was probably much discussion; the accused may even have exchanged smuggled literature. They studied; they wrote. Kozmin suggests this prison experience was an awakening for Petr, but there is little evidence that Tkachev emerged from the short incarceration as "a decisive revolutionary," as Kozmin puts it.[18] Nevertheless, prison did permit him his first close contact with the radical university students of St. Petersburg. In that sense it may have educated the young radical. Surely he met one student there who became his friend and who was revolutionary enough for both of them. Tkachev himself never reported anything about his experience save Suvorov's conviction that the students were lucky, that in the future egghead radicals would find a worse fate at the hands of the loyal peasantry: "The government will [in the future] deal otherwise with you. It will not nourish you with prison fare but turn you directly over to the people. The people will be able to make short work of you."[19]

Alexander himself cut short a trip in the south of Russia to return and deal with the student question. His mood led him to sympathize with the young rioters. He decried Putiatin's regulations, insisted upon leniency for the prisoners, and set up a committee to formulate a new statute for all of Russia's universities.[20] The disciplinarian admiral-educator was dismissed. The punishments imposed on the demonstrators were on the whole reasonable. Five of the students (supposedly revolutionary ringleaders) were banished from St. Petersburg and for-

---

18. Kozmin, *Tkachev*, p. 19.

19. Tkachev, 3: 53.

20. There is a good description of the formulation of the university statute in William L. Mathes, "N. I. Pirogov and the Reform of University Government, 1856-1866," *Slavic Review* 31, no. 1 (March 1972): 34-36. Mathes points out that the original judgment of the committee was revised conservatively at every subsequent stage of the statute's review.

bidden to return, and most of the others were expelled and released under parental guarantees. Tkachev was released to his mother who was then in the capital city; he was not even required to return to Velikie Luki and the family estates.[21] The onus of expulsion was lessened because (except for a few trial days in December 1861) the university was closed pending the passage of the new statute.

And so it remained for nearly a year, a period in which few specifics about Tkachev's personal life can be determined. For a time (a few months in the spring of 1862) he attended a free university sponsored by the students and sympathetic professors. Twenty professors had agreed to lecture, but the project was closed by officials when the historian Professor P. V. Pavlov, one of the student favorites, gave an antigovernment talk at a literary meeting. An ardent supporter of intellectual freedoms, Pavlov had carefully showed his speech to the censor and received proper permission. But during his delivery, to the students' delight, he proceeded to throw caution to the winds by strongly accenting certain suggestive words and phrases. The excited audience went so far as to sing the Marseillaise. Pavlov was shortly arrested and exiled, and the free university came to an end in March 1862.[22] Attempts to revive it were frustrated when the government became alarmed by a series of fires in Moscow, thought to be the work of student arsonists.

Tkachev was thus forced to continue his studies on his own. Kozmin suggested that he now perfected his knowledge of foreign languages.[23] His interests continued to focus on jurisprudence, and he expanded his readings into the areas of economics and statistics. Frequent references to works by Western authors in his early articles demonstrate that he was following the example of Chernyshevskii and devouring writings from the West, to which he certainly added eagerly read articles from polemical St. Petersburg journals. He buried himself in books and papers; they were his first love. Evidence of the discipline and intensity of his work lies in his later university record. Eventually the students expelled in 1861 were permitted to submit the dissertations required for their university degrees, and in 1868 Tkachev did so, probably never having attended a formal class. He was awarded the status of a candidate in law. He never finished the other requirements for his degree, for by then he was too busy.

---

21. This verdict is misrepresented as exile to Velikie Luki in several articles on Tkachev, all apparently based on an inaccurate account in *Obshchee delo*, reprinted as "Materialy dlia biografii P. N. Tkacheva," *Byloe*, no. 8 (1907), pp. 158-72.

22. Lemke, *Ocherki osvoboditelnogo dvizheniia*, pp. 7-13. See also Coquart, p. 173; Annenskaia, p. 54. Chernyshevskii was apparently in attendance at this particular meeting.

23. Kozmin, *Tkachev*, p. 19.

In the spring of 1862, to the great pride of his family, Petr published his first article. He was not yet eighteen when it appeared in *Vremia* (Time) for June.[24] *Time* was a conservative journal edited by Fedor Dostoevskii and his brother, and its editorial policies were dictated by the neo-Slavophile, religious, and nationalistic attitudes of the famous novelist. Indeed in *Epokha* (Epoch), the Dostoevskii journal that was a successor to *Time* and to which Tkachev would also contribute, Fedor Dostoevskii was to write:

The study and analysis of our social and rural problems from a Russian national point of view will as before remain the chief aim of our publication. We are convinced as before that there can be no progress in our society until we become real Russians. And the mark of a real Russian at the present time is to know what things in Russia today one ought not to abuse. One must not denigrate, one must not condemn, one must know how to love—this is what a real Russian is most in need of today.[25]

Tkachev could scarcely have agreed. Kozmin, Tkachev's biographer, found himself disturbed. Convinced that young Petr was already a dedicated radical heading for a career as a revolutionary journalist, Kozmin wondered how Tkachev could contribute to a journal edited by the Dostoevskii brothers, whose policies directly contradicted his youthful viewpoints.[26] Perhaps Tkachev's article had been rejected by the *Contemporary*, which, as a radical journal, set less stock by judicial reform. It is more likely that Petr could not yet foresee his own metier; in spite of the influence of his prison friends and that of his readings, he may still have imagined himself a jurist, working within the social framework rather than attempting to destroy it. The mystery of his choice of vehicle remains unsolved and fortunately unimportant.

Indeed Petr's first article was far from a radical departure. Like all Russian lawyers, young or old, he was interested in the court system to be set up by the new judicial reforms. For a time even the government encouraged commentary, suggestions, and criticism. Tkachev's particular concern in his first published writing was libel, its definition, and its penalties. He had read and was irritated by an article on ideal press laws written by Ivan Aksakov in the conservative journal *Den* (Day). Although *Time* was at least equally conservative in policy, it accepted and published Tkachev's response.

---

24. P. N. Tkachev, "O sude po prestupleniiam protiv zakonov pechati," *Vremia*, no. 6 (June 1862), pp. 40-50.

25. *Dostoevsky's Occasional Writings*, ed. David Magarshack, p. 249.

26. Kozmin, *Tkachev*, pp. 44-45. Soviet scholars have recently suggested that he may have had some influence with Dostoevskii through a teacher at his gymnasium, N. N. Strakhov, or another friend, A. E. Razin. See Petr Nikitich Tkachev, *Sochineniia v dvukh tomakh*, 1: 17-18.

To his credit, in assessing the merits of libelous action Tkachev was keenly aware of the importance of freedom of the press.

In a well-constructed state, everything must be subject to discussion. Common sense tells society that if it wants to act rationally, in accordance with healthy reason, then it must broaden as far as possible the limits of free criticism. And the freer this criticism, the greater the quantity of subjects and persons subjected to its scrutiny, the more reasonable will be social relationships [and] the smaller the danger that will threaten the state. Free discussion about everything that goes on around us is the inalienable right of man; to deprive him of it is to wage war on reason, to violate the urgent need of any civilized man—the need for criticism.[27]

If libel suit were too easy to bring, the threat of court action might inhibit writers from the all-important freedom to write what they thought. Tkachev suggested caution. All libel actions in any way uncertain as to the degree of insult afforded the party bringing suit should be submitted to a grand jury, who would determine if libel actually did exist and if the case should be further tried. This grand jury would assist the public procuror in identifying and defining the libelous act. Tkachev agreed with Akaskov that for grand jurors certain educational requirements were desirable. However, he rejected his antagonist's contention that jurors in the ordinary libel courts should be chosen in equal numbers from the gentry, clergy, and merchant classes. Rather (in the first published expression of his alert social conscience) Tkachev insisted on including the popular element—representatives from the lower middle class (*meshchantsvo*) and the peasantry. He demanded that jury lists be set up based on the whole population as identified in each instance by local city or county committees. Common sense, honesty, and good conscience were the only necessary prerequisites for jurors. The grand-jury/common-jury plan should be extended throughout the whole reformed judicial system.

Petr had done his homework well. He was obviously acquainted with court procedures in both France and England. From the latter he drew his grand-jury plan although he made it clear that he viewed English courts as aristocratic (French as bureaucratic) and that Russian courts must not be so.[28] He wrote clearly and carefully. For a seventeen-year-old he organized his work well and did not hesitate to present positive ideas.

He grew bolder. He submitted two more articles to *Time*, and they were accepted for publication in July and November of the same year.[29] These dealt with the peace courts, the courts of lowest instance in the

27. Tkachev, "O sude po prestupleniiam . . . ," pp. 41-42.
28. Ibid., p. 44.
29. Tkachev, "O mirovykh sudiakh," *Vremia*, no. 7 (July 1862), pp. 83-92; and idem, "Mirovoi sud," *Vremia*, no. 11 (November 1862), pp. 74-87.

Russian judicial system. Tkachev demanded that the courts protect the poor. If a rich man brought his case against a poor man to an expensive trial, the richer should be forced to pay the fees. The amount of money involved should not determine which cases should be assigned to lower courts or to higher (where, Tkachev felt, the poor were better protected). The gentry should have no special part in appointing peace court judges. Rather these officials should be chosen by the population at large, for the office demanded no special knowledge of law but only common sense, conscience, honesty, literacy, and the respect of society as a whole. Justices should be paid by taxes assessed upon the entire community.[30] Citing Jeremy Bentham, Tkachev proceeded to criticize the court systems of other countries. Russia's courts, he repeated, must not be aristocratic like those in England, the "classic country of the aristocracy," where,

thanks to a special course of historical life, an economic way of life has developed [that is] in the highest degree unfavorable for the *masses*, for the simple toiling people, and in the highest degree favorable for the minority, the happy ones who in the most unscrupulous manner exploit the labor of the majority. The landed and industrial aristocracy, having developed there to a monstrous degree, casts its shadow on the mass of *poor* [*chernyi*] people, the mass of the proletariat; and this is why for a long time it has seemed to us [Russians] that the government structure in England is the ideal government structure. For the aristocracy, for the rich, the bankers, for the *owners* it is really extraordinarily apt, profitable, and we, taking this aristocracy, these factory-exploiters, these proud dandies, these elegant gentlemen for the English people, naïvely admire English institutions.[31]

Fearlessly, Tkachev referred to the Russian legal system as a lottery in which you took your chances. He went on to accuse Russian jurists of viewing law through the prism of dead theories, of being incapable of creative thinking, of talking in terms always remote from reality.[32] He was to develop these themes more carefully later. But at the early age of eighteen, even under the eye of a conservative editor, Petr was already beginning to sound like Tkachev.

Unfortunately, his writing did not continue unimpeded. In November 1862 Tkachev's budding career as a legal journalist was rudely interrupted when he was arrested for the second time. This time the police had more damaging evidence against him. They were able to connect his name with that of an older, radical ex-student, and a search of his quarters turned up several pieces of illegal literature.

Tkachev had met Leonid Olshevskii at Kronstadt the previous year

30. Tkachev, "O mirovykh sudiakh," p. 85.
31. Tkachev, "Mirovoi sud," p. 78.
32. Tkachev, "O mirovykh sudiakh," p. 84.

when both of them were imprisoned in connection with the university riots.[33] In December 1861 Olshevskii had received stronger punishment than his younger colleague; he had been banished to his native district of Kovno and forbidden to return to St. Petersburg. Several months later he petitioned for permission to end his exile, and in the spring of 1862, when the authorities acceded to his wish, he and Petr resumed their acquaintance in the capital city. The closeness of their association remains uncertain although surely they were friends. Tkachev admitted visiting Olshevskii's rooms with some frequency, but the secret police were never able to find evidence of an organized circle or group. Kozmin feels their ties were stronger and more intimate than the police ever knew.[34]

In May 1862 the police received an anonymous letter contending that Olshevskii was distributing revolutionary pamphlets. Olshevskii was arrested, but since a search of his quarters revealed nothing suspicious he was released in a few days. Some weeks later a second anonymous letter was received by the police, and this time the routine search unearthed more incriminating materials. A seemingly innocent message could be read as a threat to the life of the tsar if certain letters at the beginning of certain words were combined in proper order. More devastating still was a proclamation entitled *To the Russian People: A Tale of Uncle Kuzmich*. Written in simple peasant language and in the form of a folk tale, the manuscript pictured an older peasant bemoaning to his fellow villagers the sad condition of the countryside after emancipation and urging his friends to take up the axe. Olshevskii thought up some excuses for the police. At first he said he had written *Uncle Kuzmich* one evening when he was drunk. Then he said it pertained to the situation in Galicia in 1848. Finally he broke down and admitted that he had read a pamphlet entitled *Molodaia Rossiia* (Young Russia), that he had written under its influence, and that he had hoped to print and distribute his *Uncle Kuzmich* throughout the country.

Soviet and other scholars have made much of Olshevskii's acquaint-

---

33. The information on Olshevkii is drawn from Kozmin, *Tkachev*, pp. 32 ff.; Venturi, pp. 299-300; Lemke, "K biografii"; and Mikhail Lemke, *Politicheskie protsessy v Rossii v 1860-kh godov*, pp. 579-96.

34. Kozmin, *Tkachev*, p. 41. Other Soviet historians make a lot of the Olshevskii circle; see Anatolii A. Galaktionov and P. F. Nikandrov, *Ideologi russkogo narodnichestva*, pp. 104-6. Most of the biographical details about Tkachev in Galaktionov and Nikandrov repeat Kozmin's account. On the other hand Vilenskaia never mentions Olshevskii or Tkachev in her account of the St. Petersburg underground in the mid-1860s.

ance with the proclamation *Young Russia* and have speculated that Tkachev may have seen it too.[35] *Young Russia* indeed expressed many ideas consistent with Tkachev's later revolutionary plans. Its authorship is uncertain, although from its Moscow origins and the outright violence it condoned some scholars have thought its author to be P. G. Zaichnevskii, then a student, later a Jacobin extremist like Tkachev.[36] This extraordinary pamphlet called on Russian youth to emulate the men of 1792, to endorse terrorism, and not to fear the spilling of blood. It demanded not just the overthrow of the tsarist government but the extinction of religion, the destruction of the family, the liberation of women, and the elimination of exploiting classes. Its author sought the communal organization of society as modeled on the *obshchina* and the *artel*. More interestingly he urged that after the seizure of power the victorious revolutionaries set up a dictatorship in order effectively to construct the new society. The pamphlet's writer was familiar with the experience of the French republicans in 1848 and feared that without dictatorship the revolution would fall into the hands of the moderates.[37]

The remarkably violent tone of *Young Russia* fired up young St. Petersburg radicals. Although Olshevskii did not keep the proclamation in his possession, he may have shown it to his friend Tkachev. Petr must surely have known it by name, for it was cited in the journals he regularly read.[38] Just what inspiration he may have found in *Young Russia* is uncertain. The older Tkachev would have endorsed specifically the principle of postrevolutionary dictatorship, a cornerstone of the

---

35. Galaktionov and Nikandrov, p. 105, claim that the Olshevskii circle grew up "under the direct influence of the proclamation *Young Russia*. See also Kozmin, *Tkachev*, p. 41; Venturi, p. 300; and J. M. Meijer, *Knowledge and Revolution*, pp. 39-40. Vilenskaia, p. 126, believes the ideas of the proclamation were rejected in revolutionary circles at this time.

36. Cf. Kozmin, *Tkachev*, p. 31; Venturi, p. 285; and many others. Coquart debates this identification, p. 175. The term *Jacobin* was consistently applied to Tkachev by contemporaries and has often been used by scholars, then and later, to describe the totality of his revolutionary plans. Although it is not a historically accurate description, it is used in this volume in its contemporary meaning for the sake of conciseness and convenience.

37. *Molodaia Rossiia* has been reprinted in Lemke, *Politicheskie protsessy*, pp. 508-18.

38. The pamphlet was once described as "crashing like thunder" on the capital city (Lampert, *Sons against Fathers*, pp. 125, 363-64 [note 43]). It was mentioned by such diverse contemporary sources as Katkov, Herzen, and *Otechestvennye zapiski;* cf. Kozmin, *Iz istorii*, pp. 264, 266-71. See also idem, "K istorii 'Molodoi Rossii,'" *Katorga i ssylka*, nos. 66 (1930), pp. 52-70, and 67 (1930), pp. 61-76.

program he proposed. Yet Tkachev did not mention *Young Russia* in his writings—not even in the detailed histories of the Russian revolutionary movement he later published in the free air of Switzerland. If he read the proclamation and was impressed, he never said so. Nor have researchers managed to discover any relationship between Zaichnevskii's Moscow circle and the young St. Petersburg student. The historian tempted to trace Tkachev's dictatorial revolutionaries of the 1870s to this early document will find little supportive evidence.

Awaiting trial, Petr's friend Olshevskii made the mistake of trying to smuggle a note out of prison to warn his associates about police surveillance. He addressed it to his roommate Nikolai Kemarskii and asked Kemarskii to tell Tkachev that he was being held. He even thought he knew the identity of the anonymous informer. Unfortunately the note was seized by an alert guard and turned over to the Third Section. Kemarskii was arrested at once (June 1862). A search of the apartment Kemarskii and Olshevskii shared revealed a brief note from Tkachev saying he had dropped by. The search of Petr's own quarters had more definitive results: in his possession were found a number of sarcastic poems and two copies of Ogarev's proclamation *What the People Need*, with its famous opening lines: "What do the people need? Very simply, the people need land and freedom."[39] Tkachev, however, was not arrested until November 17.

Petr was interrogated by the police and signed two depositions. He denied close friendship with Olshevskii and his roommate, admitting only "I have been at Olshevskii's so far as I can remember several times a week, sometimes twice, sometimes only once every two weeks; I went to Kemarskii's at the same time as they lived in the same apartment."[40] They never talked of politics, he said in a rather obvious falsehood. He had never read anything Olshevskii had written although he knew that his friend had composed a treatise on government policy in Poland. He was not acquainted with Olshevskii's friends outside of Kemarskii.

Petr also made an effort to explain the incriminating documents found in his apartment. As to the poems, he said, some of them dated back to his gymnasium days. A few of them had been given to him by a student in Kronstadt, and several had been supplied by a foreigner. He

39. These famous phrases had been published by Ogarev in *Kolokol* in July 1861 and were soon being circulated in pamphlet form. See N. P. Ogarev, *Izbrannye sotsialno-politicheskie i filosofskie proizvedeniia*, 1: 527-28. That Tkachev possessed Ogarev's work in two copies probably caused the police to suspect that he planned to pass it along.

40. Lemke, "K biografii," p. 152. Tkachev made his first deposition only after being urged by a priest (Lemke, *Politicheskie protsessy*, pp. 585-86).

had copied them himself, always on the spur of the moment, and kept them for laughs–for their "loud phrases and empty blabber."[41] For his possession of the Ogarev proclamation Tkachev had a more ingenious explanation.

About a year ago I became acquainted with a certain gentleman in the public library, acquainted to the extent that on our meetings we bowed, we chatted–but no more; he did not know my family name nor I his, nor did he and I know where each other lived. One time in the evening–I remember that this was before some sort of holiday, it seems before Easter–when I was getting ready to leave the public library, this gentleman arrived there; seeing me, he came to me, drew me aside, and asked had I read Ogarev's work, *What the Russian People Need*. I answered that I had not. Then he thrust a page of some sort of rolled up paper into my hand and left. It surprised me that a man whom I knew so slightly and who knew me so slightly had given me forbidden works in a public place. . . . I read through the work and it did not produce any particular impression on me because I am in general not in agreement with the thoughts of Mr. Ogarev although, by the way, in the basic idea of this proclamation I saw nothing seditious or antigovernmental. The basic thought is that the people need land and liberty. But has the government not several times clearly and openly expressed this thought? How else can one explain the other humanitarian measures taken by the government to improve the way of life of *pomeshchik* peasants, to secure them land for future use? Having read Ogarev's work, I rolled it up and put it in my pocket, for I wanted to return it to the gentleman who had given it to me, but it so happened that I did not meet him for two or three weeks; because of the holiday, the library was closed. And then I went to the village with mother and forgot about Ogarev's work, forgot even that I had it. . . .[42]

It is difficult to imagine that the device of the mysterious stranger was swallowed whole by the secret police.

Tkachev's case, together with Olshevskii's, was investigated by a special committee under the chairmanship of A. F. Golitsyn and thence referred to a department of the Senate (the supreme court of the land) for decision in January 1863. The Senate sentenced Olshevskii to a year in prison and thereafter to exile. For Tkachev the penalty was far less

41. Lemke, "K biografii," p. 155. Tkachev made fun of these poems, commenting about one ("Christ Is Risen") that the author "is so carried away that he has forgotten what time we live in, saying, for example, that angels sing, forgotten whether the point of the day is liberation or resurrection [*osvobozhdenie ili voskresenie*]." Soviet scholars believe these poems to have been written by Tkachev himself (see N. Belchikov, "Stikhotvornye opyty P. N. Tkacheva," *Russkaia literatura*, 1958, no. 4, pp. 178-87) and have reprinted them in the 1975 edition of Tkachev's *Sochineniia*, 1: 558-69. Lemke apparently disagreed, for when he published the ode to A. Mikhailov in *Politicheskie protsessy*, pp. 136-37, he termed the author anonymous. In any case the poems were unsophisticated in style, mostly radical in tone, and often dedicated to revolutionary heroes of the early 1860s.

42. Lemke, "K biografii," pp. 153-54. Tkachev's description of the innocuous content of Ogarev's proclamation is hardly borne out by a reading; indeed, the tsar is blatantly compared with Judas Iscariot (Ogarev, 1: 530).

severe, for the police had been unable to prove any conspiratorial association between the two young men. The judgment amounted to a reprimand.

The former student of St. Petersburg University Petr Tkachev, nineteen years, accused of association with the student Olshevskii in his criminal schemes and of visiting Olshevskii with criminal intent at the time of his stay in the Second Overland Hospital, is freed by the Court; but for possessing the inciting proclamation entitled *What the People Need* and for not reporting it to the proper person, he will be imprisoned for three months.[43]

Mikhail Lemke's phraseology indicated that Tkachev was released on January 31, 1863; at least on that date he was given a farewell warning and exhortation for good behavior by the Senate. Lemke further records that the verdict was sent to the State Council for approval and that the minister of justice returned it to the Senate so approved in October 1863. The decision then went to the tsar for confirmation, but the tsar did not act on the matter for over a year (October 1864), according to Lemke's statistics. The confirmed decision was then communicated to those involved in an open meeting of the appropriate Senate department on November 5, 1864.[44] The incredible time lapse between the sentencing and the final communication is conceivable within the Russian bureaucratic system. Less certain is the actual stage of the procedure at which Tkachev was released from prison. The date given by Lemke seems unlikely in that Petr had not yet served the requisite three-month term. Either he remained longer, as other observers suggest, or he was released and returned to prison to serve out his sentence later after it was confirmed by the tsar.[45]

Wherever he was, Petr became nineteen in June 1863. He was young

43. Lemke, *Politicheskie protsessy*, p. 595.

44. Ibid., pp. 585-86, 596.

45. The somewhat vague statement by the editors of the 1975 edition of Tkachev's *Sochineniia* seems to confirm Lemke's opinion that Tkachev was released after investigation in February 1863 and returned to prison to serve his three-month term only after final judgment on his case was passed by the Senate and confirmed by the tsar in November 1864; see Tkachev, *Sochineniia*, p. 13. Although this procedure seems unusual, it would explain why Tkachev's works appeared regularly in the press from April 1863 through the following year. Nevertheless Annenskaia remembered that Tkachev was in prison for almost a year (p. 62); Coquart seems to believe that he was still behind bars in autumn 1864 (pp. 189, 194); and Venturi, surely inaccurate, stated that Tkachev was sentenced to three years in prison (pp. 252, 390). Another misunderstanding has to do with the relationship of Tkachev to Pisarev and Petr Ballod, who were arrested in the spring of 1862. Although they were all sentenced at the same court session (owing to their apparent violation of the same law), the men had not actually associated. It is not certain that Tkachev ever personally knew Pisarev, on whose journal he was later to work. Cf. Lemke, *Politicheskie protesessy*, p. 579.

by many standards, but young men matured rapidly in his day. His appearance was far from prepossessing, and few of his contemporaries were later to remember him at all. He was quiet, and he seems to have retained his pleasure in being often alone, to have preferred his work to the clash and clamor of St. Petersburg student life. His personality belied the acerbity of his pen. "The dreadful conspirator Tkachev was then a very sweet, thin youth," wrote one of the editors who published his works,[46] and a colleague on another journal described him as "a small man, thin, very young, modest, soft spoken, reserved, with a smiling little face, resembling an institute student moving into society for the first time."[47] His sister Annenskaia called him "gentle, not angry, but world-loving," and said that "knowing him intimately, one would not believe him also to be the ruthless critic . . . who so unceremoniously tore into the writer-artists; yet it was even more difficult to anticipate from him those fierce political theories he espoused."[48]

Yet this quiet youth was radical enough, albeit some historians (including Franco Venturi) have exaggerated Petr's role in the riots that led to his early arrests.[49] Annenskaia admits that young Petr aggravated her new husband almost beyond his tolerance; she describes her brother sitting smiling in his chair, pressing all conclusions to their extremity, and calling quietly for ultimate solutions while her husband writhed in irritation. At one time, she tells us, Petr was convinced that society could progress only when all its members over the age of twenty-five were simply eliminated.[50] Somewhere even in these early years the young "institute student" picked up his affinity for radical causes, an affinity that would lead him to become one of the most extreme revolutionaries of his generation.

Petr later identified himself with the radical students of his youth. "I myself belong to this generation," he was to write in 1874 in one of his furious letters to P. L. Lavrov,

with it I have experienced its enthusiasms and mistakes, its beliefs and hopes, its illusions and disenchantments, and almost every blow that fierce reaction inflicted

---

46. P. D. Boborykin, "Za polveka," *Golos minuvshego*, no. 3 (1913), p. 179.

47. P. P. Suvorov, "Zapiski o proshlom," *Russkoe obozrenie*, bk. 9 (1893), p. 144.

48. Annenskaia, p. 62.

49. Venturi does it by condensing Tkachev's activities over the years into a few brief sentences, as if he were constantly sought after by police for overt revolutionary activity (pp. 390-91). See also Meijer, pp. 39-40, and Kozmin, *Tkachev*, pp. 21 ff. Both Western scholars probably took their lead from Kozmin.

50. Annenskaia, p. 62.

on it has affected me either directly or in the person of my close comrades and friends. Since the benches of gymnasium I have known no society other than the society of youths absorbed in student meetings, conspiring secretly, establishing Sunday schools and reading centers, directing artels and communes, devoted to popular education, to the idea of growing close to the people, and again and again conspiring. I was always with them and among them—always except when I was separated from them by the thick casement walls of Peter-Paul fortress. Could I not know people with whom I lived with the same life for ten years, [with whom] I shared both grief and joy?[51]

Evidence belies the tone if not the words of his statement. At nineteen, whether from shyness or caution, Tkachev held himself apart. He had been arrested twice, not for leading demonstrations or for plotting a conspiracy but (on one occasion) for milling in a crowd and (on the other) for possessing illegal literature and associating with a person more actively revolutionary than himself. Undoubtedly acquainted with radicals of his generation, he carefully stayed out of their organizations. Secret police files indicate his presence at only two of the dozens of meetings that were investigated between 1862 and 1868, and recent Soviet scholarship has unearthed no evidence of conspiratorial associations in which he was personally involved.[52] On the other hand, by this early age he had proven himself able with a pen and had accomplished more than many a radical contemporary. His articles on aspects of the law were already expressing some of the principles he espoused in later life: a sense of egalitarianism, a sympathy for the poor, a demand for fair play. Tkachev's character was already taking shape. He was never to be an active leader among men, but he was often able to sway them through his writings.

---

51. Tkachev, 3: 58.

52. Recently published information from police archives confirms Tkachev's attendance at a student meeting held in the quarters of an assistant editor of *Russkoe slovo;* he was also arrested and held briefly for joining the protest crowd outside a theater on the opening of an antinihilist play. He apparently maintained contact with his old friends Olshevskii and Kemarskii. Still Soviet efforts to connect him with any revolutionary conspiratorial groups (if such groups actually existed in the mid-1860s) have unearthed no positive evidence (Tkachev, *Sochineniia*, pp. 12-17; Vilenskaia, passim).

3

Sources and Formulations

The years of the middle sixties were good years for Petr Tkachev, assuming that the successful establishment of one's name and reputation is a challenging and stimulating process whatever one's time and place. When he emerged from prison, Petr had no full-time employment, no journal to which (as in later years) he became a regular contributor. Still he was developing. His articles were appearing in many different publications. He was expanding in interests, no longer confining his work to problems of the law. Moreover, he was accumulating the elements of a *Weltanschauung*, a world view he would maintain through his lifetime—bit by bit arriving at some fundamental conclusions and preparing to fit them like the pieces of a puzzle into one another.

Tkachev wrote continually and prolifically. During the year after June 1863, in prison or out, he published a dozen articles, including a long study in three installments—one article every month. Words poured from his pen. He still enjoyed discussing law and legal questions: he wrote on prisons and courts, attorneys and crime, juveniles and incorrigibles. He contemplated foreign courts and the bases of foreign law, reviewed legal textbooks, and evaluated legal encyclopedias. But he moved in new directions too and expanded the scope of his interests. He wrote a series of articles best described by his title "Statistical Studies," articles in which he attempted to analyze from published statistics the sources of Russian criminality and poverty, the elements of her population, and the condition of her cities.[1] In Decem-

---

1. Reprinted in Tkachev, 5: 42-89.

ber 1864 he published his first review of a novel, a long, rambling summary of its plot sprinkled with self-conscious assertions about the role of the critic and tentative efforts at psychological analysis.[2]

He contributed to more journals as well. After April 1863, when *Time* was suppressed by the censor (over a misunderstanding that had nothing to do with Tkachev), the Dostoevskii brothers temporarily went out of the publishing business. The following year they began again, and Tkachev contributed an article to their new journal *Epoch*, a short-lived publication, always lagging behind with its issues and fighting the financial disaster that soon overwhelmed it. The young critic wrote a couple of pieces for the *Zhurnal ministerstva iustitsii* (Journal of the Ministry of Justice) and another for the periodical *Iuridicheskii vestnik* (Juridical Herald).[3] The most widely read journal to which he regularly contributed was a monthly periodical called *Biblioteka dlia chteniia* (Library for Reading), an old-timer that had published works by some of Russia's great literary figures and that merits special mention here.[4]

The *Library* was a well-established periodical, dating from 1834. Its editor in Tkachev's early years, a man named P. Boborykin, was by no means a violent radical in political outlook, but he was a strong liberal and deeply concerned with contemporary social thought and reform. His memoirs show him to have been sympathetic with Chernyshevskii's viewpoints on many subjects.[5] He was interested, for example, in utilitarianism; like Chernyshevskii, he sought to publish John Stuart Mill in Russian translation but ran up against the censor's disapproval.[6] Around him on the *Library* he had gathered some of the leading writers of the day, including Alexander Ostrovskii and Gleb Uspenskii, whom he later lost to his rival *Contemporary*. Boborykin maintained a moderate editorial line, and the *Library* on the whole held itself aloof from the

---

2. This article was unsigned but has been identified by Kozmin. Its title is "Geroi perekhodnoi epokhi," *Biblioteka dlia chteniia*, no. 12 (December 1864), pp. 1-29.

3. B. P. Kozmin, editor of Tkachev's collected works, has supplied a basic bibliography in Tkachev, 4: 445-54. Unfortunately the list is not complete; recent scholars have identified other works, published primarily in *Delo*. Many such articles, not included in the Kozmin collection, are used by Viktor Arsenevich Malinin in his *Filosofiia revoliutsionnogo narodnichestva*.

4. Tkachev's works appear in this journal regularly in 1863 and 1864. Unfortunately, *Library* too was doomed to imminent financial collapse.

5. Cf. Boborykin, pp. 172-205. Usakina's judgment that the *Biblioteka* was "openly hostile to the Russian liberation movement" is too harsh (Usakina, "Statia Gertsena 'Very Dangerous!!!' " p. 265).

6. Boborykin, p. 179.

intense and satirical polemics that characterized many more politicized Russian journals of the day.

It was Boborykin's policy, he tells us, to encourage beginners, a lucky policy for Petr Tkachev.[7] Tkachev's first employment on the journal was as translator; the ill-fated "Utilitarianism," never published, was among his works.[8] By September 1863 Boborykin was ready to give the young journalist more responsibility, and in that month Tkachev published a long unsigned review of a legal textbook written by one of Russia's leading juridical scholars. He followed quickly with more imaginative work: the statistical studies based on Russian government compilations, several articles on prisons, and his review of Royer's *Les jumeaux d'Hellas* for the foreign literature column. By 1864 Tkachev was adapting to Russian radical tradition: long reviews of other men's books were becoming a sounding board for his own rapidly developing viewpoints.

Many of Tkachev's most important ideas, ideas that endured through his lifetime, can be assembled by a careful reader of these first dozen articles with their deceptive legalistic titles, published in deceptively conservative journals. Among such lifetime theories was his own variety of economic determinism. He rejected the positivist theory of progress and the idea that an intellectual elite could generate human prosperity. He despised what he called metaphysics and insisted on the empirical scientific method, and he demonstrated even now a strong feeling for right and wrong, particularly in regard to social relationships. All of these leading principles in his particular vision of the world appeared in print before he attained his majority. Certain of the concepts were drawn from ideas so prevalent among young men of the sixties that it is difficult to trace them to any particular source; in some of them, however, Petr struck out on his own path in advance of his generation or contrary to it.

The idea most powerfully attractive to young Petr was what he considered the determining role of economic factors in society and in history. Searching for the dominant force of his own and past times, he hit upon and clung to the importance of the economic. In economics young Tkachev found the key to social life, literature, religion, and thus, of course, the history of the past and the progress of the future. In November 1863, when he was still nineteen, Petr wrote of economic relationships as determining the political structure of a state in one of his articles on criminal law, published in the *Library*. If the distribution

---

7. Ibid., p. 172.

8. Annenskaia tells us she once translated "On Utilitarianism"; it is likely that her brother drew on her work, especially since Boborykin was overwhelmed with the speed with which he fulfilled the assignment (Annenskaia, p. 57).

of wealth was inequitable, government power too would be unequally shared, or, as he put it exactly, "an economic way of life based on a principle favorable to inequitable distribution of wealth carries this aristocratic element into the political structure."[9] Trained in the law, Tkachev carried his axiom into legal relationships.

Positive law, juridical relations comprise one of the aspects of social life. In order to understand this aspect, it is necessary to form for oneself a clear, precise conception of those basic principles and foundations that give, so to speak, the tone and direction to *all* the public life of society. What sort of principles are these? *Economic.*[10]

He went so far as to view economics as the basis not only for law and social life but for religion, literature, and philosophy. "All social life in all its manifestations, with its literature, science, religion, with its political and juridical way of life, is nothing but the product of certain economic principles that lie at the basis of all these social phenomena."[11] The very course of history was determined by changes in economic relationships, and progress could be measured through their improvement.

Given economic principles, developing sequentially, combine human relationships in a certain manner, give birth to industry and trade, science and philosophy, corresponding political forms, the existent juridical way of life, give birth, in a word, to all our civilization, *create* all our progress.[12]

Carried away by the scope of his generalizations, the young Tkachev did not pause to define his terms clearly nor to break them down into explicit examples. Only with respect to his own fondest interest did he attempt further explanation. Poverty and crime, the phenomena to which his early statistical studies were devoted, he viewed as socioeconomic problems, not as the results of individual laziness in the one case nor individual immorality in the other. The poor and the criminal, he wrote, owe their status to a surplus of labor, to society's failure to provide enough remunerative work for everyone. "All those excluded from the overflowing market," he wrote in 1864,

all those deprived of the power and possibility of trying to find the desired work in the market and consequently deprived of the possibility of satisfying the demands of the human organism by legal means, are divided into two categories: the *evildoers* and the *impoverished.*[13]

9. Tkachev, 5: 469 (note with asterisk). In several earlier articles, Tkachev had made statements hinting at economic determinism, but this is one of his first clear formulations.
10. Ibid., p. 23.
11. Ibid., p. 93.
12. Ibid.
13. Ibid., p. 59.

"Metaphysical philosophers, near-sighted economists, and sentimental philanthropists" were wrong in regarding poverty as individual,
inevitable, and ubiquitous. Charity toward the poor was merely a superficial palliative "based on a fallacious and untrue view of the causes
producing poverty"[14] and would never really help. It was not the individual but the entire system that malfunctioned. Tkachev held a similar
view towards criminality, arguing that the rate of crime was a function
of social and economic conditions, of "disorder and malstructure in the
economic way of life of the people."[15] Thus punishment for crime was
no solution; rather it was "useless, consequently unjust; illegal, consequently it should not exist."[16]

Beyond his investigations into poverty and criminality as socioeconomic phenomena, Petr did not explain further. The breadth of his
statements on the determining role of economics in society outcom-
passed the examples he was willing to give.

Where would a young man in St. Petersburg have picked up such
ideas? Theories of socioeconomic determinism were flourishing in
Petr's times, and he might have derived his ideas from many different
sources. Chernyshevskii, whom Tkachev later credited with influencing
his entire generation, was an environmentalist. As early as 1856 in a
famous article on Lessing, Chernyshevskii had suggested that political
institutions and philosophical schools were the product of their social
and economic environment, of the specific historical context of their
times. Any philosophy concerned with "the common aspirations of
mankind," he wrote, must always be "the daughter of the epoch and
the people among whom it arose."[17] In 1860 in *Contemporary* Chernyshevskii published his essay on "The Anthropological Principle in
Philosophy," an investigation into Feuerbach's materialism, which
Chernyshevskii greatly admired.[18] "Political theories," young Petr must
have read among the words of his early idol,

like every philosophical doctrine, are always created under the most powerful
influence of that social situation to which the philosophers belong, and each philosopher was a representative of some one of the political parties struggling in his
time for predominance over the society to which the philosopher belonged.[19]

---

14. Ibid., p. 87.
15. Ibid., p. 472 (note 13).
16. Ibid.
17. Quoted in B. G. Baskakov, *Mirovozzrenie Chernyshevskogo*, p. 414; see also
Lampert, *Sons against Fathers*, p. 138.
18. Cf. Woehrlin, *Chernyshevskii*, pp. 122, 131, 141.
19. N. G. Chernyshevskii, *Antropologicheskii printsip v filosofii*, p. 8.

Most scholars attribute Tkachev's economic determinism to the prime influence of Chernyshevskii.[20]

There were others who spread a similar gospel. Iurii Zhukovskii, a critic on *Contemporary*, by 1864 had expressed a brand of economic determinism similar to Tkachev's and attempted to apply it in historical interpretation. Zhukovskii's book, *Political and Social Theories of the Fifteenth Century*, antedated Tkachev's early formulations, but Zhukovskii was a prolific journalist and Tkachev must have been acquainted with his ideas long before he reviewed the published volume in 1865.[21] V. D. Spasovich, a noted criminal lawyer and professor at St. Petersburg University, published a controversial textbook on criminal law in 1863; Tkachev read it and reviewed it with more than his usual enthusiasm in *Library* (September 1863).[22] Spasovich was convinced that law was not based on transcendental absolutes but rather formulated from the realistic social and economic milieu. Tkachev adopted the environmental view of the origins of law in a later article of his own, having anticipated his conclusions to a great extent in his Spasovich review.

Foreign sources too might have played their part. By 1862 Tkachev was acquainted with the works of a German jurist named Heinrich Dankwart; he reviewed Dankwart's book on civil law later when it appeared in Russian translation.[23] Dankwart clearly associated law with certain economic relationships without, however, entirely rejecting the moral bases of legal doctrine. Tkachev was greatly impressed with *National-Oekonomie und Jurisprudenz;* he praised Dankwart not once but several times in his early articles. In addition, the young critic himself stated (1863) that he found elements of the economic explanation of social phenomena in the works of Adam Smith.[24] Indeed, the second volume of the *Wealth of Nations*, to which Tkachev specifically referred, deals with economic history and the importance of economics in

---

20. See, for example, Malinin, p. 118; Galaktionov and Nikandrov, p. 104. The latter work puts it as follows: "Chernyshevskii facilitated for [Tkachev] the mastering of the basic principle of the materialistic concept of history, formulated by Marx in the preface of *Towards a Critique of Political Economy.*"

21. See Tkachev, 1: 69-77. Kozmin presents additional information in his long footnote 5, pp. 433-35.

22. "Bibliografiia: 'Uchebnik ugolovnogo prava' sostavlennyi V. Spasovichem," *Biblioteka dlia chteniia*, no. 9 (September 1863), pp. 47-64.

23. The book was first published in Germany in 1859. Tkachev mentioned it with approval in his Spasovich article, ibid., p. 56, and thereafter on a number of other occasions. His review of Dankwart's *National-Oekonomie und Jurisprudenz* is not reprinted by Kozmin, but is described in Tkachev, 5: 470-71 (footnote 6).

24. Tkachev, 5: 92.

any society. Very likely many of the books he read, particularly the works of Chernyshevskii and those of Dankwart, combined to convince young Petr that economic relationships were the source of all evil, good, and social development.

Tkachev was probably the first Russian to mention Karl Marx in a published article; this, and the similarity of his early statements to Marx's famous "superstructure" analogy have misled scholars into imputing his early economic ideas to the influence of his great Western contemporary. Even a leading Soviet historian once dubbed Tkachev the first Russian Marxist.[25] Careful investigation does not confirm this viewpoint. Certainly by 1865 Tkachev had read Marx's first clear and widely available statement of economic determinism in the introduction to *Zur Kritik der politischen Oekonomie*, published in Germany six years before. With enthusiasm young Tkachev quoted the famous words: "The sum total of these relations of production constitutes the economic structure of society, the real foundation on which rises a juridical and political superstructure."[26] The words seemed to Tkachev to confirm what he himself had long preached and what, he said, every thinking man must now recognize.[27] Nevertheless, it is difficult to believe that the origin for Tkachev's early statements should be sought in Marx. In the first place Tkachev was a prolific citer of sources and had he known Marx in 1863 when he made his original assertions, he undoubtedly would have said so. His very enthusiasm in 1865 indicated that Marx was new to him; a year before he had expressed regret that so few writers were applying the principles of economic determinism on a broad basis to contemporary life and history.[28]

In the second place, Tkachev's own economic determinism never took on any truly scientific definition and never considered economics in Marxist terms of productive relationships. Rather it tended in some instances to become psychological (a man thought first of his pocket-book) or in others social (a government leaning on the gentry for support would necessarily favor the gentry in its economic policies). As A. Walicki has put it,

This specific "economic materialism" of Tkachev did not amount to Marxism; it consisted rather in a peculiar mixture of some elements of Marxism with a rather

---

25. M. N. Pokrovskii, *Ocherki russkogo revoliutsionnogo dvizheniia XIX-XX vv.*, p. 62.

26. Tkachev, 1: 70, in his own footnote. The sentence is from the introduction to the book; see Karl Marx and Friedrich Engels, *Werke*, 13: 8-9.

27. Tkachev, 1: 70.

28. Cf. ibid., 5: 24, 90.

primitive utilitarianism, grossly exaggerating the role of direct economic motivation in individual behavior.[29]

Most contemporary Soviet scholars deny that Tkachev was any kind of Marxist at all.[30]

If Petr's early economic theories probably reflected a blend of Dankwart, Chernyshevkii, and the general beliefs of his day, in another important area the young critic parted company with his contemporaries and did not hesitate to let them know it. His early works deplored the intense interest in science that so inspired his friends and attempted to refute the positivist theory of progress through scientific achievement that many of his colleagues were eagerly endorsing.

The air of St. Petersburg was indeed full of excitement about the new strides of Western science, and many young people around Petr were swept up in enthusiasm. Although Dmitrii Pisarev, perhaps the greatest Russian popularizer of science, was only beginning his career in 1862, the passion for science already gripped the younger generation. Among Russia's most hotly debated writers were the German popularizers of scientific discoveries and their meaning. Ludwig Büchner's mechanistic *Kraft und Stoff* was prescribed reading for a whole generation; university students long recalled their excitement when they first discovered the book. Young people read Jacob Moleschott's physiology, and it was fashionable to define behavior and even morality in terms of physiological reactions. Spasovich had done so, and Tkachev had approved.[31] Chernyshevskii endorsed a mechanistic explanation of human behavior.[32] Dobroliubov wrote a long article entitled "The Organic Development of Man in Connection with his Mental and Moral Activities."[33] By 1863 the Russian translation of Henry Thomas Buckle's scientistic *History of Civilization in England* had gone into a second printing. Darwin's *Origin of the Species* became widely known

29. Andrzej Walicki, *The Controversy over Capitalism*, p. 141.

30. Ibid. Malinin, p. 119, speaks of Tkachev's "simplification" and "vulgarization" of Marxist concepts within the framework of his "mechanistic" interpretation. The economic historian A. L. Reuel has an early and thoughtful analysis: "Ekonomicheskie vzgliady P. N. Tkacheva," *Problemy ekonomiki*, no. 4 (1938), pp. 142-61. After some sharp criticism of his early works, B. P. Kozmin came to a similar conclusion in "K voprosu otnoshenii P. N. Tkacheva marksizmu," *Literaturnoe nasledstvo* 7-8 (1933): 117-23. See also my own article "Tkachev and the Marxists," *Slavic Review* 29, no. 1 (March 1970): 22-34.

31. Tkachev's review of Spasovich, *Biblioteka dlia chteniia*, p. 57.

32. Woehrlin, p. 131.

33. Published in Nikolai Aleksandrovich Dobroliubov, *Selected Philosophical Essays*, pp. 69-101.

among the Russian intelligentsia; Tkachev was familiar with it in 1862. Herbert Spencer's works began to be translated into Russian as early as 1860.

Caught up in his concern for people and society, driven by his demands for improvements in social conditions rather than discoveries in the laboratory, young Petr Tkachev disliked the whole business. To his credit he said so outright, although it meant swimming against a powerful tide. What was so important about science that men should forsake the study of society for the study of the cell? "It is strange indeed," he wrote in 1864,

that frequently we see jurists reading books on natural history, philologists concerning themselves with physiology, historians listening to lectures on chemistry, but we never see naturalists, philologists, or historians reading juridical handbooks. . . . Is not the knowledge and study of social sciences just as important? . . . Not at all minimizing the great significance of natural sciences, we for our part still assert with complete conviction that study and dissemination among the masses of social, primarily economic, sciences, and—as it has the deepest, inseverable connection with them—juridical science may be more important at the given moment, may lead to more decisive and fruitful results than all other knowledge.[34]

Even in these early years Tkachev may have feared that the study of nature's ways might divert man from the fighting of the revolutionary cause.

Specifically mentioning Buckle by name, Tkachev early attacked the idea that social progress occurs through the accumulation and dissemination of knowledge. Tkachev did not believe that the acknowledged march of science, the accomplishment of an intellectual elite, would automatically create a better world. He snarled at Buckle. "Wise heads reveal some sort of truth," he interpreted the English historian as saying. "The truth little by little begins to spread—from the *intelligent* it transfers to the stupid, from the minority to the majority, and the revolution is completed, so to speak, by itself."[35] The idea only made him angry. "Of course," he wrote,

all this caters to our optimistic tendency. We love to lull ourselves with thoughts about progress. Thus we love to listen to those thinkers who turn our attention exclusively to that sphere of human activity in which progress actually is inevitable. Indeed, who dares to doubt the progress of our knowledge? . . . How can we not love those thinkers who point out to us . . . this victorious procession of the human spirit through the great arena of history?[36]

To one who hoped for drastic change, the tortoise-slow spread of knowledge outward from the intellectual elite seemed frustrating indeed.

34. Tkachev, 5: 26–27.
35. Ibid., p. 91.
36. Ibid.

The intellectual elite struck Tkachev as parasitical rather than heroic. He painted a picture of the unwashed and unpolished masses giving of the sweat of their brows to "deliver comfort and solace to us who make progress."

Here are the thinkers—the optimists; they assure the unbelievers that progress of the intelligentsia is deeply, directly connected with social progress, that the latter is nothing but the result of the former, [that] they can rest content, and, divorcing themselves from impious thoughts, peacefully continue their occupations in laboratories, in libraries, in academies, universities, write scholarly treatises and articles, make eloquent speeches, express noble feelings in scholarly gatherings.[37]

Needless to say, Tkachev's own idea of true progress rested on the firm old cornerstone of material socioeconomic improvement. What he called economic factors determined society's shape and movement.

If these [economic] principles in themselves are unjust and unreasonable, then their consequences too will not be distinguished by better qualities; if in their foundation they include the seed of slavery and despotism, then the tree of civilization bred from them will scarcely bear better fruit. Consequently this theory [of mine] conceives of social progress only under one condition, if the principles generating the perpetual movement and metamorphoses in the social world are reasonable and just; if not, says this theory, then there can be no progress. There is movement, there is change, there is development, but no progress in the sense of betterment. On the contrary, the farther and farther a bad principle develops, the worse and worse the consequences to which it leads us. Progress itself, that is, improvement in a good direction, appears only when instead of a bad or unreasonable principle a good and reasonable principle lies at the basis of everything. In the development of this principle there will be progress.[38]

The same dislike for the remote, the scholastic, and the impractical led young Tkachev (along with many of his generation) to dislike speculative—what he called metaphysical—philosophy. Tkachev was above all a rationalist. For all his dislike of scholastic science that held itself remote from human affairs, he had confidence in science's knowledge and above all in its methods. As one recent scholar has pointed out, he adhered to the cult of reason; he insisted on subjecting knowledge to rational test and empirical examination.[39] Throughout his life he rejected metaphysics as impractical and unprovable.

He began his attacks in these early years via his original interest in law. The interesting article "Juridical Metaphysics," published in *Library* for December 1863, represented Tkachev's major effort to define the fundamental nature of law.[40] He had attempted definitions once before—in his review of Spasovich's textbook—and obviously

---

37. Ibid., p. 92.
38. Ibid., p. 93.
39. Malinin, pp. 13-14.
40. This article is reprinted in Tkachev, 5: 15-41.

enjoyed it. Now he was ready more carefully to categorize legal theorists and their views. Reviewing three Russian encyclopedias of law, he found the authors defining their topic historically or philosophically. The historical school sought the essence of law in the evolution of common law, which its proponents tended to base on national character or on popular genius. To Tkachev the concept of popular genius (unless securely lodged on specific socioeconomic factors) was no more than a magic formula evoked by sly jurisprudents to explain away certain difficult questions. On the other hand philosophical jurisprudence, as young Petr saw it, viewed law as emerging from some facet of human nature (man's striving for a common life, man's striving for freedom, man's striving toward beatitude) or from a kind of infallible axiom or from some transcendental, superhuman moral force. All of these theories were idealizations, deriving law from the immutable and axiomatic, the absolute and abstract. To this young jurist the theorists were wrong: law was the product of a concrete social world rather than a cosmic principle with an existence of its own.

The whole error of juridical philosophy consists precisely in the fact that it has seen the juridical life of society separately from social life in general, that it has not wanted to see the connection between the legal and economic relationships of people, that, isolating the former from the latter, it has developed and constructed [legal relationships] by means of speculative abstractions, considered them something self-sufficient, independent, although in essence they were dependent and conditioned in all respects.[41]

He accused certain legal philosophers of raising to the level of axiom those positive laws or statutes that were not axiomatic at all but simply a reflection of social relationships. He had written the same thing in regard to Spasovich,[42] and he would say it again. One of Tkachev's favorite complaints was always that, determined to construct an ideal rational system, man ended by merely rationalizing the system around him.

Tkachev's own contention, of course, was that "life has created law."[43] The environment had determined. Philosophers only justified what they saw.

The life of the ancient world created slavery, and philosophy supported it; the Middle Ages developed the principle of hierarchical subordination, the principles of feudalism and serfdom; scholasticism justified and rationalized these principles; finally in the reality around us now there exist many similar circumstances, the

41. Ibid., pp. 23-24.
42. Tkachev's Spasovich review, *Biblioteka dlia chteniia*, p. 49. His review in many ways anticipates "Iuridicheskie metafiziki."
43. Tkachev, 5: 28.

reasonableness and usefulness of which are unconditionally denied by experimental and social sciences, like, for example, statistics and political economy—but circumstances that are supported and justified by philosophy.[44]

Legal philosophers emerged not only foolish but hypocritical and blind to real justice as well.

Tkachev did not on principle reject the idea of setting into formulae those "general fundamental laws that create and regulate the legal life of a nation," as he put it.[45] However, he was convinced that such conclusions could not be based on some sort of metaphysical, speculative formula; instead they had to be achieved by empirical investigation.

Philosophy seeks out general immutable laws that direct, explain, and condition given phenomena of reality. But these laws, being the last, final conclusion of experience [as] revealed or rather observed and explained not by means of speculation, not by means of unproven hypotheses, but by pure empiricism and by *experimental* analysis—such laws can and must be raised to the stage of mathematical certainty, of mathematical axioms, such laws, factually verified and proved, can and actually do serve to explain not only the past and the present but even the future.[46]

Tkachev was still young. He and his contemporaries were to dedicate years and lifetimes to the fascinating possibilities of discovering some great system by which nature and man might be known to operate. In 1864 Petr could hardly foresee the intellectual agonies he would endure in his attempts to reconcile immutable law with voluntaristic revolution.

Young Petr himself based his idea of the origins of law on the natural freedom of man: "Each man is free, and all peoples are equally free."

This consciousness of general freedom, embedded in our soul, is reflected in the relationships of people to each other. Considering ourselves morally-reasoning and free beings, we also begin to consider other people as morally-reasoning, begin to recognize also in them the same freedom that we respect in ourselves, and thus appears the need to limit our freedom, from which emerges an understanding of rights and obligations and consequently of laws. The uniform definition and equalization of our relationships to each other is called justice. Thus the concept of justice is, as the reader may easily see, a consequence of urgent, practical necessity, a consequence of real-life relationships, a consequence of the purely accidental collision between people endowed with freedom.[47]

Although he did not admit it, Tkachev's views fell within the category he himself had once scornfully labeled philosophical jurisprudence,

---

44. Ibid., p. 29.
45. Ibid., p. 41.
46. Ibid., p. 40.
47. Ibid., pp. 39-40.

for he was interpreting law as based on a facet of human nature, in this case man's striving for freedom. He contradicted himself, and not for the last time. Throughout his life he would slip into broad generalizations while criticizing others for indulging in the same pastime.

Tkachev's views on speculative philosophy were common to his generation. Two decades earlier Herzen and the men of the forties had made long, introspective, and often personal treks from Schiller to Schelling and from Schelling to Hegel. But by 1860 even Herzen had set aside philosophical speculations and become absorbed in questions of politics and society. Chernyshevskii stood even more firmly in the nonphilosophical camp. After his early years as a Hegelian he devoted less and less time to purely speculative philosophy. When he was not considering the actual problems of social reform, he immersed himself in studies of social and political theory; in his writings matters of philosophy occupied few pages and most of them were didactic paraphrases.[48] Likewise for most of the radicals of Tkachev's generation— the Zaichnevskiis and Ishutins, the Axelrods and the Zasuliches—philosophical speculation does not seem to have existed. They never reasoned out their rejection of idealism because they never found it worth studying and rejecting. Like Tkachev they studied social theory but sneered at metaphysics. Like him they scorned all but the empirical method of proof. Yet their passions and emotions often led them to espouse those very ethical and moral values they rejected in others. This "generation of materialism," to use Carlton Hayes's phrase, had an ethos of its own.

If Tkachev slipped into defining law on the same philosophical basis he criticized in others, he came face to face also with the dilemma of the environmentalist. Other people's morality, he was sure, was dictated and perverted by the standards of their times.

. . . Everything that is endorsed by contemporaries and, worse, by contemporary philosophers who have . . . the clearest concept of their own "moral, reasonable nature"—all this is moral, reasonable, and legal. In the ancient world slavery was moral, in the Middle Ages the Inquisition and torture were moral, until the peasant reform serfdom was moral in Russia, the inhuman, barbaric punishments that existed and that still, unhappily, now exist in the criminal codes of societies contemporary with us are moral; in a word, everything dull, senseless, ignorant, and routine is moral if only it succeeds in setting deep enough roots in our social way of life, if only it eats enough into our flesh and blood so that philosophy and learning do not dare to protest, cannot and do not want to raise their voice on behalf of profaned and crucified truth. A fine criterion—but let it work itself out![49]

---

48. Woehrlin, pp. 140-41. Lampert says Chernyshevskii became more interested in the sources and applications of abstract ideas than in the systems themselves (Lampert, *Sons against Fathers*, p. 144).

49. Tkachev, 5: 38-39.

Tkachev never paused to speculate on his own ethic within his own environment. Indeed his relativistic view of morality never prevented him from developing a strong sense of right and wrong. The feeling for social justice that young Petr expressed when he was still in his teens was to become a cornerstone of Russian populism. In fervent writings the radicals of Tkachev's generation attacked the evils of systems that could tolerate serfdom or poverty. Tkachev himself spoke most passionately and dramatically on behalf of the poor—those who, by his own definition of poverty, owed their sufferings to society's economic malfunctions. Like Chernyshevskii he drew on the West for his examples of their worst agonies.

In the market of human labor, the crush is unbearable; each with his supply [of labor] is striving there. The price for labor, determined here as in all other markets by *supply and demand*, descends ever lower and rapidly threatens to reach its extreme limit, its very minimum; and in certain branches of labor and in certain limited markets, it already has reached it. In the West, in the great industrial centers, the factory worker scarcely earns his crust of bread, barely earns the means of satisfying his primary, necessary wants. The workers little by little are being converted into hungry proletarians. And each year in addition ever new and ever changing crowds swell the marketplace and with each year the pressure there becomes more and more unbearable.

Small wonder! *Labor* is considered the patent for life, labor gives the right to existence, to a share of the common quota of human happiness. A proletarian by his labor earns for himself a daily piece of bread, but if he does not work he would not have even this little piece! Everyone needs bread. Everyone needs the possibility of satisfying the demands of the human organism. But bread and the means for satisfying human demands are bought at the price of labor; thus all thirst for labor and are greedy for it. However, "many are called but few are chosen." *Supply exceeds demand.* There is not enough work for all, the privilege of earning bread "by the sweat of his brow" is not extended to everyone. Here as everywhere, the strong, the cunning, the audacious force their way ahead, but the weak and the faint-hearted, the infirm and in general the "poor in spirit and in flesh" remain behind.[50]

His articles on poverty and crime demonstrated deep sympathies for the downtrodden. Tkachev did not yet blatantly propose a solution, but there was strong suggestion between his lines. Palliatives would not help, he said, scorning those who suggested them.[51] He hinted that private ownership did not help either.[52] The long-term cure stemmed from his conviction that poverty and criminality would not be ended until the socioeconomic inequalities that produced them could finally be eliminated.

Thus did Tkachev begin his career as a writer and a critic. In many

---

50. Ibid., p. 58.
51. Ibid., pp. 62-63.
52. Ibid., p. 19.

ways he was a man of his generation: at the age of eighteen one could scarcely expect otherwise. He had a strong sense of social injustice as did his young radical contemporaries, the more so because he did not believe poverty or its consequences originated with the individual. He was already developing a sociological approach to his work, tending to view evils in their social context and interested more in broad social groups than in individuals or elites. His economic determinism, the hallmark of his early thought, lay at the root of his rejection of the popular positivist theory of progress through science; Tkachev's work was never characterized by such optimism for the future. He disliked any metaphysical speculation, as he put it, and demanded that conclusions be reached by a strictly empirical method firmly rooted in reality. Yet he did not reject moral judgment even though it might be based on just those indefinite idealistic and absolutist aphorisms he generally deplored.

Before he was twenty Tkachev had published over a dozen articles, many in the form of long reviews. He was beginning to establish himself as a writer in the legal Russian press, and his work for *Library* was of great importance as he did so. He had hardly become rich and he was not yet famous, but at this early age he must have delighted in the knowledge that he had discovered his metier.

4

Tkachev, Pisarev,
and the *Russian Word*

The years 1865-66 in Tkachev's life were dominated
by a new and vital association with Dmitrii Pisarev and the nihilists. It is
important and difficult to assess the influence of nihilism on Tkachev's
early thought for a variety of reasons. Nihilism itself had many facets;
Pisarev's ideas were sometimes original but often common to his radical
generation; and during this period Tkachev avoided considering many
of the important issues involved. Surely during his brief period of
association with Pisarev's journal Tkachev doggedly retained his own
particular point of view and transferred many ideas from his earlier
works into his articles. He did not actually become a nihilist in the
sense implicit in the world view of Pisarev, nihilism's most famous
defender. On the other hand, his experience with nihilism contributed
to his intellectual development and expansion into new realms of
thought. Among his contemporaries it determined his own image for
years to come and inaugurated personal and literary associations of
lifetime duration. These brief years, then, see Tkachev's maintenance of
his own stance, his first ties with new colleagues, his adoption of a few
of Pisarev's ideas, and the composition of one of his most interesting
early works.

With the financial collapse of the *Library for Reading* at the beginning of 1865 Tkachev found himself without a regular outlet for his
journal articles. Although he did not sink into destitution, he must have
felt a considerable blow when his immediate source of income was cut
off. What seemed like a promising career as a legal analyst and statistical interpreter was nipped in the bud. The new year could hardly have

seemed happy or prosperous to the young critic. For months his work
lagged, and no articles of his authorship have been identified for most
of 1865.[1] His big break did not come until autumn when, owing to his
reputation in journalistic circles and to a propitious combination of circumstances outside of his own control, Tkachev was offered a position
as a regular contributor to the monthly St. Petersburg journal *Russkoe
slovo* (Russian Word). It was his first association with the radical press,
where he was to find a home for the rest of his life.

   Russian Word was one of the two leading publications of the radical
left. As compared to its rival the *Contemporary*, the journal of Chernyshevskii and Dobroliubov, it was a publication slanted to the younger
set and was the mouthpiece of what came to be known as nihilism. Its
editor was G. E. Blagosvetlov, with whom Tkachev began a lifetime
association.[2] One of the most interesting publicists of his generation,
Blagosvetlov was set up as editor of the *Russian Word* by the journal's
owner, Count Kushelev-Bezborodko, who remained in the background
and later sold out his interest. After a few disappointing editorial starts
the count had discovered Blagosvetlov in Western Europe, where the
younger man was making a typical grand tour, living in Paris (where he
met Turgenev) and in London (where he knew Herzen and Ogarev).[3]

   Blagosvetlov was an ardent Westerner, a positivist, and a Benthamite
utilitarian. The editorship of a journal placed him in a position to work
towards realization of his own most important goals, for Blagosvetlov's
hopes were defined more in cultural-educational than in sociopolitical
terms. He aimed to create an educated Russian elite who would worship
liberty and science, draw close to the West, and thus elevate the cultural
level of Russian society and the critical power of Russian thought.[4] As

   1. Tkachev, 4: 449.
   2. Blagosvetlov still awaits a biographer in any Western language. The most
easily available sketch of his life and beliefs may be found in Coquart, *Dmitri
Pisarev*, pp. 66 ff. B. P. Kozmin has published an article entitled "G. E. Blagosvetlov
i *Russkoe Slovo*," in *Sovremennik*, bk. 1 (1922), pp. 192-250. Additional material
is presented in the essay introduced by G. Prokhorov under the title "P. N. Tkachev
ob izdatelskoi i literaturnoi deiatelnosti G. E. Blagosvetlova," in *Shestidesiatye
gody*, but Prokhorov is not convincing in his argument that the following article
was written by Tkachev. There is some excellent material in Feliks Kuznetsov,
Publitsisty 1860-kh godov: Krug "Russkogo Slova."
   3. On Count Kushelev-Bezborodko and his early difficulties with his journal's
editors and policy see *Istoriia russkoi zhurnalistiki XVIII-XIX vekov*, ed. Berezina
et al., pp. 368-70.
   4. For these and his other attitudes Kozmin called him a "priest's son, speculat-
ing in radicalism" (Kozmin, *Tkachev*, p. 136). The similarity between Blagosvetlov's
ideals and those of young Pisarev is apparent in Coquart's discussion, although
Coquart asserts that Pisarev developed his ideas independently before he came to
know his new editor. See Coquart, p. 74.

an editor, he was efficient, imaginative, irascible, bullheaded, and eventually very influential. He performed his greatest service for the Russian literary world in discovering a talented young University of St. Petersburg student who had written his dissertation on Platonic idealism: Dmitrii Ivanovich Pisarev.

Pisarev cometed across Russia's literary heavens for a period of only a few years, but his flash and style, his ebullience, and his vitriolic rejection of traditional social mores made him the leader of the radical young people reaching maturity in 1865. His influence among radical youth without doubt overcame and eclipsed that of Chernyshevskii. He was the angry young man of nihilism, the audacious cynic who startled the literary world by his deliberate adoption of Turgenev's designation for Bazarov (*Fathers and Sons*), and by his daring espousal of those very qualities in Bazarov that had led other radical reviewers to consider the character an insulting caricature and to reject Turgenev as a traitor to the radical cause. Pisarev made his mark with his review of *Fathers and Sons*, which appeared in the *Russian Word* in March 1862. By what may or may not have been a coincidence, the *Contemporary*'s review of the novel appeared in the same month. The *Contemporary*'s editorial board had a long-standing feud with Turgenev, as Pisarev must have known; it was no surprise that M. A. Antonovich of that journal panned the novel as an attack on the young generation. Where Antonovich condemned, Pisarev praised. Through the influence of Pisarev's pen, Bazarov came close to replacing Chernyshevskii's Rakhmetov as the idol of the young generation.[5] Pisarev's enthusiastic adoption of nihilism drew a youthful following around him. Tkachev later claimed to belong to it.[6]

In its heyday Russian nihilism had two faces: an intellectual creed defined by Pisarev and a behavioral style devised by his followers. As a life style the term nihilist came to denote the flouter of conventions. In the early 1860s young Russian radicals came to flaunt slovenly dress. Women cut their hair, talked back to their parents, and, as Tkachev once wrote with a sigh, acted so independent you could hardly distinguish them from men ("O tempora, o mores!").[7] Couples lived together

---

5. Cf. Coquart, pp. 132-40, where he contends that word of Antonovich's review had been leaked to Pisarev, enabling the latter to compose his own in its deliberately hostile frame. See also Dmitrii Ivanovich Pisarev, *Selected Philosophical, Social, and Political Essays*, p. 705 (note 6). The character of Bazarov stood at the center of these arguments. Turgenev protested in vain that he felt sympathetic toward his young Frankenstein: *Turgenev's Letters*, ed. Edgar H. Lehrman, pp. 133, 135, 138.

6. In a crowded courtroom where he was on trial (B. P. Kozmin, ed., *Nechaev i nechaevtsy*, p. 172).

7. Tkachev, 5: 199.

openly in relations not sanctioned by church or state; communal living groups sprang up among university students. The nihilist existed to shock; he exploited the generation gap and enjoyed doing so.

And shock he did, conservatives and liberals alike. A Third Section secret agent described a female nihilist in unflattering terms: "She has cropped hair, wears blue glasses, is slovenly in her dress, rejects the use of comb and soap, and lives in civil matrimony with an equally repellent individual of the male sex, or with several such."[8] M. E. Saltykov-Shchedrin, a satirist who worked on Pisarev's rival journal *Contemporary*, dismissed the nihilists as enfants terribles—not a bad description for Pisarev himself—who would grow out of it. Shchedrin's nihilist was a hypothetical lop-eared youth.

"I am a democrat," the lop-eared one says to you, and demonstrates this by going around in his overcoat and blowing his nose without the aid of a handkerchief. "I am a nihilist and do not have any prejudices," another lop-eared one tells you, and demonstrates this by being ready at any time of day to run out naked into the street.[9]

Shchedrin's lady nihilist dissected a human cadaver to the joyful rhythms of song and dance, an inspired amalgam of Turgenev's Bazarov (who found life's meaning in dissecting a frog) and Chernyshevskii's Vera Pavlovna (who was an advocate of Fourier-type joyful labor).

The disapproval of *Contemporary* was not confined to nihilist behavior styles but extended to intellectual nihilism as well. The new decade saw a growing rift between *Contemporary* (the vehicle of Chernyshevskii before his arrest in 1862) and *Russian Word* (dominated by Pisarev who wrote from his prison cell), a rift that reached its climax in 1865 shortly before Tkachev joined the staff of the latter periodical. The bitter rivalry that grew up between the two journals became a cause célèbre; Dostoevskii happily termed it a schism among the nihilists, and Pisarev's biographer Armand Coquart considered it "the Byzantine discord of a party without experience which, scarcely constituted and menaced from all sides, foolishly squanders its strengths in order to destroy itself."[10]

The vitriolic, intense, and near-libelous public debate between the journals centered around everything and anything; if a critic on the one affirmed, a critic on the other denied. They argued continually about

---

8. Quoted in Lampert, *Sons against Fathers*, p. 310.

9. Quoted in B. P. Kozmin, " 'Raskol v nigilistakh': Epizod iz istorii russkoi obshchestvennoi mysli 60-kh godov," in *Iz istorii revoliutsionnoi mysli v Rossii*, p. 29.

10. Coquart, p. 292. Dostoevskii used the phrase in *Epokha*, no. 5 (1864); see Kozmin, *Iz istorii*, pp. 20-21.

the character of Bazarov and their differing interpretations of nihilism. They argued about the meaning of art, the capacity of Negroes, the social repercussions of Schopenhauer, whether John Stuart Mill represented the viewpoints of the English bourgeoisie, and whether Blagosvetlov in editorial policy was simply fawning before Count Kushelev-Bezborodko. Clever personal attacks were barely disguised by satire. Pisarev, who languished in prison during almost his entire literary career, was at one time defended by his vigorous and dominating mother. The controversy might have recapitulated that between Herzen and Chernyshevskii a few years before, except that the arguments degenerated into matters so trivial that even letters to the editor occasionally urged that the polemic be halted.[11]

The more interesting question is why it arose in the first place. Even in the midst of the arguments *Russian Word* editorially admitted that both journals sought the same goals.[12] In a perceptive article not published until later, N. V. Shelgunov, a critic for *Russian Word*, insisted that Pisarev and Dobroliubov, personifying his journal and *Contemporary* respectively, sprang from the same source and that each could with equal justification claim to be heir to the tradition of Russian radical criticism.[13]

From a cursory reading of the polemics, one might well conclude that personality disagreements, individual styles, and simple competitiveness were the dominant issues, so petty was some of the subject matter and so vitriolic were some of the personal attacks.[14] From a difference in journalistic style, the staffs of both journals traveled from disagreement to hostility to vindictiveness, finding that once begun such tensions were impossible to erase. Furthermore, the *Contemporary* was battling for prestige and a reading public that the *Russian Word* was beginning to steal. Indeed, the older journal was clearly on the defensive, its triumphs lost in the past and its influence slipping, an occasion frequently evoking bitterness. The *Contemporary* was suffering from a lack of imaginative leadership. True, the poet Nekrasov, its long-time editor, was still at the helm, but fortune had deprived him of his essential rudders. Still in his twenties, Dobroliubov died of tuberculosis in 1861. Chernyshevskii went to prison in 1862, and although his novel

---

11. Kozmin, *Iz istorii*, pp. 32-33; Coquart, chap. 10, passim. On this polemic see also Berezina et al., *Istoriia russkoi zhurnalistiki*, pp. 381-84.

12. Kozmin, *Iz istorii*, p. 35.

13. "Neizdannaia statia N. V. Shelgunova o Dobroliubovtsakh i Pisarevtsakh," *Literaturnoe nasledstvo* 25-26: 402-3.

14. Coquart himself, usually a keen observer, tends to belittle any thoughtful basis for the schism (Coquart, p. 292).

What Is to Be Done? (written in prison) roused radical students to passionate excitement, his association with his journal was forever terminated. Those remaining were scarcely a match for the vitality of Blagosvetlov and the sharp tongue of Pisarev. St. Petersburg's radical youth was turning its attention from an older idol to a new. The struggle may have seemed a matter of life and death to *Contemporary*'s staff. The journal was clearly slowing down; it was becoming a cautious father, fighting to best its impatient son. Its unenviable position must have played a role in the vehemence of its attacks.[15]

Actually the gulf between the two journals was much greater than a breach caused by rivalry for circulation or discord of personalities. Kozmin has caught its importance.[16] As Chernyshevskii's influence faded from the *Contemporary*—and it faded so far that Shchedrin on occasion made snide remarks about the novel *What Is to Be Done?*— the *Contemporary* moved steadily in a direction contrary to that of *Russian Word*. It began ever more clearly to adopt the spirit that one day would be called populism: a collectivist, Russian-oriented, peasant-concerned, and occasionally anti-intellectual tradition only beginning to arise in the 1860s. The *Contemporary*'s pages reflected the journal's initial confusion and then later demonstrated its waning interest in Western individualism, scientism, and intellectual elitism, its adoption instead of a sociological approach, the peasant cause, and radical hopes for widespread social change.

The multiple differences between nihilism and populism merit great attention from scholars, but their discussion is hardly in order here. Surely both strains of thought had sprung most immediately from the wide-ranging mind of Chernyshevskii, with his broad and often uncoordinated interests that encompassed both the West's scientistic intellectuals and Russia's illiterate peasants. Indeed Chernyshevskii has been occasionally lumped with the nihilists by some scholars as he has been termed a populist by others. Had he continued his productive life, the designations might not have seemed so mutually exclusive as they did to his contemporaries, as in the following description by Shelgunov:

Dobroliubov [of *Contemporary*] concerns himself more with society, Pisarev with the individual. Dobroliubov shows the way to social aspirations; Pisarev compels thoughtfulness on individual behavior. Dobroliubov wants to rouse energy, Pisarev to teach people to think. Dobroliubov regards things around him critically; Pisarev

---

15. These trials and tribulations are well recorded by Coquart, pp. 274-76. Shchedrin himself quit *Contemporary* in 1864; he and Chernyshevksii had never been great friends. Herzen thought Shchedrin may even have betrayed some of Chernyshevskii's friends to the police in 1862 (Kozmin, *Iz istorii*, p. 26).

16. In his excellent article in *Iz istorii*, especially pp. 35 ff.

wants to teach the reader himself to look critically at life. . . . Dobroliubov acts
through passion on the mind . . . [Pisarev] thinks that first it is necessary to
correct judgment and teach people to think.[17]

Western intellectual rationalism and Russian populist aspirations did
not necessarily travel hand in hand.

In 1865 when he joined the staff of *Russian Word* Tkachev must
have been aware of the journalistic polemics and their significance. If he
agreed more with *Contemporary*, he could hardly afford to be discrimi-
nating. Moreoever, *Russian Word* was a dynamic, challenging publication, and Pisarev was the talk of the young generation. Tkachev must
have been flattered and excited by his new job. He owed his appointment to one of Blagosvetlov's typically bullheaded maneuvers. The
irascible editor had quarreled with his staff. At the core of their argument lay his congenital parsimony as well as his habit of making sweeping copy changes without consulting his writers. Two of his leading
writers quit; from his prison cell Pisarev considered making common
cause with them but eventually lost his nerve and hung on with waning
enthusiasm.[18] One of the writers had specialized in economic problems;
Tkachev's interests made him a perfect replacement. In January 1866
Blagosvetlov added the young critic's name to the list of writers in his
editorial statement, albeit at the bottom.[19] Tkachev was employed
to write a column on new books. Blagosvetlov's personnel difficulties
were Tkachev's great good luck, for in spite of the brevity of Petr's
association with *Russian Word*, the experience was of lasting importance to him.

Circumstances had placed Tkachev in the wrong camp. In the conflict between the old and the new, he stood clearly on the side of
Contemporary. He worked for Pisarev and Blagosvetlov, but his heart
never sold out to intellectual nihilism. A colleague on *Russian Word*, he
belonged more to its rival journal. Pisarev never came close to replacing
Chernyshevskii as an influence in his thinking.

---

17. "Neizdannaia statia Shelgunova," p. 403. The fundamental differences
between the two rival radical journals became clearer as years progressed. In 1867
after both had finally been forced to cease publication, Nekrasov, ex-editor of
Contemporary, made his political preference known by taking over editorship of
Fatherland Notes. He built it into a key journal in the classic populist cause. When
Pisarev emerged from prison in 1867 Nekrasov hired him but their brief association
was notoriously unhappy. Blagosvetlov at the time recognized that Pisarev was not
the same; at least one contemporary attributed the change to Blagosvetlov's own
skill as Pisarev's editor on *Russian Word* (*Shestidesiatye gody*, pp. 225-27).

18. Coquart, pp. 202-8, 285, 358-59.

19. L. A. Plotkin, *Pisarev i literaturno-obshchestvennoe dvizhenie shestidesiatykh godov*, p. 312.

To begin with, Tkachev was never opposed to the new life style of the nihilists. On the contrary he identified himself with it insofar as nihilism represented a code of behavior, a flouting of conventions, and a dislike of contemporary society and its standards. Petr was four years younger than Pisarev, the very age of those people most strongly influenced by nihilism's ill-defined iconoclasms and explicit fads. At an uncertain date he took an attractive young lady for his common-law wife; they seem never to have considered marriage. On several occasions he arranged fictitious marriages, those legal but unconsummated unions designed to free young women from the financial and legal domination of their parents. Tkachev's sister Annenskaia was a nihilist of a thoughtful sort and had drawn around her a circle particularly concerned with women's rights, one of Pisarev's strongest passions.[20] Tkachev was never one to expose his private life to public view, but he obviously enjoyed the behavior of the radicals around him.

Pisarev, Blagosvetlov, and the intellectual beliefs of the nihilists were different. Tkachev could not conscientiously accept them. Actually he had been exposed to the same influences that inspired his colleagues: the German mechanistic materialists who were universal reading for his generation; Buckle, whom he read and translated; positivism, utilitarianism, and scientism.[21] But by no means had he accepted these creeds. He was critical of some and had not written of others. He shared a few beliefs with Pisarev, but he shared more with Chernyshevskii. In *Russian Word* Blagosvetlov let him express his viewpoints, and Tkachev was careful not to make his disagreements with Pisarev seem too sharp.

Both these rebellious young colleagues, after all, held some important views in common. Foremost among them was their desire to construct a new world even though this necessitated the total destruction of the old. Pisarev put it furiously in his famous and often-quoted words: "Here is our ultimatum: What can be smashed must be smashed. What stands the blow is good; what flies apart is rubbish. In any case, hit out right and left; no harm will or can come of it."[22] Pisarev's violence never bothered Tkachev; he did not fear it nor find it shocking. Within a few years he was to assert that only violence could reform

---

20. Annenskaia, p. 63.

21. Tkachev, 5: 16. *Etiudy G. T. Boklia*, edited by Tkachev and published in St. Petersburg in 1867, contains an introduction written by the editor and one article (on the influence of women in science) translated and annotated by him as well. As reported above, Tkachev and his sister had once translated "On Utilitarianism" for *Biblioteka dlia chteniia*.

22. Quoted in Lampert, *Sons against Fathers*, p. 312.

society to make the future richer, more reasonable, and more just. Tkachev had a stronger sense of the past than Pisarev; he might more willingly have built on tradition. But Pisarev's optimism about what he called the great and bright destiny of mankind[23] to a great extent compensated for his mistrust of what had gone before. Tkachev was gloomier about the future, but in 1865 he had not yet said so.

Like Pisarev (and a whole Russian generation) Tkachev prided himself on his hard-headed, common-sense thinking. The cult of reason attracted both of them. The two were both materialists in the tradition of Russian radical critics. "We want to know what is and do not want to surmise about what may be," Pisarev once wrote,[24] and again: "Speculative philosophy is a waste of mental powers, a senseless luxury which can never be understood by the masses which stand in need of daily bread."[25] His essays on Platonic idealism indicate that Pisarev had explored philosophy;[26] Tkachev had never bothered. Yet the two men reached similar conclusions. Tkachev admired people, he wrote in *Russian Word*, who faced facts as they were and deplored deceptive abstractions.[27] Like Pisarev, he despised the idealist who

never takes facts in their pristine, uncolored aspect; he always looks at them through the prism of some sort of ideal that has been hammered into his head by his upbringing or obtained by his own thinking. Thus reality appears to him as the distorted and formless imaginings of his unbridled fantasy. One can compare the idealist with a man whose vision has gone bad, gone bad in such a manner that he sees all objects appearing before his eyes upside down or—to take an example closer to the matter at hand—immersed in some kind of strange and mysterious ether that diffuses brilliance and perfume all over. No matter how frightening a similar illusion of vision would be, it still could never give practical life to that mass of evils the idealistic illusions of the mind carry.[28]

Such an idealist, Tkachev hinted in an unpublished fragment, was Sir Thomas More with his unrealistic vision of Utopia. Tkachev himself preferred Machiavelli for his cool assessments of power and politics.[29]

On one final point Tkachev and Pisarev were in agreement: both rebels deplored art for art's sake and adopted utility as a standard of artistic value. Tkachev was not yet ready to follow Pisarev in the latter's famous denial of aesthetics nor in the setting of realistic criteria for literary criticism, a topic the younger man did not take up until later in

---

23. Pisarev, p. 235.
24. Ibid., p. 105.
25. Ibid., pp. 153-54.
26. Ibid., pp. 45-71.
27. Tkachev, 5: 200.
28. Ibid.
29. Ibid., 1: 71-73.

life. Clearly, however, Tkachev agreed with Pisarev (and with Chernyshevskii and with his whole generation) that the only valid criterion for
judging deeds or ideas was their social usefulness, their actual measurable results in operation. Pisarev was influenced by the Benthamite
ethic, and so was Tkachev. "Any book devoid of social significance is
no more, no less than idle twaddle," wrote the latter, the heir to a long
Russian radical tradition.[30] Returning to his old field, Tkachev deplored laws that were empty phrases because they did not reflect
social realities.

By law, for example, everyone has a right to ride in luxurious carriages, to drink
champagne every day, to read Kuno Fischer and to delight in the operas of Serov.
But in reality, this right is actually practical only for the very few. Put everyone in a
similar condition in regard to development and material security, and you give
everybody *real, factual* equality of rights and not that false, fictional equality of
rights that scholastics-jurists invent with the deliberate aim of fooling the ignorant
and deceiving the simple.[31]

Like Pisarev Tkachev knew his Proudhon and admired the old anarchist's conviction that unrealizable political rights could be no more
than shams. Chernyshevskii had seen the same in his studies of European government. Tkachev put it in different words:

Remove this harmful dualism between fictional right and active, achieved right,
that is, look on a right not as on some sort of ideal potential but as the real, actual
possibility of satisfying one's needs, and then equality of rights [*ravnopravnost*]
will become synonymous with equality of strength [*ravnosiliia*].[32]

Pisarev would hardly have objected. Nevertheless, on more issues than
they agreed upon, Tkachev and Pisarev disagreed and stood irrevocably
on opposite sides of the fence.

Most importantly these unusual colleagues had developed very
different views of the moving forces in history and civilization. To
Tkachev the only foundations of history, the key criteria on which
human progress must be evaluated, lay in measurable socioeconomic
realities. His analysis of Europe's productive forces, published in
Russian Word for December 1865, was based on his earlier conviction
(now repeated) that economic factors lie at the core not only of legal
and political institutions but of cultural phenomena as well.[33] Approaching Europe's difficulties from a socioeconomic point of view that
had little in common with Pisarev's premises, he determined (by a
doubtful piece of logic) that the average European per capita income

---

30. Ibid., 5: 180.
31. Ibid., 1: 75.
32. Ibid. Cf. Woehrlin, pp. 238-39.
33. This article is reprinted in Tkachev, 5: 152-70.

lay at subminimum basis for subsistence. Inspired by Proudhon, whose *War and Peace* he quoted liberally throughout, Tkachev saw the problem as one of underproduction, maldistribution, and excessive taxation. His suggestions for eradicating poverty sought egalitarianism in distribution of wealth and elimination of social parasitism. He would, he said: (1) make the producer the owner of whatever he produces, Tkachev's first public statement of anything approaching socialism or, more accurately, a roughly equitable distribution of wealth; (2) add nonproductive persons to the labor force in order better to exploit resources and enlarge the national product, a recommendation hardly consistent with his previous assertions that excess labor force produces poverty; and (3) decrease extravagant and unproductive government expenses, thus permitting reduction of the taxes that must be assessed against the productive class. These remedies Tkachev drew straight from Proudhon, although he carefully rejected a number of the anarchist's other ideas (the inevitability of poverty, the importance of education and temperance). They indicate once again that Tkachev stood by his socioeconomic view of the world.

His socioeconomic environmentalism dominated Tkachev's evaluation of the past as well as his critique of the present. Unlike Pisarev Tkachev was fascinated by social history and consistently judged human progress in a sociological light. One of the most interesting of the young journalist's writing during his *Russian Word* period was never finished and remained unpublished until Kozmin found it more than half a century later in the archives of the Third Section.[34] In this long article entitled "Essays in the History of Rationalism" Professor Michael Karpovich has seen the germs of Max Weber's later identification of Protestantism with emerging capitalism.[35]

Tkachev's subject was the gradual defeat of Catholic dogma by the new doctrines of capitalism that appeared with changing social and economic relations. The topic gave him the opportunity to advance again the primacy of economic factors, a theme stated here on many occasions. The Church's control over moral and intellectual life was challenged, Tkachev wrote, by a new economic system that changed men's outlooks on Catholic dogma in accordance with a new ethic. Among the landmarks of Catholic belief destroyed by rising capitalism

---

34. "Ocherki iz istorii ratsionalizma," first published by Kozmin with his own foreword ("K voprosu") and notes, *Literaturnoe nasledstvo* 7-8 (1933): 117-62; it appears in Tkachev, 5: 104-51.

35. Michael Karpovich, "Forerunner of Lenin: P. N. Tkachev," *Review of Politics* 6, no. 3 (July 1944): 339 (note). Kozmin pointed out this similarity in "K voprosu."

were the prohibition of usury, intolerance, self-renunciation and asceticism, and prohibitions in the area of entertainment. Usury became acceptable when the agricultural society based on exchange gave way to an urban factory system that recognized the value of money. Intolerance of other religions, especially anti-Semitism, was broken when trade brought contacts among various nations, classes, and religions; the Jews represented the new society and in spite of Catholic persecutions were eventually recognized under its laws. Self-renunciation and asceticism, based on the idea of reward only after death, collapsed in the face of an increasingly comfortable life on earth; they were replaced by the capitalistic, materialistic standard of individual benefit and personal gain. Even the rising demand for entertainment, the mark of the growing affluence of urban society, had its effect in relaxing prohibitions of the Church. The lesson of history, Tkachev concluded, is

People, if you are dissatisfied with the sterility of your learning and the crass egoism of your morality, if you suffer under the yoke of various prejudices, social and religious, turn to your economic relationships, change them, and everything else will change itself.[36]

The conclusion is familiar, but the article is Tkachev at his best, well researched and clearly stated, undoubtedly one of his finest and most original pieces of writing.

Pisarev probably never read it. If he had, he would not have denied Tkachev's conviction that progress could be achieved through economic action. The nihilist too was an admirer of Proudhon and occasionally paid lip service to the importance of economics, drawing ideas from his favorite French author.[37] He sometimes wrote of the poverty-stricken masses but usually (as his biographer Coquart pointed out) managed quickly to divert his readers to more propitious topics. He wrote a long essay on the history of labor; his reading of Chernyshevskii's *What Is to Be Done?* convinced him that willingness and ability to work were among man's most important qualities.[38]

But Pisarev was never a sociologist and never pretended to be one. Even his "Essays in the History of Labor" tended to focus on individuals rather than groups. Whereas Tkachev considered and rejected cooperatives as a means toward social and economic progress (he determined that they were merely a palliative for the evils of capitalism

---

36. Tkachev, 5: 136-37.
37. Coquart lists Proudhon as one of the three prime influences in the development of Pisarev's thought (Coquart, pp. 165-66, 422-23).
38. This long, rambling article is published in Pisarev, pp. 172-294. See also pp. 637-40 and scattered references to Chernyshevskii's heroes in the essay "The Thinking Proletariat."

and a dubious palliative at that),[39] Pisarev delighted in them and rejoiced in the stimulation and excitement that happy communal work could bring to Vera Pavlovna and her lovers.[40] Tkachev described the evils of the European factory system—decrying monotony of labor, poverty, unemployment, business crises, and the growing gap between rich and poor[41]—but Pisarev worried about the emotions of an individual worker and concluded that education and consciousness, the merger of "scientific development and physical labor," could save the working class.[42] Tkachev defined historical progress in economic and social terms, but Pisarev was convinced that the progress of civilization arose through the continual expansion of knowledge and through the growing creative capacity of men's minds.[43] Like the positivists, he was sure that science, knowledge, and analysis were the driving forces of history. History was the history of ideas; "les idées marchent," as Coquart put it.[44]

Indeed Pisarev's potential social mission was diverted by his intellectual interests, and Tkachev probably realized it. Tkachev had long since attacked ivory-tower intellectuals who spent their lives in isolated laboratories. Pisarev, on the other hand, admired them. He was caught up in his generation's excitement about Moleschott and Büchner, Vogt and Buckle, and in 1861 and 1862 wrote articles on them. Science fascinated him. In 1864 he popularized Darwin in an essay, which, carried a little farther, might have approximated the length of the *Origin of the Species* itself. He devised curricula for gymnasium studies, focusing on mathematics and the natural sciences, curricula in which one of Tkachev's favorite subjects, history, was rejected as not scientific enough.[45]

His fascination with science determined Pisarev's intellectualism and led him to the conviction that the finest future lay in the direction of knowledge. "Knowledge," he wrote, "constitutes the only key that opens all broad and rational activity, of whatever sort, theoretical or practical, scholarly or social."[46] History, he was certain, demonstrated that "supremacy in society is acquired and retained by that class or

---

39. Tkachev, 1: 84.
40. Pisarev, pp. 637, 638, 641.
41. Tkachev, 1: 79 ff.
42. Coquart, p. 328.
43. Ibid., p. 304; Pisarev, pp. 23, 34.
44. Coquart, p. 90.
45. Ibid., pp. 175, 321-25; the emphasis in Pisarev's curricular requirements shifted as he studied Comte's tables on the importance and derivation of different sciences.
46. Quoted in ibid., p. 420.

circle of people that possesses the greatest amount of developed intellectual powers,"[47] a statement clearly in conflict with Tkachev's
socioeconomic determinism. The first task of his epoch, Pisarev believed, lay in the creation of an intellectual elite who would diffuse and
disseminate knowledge to as many people as possible. He was doing his
part. He realized that the process was slow and difficult, but he did not
lose faith.

> Knowledge is distributed very unequally among the different strata of society; it
> penetrates into the lower strata very slowly and, remaining in the upper strata, is
> often turned into a pretty toy to distract an idle mind, but impotent to contribute
> to any productive labor. In one section of society there is a mass of useless knowl-
> edge, while at the same time human strength is strained to utmost exhaustion in
> another, strained in blind, mechanical, and therefore ungrateful labor. Unite knowl-
> edge with labor; give knowledge to those who will necessarily derive from it all the
> practical use it can contain and you will see the riches of the country and the
> people increase at an incredible rate.[48]

He spoke of riches, but that was a secondary problem. Basically
Pisarev's ideal society of thinking people (like Blagosvetlov's) was one
in which knowledge had spread to thousands and millions, where each
man acted independently and autonomously as he knew best, where the
ideas of each were examined carefully and critically by all.[49] That
would be the millenium.

Tkachev saw it otherwise—perhaps more cynically, for he never
entertained the belief that knowledge could actually be spread throughout the broad masses of population. An individual, he thought, must
be judged by his usefulness to the social cause, and unless a scientist
had invented a new plow and seen to its distribution, his contribution
could not be positively evaluated. Tkachev never spared his pen in
attacking drones who did not contribute to society; he found them
primarily among the highly educated elite, the group Pisarev most
admired and to which both young critics belonged. Tkachev was convinced that society was foolish to support and admire high-thinking
parasites. An intellectual by profession and training, he detested effete
intellectualism.

In his *Russian Word* articles economic theorists came in for his
special scorn. Not only were they noncontributors, they dreamed up
theories in support of the ruling social class and became its fawning
sycophants.

---

47. Pisarev, p. 294.
48. Ibid., p. 273.
49. Coquart, pp. 159-60.

In their teachings and theories, as in a mirror, have been reflected the slightest changes of spiritual attitude of that class that wined and dined them, bought their writings, gave them pensions and laurel wreaths, that is, honorary decorations and cushy jobs.[50]

Far from regarding economists as admirable scholars attempting to apply the methods of mathematics to the social world, Tkachev deplored them. As the bourgeoisie solidified its position, the economists became increasingly middle class in outlook and increasingly insolent in attitude. Criticizing one book on economic theory, Tkachev found its author reprehensible and amoral. Economists had finally dropped their pretenses, he growled. They have been forced to admit that price is not a function of value but determined by the cold forces of supply and demand; they concede that wages have nothing to do with man's needs for subsistence, that land has no special Ricardian quality, and that capital is no more than profit—in short, that moral values have no place in the workings of capitalism, which is instead dominated by inhuman forces.[51] Pisarev, had he cared to look, might have applauded the application of scientific methods to economic analysis; Tkachev could not.

Philosophers, writers, and journalists fit equally well into Tkachev's list of parasitic intellectuals who were merely mirrors of society and served no useful purpose in the modern world. In his bitter, sweeping denunciations he eclipsed even Pisarev, who for all his acerbity retained a lifelong curiosity about individual behavior. Tkachev's attacks on parasitism, which he seems to have adapted from Proudhon, resulted in part from his view of national wealth as a fixed amount that must be divided in shares among the population. Thus any share (or increased share) seized by or given to nonproductive individuals reduced by that much the share of each positive producer. The worker, Tkachev was convinced, was physically worse off for every ivory-tower intellectual or philosopher society chose to support.

From the lowest worker [*chernorabochii*] they take the last groschen, and on these groschen they support philosophers, who in exchange for these groschen that have been taken give the lowest worker *nothing* but printed pages, stained with some sort of stupid phrases, which lack any human meaning. Is this not paying with false medals for real gold?[52]

The useless, isolated, laboratory intellectual and the fake theorist who really only reflected conditions around him remained Tkachev's

---

50. Tkachev, 1: 60.
51. Ibid., pp. 61 ff.
52. Ibid., 5: 172.

whipping boys throughout his lifetime. Science for the sake of science was no better than art for art's sake alone.[53] Pisarev, the utilitarian, agreed about art. But for science, for knowledge, Pisarev took an opposite stance. He seemed to feel that no science was lost, that all knowledge eventually was preserved and became essential to the pattern of progress.[54] Anything man learned, immediately useful or not, would end by nudging society forward toward the intellectual perfection Pisarev sought.

What is more, Pisarev was an individualist, always interested in personality and psychological dynamics. In his early years he was particularly fascinated by the emancipation of individuality, which he saw as an involuntary, unconscious progress towards self-perfection.[55] "Respect the human personality in yourself and others" was to Pisarev the simplest and most obvious of rules.[56] In his writings he could not help talking in terms of individuals; efforts on the part of Soviet scholars to turn Pisarev into a sociologist have fallen flat.[57] Tkachev always fit people together or bound them into their social class.

Nowhere is this difference between Tkachev and Pisarev—the sociologist and the individualist—better demonstrated than in the treatments both men accorded the same book, a history of eighteenth-century literature written by the German scholar Hermann T. Hettner. Tkachev reviewed the book (and eighteenth-century French literature) in the "Book List" column of *Russian Word* for January 1866.[58] Pisarev used it as a basis for his long article "Popularizers of Negative Doctrines," which appeared in the collection *Luch* (Ray), March 1866.[59]

Tkachev's approach to Hettner was hostile. His environmentalism determined his dislike. Although he admitted that Hettner's interpretation was preferable to some, he was immediately annoyed that the author had not recognized the influence of socioeconomic conditions, particularly the rise of the bourgeoisie, on eighteenth-century French philosophers. Hettner should have analyzed the economic situation

53. Ibid., 1: 88.
54. Coquart, p. 346.
55. Ibid.; Pisarev, pp. 58-60.
56. Pisarev, p. 90.
57. See for example Plotkin, pp. 293-94 and elsewhere; A. I. Maslin, *D. I. Pisarev v borbe za materializm i sotsialnyi progress*, chap. 4. The relationship of educated individuals to the gray underdeveloped masses—like the dichotomy between Western rationalism and peasant *narodnichestvo*—caused many a sleepless night for Russian radicals like Lavrov and Mikhailovskii.
58. Tkachev, 5: 177-89.
59. Pisarev, pp. 497-563.

first and on that basis explained the motives of the writers he discussed.[60] He, Tkachev, did so. At the turn of the seventeenth century,
French writers reflected the bourgeoisie in looking to the monarchy
for support (Bossuet, Fénelon, Racine, Corneille). Then as the bourgeoisie became more powerful, they mirrored its demands in their
violent attacks on monarchy and church (Holbach, Helvétius, Voltaire,
and Rousseau). Voltaire's great popularity arose because more than
any of his contemporaries he was the epitome of the bourgeois, the
personification of the new class, hardly attractive in Tkachev's eyes.

The bourgeois never can be consistent because by nature he is cowardly and indecisive; he fears strict logic because at the basis of his activity lies not a theoretical
principle but the banal practicality of the small tradesman. Thus are explained all
the seeming anomalies of his actions; he is a freethinker and at the same time
frightens his workers with priests and crosses; he makes fun of church ceremonies
and at the same time fulfills them with the punctiliousness of the bigot; he con-
structs philanthropic institutions and discourses a lot about humanity but at the
same time kills his worker by starvation; he hates any monopoly and privilege and
at the same time demands that a monopoly of strikes [lockouts] be granted exclusively to factory owners; he plays at being a liberal and is indignant against the
despotism of government and at the same time fawns before this government and
openly repudiates those who undermine it in principle. This motley amalgam of
meanness, inconsistency, and obtuseness is called in his jargon *practicality*. He
possesses this invaluable quality in its most perfect degree.[61]

Voltaire was not Voltaire so much as he was bourgeois in effigy, a
representative by irrefutable law of a class Russian radicals despised.
Tkachev insisted that even this great individualist fell prey to his
environment.

Pisarev's approach differed. Never without his prejudices and his
foregone conclusions, he seemed in comparison to his colleague to have
no axe to grind. Far from denigrating the men of the Enlightenment,
he obviously enjoyed them. He took them at their own value, seeing
them not as representatives of a social class but as individuals, people
who were battling for what he considered important principles. Pisarev
admired Voltaire, "the tireless fighter, the great publicist, who has
not a peer in history and whose name still inspires European pietists
with the most comical horror."[62] Rather than condemn Voltaire
for cowardice, he commended him for courage, particularly in the Calas
affair. Pisarev must have read Tkachev's review before he wrote his
own; he was subtly chastising the younger man.

---

60. Tkachev's recommended procedure is not unlike that adopted by Soviet
historians of the twentieth century.
61. Tkachev, 5: 186-87.
62. Pisarev, p. 508.

Whoever values Voltaire's activity must not reproach him with his cunning, his fawning, or his obsequiousness: all these maneuvers helped toward the success of the main cause. . . . In the realm of thought Voltaire did not make the slightest concession to anybody, and nobody dared to demand such concessions of him. But on the other hand Voltaire was as flexible and elastic as a steel spring in his methods and attitudes. . . . This elasticity and flexibility are one of the principal causes and one of the most important aspects of his significance.[63]

In this instance it was Pisarev who was flexible, not Tkachev. The nihilist enjoyed Hettner's book and commended it to his readers; there was much to learn from it, he said.[64] The tone of his article is far removed from that of Tkachev's. The latter was already more dogmatic and doctrinaire in his analyses. If he was more systematic than Pisarev, whose vitality and enthusiasm frequently caused him to react in many directions at once, he was also more heavily didactic and lacking in fire. Pisarev would take a man for what he was. Tkachev remained hidebound by his insistence on the determining power of socioeconomic factors.

Pisarev's interest in individuals and science led him early to consider the role of the single human being in a Darwinian universe, a universe basically operating by predetermined processes. The German popularizers of science whom he admired depicted a mechanistic world: man was a machine responding to stimuli, his behavior a matter of glandular secretion, his immorality explicable by his body chemistry. The idea had appealed to Dobroliubov; Chernyshevskii too had speculated about the theories of mechanism as against those of life force. Pisarev was certain that the laws of the universe were irrevocably predetermined.

We can neither believe nor doubt as we please; our thoughts develop in a certain order, independently of our will; even in the process of thought we are restricted by the conditions of our physical makeup and the circumstances of our development.[65]

And again:

All laws of nature, the simple and the complex, the studied and the unstudied, the physical and the psychological, are equally unshakeable, equally extensive, and equally impatient of exceptions, for they all equally derive from the necessary and eternal qualities of boundless matter.[66]

Yet in spite of his intellectual conviction, emotionally Pisarev could not abandon the individual to a predetermined, mechanistic fate. He was too interested in people. "I think humanity can be fully revealed,"

63. Ibid., p. 515.
64. Ibid., p. 563.
65. Quoted in Coquart, p. 425.
66. Pisarev, p. 329.

he wrote, "only in a whole individuality which has developed absolutely naturally and independently, untrammelled by service to various
ideals."[67] Adopting a universal determinism applied to mankind in
general, he still emphasized the individual as a vibrant and dominating
force. "These two theories are poorly wed," comments his biographer
Coquart.[68] Even contemporaries thought so. Individualism was as much
a cornerstone of literary nihilism as scientism in spite of the generally
irreconcilable nature of the two in these Darwinian times.[69] Pisarev
struggled to bring them together or more often chose whichever theory
seemed applicable at the moment.[70]

Tkachev was not ready to plunge into such difficult peregrinations,
but in 1865 he made a beginning. He must have asked himself the
eternal questions: Was the course of universal history actually writ
irrefutably in the stars? Was the progress of society based on a mysterious predetermined set of rules such as Darwin claimed for the biological development of the species? Unlike Pisarev, Tkachev decided it
was not. Society did not operate like nature at all.

Naturalists deal with the phenomena of nature, which always and everywhere acts
monotonously and regularly. From such phenomena one can, of course, deduce
unchanging and constant laws. On the other hand, there is nothing constant and
regular in the phenomena of social life. Much here depends on simple accidents,
much on the caprice and willfulness of certain people, the plenipotentiaries of the
government.[71]

As society differed from nature, so humanists must differ from
scientists. They must never, he wrote, accept society as the physicist
accepts kinetics. Rather they must insist on pronouncing value judgments.

The naturalist deals with the facts of physical nature, with facts arising outside the
will and interference of man. For him, the only important question is the question:
How and why does this or that phenomenon exist? The question of whether this
phenomenon is bad or good, whether it is beneficial for men or not, has for him no
essential significance. Thus he approaches the study of phenomena of reality with a
clear conscience, so to speak, without any intention to prove, come what may, that

---

67. Ibid., p. 113.

68. Coquart, pp. 158-59.

69. Even contemporaries were quick to recognize the individualism inherent in
Pisarev's nihilism. See for example Alphons Thun, *Istoriia revoliutsionnogo dvizheniia v Rossii*, p. 52; S. M. Kravchinskii, *Underground Russia*, p. 14.

70. As Coquart pointed out, he finds the individual commanding history with
absolute freedom in the case of Gregory VII, but he quickly re-establishes determinism in attacking Raskolnikov's beliefs (*Crime and Punishment*), which he
regarded as complete absurdities (Coquart, p. 426).

71. Tkachev, 1: 63.

what exists is bad or good. Jurists and economists are in a completely different situation. If they are not heartless idiots, then the question of whether what exists is good or bad cannot be ignored by them. For any person studying social life this equation must inevitably stand in the forefront. An objective relationship to the subject of study here is scarcely thinkable.[72]

Tkachev had made a commitment, but he had hardly avoided Pisarev's dilemma. At best he had put off considering it. Denying the existence of immutable natural laws in human history and experience, he stood on the side of voluntarism. Yet how could one believe that economic forces predominated, driving even man before them, and still contend that history had room for human caprice and freak accident?[73] The man who loved the individual called himself a determinist; the man who did not ended by granting the individual full freedom within history's unpredictable march. Pisarev, wrestling with the problem, tried to compromise. Tkachev was not yet ready to think it out. Elements of a *Weltanschauung* mixed and unmixed in his writings, but it was not until later that he made a real effort to put them together. In 1865 he was just twenty-one; he had years to go.

Yet the ideas were germinating, most of them outside of Pisarev's influence. Early in 1866 Tkachev set down on paper in a review (intended for an issue of *Russian Word* that was never to appear) his approval of revolution—and revolution by conspiracy, the hallmark of his later violent Jacobin plans.[74] The lessons he drew from the history of France between 1815 and 1848 can hardly be missed, and the analogy to Russia comes close to being stated outright. Tkachev began by warning his reader that the political overthrow of a government does not always solve all problems; few of the recent French revolutions brought about vast changes. They did demonstrate, however, the deceptiveness of the government's position, the weakness hidden under its show of strength.

Today a government is strong and powerful, deploys huge armies, millions of gendarmes and police, maintains in its hands all the moral and material powers of the nation—tomorrow, in one night, it can lose all its power, be left without a roof and shelter, lie at the feet of those whom only yesterday it could shoot down or hang publicly.[75]

---

72. Ibid., pp. 62-63;

73. Walicki, p. 141, correctly seizes on this problem as fundamental in Tkachev's thought. Chernyshevskii struggled with the same point and never decided whether change in economic systems depended on "an objective historical process or on the free choice of rational men," as Woehrlin puts it, p. 225.

74. This review, preserved in the archives of the Third Section, was confiscated when *Russian Word* was closed in 1866. See Tkachev, 5: 190-96, 478 (note 43).

75. Ibid., p. 193.

In its struggle for self-preservation a desperate, insecure government might attempt to sway its opponents or may make concessions to them at first. Then—like the government of Louis XVIII after the assassination of the Duc de Berri or like that of Charles X after 1824—it could move to suppress its foes in a period of reaction. In France repression only led to the formation of secret revolutionary societies. In 1830 a revolution broke out.

True, the uprising did not succeed. But one should not blame the secret societies for this failure; in their fiasco no one should see proof of the valuelessness or fruitlessness of all secret and underground agitation. Sometimes uprisings have failed from purely accidental conditions, which either might or might not exist. . . . The government of Louis Philippe . . . understood that conspiracy is the only possible means of struggle with a victorious opponent.[76]

The article ends boldly, "The lesson is also instructive."

Tkachev developed the idea of conspiracy as a revolutionary technique more carefully after 1875, but its brief mention here indicates the focus of his early thinking. He was not alone or unique in his conspiratorial hopes: secret circles were apparently widespread among radical students of the early 1860s and conspiracy to overthrow the government had been endorsed by such radicals as Herzen's friend Ogarev.[77] If Tkachev had already perfected his careful plans (the disciplined party, the postrevolutionary dictatorship), he has left us no hints. It seems unlikely that he had reached his final conclusions by 1865. Clearly, however, his mind was turning in revolutionary directions. The voluntarism that assumes the ability of man to sweep history his way; the conviction that a government might represent only token, sham power; the idea that secret societies could lead to successful revolution—all these were recorded by the young critic in published articles and unpublished fragments. For all Pisarev's nihilism, for all his cries about smashing images, Tkachev outdid him in anger. The practical demands of his writings surpassed Pisarev's more philosophical hopes for destruction.

The two critics remained aloof from each other, but in several lesser ways the younger man learned from his colleague. One of these was feminism: by the end of 1866 Tkachev had progressed from outright denial of woman's capacities as judged by the physically smaller size of her brain (and, of course, muscles), to a sympathy for

---

76. Ibid., p. 195.

77. This was in his famous pamphlet once seized by the police in a search of Tkachev's quarters. Vilenskaia, *Revoliutsionnoe podpole*, found no trace of Tkachev's membership in any secret circles, but he may carefully have kept his associations underground.

prostitutes as outcasts from the society that created them, to a tolerant and amused view of the emancipated woman, and thence to her champion.[78] Further, in a few paragraphs at the beginning of one of his articles Tkachev made an attempt at lightness and entered into the spirit of current journalistic polemics.[79] Perhaps Blagosvetlov had encouraged him. The lesson did not take. Through his life Tkachev's polemics were characterized more by ponderosity than by wit. Earnest fire could hardly be doused by a few sprinkles of light rain.

Still in the brief months of their association Tkachev demonstrated little affinity for Pisarev's intellectual nihilism. He was not inclined to follow Pisarev's lead toward a world dominated by science, knowledge, and ideas. Rather he scorned the thought that progress would be achieved automatically through the accumulation of knowledge; that would have left men complacent bystanders merely waiting for the world to turn. Tkachev refused even to admire the intellectual elite, whom he regarded as slaves to society's mores, parasites on society's wealth, indifferent to society's problems. Even less was he taken with Pisarev's enthusiasm for people as individuals. He insisted instead on his own favorite socioeconomic interpretation of history and society, dedicated as it was to class rather than individual analysis, to sociology rather than psychology. The mechanistic view of man and society with which Pisarev flirted Tkachev rejected outright in favor of the concept of history as accident, turning on whim and caprice. That his own stance seemed contradictory did not bother him. It is tempting to believe that the need for revolution was already his most compelling motif and that he would sacrifice logic to allow room for revolution in his view of the world. Indeed he espoused even more clearly than his colleague the fundamental principle that revolution—probably by conspiracy—must be made.

Pisarev and Tkachev never quarreled openly, neither face to face nor in print. Indeed, on many of the issues where their views conflicted, Tkachev judiciously held his tongue. His analysis of some of Pisarev's favorite themes—utilitarianism, elitism, anarchism—was reserved for a future date. Tkachev probably admired his colleague in spite of their differences of opinion. Five years later, to a crowded and sympathetic courtroom, Tkachev proudly stated, "I am a nihilist,"[80] but he did not mean he was a follower of his colleague on *Russian Word*. Rather he used the term to mean rebel, iconoclast, defier of convention—a common enough meaning among his generation. He himself never

78. References are to Tkachev, 5: 59, 96-103, 199; see also chap. 6, below.
79. This brief venture is in Tkachev, 5: 197-206.
80. Kozmin, *Nechaev i nechaevtsy*, p. 172.

conceived of the term in a specific definition; he once wrote that nihilism was many things to many people. The rebellious nihilist life style was the major facet that Tkachev actually adopted.

In his association with the *Russian Word*, Tkachev stood on the side of the *Contemporary*. Working with Pisarev did not change his mind; he maintained his own identity and his own line. Yet he benefited greatly from this brief experience. *Russian Word* pulled him out of isolation, transported him into the world of literary criticism. He found himself in the middle of great debates and petty polemics; he watched the battle, timidly tried his hand at it, and probably even enjoyed himself. He had become by now a commentator on the whole political and economic scene. Here he made his reputation, and his name became known if only through association. Years later contemporaries identified him as a colleague of the famous Pisarev, as a critic on the famous— or infamous—*Russian Word*.[81]

Tkachev's association with the journal was terminated through no fault of his own. *Russian Word* was already in trouble when the young critic joined its staff. It received its first warning from the censor after its October 1865 issue, for Pisarev's article "A New Type," a highly favorable evaluation of Chernyshevskii's novel *What Is to Be Done?* in which Pisarev rather unsuccessfully attempted to merge Chernyshevskii's hero Rakhmetov with the nihilist Bazarov, of whom he was so fond. The second warning came the following month, probably because of an article on cooperatives written by Shelgunov. On February 18, 1866, the journal was suspended for five months on the basis of its January issue; such a suspension was the penalty for a third offense under the Russian press laws. Before June, when the *Russian Word* might have reappeared, Karakozov had attempted to assassinate Alexander II, and in the tightening of controls that followed, the journal, together with its rival *Contemporary*, was permanently suppressed.

Blagosvetlov was not one to give up. Prohibited from editing any more publications, he set Tkachev up as a puppet editor and in March 1866 printed the first volume of a new journal entitled the *Ray*. Most

---

81. A coprisoner in the Nechaevist case, receiving a smuggled note from Tkachev, exclaimed, "It was from Tkachev, the famous critic from *Russian Word*" (L. P. Nikiforov, "Moi tiurmy," *Golos minuvshego*, no. 5 [1914], p. 187). Lev G. Deich pinpointed this as a key period in Tkachev's life, one he praised in contrast to later years (*Russkaia revoliutsionnaia emigratsiia 70-kh godov*, p. 81). The obituary in the Bakuninist periodical *Obshchee delo* (Geneva), republished by Lemke in "Materialy dlia biografii P. N. Tkacheva," p. 159, praises his work on *Russian Word* as demonstrating "belligerence and talent" and as the basis for public recognition of his literary skill.

of the contributors were staff members from *Russian Word*, and the *Ray* included several long essays by Pisarev himself.[82] Tkachev edited but did not write.

The first issue of the *Ray* saw the light of day; the second, for which Petr had prepared an article, did not. In the course of its preparation, the printing house was invaded by police and the presses and pages confiscated. As editor Tkachev was brought to court. There is no published record as to the results of this case; he was probably reprimanded and perhaps fined. A few months later he suffered another bout with the authorities when he was picked up in a crowd of demonstrators picketing an antinihilist play; again records have not been published, but if he was imprisoned, it was for a relatively short period.[83]

In the autumn of 1866, together with a number of colleagues from *Russian Word*, Tkachev wrote for a short-lived journal entitled *Zhenskii Vestnik* (Women's Herald), publishing in two issues a long article on the economic position of women.[84] For some reason the article never was finished and his name was dropped from the *Herald*'s pages, but his contribution was enough to make him a hero with many ardent young members of the opposite sex. It is possible that his contacts from *Russian Word* aided him in editing and translating the several volumes that appeared under his name in 1867: a book of essays by Buckle

---

82. Among them was the Heffner review discussed above. *Luch* was designed as a continuation of *Russkoe slovo* to the extent that it was sent (as was *Delo* later) to subscribers to fill out their unexpired subscriptions to the previous journal. See *Shestidesiatye gody*, p. 231.

83. Ibid., p. 430; Deich, *Russkaia emigratsiia*, p. 82. The exact sequence of these arrests is uncertain since Deich and others refer to Tkachev's arrest "after the Karakozov attempt" on the emperor's life without indicating whether this was in connection with a demonstration or with his editorial tasks on *Luch*. The *Luch* case was apparently not finally judged until years later when Tkachev was already serving his sentence in the Nechaevist case. Kozmin reports that the staff of *Russkoe slovo*, including Tkachev, attempted to arrange for the publication of an émigré journal during this same period (B. P. Kozmin, *Revoliutsionnoe podpole v epokhu "Belogo terrora,"* p. 178). During this period Tkachev may have had connections with the student commune called "Smorgon Academy," a group devoted to the reading and studying of radical and revolutionary literature, although the report of this connection comes years later and secondhand, from Varlaam Cherkezov (one of the Nechaevists) to Max Nettlau (a biographer of Bakunin). Police records apparently do not confirm this connection. See Kozmin, *Revoliutsionnoe podpole*, p. 117.

84. "Vliianie ekonomicheskogo progressa na polozhenie zhenshchiny i semi," *Zhenskii vestnik*, no. 1 (Autumn 1866); no. 2 (Autumn 1866). This article is not included in Kozmin's published collection of Tkachev's works.

(of whom Tkachev did not approve), and the first volume of a collection on judicial errors.[85]

But the challenge of working with Pisarev was over and done with. Although they were colleagues, it is probable that the only occasion of Tkachev's face-to-face meeting with the enfant terrible was under far different circumstances, when in 1862 the Tkachev-Olshevskii case was considered by the courts together with Pisarev's and sentence was pronounced on both journalists at the same court session. When Pisarev was released from prison in 1866 he was already on strained terms with Blagosvetlov. Although the two made it through another year of association, no one was surprised when Pisarev finally switched his allegiance to *Otechestvennye zapiski* (Fatherland Notes), a journal with an interesting future in the Russian radical movement but with few nihilistic inclinations. Tragically, the road back to reality after his isolated years behind bars was more than Pisarev's high-strung, turbulent personality could travel.[86] He died—probably a suicide, drowned in the Baltic Sea— in 1868. He was twenty-seven.

More important to Tkachev's immediate future was his association with Blagosvetlov. Late in 1866 one of the contributors to the late *Russian Word* managed to get permission to begin a new periodical, permission that had been repeatedly denied to Blagosvetlov himself. N. I. Shulgin contacted his previous colleagues, and Blagosvetlov became the de facto editor of the new journal, notwithstanding considerable uncertainty on the part of nervous and suspicious authorities.[87] *Delo* (Cause) proved to be less menacing to the government than *Russian Word*, and it lasted upwards of twenty years. Tkachev joined its staff as a literary critic and stuck with it all his life, even after he fled Russia in 1873. From 1866 until his arrest three years later, he published in the *Cause* some of his most important articles, many of them dealing with issues familiar to Pisarev. The journal never attained the popularity of its predecessor[88]—possibly because Tkachev's style and wit never approached that of Pisarev and a vital spark was missing—but

---

85. Both were published by the Lukanin press; Tkachev, 4: 499-50.

86. For a description of *Otechestvennye zapiski* during this period see *Istoriia russkoi zhurnalistiki*, pp. 409-17. Coquart has described the tragic demise of this violent spirit. Pisarev's love affairs—intense, tragic, and often conducted by mail— played their role. Pisarev described himself after his release from prison as friendless and alone, with no colleagues he really respected (Coquart, pp. 357-62).

87. *Istoriia russkoi zhurnalistiki*, p. 429.

88. Several sources agree that *Delo* took second place to *Otechestvennye zapiski*. See *Istoriia russkoi zhurnalistiki*, pp. 428-29, and Nikolai Ivanovich Sokolov, *Russkaia literatura i narodnichestvo*, pp. 104-5.

in it appeared some of the most important statements of his Russian years, those years in which he was finally marshalling his thoughts into a more or less cohesive whole.

5

The West: Utilitarianism,
Capitalism, and History

Tkachev's association with the *Cause* in 1867 marked the beginning of the most important decade in his life. To the historian reviewing his accomplishments, the apex of Tkachev's work came in the mid-eighteen-seventies when he finally set down on paper the revolutionary plans he had long been devising. But the principles, the background, the intellectual foundations for these plans stemmed from the years of studying, reviewing, writing, and reconciling the contradictory elements of the particular view of history and society that he strove to define. Tkachev was only twenty-two in 1867, but Dobroliubov had died at twenty-five, Pisarev at twenty-seven. In Russia a young man was expected to mature early; he had no time to waste. So Tkachev moved rapidly ahead, studying, assimilating, and trying to arrange his thoughts.

He began with the West. Like Chernyshevskii, Pisarev, and most radical thinkers of his generation, he found his inspiration among Western writers and philosophers. Rationalism, materialism, and (in spite of his reluctance) scientism all appealed to him as they appealed to his contemporaries. In his years on the *Cause* he considered utilitarianism, positivism, socialism, and Western history. He tackled problems that had baffled great minds for generations, but to his credit he worked at them independently and courageously. From his writings basic principles clearly emerged. Firstly he found little to admire in the Western way of life but much to respect in Western intellectual achievements. Given his environmentalistic conclusion that ideas follow from socioeconomic conditions, this dichotomy, which he shared with his radical generation, seemed doubly strange.[1] Secondly, Tkachev began all his analyses with the conviction that society must be changed. No concept expounded by any thinker could command his approval if it contradicted this basic premise. Logic and consistency must if necessary be sacrificed on the altar of radical change—revolution, Tkachev would have said, if the censors had allowed him to do so.

To his credit Tkachev understood the importance of definitions. One could scarcely condemn until one could define. His materialistic relativism denied the existence of an abstract, absolute definition of good and evil, yet his judgments could scarcely proceed without one. His initial questions, then, led him to a study of utilitarianism, the most influential ethical theory in his generation.

Chernyshevskii more than any other writer of his times had introduced the Benthamite utilitarian ethic to his countrymen, especially as that ethic was interpreted by John Stuart Mill. Espousing the doctrine that "good means utility" and that actions should be scrutinized in terms of their usefulness and benefit,[2] he followed Belinskii in subjecting even art to such criteria. Like Mill, Chernyshevskii had found utility hard to define and became convinced that pure pleasure was not a sufficient motive for man's actions. His doctrine of "rational egotism," the requirement that an individual should indulge himself by indulging society, was a variation of Mill's interpretation of Bentham's way.[3] Pisarev's enthusiasm for utilitarianism eclipsed even Chernyshevskii's, and some scholars have concluded that Tkachev's philosophy stemmed directly from Pisarev.[4] It seems more likely that in this as in all matters Chernyshevskii had the greatest influence. Tkachev surely read them both.

The young critic greatly admired the utilitarian ethic, the principle that value must be assessed by social utility and that good is that which makes people feel happy. To Jeremy Bentham, Tkachev accorded the

1. It might be noted that Tkachev's favorite, Chernyshevskii, was among the many Russian critics of Western capitalistic society. Woehrlin discusses this criticism on pp. 186-88, 204-6, and passim.

2. N. G. Chernyshevskii, Selected Philosophical Essays, pp. 125, 128.

3. Woehrlin, pp. 132-34; Lampert, Sons against Fathers, p. 153. Chernyshevskii's demand for "rational egotism" was a reflection of Mill's analysis. Mill wrote that justice was "vastly more important and therefore more absolute and imperative than any other social utilities as a class . . . and which therefore ought to be distinguished from the milder feeling which attaches to the mere idea of promoting human pleasure or convenience" (John Stuart Mill, "Utilitarianism," in Utilitarianism, Liberty, and Representative Government, p. 60).

4. Cf. Galaktionov and Nikandrov, Ideologi russkogo narodnichestva, p. 104; Malinin, Filosofiia revoliutsionnogo narodnichestva, pp. 82-83, argues the point.

highest praise that any man received from him during these years: Bentham was a great thinker, not just of his own but of all times.[5] But like all utilitarians (including Mill and Bentham himself) Tkachev was concerned with social welfare and the difficulties of reconciling the happiness of the individual to the happiness of society as a whole. For one person, as he pointed out, the definition of happiness was not very complicated. Placed in a social context, however, the measurement and evaluation of happiness was

extremely complicated; it is insufficient to define the relationship of a given act to the happiness of a given individuum; it will be necessary to follow its direct and indirect influence on the happiness of all other members of society.[6]

If conflict arose between individual and society, Tkachev asserted, the principle of social welfare must stand foremost. But unfortunately social utility as a criterion for specific judgments was as subjective and indefinite a concept as social happiness itself.[7] Bentham went through many permutations attempting to classify degrees of suffering and pleasure with the aim of balancing an individual's feelings against the reactions of others throughout all of society.[8] Tkachev did not approve of the results: the scheme was dry and pedantic, he wrote, filled with subjective arbitrariness, and "one of the weakest sides of the theory of social benefit."[9] Bentham's identification of happiness with security reflected what Tkachev called inflexible conservatism.

How is it possible to increase the sum of common happiness if certain institutions oppose it and if a legislator cannot touch them without violating the principle of security, without which happiness is also impossible? . . . In the sphere of civil as well as in the sphere of criminal law, Bentham's theory of "social benefit" recognizes as *beneficial* everything that exists, beginning with barbarian punishments to barbarian monopolies and privileges.[10]

Obviously happiness should not be defined as security and social benefit should not be found in the maintenance of tradition.

Tkachev had his own solution, a solution clearly based on his own interpretation and one that remained a cornerstone in his private utopia for the rest of his life. If the conflict of the individual's benefit with that of society should stand in the way of personal and private happiness, then that conflict should be eliminated. A society should

---

5. Tkachev, 5: 376.
6. Ibid., p. 373.
7. Ibid., pp. 374-75.
8. These agonies are reflected in Jeremy Bentham's *An Introduction to the Principles of Morals and Legislation*, chaps. 3-6.
9. Tkachev, 5: 378-80.
10. Ibid., pp. 388-89.

be devised in which the interests of the individual would merge into social interests, where the one would automatically and willingly act to the benefit of the whole. When human interests attained complete solidarity, then the happiness of one would mean the happiness of all. Solidarity of interests was the key to development of pleasure, benefit, and character. Indeed how could one act in accordance with the Golden Rule, young Tkachev demanded, if one's own interests were antagonistic to those of one's neighbors?

> If this solidarity does not exist, if, on the contrary, [human interests] are opposing and filled with mutual antagonism—then this moral "retribution," in spite of all its practical utility, cannot be realized in actuality. . . . Human reason . . . can lead to the introduction of peace, love, and harmony between people only in the event that the economic interests of these people, these mainsprings, these prime movers of all their thoughts and actions, will not stand in mutual antagonism, when complete and unbreakable solidarity will be established between them.[11]

Without such solidarity it was futile for Bentham to speak of harmonizing the egotistical actions of individual members of society. Tkachev's utopia sprang from this initial study of utilitarianism. The exact meaning of "solidarity of interests" and how such a state could be attained he left to further study. But he was sure that the Benthamite ethic, the definition of good in terms of human pleasure and happiness, belonged "without argument among the greatest and most fruitful doctrines to which human reason has ever risen."[12]

The necessity of steering the world toward its future directed Tkachev to a study of the past. The definition of progress, past, present, and future, was the deepest concern of Western philosophers from Buckle to Comte, from Darwin to Marx. The search for the nature of social movement, the essence of the forces or individuals that propelled man forward, the answer to the old conundrum of man pitted against irrevocable destiny, had troubled Tkachev before as it had troubled all men seeking the key to man's past and his future. In his *Russian Word* days Tkachev had begun to think about these eternal questions and their elusive answers.[13] Now in the *Cause* he came to some positive conclusions.

In the first place man was not like animals. Social evolution did not recapitulate physiological development and laws of biology could not be applied to man. Tkachev drew his conclusions from his reading of Herbert Spencer and to a lesser degree from Quételet's *Du système*

---

11. Ibid., 2: 16-17.
12. Ibid., 5: 389.
13. See chap. 4, pp. 68-70, above.

sociale et des lois qui le régissent.[14] Although he admitted the intelligence and acuity of Spencer, he delighted in satirizing analogies between biological and social evolution. He groaned at the thought that society has a childhood, a period of maturity, and an old age. He scorned those writers who viewed the state as organic, granting it arms, legs, and other human parts. Spencer's theory that society, like a man, was produced from two types of cells (generating its lower and upper classes) he rejected out of hand.[15] Man could not be compared to a simple organism; he was not the helpless product of biological rules. The difference was that he could break rules, for (unlike the amoeba) he was able to control his own destiny. He stood above biology. Like Marx's man he made his own laws.

The social organism differs from any other organism in that it is capable of perfecting itself. No other living organism can do this because the laws by which it develops are not created by its self-willed action; they are granted it as if from outside— they [the laws] exist before it and will remain after it. The laws of organic and nonorganic evolution are eternal, uniform, unchanging, and immutable; organic and inorganic bodies can exist only under the condition of blind and continual submission to these laws. On the contrary, the laws by which society is governed are not distinguished by any one of these traits; appearing always as the products of society itself, that is, the products of human will and human reason, they arise and are destroyed together with society.[16]

In biology development proceeded by definable laws, and Tkachev never denied them. In society, on the other hand, he was not certain that progressive development was inevitable at all. Belief in continual and automatic progress, comparable to the constant evolution of the species, was not just a fallacy but an opiate, lulling man and enervating him. Tkachev never tired of telling his readers:

Thus we find a beautiful way to reconcile the bitter pessimism evoked by actual life with the sweet optimism that seeks to see life in the manner the optimist desires. Having recognized the existence of historical progress as an indisputable fact that virtually does not demand proof, we create for ourselves a little bridge that entirely inconspicuously transfers us from pessimistic agitations to optimistic

---

14. Tkachev's early review of the first six volumes (1860-67) of a seven-volume Russian edition collecting Spencer's works is republished in Tkachev, 5: 298-303; he was to consider Spencer at greater length later. Quételet's book had originally been published in France in 1848; the Russian edition was reviewed by Tkachev, as reprinted in ibid., pp. 304-11.
15. Ibid., pp. 298-303. The exactitude of Spencer's biological-sociological analogies is titillating to the modern reader. There is an excellent selection in Herbert Spencer, *The Evolution of Society*, especially chaps. 1-7.
16. Tkachev, 5: 302; see also idem, 1: 234-35.

self-satisfaction. But it is obvious that such recognition can only fully calm and console us when we assume historical progress to be not only a simple *fact* but an immutable law.[17]

Tkachev's contention was that unlike biological evolution, man's motion forward (if it occurred at all) was uneven and could not be counted on. His conviction led him to oppose with violence two other sets of progressists whom he encountered in his early years on the *Cause:* the Comtean positivists, to whom progress was inevitable and occurred through the accumulation of knowledge, and certain economists, to whom progress, equally inevitable, could be defined in terms of what they saw as economic advances under capitalism.

Positivism Tkachev had considered before, but in the *Cause* he first tackled Auguste Comte, the *"quid pro quo* positivist," as he called him.[18] Tkachev's respect for Spencer, whom he considered the most talented popularizer of positivist philosophy,[19] did not in the slightest degree extend to Comte. Positivism had found much support among Tkachev's radical contemporaries. It represented to most of them a rejection of idealism, an espousal of materialism and rationalism, and a clear demand for specific, empirical knowledge. People talked about the positivist method, meaning the scientific approach to research, and suggested that it be applied to the study of social phenomena. Tkachev's own sympathy with all these trends might well have made him a supporter of Comtean interpretations.[20]

Instead he was blinded by two facets of Comte's philosophy: the role of ideas in history and the nature of the government Comte proposed. The latter he never mentioned, but he read Mill's critique of *August Comte and Positivism* and surely recognized (as did Mill) the aristocratic nature of the ideal Comtean state. On the role of knowledge in history he had spoken negatively before. Here lay the basis for Tkachev's most violent attack on the French philosopher. Comte had sought out, Tkachev wrote, the one facet of history in which progress was actually inevitable and then proceeded to define all historical change on the basis of this element alone.[21] He was wrong, for knowledge did not provide a key to history.[22] In the first place, knowledge

---

17. Ibid., 1: 234-35.
18. Ibid., 2: 36.
19. Ibid., 5: 299, 327; cf. Malinin, pp. 29-30.
20. Malinin has a good summary of the early populist views on Comte, pp. 28-29.
21. Tkachev, 5: 328.
22. Mill accepted Comte's notion that intellectual movement is "at the root of all the great changes in human affairs." See John Stuart Mill, *August Comte and*

did not cause action; individuals were seldom moved to activate ideas. "Ideas are active movers only when they coincide with our personal interests," Tkachev wrote; "in all other cases they represent a purely passive element or a decorative one, to speak more exactly."[23]

What was more, as he had asserted before, human progress could simply not be defined as the accumulation of knowledge any more than it could be defined as the biological mutation of the species.

In spite of the undoubted progress of science in Western Europe, material well-being of the masses far from corresponds to this progress; on the contrary, according to the testimony of several journalists who have studied the way of life of the French and English working classes, the rapid development of machine production, technical perfection, and the excessive division of labor evolved without doubt by the progress of our knowledge in many regards worsen the situation of the workers and promote the lowering of the moral level of their milieu.[24]

His dislike of the concept of ideas as the moving force of progress caused him to call Comte a bourgeois metaphysician, a double insult by Tkachev's light. Comte was hiding his metaphysical tendencies, refusing to cope with the really essential philosophical questions, and trying in vain to separate positivism from metaphysics, "from its own true mother."[25]

Tkachev at least recognized the accumulation of knowledge as inevitable. On the other hand, progress in any economic definition could not be considered inevitable at all. For the *Cause* Tkachev reviewed the French economist Jerome Blanqui, whom he considered a hypocrite and a bigot (language not atypical of some of his sharp attacks).[26] To see any progress in capitalism, to imagine the embryo of everything perfect in the bourgeoisie, to look on economics as a beautiful science (as Tkachev interpreted Blanqui) was indeed ludicrous. Economic modernization and progress were not at all the same.

The principle of slave labor and the principle of free labor, the principle of the mercantile system and the principle of free industry, the principle of authority and the principle of competition—what a huge difference, what striking progress! But

---

Positivism, p. 104. This concept of Mill's may well have caused Tkachev's mistrust of the English political economist.

23. Tkachev, 5: 330. Mill said just the opposite in *Auguste Comte*, pp. 104-5: "To say that men's intellectual beliefs do not determine their conduct is like saying that the ship is moved by the steam and not by the steersman. The steam indeed is the motive power; the steersman left to himself could not advance the vessel a single inch; yet it is the steersman's will and the steersman's knowledge which decide in what direction it shall move and whither it shall go."

24. Tkachev, 5: 329.

25. Ibid., 2: 36; cf. Malinin, pp. 29-31.

26. Tkachev, 5: 461, 464.

look at the practical consequences that emerge from them, and you will be instantly disenchanted; you will be convinced that the difference is not very great and that there is absolutely no progress; you will be convinced that under the trim clothing of beautiful theory hides an ugly being, and you will then understand the real meaning of these beautiful theories and also of this glistening progress.[27]

Clearly by Tkachev's standards progress only occurred when improvements in the way of life of the working classes could actually be measured and determined. Progress was not to be defined by changes in economic techniques, by the accumulation of scientific knowledge, nor in terms of biological development. Tkachev's own specific definition of the nature of progress determined his apparent conviction that history had seen no progress at all.

Beyond the measurement of progress to which he was led by his studies of the positivists, Tkachev considered the nature of historical change. In doing so, he turned to history itself. Like many scholars of his time he began by dividing history into periods. In some of his works he considered legal changes as the basis for periodization.[28] More often he divided man's past into eras based on economic development. He described in turn the general traits of primitive society, feudalism, and capitalism in terms of property and property rights, labor, and social relationships,[29] but of the three periods he concentrated his own work on the feudal system. His earlier study "Essays in the History of Rationalism" was matched in interest and length by "German Idealists-

27. Ibid., p. 464.

28. See for example ibid., 1: 106-7; and 5: 370 ff. In ancient and tribal times, Tkachev wrote, law was based on physical force and men were roughly equal. No outside enforcement authority was necessary since physical defeat sufficed as punishment. However, war between tribes eventually brought inequality and slavery, and law soon became based on wealth. Now natural law gave way to juridical law. Authorities and compulsions had to be set up. Tkachev considered German law vastly inferior to Roman law; he thought the former was based on the concept of absolute ownership of landed property.

29. Tkachev's clearest enunciation of the economic stages of history is in an article entitled the "Feminine Question" inserted in a book of essays translated and edited by Tkachev himself. Kozmin republished this article in ibid., 1: 370-402; see also 1: 444-45 (note 54). Primitive society was the early stage of history in which physical force ruled, rough economic equality was maintained, and each lived by his own labor. Gradually those physically stronger forced the weaker members of society to become slaves. The second stage of history was distinguished by the hegemony of immovable capital, particularly land; material wealth replaced physical force as the ruling element. In the third and present period of history, movable capital (money, etc.) forced men to sell their labor, but labor (now free from serfdom) merely fell into another dependent status. Its "fictional, nominal freedom" did not give it a chance on the market place dominated by money.

Philistines" published in the *Cause* in three installments in 1867.[30] Based primarily on Wilhelm Zimmermann's *Der grosse deutsche Bauern-krieg*,[31] a monumental work on the sixteenth-century German peasant wars that Tkachev and several friends had translated and published serially, Tkachev's article had as its theme the molding of German character by social environment and historical development. In it appeared the Russian critic's interpretation of the nature of historical change.

In his study of medieval Germany Tkachev began by isolating a dual nature in the German character amounting nearly to schizophrenia, as he termed it. Germans, he wrote, ranged from narrowly practical to idealistic, from the burgher who thought only of his money to the great dreamer, from extreme realist to extreme idealist.[32] Germans were distinguished by phlegm and energy, sentimentality and strictness, high principle and ignorant superstition. Tkachev's study attempted to explain these contradictions by identifying their source.

Indeed the two extremes—philistinism, as he termed the worldly attitudes, and idealism—were not so far apart as they seemed. Both were socially unproductive; neither could rise to influence or improve society. Both were distinguished by their apathetic indifference to others, for both centered around the individual ego. Germans of the Middle Ages did not think of public interests, Tkachev wrote, but only in terms of private ones. Society as a whole hardly existed for the philistine and the idealist.[33]

Like a snail hiding in a shell they conceal themselves from life; one in its office books, the other in the sorrowless world of its futile fantasies. If we compare society with a living tree and its citizens with boughs, then we must liken the idealist and the philistine to dry twigs needlessly impeding the growth of the tree.[34]

---

30. This long article is reprinted in ibid., 1: 101-72.

31. Zimmerman's book was a favorite of the radicals because of its interpretation of the peasant movement as the "spirit of freedom and light"; see *Der grosse deutsche Bauernkrieg*, p. 9. Friedrich Engels wrote a laudatory introduction, which is included in the new edition cited. In addition Tkachev read and reviewed several other works dealing with the same period. He discussed V. G. Rill's *The Fourth Class or the Proletariat* in Tkachev, 5: 344-59, and Theodor Girzinger's work *The Jesuits* (only one volume of which had been published in Russian) in Tkachev, 1: 258-73.

32. Tkachev once referred to contemporary Germany as standing "at the forefront of European civilization yet not emerged from the Middle Ages" (Tkachev, 5: 344).

33. Ibid., 1: 170-72.

34. Ibid., p. 105. Tkachev may have remembered this pleasant analogy as used by Dobroliubov; see "Provincial Sketches" in Dobroliubov, *Selected Philosophical Essays*, pp. 57-58.

He suggested that every philistine covered his attitudes with some sort of ideal, and every idealist was more or less a philistine for want of social purpose.

Tkachev blamed these antisocial characteristics basically on the decentralization and individualization that resulted when German law was substituted for Roman. German law, he wrote, emphasized the rights of individual landowners rather than the rights of the centralized state. It necessarily resulted in the splintering of society and encouraged particularistic interests rather than a sense of broad social justice. Idealism grew from the isolated parasitism of local landed noblemen as a cloak for their pettiness and a manifestation of their general boredom with the superficial idealization of women, love, knightly bravery, and erotic adventure known as chivalry. Monks, isolated in remote monasteries, turned to scholasticism and developed their own brand of abstract idealism; to Tkachev they elevated superstitions into abstract principles, muddied otherwise clear thoughts, and transformed the simple into the mysterious.[35]

In neither case did idealism truly permeate society. For the monk as for the knight it became a screen for the grossest depravities.

Hand in hand with the idealistic viewpoints of chivalry went the deepest depravity . . . the delicate dreamers dedicating their whole lives to self-imposed service of some sort of beauty, having created from love of woman some sort of elevated cult, were in essence very ordinary dissolutes, drunkards, and gluttons, petty tyrants foolishly wasting the sweat and blood of their slaves on their silly fancies. In exactly the same relationship to their ideal viewpoints stood the scholastics. For them as for the knights idealism was only a sterile game at which they played either from nothing to do or to justify their animal impulses.[36]

Thus German idealism was born into the feudal world of knights and monks. On the other hand the petty, narrow practicality that Tkachev described as philistine was centered in the medieval cities. In these new urban areas Tkachev found a spirit of "philistine isolation from everything that lay beyond the limits of the city or beyond the quarter of the guild."[37] Because the new cities had been founded on the principle of individual labor, there was little room for more than hard work and practical employment in the narrow circle of each burgher's life. The leisurely speculations of the knight and the monk were not for the busy, secular, worldly minded urban bourgeois. Philistinism in Tkachev's view arose from conditions of city life as idealism grew out of agrarian feudalism.

35. Tkachev, 1: 123-24.
36. Ibid., p. 124.
37. Ibid., p. 129.

Having defined these ingredients of German national character, Tkachev proceeded in this article (and in conjunctive reviews) to set forth his own concepts of the historical process. First and foremost, as in his earlier "Essays in the History of Rationalism," he interpreted the entire Reformation in an economic light. Most contemporary historians had failed to recognize the Reformation's economic significance, he wrote.

Historians look on the Reformation as a progressive movement of human thought; as [the mind's] surge to free itself from the iron chains of the scholasticism of the Middle Ages, when in essence this [Reformation] was one and the same scholasticism—only in a different form and with different content.[38]

Scholastic philosophers before the Reformation had idealized the agricultural social orientation of feudalism into a dogma,

from which was developed teaching on the authority of the pope, on the enslavement of human thought, and on the ecclesiastical hierarchy. To rise up against these teachings meant to rise against medieval feudalism because the [teachings] were only the ideal, symbolic expressions of [feudalism]. Such was the deep tie between feudalism and Catholicism. On the other hand, the principles of urban industry had very little in common with the principles of feudalism because Catholic dogma could not be especially useful for the burgher; he had to seek other sanction and other justification for himself. Urban industry, denying serfdom, brought to life a new view of labor; it looked on the worker as on a living machine—the more independent the use of this machine, the fewer constraints it entails, the more profitable it is. . . . Thus urban industry above all strives to break the chains that attach the machine to its owner; it demands that the owner use it only while he finds it profitable for himself and that this temporary usage does not impose upon him any obligations in the future. This demand it passes off as seeking "freedom of labor and movement, freedom of person." Lutheranism raises this freedom to dogma and on this dogma bases its teachings relative to interpretation of the Bible and papal authority.[39]

Thus with the rise of the cities, the agricultural system ceased to represent an ideal. Attacking feudalism and substituting his own values, the burgher denied the Catholicism that feudal lords supported and that meant little to himself. Burghers were hostile toward idealism and irritated at the impractical mysticism of the Church. They liked exactness and accuracy and had no time for rites and rituals. To the principle of hierarchy they opposed that of equality and freedom, "and this protest was nothing more than a denial of the recognized economic principles of feudalism."[40] Religion was merely a symbol of medieval life, but the attack on the symbol was actually an attack on the essence

38. Ibid., p. 134.
39. Ibid., pp. 134-35.
40. Ibid., p. 137.

of feudalism. Protestantism "was the fullest and most multiform expression of the interests and demands of urban industry, a new social element already attaining mature manhood toward the end of the fifteenth century."[41]

Tkachev hardly admired Protestantism. It was, he wrote, as arid as the Catholicism that preceded it. Luther was a "stupid, ignorant monk who, forgetting his own peasant origin, disavowed the peasantry in order to throw himself into the arms of kings and burghers."[42] Tkachev identified him not with humanism but with the narrow, dry philistinism he had described. The young Russian disliked Luther for his firmness against heresy, for his insistence on Christian submissiveness, and for his willingness to shed blood for the new faith. Protestantism clearly stood for urban capitalism, for principles Tkachev firmly opposed. Little could be said for philistinism or Lutheranism beyond identification of the one with the other.

Tkachev's portrait of the medieval peasant was the second notable element emerging from his study of the Reformation and the German peasant wars. In a world where feudal lords represented idealism and urban burghers personified philistinism the peasant manifested the only admirable *Weltanschauung:* that of the realist with "a sober attitude toward questions of life that is as far from abstract idealism as it is from narrow philistinism."[43] Only the peasant had the breadth of vision and the spirit that might have renovated the German social conscience.

The peasants . . . felt between themselves a vital link: they did not shrink into the particular interests of a given village area, they considered each other as brothers—brothers obligated to aid and support one another in all needs and difficulties, and they demonstrated this in the so-called "peasant wars."[44]

From peasant demands it was clear that

the peasants strove not only for betterment of their own situation but also for introduction of certain general governmental reforms; thus they demanded judicial reforms and the change of the death penalty. This matter shows that they understood the solidarity of their interests with the interests of other classes in general; they understood that their situation could be changed only as a consequence of general, more or less radical reforms, and not as some sort of partial measures. . . . In their social world view the peasants stood above all other classes.[45]

41. Ibid. In his review of Girzinger, Tkachev noted a conflict between Jesuit tradition and that of the early urban bourgeoisie, thus again setting the urban population into an anti-Catholic framework. See ibid., p. 263.
42. Ibid., p. 139.
43. Ibid., p. 131.
44. Ibid.
45. Ibid., p. 143.

Much of Tkachev's article demonstrates a view of the peasant that in another writer he might have seen as vision distorted by rose-colored glasses.

Tkachev found other lessons in his readings on the fifteenth century. Reviewing Theodor Girzinger's work on *The Jesuits*, one volume of which appeared in Russian translation in 1868, he found cause to consider the role of the individual in history.

Although personality and personal activity also play a very important role in all those historical metamorphoses that are called historical progress, although personal action can destroy that which centuries have created and set a new path for the further development of humanity, however [such activity] always must be based on some sort of actual social elements, it must find support and justification in the given conditions of the economic way of life of a people. Without this support, without this firm soil underfoot, it is totally impotent and everything that it produces will have only a passing ephemeral significance. Thus no history—if it is really history and not biography—should ignore the economic factors, [none] can nor should leave without consideration those general economic foundations of social mores among which one or another personality is acting.[46]

Basically rejecting the role of the individual in historical development, Tkachev still left the back door open. Under certain circumstances an individual could exert his power; freakery could occur. In Tkachev's studies of the peasant wars he found proof that history often depends on accident. The deed of one man could be vital. A man killed by an assassin, a bullet gone astray, a battle that might have been inconclusive but for the heroism of a handful of individuals—these accidents seemed to Tkachev decisive factors that changed the course of events in the fifteenth century.

We beg the reader to dwell on this fact. See on what stupid and meaningless accidents this glorious historical progress depends. Two traitors, several strokes of the dagger, the death of one man—and progress stops, worse yet, turns into regress. Had there not been two Spaniards who had agreed to deliver the head of the popular leader to Innsbruck for money, or had they not succeeded in the attempt, history perhaps would have traveled a very different path from that it now walks along. In the short period of the peasant movement on several occasions the result of the uprising depended on similar kinds of accidents.[47]

Greatly overestimating the resources of the peasantry, Tkachev blamed the failure of the revolutions on bourgeois betrayal, which he thought had "a purely accidental character; it could either be or not be; the popular party had as much and even more chance to win as to be beaten."[48] History was here not dominated by rules or logical

---

46. Ibid., p. 259.
47. Ibid., p. 255.
48. Ibid., p. 260.

progression. It remained in the frivolous hands of whimsical and unpredictable destiny.

But Tkachev himself had propounded another theory of history: that man and his institutions must develop in accordance with the economic environment of the times. How, then, could the peasant be victorious? The times belonged to the aristocracy and the burghers. Tkachev himself had stated that the bourgeoisie was riding a rising wave although urban capitalism was just in its infancy. Could the economic chain be interrupted? Could the peasants overturn a developing economic system in an overnight military victory?

Tkachev argued that they could. Unwilling completely to reject his assumption of the primacy of economics in society, he was less willing to recognize the evolutionary view to which this assumption led. He answered in both directions. Social history must generally proceed logically and developmentally; in one of his reviews Tkachev wrote of the inevitability of the fall of medieval feudal civilization. But still this radical critic was not (he insisted) a historian gradualist, proposing that "any human society to attain higher forms of political development necessarily must live through all the lower." Such a gradualist theory, Tkachev wrote, was "historical hierarchy," "a scholarly phantasmagory thought up by flabby and complacent optimism for its own comfort."[49] Rather Tkachev insisted that occasionally history can turn on accident and society can proceed by leaps rather than slow steps. The peasant might have been victorious. Moreover had he won his battle, the victory would have "transferred the German nation directly from the sixteenth into the nineteenth or even, if you will, into the twentieth century."[50]

Tkachev obviously viewed some developments as inevitable and others as not. In terms of the peasant wars he thought a victory of the peasants over the feudal nobility to be possible. The fifteenth-century burghers, on the other hand, could not have defeated feudalism; their defeat by the feudal aristocracy (as he interpreted the wars' results) was what he called "fatal, logical, inevitable necessity." Tkachev sensed the difficulty himself.

Obviously we are expressing totally contradictory positions, obviously we are defending blatant paradoxes. In one case we show the possibility of *historical jumps* [*skachki*] ; in another we retain the theory of *gradual* historical development. Why could the peasants win in the sixteenth century and reconstruct the entire social way of life through their sociodemocratic program but the urban bourgeoisie have to wait patiently for its victory for another full two centuries? If in the first case a

---

49. Ibid., p. 248.
50. Ibid.

historical jump was possible, why was it not possible in the second? And here is why: the peasantry was fighting for change of the very principle lying at the basis of the given social way of life—the bourgeoisie, however, retaining the inviolable principle, was striving only for acceleration of certain of its logical consequences.[51]

One could not change the evolutionary development of society once a pattern was established. However, should the pattern be broken, history might jump from an old track to a new. Never able to skip the inevitable intervening rungs, history might begin to climb a totally different ladder.

Any given economic principle develops by the laws of its logic and to change these rules is just as impossible as it is to change the laws of human thought, the laws of our psychological and physiological functions. In the area of logical reasoning it is impossible to skip from the first premise to the last without the middle—exactly as in the sphere of the development of a given economic principle, it is impossible to jump from the lower stage directly to the higher without [passing through] all intervening ones. . . . It is a totally different thing if [one], setting aside the old principle, will strive to exchange it for a new. This striving can very easily be crowned with success, and in his action there will certainly be nothing utopian.[52]

Tkachev's theory of historical jumps enabled him to mitigate the strict doctrine of determinism without totally abandoning the concept of man and society as subjugated to some unspecified developmental law. Clearly the sideways leap to the next ladder permitted possible peasant success in the fifteenth century as it opened the door to the success of voluntaristic action at any time in history. In Tkachev's view there had to be some way of avoiding what seemed inevitable. Revolution could not be denied the possibility of victory. The theory of historical jumps was Tkachev's novel way out.

For this young radical, in spite of his historical studies, was more interested in contemporary man than in the fifteenth-century peasant. His concern was not the overthrow of feudalism but the defeat of Western capitalism and, as he later acknowledged, the avoidance by his native land of capitalism's evils. From the potential victory of the fifteenth-century peasant it was a short step to the posssible success of revolution in his own times. For the *Cause* Tkachev studied not only the economy of feudalism but the principles of that contemporary system he so hoped to see eclipsed.

Examining the doctrines of bourgeois economists, particularly those

---

51. Ibid., p. 260.

52. Ibid., pp. 260-61. Galaktionov and Nikandrov find a similarity between Tkachev's theory of historical jumps and Pisarev's division of historical movement into two types: chemical, which is gradual development, and mechanical, comprising revolutionary change. A historical jump would fit into the latter category (Galaktionov and Nikandrov, pp. 115-16).

of the liberal school, Tkachev attacked these Western writers first and foremost for their inability to rise above the capitalist system. Like the philosophers he had considered in his *Russian Word* days, economists attempted to unearth the principles of capitalism and then claimed these principles as immutable in time and space. They could not recognize that under a different system man would himself become different; rather they accepted his contemporary flaws—competitiveness, restlessness, greed, amorality in regard to fellow man—as inevitable facets of human nature. Having made certain empirical observations, the liberal economists elevated these contemporary mores to the level of eternal law. As Tkachev put it,

> The empirical fact, born of empirical conditions, which may exist or may not exist, they took as an unconditional, eternal, immutable fact—and this pseudo-immutable fact they set at the basis of their whole system; on it they based their science.[53]

Thus the economic and psychological rules propounded by bourgeois economists actually arose from capitalism, but these economists were unable to realize that another order might alter the entire nature of man.

Between 1867 and 1869 Tkachev reviewed for the *Cause* the Russian editions of the works of Adam Smith, Malthus, and John Stuart Mill. Of the three the young critic reserved his heartiest dislike for Malthusianism, "that most backward and pernicious doctrine of the old economic school," as he termed it in one article.[54] Tkachev did not entirely disagree with Malthus; he approved of Malthus's concepts of the lack of correspondence between food supply and population and shared the economist's lugubrious predictions for the future of bourgeois society.

> Among the proletarians of contemporary Western European society full disharmony between the means for existence and demands really exists; economic progress does not weaken this disharmony, but on the contrary continually increases it because with the broadening of factory industry, with the increase in competition of capitalists, with the development of technical perfection, the sum of products must rapidly increase and together with this the price of them must fall lower and lower, that is, the costs of production, in other words, worker pay, must perpetually be decreased.[55]

He did take exception to the Malthusian ratio (geometric to arithmetic progression) of population and nutritive increases. But his most violent onslaught he saved for Malthus's conviction that the evils of overpopulation and undernutrition were inevitable. Malthus had taken

---

53. Tkachev, 5: 315.
54. Ibid., p. 305.
55. Ibid., p. 458.

a fact of his particular capitalist society and found it to be immutable, Tkachev wrote. Doing so, the English social philosopher clearly acted under the influence of his particular environment.

Social and moral ideas, theories, ideal laws are not so much the product of independent logical development of the human mind, the product of intellectual progress, as the product of certain social relationships, certain economic interests that enslave the mind, that force it to work not *by itself* but *according to their own* logic, that prompt it as to what should be said and proved, that make of it their servant.[56]

Tkachev could not believe that poverty was necessary. Instead he was convinced that a change of capitalist forms could produce a different and better system. The solution lay in redistribution of wealth. Malthus's insistence on solving the problem by regulating demand (decreasing the number of mouths to feed by catastrophe, illness, or unnatural restraint) rather than by redistributing available supplies Tkachev viewed as a clear reflection of ruling capitalist philosophy.[57] Poverty could best be cured not through increasing production or decreasing population but by a more equable distribution of goods.[58]

Tkachev criticized Adam Smith on the same basis: for taking human nature as it existed to be immutable rather than regarding it as a temporary product of an unfortunate environment. In an 1868 review Tkachev concerned himself not only with *Wealth of Nations* but with Smith's work entitled *Theory of Moral Sentiments*. He caught Smith's own duality of approach: in the essay on morals Smith found man devoted only to virtue while in the treatise on economics man was motivated only by cupidity, in each case excluding all other possible characteristics. Smith had in each essay isolated certain traits from the whole. Obviously, Tkachev snarled, it was a hypothetical man Smith had in mind in both books; obviously he endowed this man with rigid, exclusive, immutable form. He and other economists

translate the hypothesis into fact and on it construct their entire theory, as if the given relationships are explained by and emerge from the basic essence of human nature, as if man in the economic sphere will always act under the influence of selfish motives, will always be dominated by the wish to work as little as possible and to acquire, as much as possible, as if he never will be vigorous enough to emerge from the congenital role of shopkeeper and landlord, so, consequently, the given relationships in both traits are immutable, and, so to speak, eternal.[59]

---

56. Ibid., p. 459. This statement is very similar to Chernyshevskii's expression of environmentalism: see his *Antropologicheskii printsip*, p. 8.

57. Tkachev, 5: 452.

58. Reuel has used this as one example of Tkachev's non-Marxist understanding of economics. See his "Ekonomicheskie vzgliady P. N. Tkacheva," p. 148.

59. Tkachev, 5: 394.

Tkachev, on the contrary, was convinced that cupidity was only one manifestation of ego and that man's ego (which he seemed to consider enduring and innate) could be satisfied not only through satisfaction of his greed but through acts of benevolence and the achievement of other goals. In a series of arguments that seem superficial and immature, he attempted to prove that such an innate human emotion as sympathy was actually a manifestation of ego, thus demonstrating, he believed, that ego could indulge itself by actions that were profitable and valuable to human society.[60] Cupidity, he wrote, was merely that product of egotism elicited by contemporary economic mores. Tkachev was actually arguing that man was perfectible, that the blatant evils of his nature were not innate but temporary, as called forth only by the horrors of capitalistic demands.

He restated his point in connection with Stuart Mill's economics. In doing so, he was entering into a polemic that had raged among Russian radical critics since Chernyshevskii had translated and published Mill's *Principles of Political Economy* in *Contemporary*. The book became, Kozmin tells us, the "manual by which Russian youth became acquainted with political economy."[61] In 1860 Chernyshevskii wrote (and Tkachev probably read), "We have great respect for Mill; he is one of the most powerful thinkers of the present epoch and the most powerful thinker among the economists who have remained true to Adam Smith."[62] But Mill remained, in Chernyshevskii's view, timid in his approach to fundamental problems because he was unable to rise above his middle-class origins.[63] The debate over Mill as an economist attained wide proportions in the radical press, reaching a climax in 1865 in the violent arguments of N. V. Sokolov (then of *Russian Word*), who called the *Principles* "a code of commercial crimes, a statute of usurers, and a credo of profiteers," and M. A. Antonovich of *Contemporary*, who called Sokolov ignorant.[64]

Tkachev took his side with the doubters. He was irritated that Mill (like Smith) viewed greed and selfishness as eternal traits of human nature, a matter in which Chernyshevskii, incidentally, had agreed with

---

60. Ibid., p. 396.

61. Ibid., 1: 450 (note 61).

62. Chernyshevskii, *Selected Philosophical Essays*, p. 57.

63. See the excellent analysis in Frederick C. Barghoorn, "The Philosophical Outlook of Chernyshevskii: Materialism and Utilitarianism," *Slavic Review* 6, nos. 18-19 (December 1947): 46.

64. Tkachev, 1: 451 (note 61).

Mill.[65] Tkachev did not; he repeated that cupidity was induced by contemporary economic forms.

Such a mood of the human spirit is called forth and conditioned by those economic circumstances in which man acted . . . with other conditions human egotism would have no need to express itself in this repulsive, selfish form.[66]

To his credit, Tkachev wrote, Mill recognized certain circumstances as conditioned by environment; among these was the distribution of wealth, which to Mill was not permanent and immutable but a result of contemporary mores. On the other hand Mill could not imagine an economy without profit, competition, and prices as well as wages conditioned by supply and demand.[67] Here again, Tkachev believed, the Englishman was writing into law a circumstance that was actually temporary and changeable, depending on broad economic environment.[68]

In another essay Tkachev expressed the point even more clearly: man was an environmental being and his environment determined his nature. It was capitalism that was at fault.

Human egotism consists in the striving of man toward his personal happiness; if this happiness is possible only with the unhappiness, the ruin of his neighbors, it forces a man to seek their unhappiness and ruin; if, on the other hand, it is possible only with their happiness and success, it forces man to strive for the happiness and success of his brothers. Thus the forms of existence of this emotion can be just as varied as those external conditions of human existence under which they are manifested are varied; in them there is nothing constant, eternal, immutable.[69]

He went on to debate the contention of Ernst Becher, a German social-democrat, that the competitive spirit is innate in man.

If [competition and ego] arouse in man antisocial feelings hostile to the true bases of social life, that means they are unreasonable, means they contradict the natural

---

65. "All deeds, good and bad, noble and base, heroic and craven, are prompted by one cause: a man acts in the way that gives him most pleasure. He is guided by self-interest" (Chernyshevskii, *Selected Philosophical Essays*, p. 124; cf. Woehrlin, pp. 132-34).

66. Tkachev, 5: 315.

67. Tkachev was being harsh with Mill, who did not actually believe competition to be as important in society as many observers. See John Stuart Mill, *Principles of Political Economy with Some of Their Applications to Social Philosophy*, particularly bk. 2, chap. 1 (dealing with socialism, communism, and private property) and bk. 2, chap. 4 (dealing with competition).

68. Tkachev, 5: 315-20.

69. Ibid., 1: 419.

inclination of man toward social life, that is, they contradict human nature. But what is unreasonable and unnatural cannot exist eternally.[70]

Tkachev's argument against competitiveness as a permanent trait of human nature is weakened by his contention that man does indeed have certain natural inclinations, such as a drive toward social life. But he believed it possible to discriminate between those human traits that were natural and those that were temporarily induced by the contemporary, changeable environment. Unfortunately, he was unable to evolve any clear set of criteria by which the one might be distinguished from the other. Tkachev suggested that when man was reacting as all living things react, he must be responding to a general law of nature rather than to his particular milieu. All living things die; therefore man dies in response to a general law. The strong always prevail over the weak.

Strength has always ruled and always will rule—this is the general law regulating the relations of all living beings between each other; to stand against it is pointless; to complain about it is stupid. Without it progress is inconceivable, without it there is eternal stagnation and eternal somnolence.[71]

This law could be recognized as immutable, Tkachev contended. However,

in the area of social relations [it] is distorted and loses its reasonable sense. Here it stops being a mover of progress and social perfectibility because the concept of *force* stops expressing itself through the idea of actual individual force, individual perfection; not more perfect, more intelligent people, closer to the ideal of man, but people possessing a greater quantity of means for existence are considered powerful.[72]

A given culture thus might pervert a general law, but the general law would stand. Beyond the rules of death and the superiority of the strong Tkachev found few unpleasant human traits to be inevitable. Man was, he wrote, an environmentally conditioned being; shedding his environment he might free himself from everything negative and evil. He had the will and power to perfect himself. It is a doctrine any idealistic social reformer must espouse or else admit his efforts to be futile.

Tkachev criticized the bourgeois economists for many affirmations beyond their views of human nature. He attacked the labor theory of value as endorsed by Adam Smith and John Stuart Mill, pointing out that labor is only one cost of production and that others (such as equipment) must be accounted for.[73] He sneered at the idea that the

---

70. Ibid.

71. Ibid., 2: 26.

72. Ibid.

73. Ibid., 1: 96-97. He soon contradicted his own denial of the labor theory of value.

greedy actions of different men neutralize each other, leading the economy to its highest peak of perfection and bringing happiness and well being to its participants. "This harmony," he wrote bitterly, "is the purest illusion," and he quoted Adam Smith himself on economic conditions in England. He regarded as utopian the idea that solidarity and confluence of interests necessarily exist; economists who claimed so were permitting their hopes to overcome their empirical common sense.[74] He did not believe that the laws of supply and demand, which Western economists viewed as determining market value, represented anything like a rough justice,[75] and the amorality of determining wages by external forces instead of intrinsic worth horrified and infuriated him. The importance of exchange in economics he condemned as a return to the Biblical law of an eye for an eye, and he accused economists (among them Proudhon) who viewed exchange as the most important factor of any economy of reviving "the old principle of revenge from the area of criminal law, where its insolvency is already fully recognized."[76] He detested what he considered the spirit of total individualism and free development of the human personality to which the bourgeoisie still "sings hymns"[77] because this freedom was a sham and its unconditional rule "proves profitable only for those who have the possibility and leisure fully to enjoy this freedom."[78]

To Tkachev, clearly, the capitalist society of the West was all wrong. It had created a man who was competitive, destructive, and cruel. It had deprived the toiler of the modicum of security that was his under feudalism, and the contemporary worker

is not in a state to say what awaits him tomorrow and thus constantly feels the precariousness, the hopelessness of his situation—any minute he may be deprived of work and become a beggar. Consequently *insecurity*, from the private, occasional phenomenon it was in the Middle Ages, has become in the West a phenomenon, so to speak, constant, normal, emerging from the very essence of present economic principles.[79]

At best bourgeois society had sponsored certain scientific advancements. Who cared, when it had created neither material nor moral well being?

What solutions, then, did Tkachev offer? What kind of society might replace that of the Western bourgeoisie and truly offer man the opportunity to perfect himself? Writing in the legitimate Russian press,

---

74. Ibid., 5: 405-6.
75. Ibid., p. 405.
76. Ibid., 1: 90.
77. Ibid., 2: 10.
78. Ibid., 5: 358-59.
79. Ibid.

Tkachev had little opportunity to set forth his specific hopes. He did, however, make one possible alternative clear in the introduction and notes he provided to his translation of a work by Ernst Becher, a German Lassallean.

Becher's *The Worker Question in Its Contemporary Significance and the Methods for Solving It* as translated and edited by Tkachev appeared in St. Petersburg in 1869. Tkachev added as appendices Proudhon's plan for a popular bank and the constitutional statute of the International Workingmen's Association, the Marxist International established in 1864. The publication was strongly criticized by the censor and featured as a point against Tkachev in his later trial as a Nechaevist.[80]

The introduction and notes to Becher's book make it clear that Tkachev viewed labor as enslaved to capital, a situation he regarded as destructive of social life in general and conducive to agony and anarchy in society. Labor was robbed by capital of the fruits of its work. Forgetting that he had just strongly denied the labor theory of value, Tkachev wrote:

Labor is, always was, and [always] will be the *sole* source of any production; consequently, it should have all rights to [products] ; but in reality, between [labor] and that which is produced stands the middle man, who with the aid of various privileges based on dry fictions and without taking even the slightest personal role in production himself, appropriates [the products] all to himself, doling out to labor merely whatever he finds profitable for himself.[81]

The solution to this gross injustice was to guarantee that labor might retain the produce of its toil, to merge the worker with the owner. Although he had previously denounced cooperatives as a mere palliative lacking the capacity to correct the evils of the economic system, he here seemed to agree with Becher that producer cooperatives might help. Such associations would eliminate the middleman-capitalist and permit the workers to share all possible profits from their labor. In this statement lay Tkachev's earliest clear espousal of socialistic principles. He was at least temporarily willing to follow the lead of Ferdinand Lassalle.[82]

---

80. Kozmin published Tkachev's introduction to Becher's book and the footnotes he appended to the manuscript in ibid., 1: 403-29; his long note on the censor's reaction is in ibid., pp. 448-50 (note 59). For a discussion of Tkachev's involvement in the Nechaevist case see chap. 7, below.

81. Tkachev, 1: 406.

82. Tkachev's interest in artel or cooperative production was common to many young people of the times. Chernyshevksii's famous novel *What Is to Be Done?* concerns, among other things, a young women's artel; real-life sketches of many of

In order to set up producer cooperatives, material aid and financial backing were essential. Becher realized it, and Tkachev agreed. The question of where such aid might be found had gained considerable attention from such proponents of the cooperative ideal as Lassalle, Louis Blanc, and Proudhon. Along traditional Lassallean lines Becher suggested that the state arrange for credit, either through a specially created bank or by requiring that private banks make moneys available. Tkachev roused the bête noire of the cooperativists when he expressed doubts that any government would choose so to aid the worker movement. After all a state's character and activity were determined by its economic milieu, and the workers could hardly expect a free ride from a government dedicated to the ruling bourgeois class.[83] Were the state a workers' state such aid would of course be forthcoming. Lassalle hoped that universal suffrage might make it so.

But Tkachev disagreed with Lassalle. There was a principle involved, a principle Tkachev had recognized in his own kind of socioeconomic determinism and had found clearly expressed in his early reading of Marx. The class that dominated the economic system of any society must necessarily also be politically dominant. The acquisition of power by a lesser class thus would seem to be impossible until the economic order was overthrown. Tkachev isolated the dilemma he found in Becher's reasoning.

We are again falling into a magic circle. Political rule, as Becher very correctly shows, taking exception to Lassalle, is possible only under conditions of economic independence; slaves in the economic sphere remain slaves in the political sphere, whatever juridical rights you invest in them. . . . Can the workers acquire political power without having economic power? On the other hand, can they acquire economic power without having political power?[84]

Tkachev answered with his old conviction that laws could be violated and the ordinary course of events could be subverted by human intervention.

Actually, *by the natural order*, only those classes always rule in the political sphere that rule in the economic sphere; actually, real benefit from political *rights* is possible only under economic independence. But the natural order can be temporarily broken, for, of course, political power is not always political right. Of

---

them are to be found in Vilenskaia. Walicki, p. 53 and elsewhere, follows Lenin in his belief that the defense of unspecialized labor and the small producer along with what he calls sociological romanticism, or a desire to return to pretechnological industrialism, are common to those he calls classical populists; see pp. 56-59. Tkachev did not return to his support of Lassallean-style cooperatives in future writings.

83. Tkachev, 1: 410.
84. Ibid.

course, breaking the natural order is possible only for a short time, but however short the time, it still will be sufficient to institute an economic reform that . . . boils down to a simple governmental decree. Thus the knot is untied by itself and the magic circle is broken.[85]

Thus the workers ordinarily could not control the state without first becoming the dominant economic force in society in accordance with Tkachev's view of the state as superstructure. However, it was possible for them to seize power on a temporary basis, if only long enough to pass legislation establishing themselves as the dominant economic class. In doing so, they would reinstitute the essential hegemony of the same group in both political and economic spheres.

As in his theory of historical jumps Tkachev showed himself willing to forego a general rule for the purpose of expediency. The takeover by the workers without proper economic status is analogous to the possible peasant victory in the sixteenth century. Both hypothetical situations reflected Tkachev's voluntarism. Both solutions were born of his impatience to change the world over and above the course of its natural evolution. Breaking the magic circle in 1869 prepared the ground for Tkachev's later belief in overthrowing the government first and making the revolution afterwards.

On matters pertaining to productive associations Tkachev remained critical of Becher. Becher retained, he believed, too much of the old order in the new. Tkachev decried his insistence that some competition should be maintained in the new society on the ground that competition was an innate human characteristic. To Tkachev, reasonable social life must deny any competitive spirit that could not be tolerated in the new society.

Reasonable human social life is possible only with the existence of complete harmony in human relationships, with the rule of peace, love, agreement, brotherhood; with the complete solidarity of the interests of all people. But the striving of man to distinguish himself, to differentiate himself from the mass, to be better and more perfect than his neighbor, however elevated and noble in itself the source of this striving, everywhere produces a struggle between people, with all its logical consequences; that is, envy, pride, vanity, the secret desire for one's neighbor's failure, the wish to harm him, to denigrate him, to raise oneself over him. With such a popular mood, with such mutual relationships between people one to another, peace, agreement, and love cannot exist between them; social harmony cannot be realized; brotherhood becomes an unthinkable Utopia; the solidarity of human interests is shattered and disappears.[86]

When Becher suggested that if the government guaranteed the

---

85. Ibid., pp. 410-11.
86. Ibid., p. 418.

income of the productive associations (Lassalle's hope) the associations might become lazy, Tkachev could not agree. Nor did he believe that incentive must be offered in the form of wage differentiation. Such differentiation was unjust, the young Russian cried; a man was not necessarily responsible for his own talents and capacities, and therefore it was unfair to reward a talented human being at a higher premium than a less capable person. Only equal distribution was fair. He urged Becher to devise a "new, more rational means for computing the value of a unit of labor." He finally suggested that the knotty problem of compensation await solution until that far-off time when all men would actually be equal in their capacities and abilities.

The task will be solved, the principle will become realized, when all people become unconditionally equal, when there will exist no difference between them either in intellectual, moral, or physical regard. Then they will all take completely equal part in the revenue from production and any special valuation of their labor will become completely superfluous; the causes that, in the opinion of the backward economists, make wages necessary at the present time will disappear of themselves.[87]

Even when worker needs were satisfied, Tkachev saw no problem in lack of incentive. Every man had inexhaustible demands, and satisfaction of some would merely elevate others to his consciousness.

As for the parasites, the drones, the minority who lived off the labor of the productive part of society, let them disappear. Becher was concerned about the principle of minority rights. Tkachev disagreed with him and took Lassalle's side. The new world would be a worker's world; there would be no room for anyone else. The workers must be the only class. They must, he cried, "become the sole center of the social order; outside of them, no one must be tolerated in the society; to them belong all rights, and outside them, nobody can have any rights or significance."[88] Thus only would disharmony be finally eliminated. Then the interests of the working class would be fully identical with the interests of all society. The harmony utilitarians sought would at last be attained.

It seemed impossible to the violent young Tkachev that Becher's plan could be realized peacefully and without force. To change an order, as did the French Revolution, force was necessary.

Therefore it is very baseless to affirm, as Becher and many others do, that force never leads to anything. Of course, this is very sad—sad that each step forward must be bought at the price of human blood, that each rational reform must be won with weapon in hand. But nevertheless, this is fact that no one acquainted with history

87. Ibid., p. 427.
88. Ibid., p. 428.

will attempt to deny and is very easy to explain with certain traits of human nature recognized by all. A man will never decide in good will without a struggle to give up to another that which he is used to benefiting from, to forego what he considers his inalienable right.[89]

Having debated the immutability of human traits, Tkachev could not refrain from reasserting it, any more than, having denied historical determinism, he could refrain from speaking of certain fatal historical trends. The insistence on force may have been a result of Tkachev's careful reasoning, but it more likely was the manifestation of his characteristic impatience.

Basically Tkachev felt that Becher did not go far enough. He underestimated himself; he did not see the entire potential of his own plans. He failed to consider the social, political, moral consequences of establishing workers' productive cooperatives. To Tkachev it was clear that (if they worked) they would provide a final answer to what Becher sought; they would indeed transform all of society. The whole system of capitalism, including its social and intellectual superstructure of family life, education, and morality, would disappear. Man would rise to higher levels; he would conceive new dimensions and new goals. The change in economic order would do no less than transform mankind, providing human beings with new security, activating those traits that permit of love, brotherhood, and harmony, evoking a finer morality, and enacting a Golden Rule. This was the society of Tkachev's dreams, his own personal utopia.

Tkachev was not a systematic thinker, and in his eagerness to proselytize for his preconceived goals he often contradicted himself. The labor theory of value, cooperatives, the innate traits of human nature—all called forth inconsistent statements in his early years. More importantly he struggled to reconcile socioeconomic determinism with revolutionary voluntarism, often violating the one to allow scope to the other.

Still his discussions of Western writers in the period from 1867 to 1869 reveal some of the goals he had in mind. His ideal society was one in which the worker dominated, the drones were eliminated, and a harmony of interests inevitably prevailed. Unconditional equality would be the social byword. The happiness of any individual would coincide with the happiness of society as a whole, and therefore all strivings for individual welfare would automatically increase the well being of everyone. Competition would not exist; nor, of course, would poverty, exploitation, greed, or hatred. All of these facets of the

89. Ibid., pp. 428-29.

contemporary scene were no more than products of capitalism; in the harmonious future they would disappear and man would arise recreated and reformed. He would organize his economic life socialistically, perhaps in the form of producers' associations, in order that the distribution of wealth might also become egalitarian. Man himself in the new world would approach perfection.

But men dare not sit back and hope that some mysterious forces of history would bring about this perfect world. The forces of progress could not be counted upon; perhaps they did not exist at all. Man was responsible for his fate, and he must bear the burden of perfecting himself and his environment. Fortunately, he could do so. Even those time-honored movements of history that seemed to be inevitable were actually subject to man's will. He had it within his power to pull all of society out of its course and set it fresh on another. He could break the rules; perhaps not forever, but at least for long enough. Tkachev was already insisting that man act, that he not remain passive or give in to his surroundings. He must take his destiny into his own hands, even if, as was likely, blood must be shed in doing so.

6

Russia: Peasants, Women, and Heroism

Tkachev's preoccupation with the thinkers of the West never meant that he had forgotten his native land. His articles for the *Cause* between 1867 and 1869—far more than in the previous period—demonstrated not only his interest in Western political and economic theories but also his concern for Russia and her people. If Tkachev throughout his life disdained most Russian writers for what he considered their lack of originality in comparison with their Western colleagues, he was deeply involved, emotionally committed to the men and women of his own country, and more immediately worried about their relationships, their lives, and their future than about their Western brothers. Within a few years young Petr wrote about poverty in his homeland and its meaning for Russia's peasantry; about the role of the intelligentsia in reform and, surreptitiously, in revolution; about the heroic men of his own generation who could lead their country toward a better world. More hopefully than at any other time Tkachev eagerly studied the young people of his country and their potential for self-sacrifice and devotion. He discovered Russia's new woman and debated her place in the sun, past, present, and future. He considered the meaning of love and the mainsprings of dedication. He became considerably more human, more concerned with persons instead of classes, more immersed in ideals that he might later consider dreams. In these writings on Russia Tkachev attained something of warmth. His hopes for his homeland shone through his articles with less bitterness and desperation than ever again.

What was his native land to this angry young man? It was, he said, a land of contrast and contradiction, mixing civilization and barbarity, backwardness and precocity, darkness and light.

The primeval stupidity and barbarianism is intermixed and interlaced with refined European civilization; backward, revolting prejudices and impenetrable ignorance with the "latest conclusions" of Western science; the most lofty and noble theories with the most backward routine practice. . . . The educated minority stands almost on the same level of development as the educated minority of Western Europe—by the tendencies ruling within it, by the mentality and direction of thought governing it, it—at least in the person of its better representatives—can occupy not the least place among the first ranks of European intelligentsia. While one part of society continues to conduct its life "in the image and likeness" of its ancestors of the fourteenth century, the other part reformulates [life] according to the latest conclusions of social science and moral philosophy, discards routine and tradition, and regards all the phenomena around it with the sobriety and fearlessness of a thoughtful critic.[1]

If Tkachev was not the first to deplore the yawning gulf between the poles of Russia's social spectrum, he was one of those who most clearly saw the difference between the poor and rich, the peasant and the gentry, the illiterate and the intelligentsia. He studied and plotted to bring them closer, to raise the one nearer the standard of the other.

He began, as had Russian reformers for generations before him, with the peasantry. Like tsar and revolutionary, plodder and visionary, scientist and poet, almost as far back as the time serfdom developed, he saw in the peasant the backbone of Russian life. Like Herzen and Chernyshevskii, Bakunin and Lavrov, Tkachev tried to assess the peasant's mentality, isolate the causes of his poverty, and estimate his potential for the future. Although he did not until later publish his long study on the importance of the commune, he wrote a number of articles before 1869 touching on the peasant and agricultural problems. Most scholarly among them is the statistically oriented study, "The Productive Forces of Russia," passed by the censor only after a lengthy, nervous evaluation and published in the *Cause* in 1867.[2]

Tkachev did not fail to recognize Russian agricultural backwardness, particularly in comparison with agriculture in the West. "Only we," he moaned, "primarily agriculturalists, sit on our forefathers' plows and harrows and continue as before to sow one field in summer, one in winter, and leave the third fallow."[3] As far as he was concerned, "our agronomical ignorance exceeds any description."[4] He criticized not only agricultural technique but produce distribution, price fluctua-

---

1. Tkachev 1: 274.
2. Ibid., 5: 208-97; see also ibid., pp. 480-83 (note 58).
3. Ibid., p. 210.
4. Ibid., p. 216.

tion, the lack of conservationist policies in regard to forest and mineral wealth, and the perennial shortage of cattle, which he accurately evaluated in its effect not only on the consumption of meat but in regard to the production of fertilizer. Agriculture, he contended, demanded certain industries to refine and prepare its products for market, to provide the tools needed in the field. "Without factories and manufacture, agricultural industry not only cannot prosper but cannot even exist," he wrote.[5] He berated Russia for not developing the supporting manufacture that her agricultural population demanded. "It is obvious," he concluded unhappily,

that they call us an agricultural country not because agriculture is well developed among us and not because we produce particularly much grain but only because we do not have any industry other than agriculture.[6]

In a final lengthy chapter Tkachev personalized his statistical data on the financial plight of the peasantry. Computing the average acreage and income of a peasant family and carefully totaling the essential annual expenses of a household, he concluded that by definition the peasant must fall into debt. He manipulated for his peasants—he cut down expenses for clothing, reduced the number of cattle, omitted the weekly contribution to the church—but the fact of poverty remained undeniable. The peasant family of 1867, Tkachev concluded, must break up; its members must find employment elsewhere. As an agricultural unit it could not possibly produce enough to remain free of debt.[7]

What did this poverty mean? What did it do to the human psyche? Tkachev answered clearly: poverty destroys a man. He cannot remain a humane being, he loses his sense of morality, he forgets how to be kind, he learns only how to fight for a crust of bread. The poor Russian peasants—indeed all of Russia's poor—were drowned in the struggle for existence. They did not have the strength to fight the ocean of poverty that overwhelmed them.

The less developed the man, the greater his dependence on the material conditions of his existence. All his thoughts, all his forces are reduced to the question of bread; and, of course, the greater the difficulties and intricacies of this question, the more fully it calls for all his attention, all his activity, all his thought. . . . All other interests, all other considerations and questions are pushed into the background, and their influence is but little reflected in his actions and thoughts. . . . Further, this explains that uniformity of character, that psychic poverty, that moral underdevelopment [of the poor]. . . . Richness and diversity of character are conditioned by diversity of the conditions of life; if millions of people are surrounded

5. Ibid., p. 241.
6. Ibid., p. 213.
7. Ibid., pp. 275-84.

by more or less uniform conditions, if they in the same measure exist under the yoke of need and poverty, then their moral, psychic physiognomy will be alike as two drops of water, similar one to the other.[8]

A poor peasant could not be expected to follow high standards of morality. He did not respect other men's property, for he knew only constant infringement of his own rights. He understood the principle of social solidarity, but however strong his principles they inevitably gave way before the demands of his stomach. He could not afford to take risks. He had to choose to satisfy his hunger, not his conscience.

This exact alternative presents itself to him each time there is a possibility and necessity of action in the sense of common interest. Consequently, common interest always disappears from view; each acts separately, each pleads only about himself, and each loses.[9]

If there was any hope, Tkachev found it in the same environmentalism that dominated his assessment of poverty. These miserable traits of the poor, these niggardly and self-centered outlooks were determined by environment. Luckily, they

do not constitute any sort of inborn characteristic of the people of the ignorant crowd; they are conditioned by those abnormal relationships into which they are placed in most events. But only let these conditions change, only let a man be transferred to a more normal situation, and all these bad traits of his will suddenly disappear, and his relations to people around him will become most peace loving and good natured.[10]

Even the ugly peasant was perfectible; even he might take his place in an ideal, harmonious society. He would respond to his surroundings; if they should change, he would one day become the ideal, harmonious man.

In spite of his optimism about the future of the poor and of mankind, Tkachev's earliest descriptions of the peasant remain some of the most realistic portrayals in the Russian literature of his day. Of course his peasant was abstract, a creature drawn from books and statistical surveys. Tkachev made no effort to describe the country people in his own personal experience; he was a literary critic, not an essayist or a storyteller. His information had the lifeless remoteness of the secondhand. Yet he saw peasant poverty and understood it better than many of his contemporaries. By 1868 he was already convinced that the poor were incapable of initiating successful revolutionary action on their own.

---

8. Ibid., 1: 340-41.
9. Ibid., p. 364.
10. Ibid., p. 363.

More realistically than his colleagues, Tkachev pitied the peasant but did not have faith in him. He reserved great scorn for writers who idealized the peasantry. He reviewed many novels and tales about peasant life—they proliferated in his time—but he refused to praise and appreciate them. He found the authors badly lacking the realistic, sociological, ethnographic outlook that he sought.

The trouble was that Russian writers reflected the conditions around them. The *intelligent* no less than the peasant was a victim of his environment. "The world view of people and the character of their activity is always determined by the circumstances of their economic way of life," he wrote in his old vein in 1868.[11] Then for the first time he admitted to exceptions, to extraordinary people who were able to rise above their environment and break the rules. "In application to an individual person," then, "this proposition allows of many exceptions, but in application to an entire class or estate, it is unconditionally valid."[12]

The Russian educated class viewed the peasantry through the prism of its own experience, conditioned in Tkachev's day particularly by the end of serfdom. With the emancipation,

the center of gravity of our intelligentsia changed; before it almost exclusively came from the solidly secure, conservative-minded estate; now this lordly intelligentsia had to retire before another, which arose from another class of people . . . and constituted something midway between a well secured and a completely insecure class.[13]

In spite of the protests of the old generation, this new generation necessarily replaced it. Because its view of the world was

the fruit of the conditions of our economic life [and] our social relations, [its rise] is naturally necessary and inevitable, whatever the representatives of the outmoded system say. Their voices will always be voices crying in the wilderness, their perfidious tricks and evil intrigues will descend on their own heads. Their time is past, and their apparent triumph unstable and fleeting; serf concepts and serf literature were necessarily destroyed with serfdom.[14]

With the old class died one group of Russian writers (among whom Tkachev mentioned Slavophiles and liberals) who had idealized the peasant. They had seen in him a great strength, the hope for the future of his country, the bearer of a powerful native and popular genius. In their novels, tales, and essays the coarse *muzhik* was transformed into a refined *paysan*. He was morally pure, uncorrupted by the stain of intellectualism.

---

11. Ibid., p. 276.
12. Ibid.
13. Ibid., pp. 276-77.
14. Ibid., p. 277.

The idealists of this sort were firmly convinced that the peasant, in spite of the unfavorable conditions of his life, in spite of all his privations, in spite even of all those injustices he must experience, always preserved purity and incorruptibility of heart, and if not in intellectual at least in moral regards stands higher, or in any case no lower, than the coddled crowd of civilized people.[15]

Serfdom, the early writers consoled themselves, could not be all that bad if the peasant remained pure and firm. The "civilized crowd" before 1861 delighted in regarding the peasant as a happy laborer, accepting his destiny and a better man for it.

Unfortunately the idealistic school did not entirely disappear with the abolition of serfdom. To his disgust Tkachev found it still represented by a group of writers he increasingly deplored. Among them he specifically mentioned Marko-Vovchek (M. A. Markovich), a close friend of Pisarev's after the latter's release from prison in 1866. She and others, misguided if not malicious, deliberately continued to deceive their readers as to the peasant's real nature. They looked gently, warmly, and sympathetically into the internal world of the peasant's heart and found it good. They emphasized his individuality and personality without dwelling on the external economic conditions of rural life. They made their imaginary peasants into heroes and heroines who spoke with the tongues of angels, kind and gentle to a man. These fictitious *muzhiks* acted, Tkachev keenly affirmed, a good bit like educated men.

Instead of the actual, real *babas* and *muzhiks*, they painted for us pictures of the civilized crowd, differing from educated readers only in that they wore peasant dress and spoke in peasant jargon. [These characters] pleased the readers because they were copies of themselves. The readers understood them and sympathized with them because they themselves, set into [peasant circumstances], would think and act exactly the same as these heroes. Thus sympathizing and suffering with them, the readers grossly erred, believing that they were sympathizing and suffering with the people; they were sympathizing and suffering with that civilized group to which they themselves belonged, and which had little in common with the actual, authentic, and uncolored people.[16]

Apart from idealizers Tkachev isolated another contemporary school of peasant writers: those who found in their subject a source of humor, grossness, ignorance, and foolishness. The writers who portrayed the peasant in anecdotes and humorous tales deliberately left their readers amused at the clumsy, comical ways of the coarse, stumbling ox. Instead of sympathizing with the peasant's fate the reader emerged chuckling. Tkachev was convinced that this school of writers (for example, Nikolai Uspenskii) operated out of fear that the peasant

15. Ibid., p. 335.
16. Ibid., p. 341.

might demand equality when he was no longer a serf. Portraying him as coarse and ignorant, they sought to discourage those members of the radical intelligentsia who hoped to make the peasant a full-fledged member of society. Tkachev admitted that the peasant was indeed gross and foolish; his own investigations convinced him of it. Nevertheless he was a tragic figure and not a comic one. His ignorance was only one facet of himself; presented without his other parts, it would deceive the reader, leaving him with an inaccurate picture and with no realistic understanding of the conditions that nourished ignorance, of the miserable way the peasant must live.

Both of these unrealistic and one-sided views of the peasantry created an illusory world about which Tkachev, the self-dubbed realist, could not control his bitterness.

Thus is created a world of illusions, in which we imperceptibly get used to living as if in the real world, finally losing any distinction between real life and the delirium of sick imagination. This is the type of *hashish* with which the civilized minority appeases its conscience and deadens its mind. The obliging novelists, poets, journalists to whom we pay money, accord praise, and even subsidize in order that they make us stupid as artistically and plausibly as possible, keep us continually in this effete drunkenness. And they fulfill their role with becoming enthusiasm.[17]

Particularly bitter was his reaction to those overestimates of the peasant and his capacity that he called the illusions of popular genius and popular self-development. He deplored the idea that the peasant had a special intuitive knowledge that educated men should absorb at his knee. It was not necessary to teach the peasantry, he sarcastically rephrased the idea,

but it is necessary to learn from it, and in the people the educated must seek a renewal of their own strengths. . . . The people's spirit, the people's genius, the people's roots—these are sacred things that the civilized crowd does not dare to touch with its impure hands, that it cannot analyze and criticize with its perverted mind.[18]

At heart, Tkachev's dislike of idealizers turned out to be a matter of practicality, like so many of his other beliefs. He admitted it himself. He had recognized at once that the concepts of a popular genius and of popular self-development would result in the intelligentsia's apathy and in the destruction of any solidarity it might feel with the interests of the poor. After all, why bother helping people who have the power to raise themselves by their bootstraps and to find their way alone?

Entrusting all hopes to the people, the idealists thus relieved themselves of the

---

17. Ibid., p. 324.
18. Ibid., p. 326.

obligation to act; everything will be accomplished, they reasoned, even without us, the people pave the way for themselves, and nothing more will remain to us than merely to merge with them and follow in their footsteps;[19]

and again, this idealization

can seed in the minds of readers unrealistic hopes and, instead of arousing in them a desire energetically to act, to act without awaiting any external, outside forces, make them set very great hopes in the people.[20]

But what, then, could the intelligentsia, the civilized crowd do? What should its attitudes toward the peasantry be? Tkachev could not go into detail because of the censorship. He did make suggestions. First of all, the educated Russian should throw away his rose-colored glasses, take the blindfold off, discard the hashish. Instead he should get to know the real peasant.

In order that [the intelligentsia] may act, it is necessary that it be fully permeated with awareness of the solidarity of its interests, its grief and joy, with the interests, grief and joys of the simple, disenchanted working masses. It must learn to suffer with their sufferings, weep with their tears; then without hesitating, it will give them all its activity, all its life, because working for them it will work for itself, because easing their fate, it will lighten its own sufferings.[21]

As to the action he spoke of, Tkachev's environmentalism again pointed the way. Education and lectures on morality would do no good, he believed, as long as the poor remained poor.

Literacy and education are a beautiful thing, but they do not bring love, peace, and harmony into family life, into the family and domestic relations of the hungry worker. However literate he is, he must always crush and press everyone he can while the basic reason for his eternal irritation and displeasure is not eliminated— his poverty and want. He will understand and will apply in practice the great rule of morality of the civilized crowd—respect others' rights—when his own rights will be respected, when from fictional they will become actual, real.[22]

The attitudes of the poor evolved not from lack of education or intellectual immaturity but from the conditions of living, conditions under which "a man was chafed every minute and every hour by failure, every minute and every hour receiving heavy slaps in the face from life."[23] Those who did not understand the true source of immorality and considered the whole problem one of education Tkachev described as Pharisees. Education simply would not help; "the demands of the stomach always will exert a stronger influence on a man's action

---

19. Ibid., p. 329.
20. Ibid., p. 338.
21. Ibid., p. 325.
22. Ibid., p. 355.
23. Ibid., p. 350.

than the demands of reason."[24] There was no way to save the poor, no way to enlighten and educate them, no way to transform them into refined, moral beings elevated by high social purpose—except to erase poverty.

But under certain circumstances the peasant could be counted on to help. With the right approach the sluggish poor could be aroused to aid in a great social cause and to act with such unity and force that success might be theirs. The peasant of 1867 knew only that he was impotent; every miserable day developed this conviction more strongly in him. He lacked confidence in the results of his protests. Such confidence must be created; the civilized crowd had to help him to see his own potential.

The poor and stupid people can act together and with solidarity in spite of their poverty and stupidity, but one condition is necessary for this; for this is needed a firm conviction of the success of the cause; then not the abstract idea but the simple, practical calculation will activate them. . . . It is necessary that they be convinced that a power is standing for them and this power will support them. Only this conviction can unite them; once united they will feel the power themselves. But until this time, consciousness of their own power can never be evoked by any synthetic measures; until this time it is ridiculous and utopian to await some sort of initiative.[25]

Thus it was up to the civilized crowd to educate the poor man to his own strength, to take the initiative to spur his action.

If they refuse to seek their own happiness themselves, if they renounce the initiative, then by this they assign it to you, they demand your aid, your instructions. And you are obliged, in our opinion, you are obliged by your own benefit to render this aid, to give these instructions. . . . The ignorant crowd is coarse, savage, brutal; it will stop being savage, coarse, and brutal when it stops being poor; it will stop being poor when it unites its private individual efforts for the *better* into a common, aggregate activity; it will become capable of such activity when it in practice is convinced that a force stands for it, ready to help it and support it. Toward the creation of this force all the striving of the civilized crowd should be directed. But where will it find it? It will find it in itself, in its knowledge, in its higher intellectual development, in the moral and intellectual conditions among which it lives and acts.[26]

The intelligentsia must assume responsibility for constructing a force great enough so that the peasant would be convinced of the certainty of victory. Feeling their own strength the peasants—or rather the poor —would rise to join the intelligentsia, and victory would indeed be theirs.

---

24. Ibid., p. 364.
25. Ibid., pp. 365-66.
26. Ibid., p. 369.

By 1868 Tkachev had clearly anticipated his own later revolutionary plans, the key to which lay in his conviction that the peasantry
would not make revolution alone. His solution, set forth as early as
these first writings for the *Cause*, was to lay responsibility upon what
he called the civilized crowd. Yet even then he hedged. He never
entirely trusted educated men; he was uncertain of their capacity for
forceful action, he feared their ivory-tower isolation from reality.
Exactly where did he lay his hopes? What particular people among
the intelligentsia would carry out the radical mission? Tkachev set forth
his answer in several long articles published before 1869. The people
of the future, the leaders of Russia towards a better world, the inspirers
of the peasantry to revolution, were not the old but the young, the
new woman and the new man of Russia's rebellious generation of the
1860s.

Tkachev was very conscious of his own generation and its attitudes.
The so-called *raznochinnaia intelligentsiia* was the only class he ever
trusted. In 1867 he saw his contemporaries in a shining light: they were
throwing off the chains of tradition, grasping with excitement at new
ideas, espousing causes with dedication and abandon, tossing caution
aside in their ardor, and asserting at every step their rights to a special
place in the sun. They congregated around universities. They planned
careers unheard of before the Great Reforms. Their hopes (and
Tkachev's) for the future reached new heights.

Moreover for the first time in Russian history young women were
moving into society, joining the male intelligentsia, and demanding
respect of their own. The movement towards women's rights—legal
recognition, personal freedom, and social equality—was a flaming cause
among the radicals of Tkachev's time. Pisarev was among its most
active proponents. Chernyshevskii had written of the status of women;
What Is to Be Done? is above all the story of a young woman's emancipation. Aping the adventures of Chernyshevskii's Vera Pavlovna, young
women of the sixties insisted on contributing to the radical cause. They
founded artels and schools. They contracted fictitious marriages, choosing any agreeable spouse and entering into unconsummated matrimony
(including even the traditional religious ceremony) in order to achieve
personal and economic independence from their families. They delighted in adding shock elements and symbols of rebelliousness to their
behavior. But they were serious in their aims. By 1870 many young
women, demanding higher education forbidden to them in Russia,
emigrated abroad in search of university training; J. M. Meijer has
studied the predominantly feminine Russian colony in Zurich, where
many women went to school and later made names for themselves in

many fields.[27] Women's rights became a cause not just for radicals but for liberals and even members of Russian aristocratic society.[28] Tkachev took up the gauntlet too.

Indeed it was the quiet, lonely young Tkachev who became the expert on women for the *Cause* in response to the spirit of women's liberation. The small, slight, smiling young man, hardly an image of strength or masculinity, devoted a number of long and sympathetic articles to the plight of the weaker sex. They were extraordinarily effective. Suvorov, a colleague on the journal, reported with some amusement that women from many provinces in Russia read Tkachev's essays with palpitating heart. Some of them made declarations of love for him through the mail.[29]

Indeed if Tkachev gathered a radical circle around him it was composed of ardent young women, obsessed with the need to liberate their sex. At least one of them wrote romantically of her excitement about her emancipation. After reading one of Tkachev's feminist articles, she had sent him a letter full of enthusiastic sympathy, and received what she termed a "glorious" letter from her hero himself. Thereafter she sought Tkachev out, visited him frequently, and wrote to her friends that their acquaintanceship might not be without benefit to the women's cause.[30] Through his feminist stance Tkachev came to know the Korvin-Krukovskaia sisters, the older of whom (Anna), revolutionary and writer, was being pursued by Dostoevskii himself, and the younger of whom (Sofia), under her married name of Kovalevskaia, was to become one of Russia's leading mathematicians. Other young women pursued him with the aim of matrimony, not necessarily with himself but with some available young man on a fictitious basis; they seemed to feel Tkachev could arrange anything.[31] The young critic was sensitive enough to understand the mental anguish and the psychic sufferings of

---

27. J. M. Meijer, *Knowledge and Revolution*.

28. Tkachev's sister Annenskaia distinguished between the nihilists' movement for women's liberation and the movement, with the same aims, sponsored by those she called aristocrats. She described one noisy joint meeting of the two groups in her own apartment (Annenskaia, "Iz proshlykh let," p. 63).

29. Suvorov, "Zapiski o proshlom," p. 145.

30. This was Anna Mikhailovna Evreinova. See Sofia Vasilevna Kovalevskaia, *Vospominaniia i pisma*, pp. 135, 181 (note 125); see also Ivan Sergeevich Knizhnik, *Russkie deiatelnitsy pervogo Internatsionala i Parizhskoi kommuny*, p. 158. Kovalevskaia herself was intrigued with Tkachev; she once wrote her husband that she was anxious for him to meet Tkachev so they could share their reactions. See *Golos minuvshego*, no. 2 (February 1916), p. 227.

31. Tkachev himself told this to the court in 1871 when he was on trial (Kozmin, *Nechaev i Nechaevtsy*, p. 167).

the oppressed female of his day, a gift that brought empathic tears
to the eyes of many a woman who was aching to call herself "new."

Tkachev had begun, of course, with his usual economic point of
view. In 1866 the ill-fated journal *Women's Herald* published his first
major treatise on women—a long, scholarly, never completed article
about the influence of economic progress on contemporary woman and
her family.[32] Tkachev's phrase was sarcastic, for he saw no actual
progress at all in the development of modern capitalism. Drawing on
Western sources (but not on Marx), he painted a dour picture of women
and children at work in England and in France, emphasizing the heavy
labor and poor working conditions, long work day, substandard food
and housing, and the breakup of the family in general. Two years later
Tkachev finished translating a collection of articles on women originally
edited by a German named A. Daul and then wrote an additional
chapter of his own to add to the collection. Tkachev's essay, entitled
"The Feminine Question," summarized woman's past and present
position in the economic world. The contemporary movement for
feminine liberation the young critic saw as "the inevitable consequence,
the fatal necessity of the logical development of the economic principles lying at the foundation of the social life of European civilization."[33] He traced the position of woman through history, finding her a
near-slave in primitive society but a full individual, virtually equal with
man, in the Middle Ages when she could own property, sit in Parlia-
ment, or become a physician. Quickly he added that lower-class women
played the role of cattle as before, forced to stay home, tend the
children, and acknowledge men as their superiors.[34]

The contemporary period of history (that in which movable capital
had taken preeminence over immovable) had seen a change for the
worse in woman's situation. With his desperate need for work and the
shortage of job possibilities, man had attempted to keep woman out of
the market place so that she could not compete with him. He wanted
her to stay home. Tkachev felt that woman's household work had been
vastly eased by machine production. She was freer to seek paid employment now than ever before, and she wanted to.

This influence of machine production was reflected on all classes of society with
more or less force, and in all families women felt a change in their situation. Before
they had their hands full of work, they did not seek nor ask it, they were greatly
burdened by it; now, however, they suddenly found themselves almost without
things to do; before they could look on themselves as necessary and useful members

---

32. "Vliianie ekonomicheskogo progressa na polozhenie zhenshchiny i semi."
33. Tkachev, 1: 373.
34. Ibid., p. 382.

of society, as a certain economic force; now, however, they were forced to become aware that they had become parasites, a heavy burden for husbands, fathers, and brothers. But in this period, when labor is recognized as the sole right for existence, parasitism is inconceivable, impossible.[35]

In spite of man's efforts woman ended by entering the market place in competition with him.

However, she had to suffer the same tribulations as her mate. Technological unemployment, low wages determined not by quality of labor but by the amoral laws of supply and demand and tending always toward the subsistence level, poor working conditions, and evils of competition made working fall short of her own great expectations. Tkachev found her prematurely old, unhealthy, dull-eyed, and often taking to wine for succor. Where women and children worked wages fell lower and even men suffered; the whole working class was paid less and degenerated as a result.[36] Tkachev admitted that the addition of women to the labor market had certain unprofitable social consequences, although

the inevitability of lowering of wages logically emerges from the very conditions of the existing system of production, and the influence of the competition of feminine labor had in this case only secondary significance.[37]

The alternative—continual subjugation in a subsidiary role—was even more devastating. Continuing as she was, woman would become a pariah, a slave of man; her subordination would lead to

lowering of her level of intellectual and moral development, her intellectual and moral rape, the development of her bovine tendencies and instincts, slovenly depravity, and, consequently, the fall of public morals, licentiousness of passions, physical exhaustion, and degeneration of the European race.[38]

It was hardly a pretty picture. Tkachev's readers might have found his alternatives to total six of one and half dozen of the other. Either woman would stay home and become bovine or she would go out to work, suffering the consequences of miserable working conditions, lowering wages for herself and others, and creating general malaise. Where indeed should she turn? Tkachev gallantly threw his strength to support women's liberation. Women must be free, he contended, to assume the full-fledged roles and responsibilities of human beings, to join the labor market, whatever that entailed. He cheered his women readers with one thought: the disruption of the laboring class occa-

35. Ibid., p. 389.
36. Ibid., p. 398.
37. Ibid., p. 399.
38. Ibid., p. 400.

sioned by woman's competition need be only temporary. The problem would be solved finally when

the view of labor characterizing the third [modern] period is radically changed, when labor emerges from servile dependence on capital, when it will no longer be measured by [capital's] arbitrary valuation, when in its turn capital too will lose all the privileges acquired by it in the period of its exclusive and unconditional hegemony.[39]

But the readers of Tkachev's generation were not so concerned about that rare phenomenon in Russia, the poor laboring woman. Indeed, the journal *Fatherland Notes* attacked Tkachev's translation of Daul on the grounds that the book concentrated too heavily on the economic aspect of feminine freedom without considering women's rights as a moral and intellectual issue.[40] Tkachev answered with a rebuttal in the *Cause:* economics, he cried, is always at the basis of social and moral phenomena.

This does not mean that I deny the historical significance of ideas and set no stakes on intellectual progress; no, it means only that I look on the historical role of ideas somewhat differently from the way it is seen by the bards of unlimited omnipotence of the human mind. Ideas (I speak of course about ideas in the area of social and moral sciences) always are the incarnation, the reflection, if you will, the theoretical reaction of some sort of economic interest.[41]

But the criticism of *Fatherland Notes* was valid. Tkachev's Russian readers were actually more interested in the problems of the young women of a different class. The women who sighed over Tkachev's wisdom and sympathy came from another social stratum: they were young, well-to-do, well-educated girls seeking a new place in an old world. Their problems were often more psychological than financial: their goals lay in freedom and recognition more than in higher pay or shorter hours. They were gentlewomen of Tkachev's own social background; he knew them and had always known them. He understood the new woman's psychological dynamics, her efforts to enter man's world, her attempts to find her identity in a society where she had been narrowly restricted in her activities and her achievements.

Who was this new woman? She was born, according to Tkachev, with the abolition of serfdom. When serf labor was eliminated Russia's middle gentry, both male and female, lost its main source of economic support. Accumulations of capital did not exist and could not provide an inherited source of wealth as they did in Western Europe. Only its own labor could preserve the gentry, that is, those strata of the nobility

---

39. Ibid., p. 402.
40. Ibid., p. 445 (note 54).
41. Ibid.

that were not very rich. Driven to seek means to live, the gentlewoman found her way blocked by tradition. She became bitter, suppressed, frustrated. She was tortured by subconscious and unformulated strivings. Unable to analyze her own needs, she yearned for something uncertain and impractical while she remained trapped in a tight circle of permissible activities. Society could use her, Tkachev cried, if only it would support her, show her a true path, point out conscious goals. "Dooming woman to immobility in her social position, limiting the circle of her activity to the kitchen and the parlor, society punishes not only her; it punishes, together with her, its very self."[42]

The new woman, as Tkachev and his contemporaries saw her, strove for independence; she was willing to sacrifice security, risk poverty, become a proletarian, live in cold and hunger, and give up her good life for the privilege of becoming self-sufficient. But working for woman's economic independence was not satisfying enough.

Her striving was much broader, more rational, more humane; enlightened and permeated with the idea of the solidarity of human interests, she set herself the goal not of attaining economic self-sufficiency merely as one or two single beings, but of realizing those common conditions under which each separately and all together could benefit by this self-sufficiency.[43]

Woman was driven by her own situation to seek greater ideals.

The less secure the situation of a person, the more accidental circumstances, lying outside his will and foresight, influence him, the more he feels his dependence on other people, the more boldly and clearly the necessity of full solidarity of human interests presents itself to him, the more naturally, the more rapidly arises in his mind the conviction that the happiness of one is impossible without the happiness of all.[44]

Indeed this striving for human betterment, this willingness to sacrifice herself and her activity for humanity was the trait most clearly distinguishing the new woman.

The striving toward bettering social welfare, toward solidarity of human interests must be the governing tendency, the governing direction of activity of thinking women. Only activity permeated with this striving conforms with her character; she alone is worthy of it.[45]

Unfortunately every dedicated woman had an Achilles' heel. Tkachev saw it as he reviewed novels written by Russian and European

---

42. Ibid., p. 286.
43. Ibid., p. 322.
44. Ibid., p. 282. Tkachev's view of what misery does to one is not consistent. Apparently it moves woman to great heights of self-sacrifice and solidarity, but in the case of the peasant it forces him to retreat from the cause.
45. Ibid., p. 322.

authors, including George Sand and George Eliot. These extraordinary, dynamic, and heroic women too often ended up discovering their greatest happiness not in freedom, economic independence, or a social cause, but in love! What is more, even the finest of the heroines, even the most altruistic of the strivers, gave herself thereafter wholly to her beloved. She ceased to think, she became slavish.[46] Doing so, she horrified young Tkachev. He could understand her feelings, he wrote patronizingly; not knowing how to find the answers to her questions, woman naturally turned to more educated, more knowledgeable, and more experienced man.[47] But loving a man, she inevitably sacrificed herself. Even when her man was a hero dedicated to her own cause, she lost herself not in his great ideals but in his arms. She betrayed the cause, she abandoned her new freedoms, she sank willingly back into the downtrodden oblivion she had once sought to escape. Love, the enemy, overcame her.

Tkachev found room in the world for love but only for a kind of love that ordinary people, *meshchane* and petty bourgeois, could not understand.

A woman loves in a man not just his body but also his mind, his world outlook; she loves his hopes and strivings, his form of thought, his ideas. The stronger and deeper this love, the more strongly and deeply she is attracted to the latter; the stronger and deeper a woman loves, the greater the force she feels in herself to obey the voice of the beloved ideas in everything; if the beloved ideas order her to reject the beloved body, she rejects without bitter tears and sickly sighs.[48]

No person, but an idea must rule her mind and soul; not love, but dedication should direct her heart. The new woman must have convictions so strong that she would not even suffer in the sacrifice of a more worldly physical and emotional relationship. Even united with a hero she must not lose sight of herself. Tkachev ended one of his longer eulogies to the new fair sex with a plea to his feminine readers: Can there be nothing for a woman besides *love?*[49] The plea apparently went deep to their hearts, and many of them, caught in turmoils of emotion in an unstable time, made the antiromantic young critic their romantic hero.

If Tkachev had found heroines, he found heroes too. As early as 1864 he had them in mind in a review for *Library for Reading* he

---

46. Ibid., p. 225. The novels Tkachev reviewed in 1878 included F. Spielhagen's *One in the Field Is Not War;* George Eliot's *Felix Holt, Radical,* and *Scandalous Marriage;* and George Sand's *Lady Markham.*

47. Tkachev, 1: 287.

48. Ibid., p. 190.

49. Ibid., p. 233.

berated a French novelist for not understanding that the men of the future would always sacrifice personal, egotistical motives for their ideals and would be distinguished by their staunchness and energy in pursuit of their goal, their high self-denial in the name of their idea.[50] In 1868 (three years after Pisarev had published his description of "The New Type" and six years after the appearance of Chernyshevskii's *What Is to Be Done?*) Tkachev considered the new hero in his own lengthy article entitled "People of the Future and Heroes of the *Meshchanstvo*," a word that in Russian referred to the petty bourgeoisie.[51]

Tkachev's man of the future, like his new woman, was daring, ahead of his times, dedicated, and working to improve the circumstances of life around him. He had little concern for himself or his own comforts. His kind had lived in history.

Among all peoples and in all ages there appear from time to time people who sacrifice their own personal profits in the name of social welfare, capable in the name of this social welfare, in the name of the great idea, of making their neighbors happy, of doing great deeds. If these people attain success, they are elevated to the pedestal of heroes, geniuses; before them [men] bow and fawn; if they break down in the struggle and fall, they are called extravagant dreamers and on their crown of thorns [men] look as on a fool's cap. . . . Their whole error consisted in the fact that they were ahead of their times in their ideas and wanted to make their neighbors happy some years or centuries earlier than the inert force of circumstances would do it. Thus it is [later] realized that these were people of the future, not wild men but very serious and positive movers among their dreaming contemporaries.[52]

Often misunderstood by society and frequently outcast, these men were driven by their cause and could not be distracted from its demands.

The distinguishing mark of people of the future consists in the fact that all their action, even the whole form of their life, is determined by one desire, by one passionate idea—to make the majority of the people happy, to call to the feast of life as many participants as possible. The realization of this idea becomes the sole task of their activity because this idea is totally merged with their concept of their personal happiness. To this idea everything is subordinated, everything is called to sacrifice.[53]

The new man differed from ordinary man not in the particular methods

---

50. "Geroi perekhodnoi epokhi," esp. pp. 22-23. The review was of Clemence-Auguste Royer's novel *Les jumeaux d'Hellas*.

51. Tkachev, 1: 173-233. Pisarev's essay on "The New Type " or "The Thinking Proletariat," originally published in *Russkoe slovo* in October 1865, has been reprinted in Pisarev, *Selected Essays*, pp. 624-75.

52. Tkachev, 1: 174.

53. Ibid.

he chose to attain his goal nor in the goal itself, but in his relationship to his ideas and in his willingness to devote himself and sacrifice himself to them.

To the man of the future the power of his love for the cause was so great as to overwhelm all his other emotional reactions.

People of the future do not disfigure themselves like the heroes of the *meshchan-stvo*, falling for the bait of love; people of the future do not run into the desert, like ascetics, from the temptations and fascinations of "this world"; they know that these temptations and fascinations for them are not in the least dangerous. . . . [A fascinating woman] cannot maintain even the slightest competition with the irresistible force of that idea that fills for them all their life and activity, because with this idea are united so many joyful and sad memories, so many plans and hopes, so many other thoughts and speculations; because this idea is so strongly tied with all their internal being that to deny it would be tantamount to self-destruction.[54]

The hallmark of this future hero was his *lack* of ambivalence about his goals. His goals were so firm and so real to him that he was not torn by passions. He was not the victim of ordinary human emotions; rather all his strengths were absorbed by one overwhelming devotion. The man of the future was not beset by internal conflicts; his life was not a constant and tortuous struggle of two opposing aims, as philistines usually believed.[55] He did not need completely to reject woman's love; he could accept it as a human experience.[56] But like other experiences not essential to his great passion he (like the new woman) was able without agony to set his love aside—even to reject his beloved or to call on his beloved to reject him should it be necessary to his goal.[57]

This Machiavellian approach to love, friendship, and even moral principles would seem cold and heartless to the ordinary petty man— indeed, only a woman of dubious emotional stability would have found such tyranny of the idea to be at once disturbing and exciting. After all, who could grant one man the right to sacrifice the happiness of others; what could justify his abandonment of his friends, his exploitation of his fellow man, or the pain he might cause a paramour who did not understand? Tkachev snarled: the world was ruled by philistine immorality and exploitation. People of the future exploit others in the name of their cause in order to attain the ideal of no exploitation and never for personal profit. Moral laws should, of course, be observed by all, but they seldom were. Under the circumstances moral laws must be considered only in relation to each other.

---

54. Ibid., p. 186.
55. Ibid., p. 178.
56. Ibid., p. 186.
57. Ibid., pp. 176, 190.

But a moral law, like everything temporal, has a relative character, and its importance is determined by the importance of that interest for the protection of which
it is created. There is no doubt, for example, that a moral law forbidding us to
torture animals is less important for us than the moral law that forbids us to pull
others' handkerchiefs out of their pockets; in its turn, the law of the inviolability of
handkerchiefs yields in importance to a law on the inviolability of honor, freedom,
life, etc. Thus moral laws are not all equal between themselves; there are laws more
important and less important. . . . Even the importance of one and the same rule
can change endlessly in different circumstances of its application.58

Should a man not respect the most important moral law, he would
resemble the Pharisees who refused to help a neighbor on Sunday because it was more important not to break the Sabbath. All morals
should be viewed "not dogmatically but critically." The high social
purpose of the men of the future justified the violation of lesser moral
principles in order to attain success. Heartlessness and even bloodshed,
Tkachev wrote, were justifiable and "not immoral as the philistines
propose, but on the contrary highly moral" in the name of the great
cause of human happiness.59 The ends justified the means.

The heroic men of the future, like the new women, were not to
Tkachev phenomenal or abnormal but rather the natural outgrowth of
intelligent reaction to social evils. They represented "just such an
inevitable result of our intellectual progress as philistinism represents an
inevitable product of intellectual weakness."60 They epitomized the
growing criticism of the society in which they lived. To become a hero
one need not have been born a genius or a freak.

The people of the future are not ascetics, not egotists, and not heroes—they are
ordinary people, and only those good ideas that they adopt and that govern them
set them in such keen contrast to everything that surrounds them that the heroes of
the bourgeoisie [meshchantsvo] can actually take them for unusual people.61

Nor were they isolated, unique, strange individuals. Indeed if they
were as rare as the philistines believed, then

there is nothing to worry about; one may admire them, perhaps, as we admire a
sparkling comet or an eclipse of the sun, but it should not be forgotten that they
are then an abnormal phenomenon and therefore to want to imitate them is stupid
as it is stupid to wish that all stars would turn into comets or that the eclipse of
the sun would never end.62

Instead, Tkachev thought, their dedication to their ideals, born of the

58. Ibid., p. 194.
59. Ibid., p. 196.
60. Ibid., p. 180.
61. Ibid., p. 181.
62. Ibid., p. 180.

evils of society itself, would remain as firm and as unwavering as the evils it combated.

The men of the future would be to a great degree individualists: that is, they would choose varied and different routes to achieve their goals. Tkachev did not attempt to dictate to them because he was aware that their temperaments and inclinations would lead them toward reform or revolution by many different paths. Their greatest similarity would be in the intensity of their dedication rather than the tactic they preferred. Tkachev recognized this diversity as a weakness, yet he would not want his heroes to close ranks and march together. Rather his association of these new men with the misunderstood heroes of history, the outcasts rejected by their own times, indicated that he believed they would be loners like himself. He did not suggest otherwise.

Tkachev's heroes and heroines remained dominated by love and not hate. Like Chernyshevskii's heroes and Pisarev's ideal men, they were humane, dedicated, elevated, moral young men and women. Their natures were noble not base; ardent not cold; constructive not destructive. Their task was not so much mercilessly to destroy the world as justly to construct it. Some of them, according to Tkachev, were gentle and warm and devoted their lives to teaching small children. Others sacrificed everything including their lives; they watched their comrades fall in battle and then gave themselves. They were individualistic to the point of disunity; they often disagreed as to procedure. What they had in common was devotion to a glorious cause. These warm and human heroes, large and small, were no obedient automatons in a coordinated revolutionary coup. In their dynamics, emotions, and dedications they sprang from the prototypes romantically envisioned by George Sand and George Eliot.[63]

Still in his writings on his native land Tkachev was moving closer to the distinctive revolutionary pattern he was later to espouse. Studying the peasant in these early years, he had recognized that the peasantry could not initiate successful revolutionary action. No solidarity could

63. Scholars have suggested that Nechaev was inspired by Tkachev's heroes when he and Bakunin wrote the notorious "Revolutionary Catechism"; this suggestion was probably first advanced by Kozmin, *Tkachev*, pp. 97-98, 160-61, 204-6. The nature of Tkachev's men of the future remains very different from that of the revolutionaries Nechaev hoped to organize. Nechaev may have admired Tkachev's heroes, but he badly distorted them in his strange mind. Venturi, *Roots of Revolution*, p. 409, feels that Tkachev's ideas were "brutally catalogued" in the "Catechism." The "Catechism" has been reprinted in V. IA. Iakovlev, *Gosudarstvennye prestupleniia v Rossii v XIX veka*, and in other sources.

unite in battle those who were tortured by poverty and oppressed by ignorance. Only one circumstance could move the peasant to violence against the state: if he were convinced that his actions would succeed in improving his lot, then he would take up the axe.

Thus Tkachev transferred responsibility for revolutionary action from the peasant to the intelligentsia. The men of his own class—the radical, educated young people of Russia—must show the peasant the way. They must demonstrate to him such power and conviction that he too would become sure of his goals and procedures. Tkachev's annoyance at the writers of his day who saw the peasant as wise, strong, or ludicrous stemmed from his fear that the intelligentsia would refuse to take revolutionary initiative. He was afraid that the new populist writers would discourage the *intelligent* from playing his role. For the future revolution lay not in the hands of the peasantry but in the hands of the educated class.

Among the young men and women of his own milieu Tkachev was sure some would be heroes. Following the example of Chernyshevskii and Pisarev he described the heroic leader: the man of dedication, conviction, and will. Here were the men and women who would make limitless sacrifices for the cause; here were the men and women eager to lead Russia to a better future. For all his pretense of realism Tkachev set his hopes in these romantic heroes. In the future he was to become more cynical as he became more disillusioned.

Studying peasant and *intelligent* in Russia Tkachev had clearly begun to formulate his own unique plans for revolution. Already he was prepared to stand on his own. Much of what he wrote was directed against the ideas of his colleagues in radical journalism: he must have had *Fatherland Notes* in mind when he attacked idealizers of the peasantry, criticized Russia's primitive agricultural techniques, and bemoaned the backwardness of Russia's industry. For even though he despised the West he was not, as he was later to become, ready to extol the privilege of backwardness, as A. Walicki has termed it.[64] Because the West was wrong did not mean that Russia was on the right track. But at least Russia had the potential for heroism, and Petr Tkachev— violent, impatient, activist—strove to drive her toward her revolutionary destiny.

---

64. Walicki, p. 107, uses this phrase as a chapter title; he is dealing with elements of the populist creed.

7

Tkachev and Nechaev

In 1869 Tkachev became involved in one of the notorious episodes of the Russian underground movement, the case of the Nechaevists. For his connection with the young and violent revolutionary Sergei Gennadevich Nechaev, and for what illegal plots they concocted together and with the St. Petersburg students, Tkachev paid with four years in prison. The issues and associations in the Nechaevist case are far from clear, obscured by lack of documentation and the often false testimony of those accused.[1] The factual material linking Tkachev and Nechaev is sparse and must be supplemented by consideration of their common aims and their diverse methods. But the case is important; it represents Tkachev's greatest brush with the law and eventually changed the course of his life if not the direction of his ideas.

Nechaev's friends in the revolutionary cause were almost all students, and many of the Nechaevists were arrested primarily for their identification with the student rather than the revolutionary

1. The records of court proceedings in the Nechaevist case were duly published in *Pravitelstvennyi Vestnik* during the trial in 1871, but certain documents admitted as evidence have vanished, according to B. P. Kozmin. See Kozmin, *Nechaev i nechaevtsy*, pp. 4-5. The latter is a collection of extremely useful depositions and reports from the Third Section, Ministry of Justice, etc. Much testimony of the accused is false, and few of the participants in the early stages of Nechaev's activities (when Tkachev was involved) told the whole truth. Corroboratory material is available in some brief memoirs published after 1905 as cited below. Tkachev himself never wrote about his relationship with Nechaev or the experience of 1869.

cause. The student movement in 1869 reached a peak similar to the riots of 1861, and the nature of this agitation determined the role Tkachev and Nechaev played.

The ferment that followed the emancipation of the serfs in Russia had given way to a period of external calm. Open manifestations of rebellion in the capital city died down after 1862. Soviet scholars, relentlessly pursuing all hints of revolutionary activity, have unearthed no further proclamations in the image of "Young Russia" and no revolutionary associations on the model of the early "Land and Freedom." The radicals nevertheless maintained their contacts. Evidence of the continued activity of young people in schools and artels abounds; Tkachev encouraged his sister Sofia, who worked as a teacher in an unauthorized artel throughout these years.[2] St. Petersburg journalists, Tkachev among them, continued their polemics and their sniping at one another. However, on the whole the revolutionary movement had sunk underground.

Even the halls of academe shared the outward quiescence that seemed to dominate Russian society.[3] A new university statute (replacing the strict rule of 1835) was adopted in 1863, the one positive result of the student protests in the early sixties. Although the law established the autonomy of professorial collegia, provided for the election of certain officials, and founded a university court of justice composed of professors, it made no provision for those corporate institutions the students had sought in the riots of 1861. Student funds to aid the needy, special student libraries, coffee shops, meeting rooms, and freedom of assembly were not written into the new law. Here and there students quietly went their way and achieved what they wanted with the tacit approval of university officials: where the rector was tolerant they operated with considerable freedom. Medical-Surgical Academy

2. Recently published Soviet documents indicate that Tkachev supported his sister by offering his living quarters as a meeting place for her school and by holding a "literary evening" to evoke interest or funds. He obviously became acquainted with some of her colleagues, for he commended one of them to his friend Olshevskii (Tkachev, *Sochineniia*, pp. 14-15). See also Vilenskaia, *Revoliutsionnoe podpole*, pp. 126, 341-42; her research on St. Petersburg and Moscow circles reveals much activity but no actual revolutionary agitation and conspiracy, as she herself points out. Kozmin echoes her opinion that revolutionary plotting had disappeared or gone far underground; see his *Revoliutsionnoe podpole*.

3. See Svatikov, "Studencheskoe dvizhenie 1869 goda," pp. 175 ff. for a good description of the student concerns. The materials collected by V. P. Alekseev in "Revoliutsionnoe i studencheskoe dvizhenie 1869 g. v otsenke tretego otdeleniia," *Katorga i ssylka*, no. 10 (1924), pp. 107-20, add little to Svatikov's excellent account.

students in St. Petersburg were under the direct supervision of the
liberal minister of war Dmitrii Miliutin; they managed their own library
and their own funds. The administration of Moscow University was
tolerant of special associations such as the Ukrainian Commune, which
set up its own bylaws, met regularly, ran a library, and maintained a
treasury.[4]

In 1866 the calm was shattered by Dmitrii Karakozov's shot at
Alexander II. Karakozov was associated with a Moscow University
circle led by a student named N. A. Ishutin. Evidence has demonstrated
that Ishutin's organization was not intent on tsaricide as the police
initially presumed, being devoted mostly to illegal readings, teaching,
and propagandizing. It had not deliberately sent Karakozov on his
mission. Nevertheless it inspired him in his unilateral attempt at assassination. He was caught and executed and made a public example.

The attempt on Alexander's life alarmed the tsar, and the police
swung into action. Arrests were made among students and radicals;
Tkachev was arrested and held briefly.[5] *Russian Word* and the *Contemporary* were both permanently closed in 1866. Censorship became
stricter; police surveillance increased. The attitude of the government
towards the universities, the breeding ground of the assassination effort,
lost much of its tolerance. The Karakozov attempt further discouraged
the tsar in his hesitant efforts at reform.

The Karakozov affair was a blow to student independence, for it led
to increased police surveillance and alertness on university grounds.
Special inspection and supervision committees jointly composed of
administrators and police were set up at each university to watch over
student activities on the orders of Count Dmitrii Tolstoy, then an
assistant minister of popular education. The committees were activated
in 1866 but formalized in a series of regulations announced on May 26,

---

4. Svatikov, p. 180.

5. Efforts of Soviet historians to connect Tkachev with what they inaccurately
call the Karakozov conspiracy (really efforts to distract Karakozov from his tsari-
cidal scheme) have not born fruit, although Tkachev was apparently acquainted
with several people who, in turn, knew Karakozov or the Moscovite student circle
led by Ishutin. The contention that the list of books and borrowers confiscated by
police in Tkachev's rooms represents the record of a conspiratorial society seems
unlikely; his sister Sofia's reading students must frequently have taken books from
Tkachev's quarters, where they met (Tkachev, *Sochineniia*, pp. 12-17). On the basis
of another document confiscated in a search of Tkachev's apartment, Philip Pomper
concludes that Tkachev and his friends had developed a cult of Karakozov after the
latter's execution (Philip Pomper, "Nechaev and Tsaricide: The Conspiracy within
the Conspiracy," *Russian Review* 33, no. 2 [1974]: 129-30). Nevertheless, this is
a far cry from participating in a revolutionary conspiracy.

1867, whereby the obligation of the police to keep order among students was clearly defined and university administrators were called upon to cooperate at all times with the authorities in their tasks.[6] Surveillance was quietly extended to embrace the activities of the professorial collegia and other intrauniversity institutions. At about the same time Tolstoy outlawed (as a waste of time, he said) certain student entertainments, including concerts and nonacademic lecture programs.

Students were annoyed at the rulings and particularly irked by the interference of the police. They had other grievances as well. Minor regulations were a source of constant irritation. No one could enter a university without showing an identification card to the guard on duty. Smoking was prohibited; now and then a more liberal rector would consider revoking this regulation, but somewhere along the line leading to the ministry of education he would be overruled. Many students thought that young, popular, liberal professors were discriminated against by university administrators. A brief protest flared in 1864 when a favorite St. Petersburg professor was replaced by an unpopular one; it resulted in the expulsion of several students by the university court.[7] Others were convinced that their professors were uninterested in them and their problems. Some claimed that they "endured no less unpleasantness from reactionary professors than from the government."[8] At the same time the living standards of most university students bordered upon real poverty. Few of them were rich; for most of them education could be attained only at the cost of great personal discomfort. Housing was minimal and crowded, food not always adequate. Stories, probably accurate, circulated about students plagued with disease, shivering from cold, or living on a below-subsistence ration of bread.

Living in St. Petersburg, where he shared an apartment with his sister and her husband, Tkachev undoubtedly continued his interest in student greivances. The revolutionary potential of the student intelligentsia could not have been lost on him after the Karakozov affair. But before 1868 Tkachev's contacts with the student movement seem to have been peripheral. True, he wrote his dissertation, but its theme—a plan for punishing juvenile criminals by a method not far removed from the present working detention home—did not demand research at the university itself. He was busy; during these years he acted as assistant to

---

6. Svatikov, pp. 181-82; Kozmin, *Tkachev*, pp. 140-42.
7. Svatikov, p. 174.
8. Ibid., p. 173.

several St. Petersburg lawyers, and he read and wrote constantly, publishing his long reviews. After all, he was twenty-four, undoubtedly in the minds of some students a victim of the generation gap. They recognized him as older and well-established; he testified later that young people sometimes came to him asking for money, employment, or the support of his pen. He was acquainted with several men close to the students who were journalists like himself.[9] He knew the St. Petersburg bookstore owned by A. A. Cherkezov, a center for the distribution of illegal literature where students often met.[10] But no testimony advanced at the Nechaev trial indicates Tkachev's intimacy with student circles before 1868. The students with whom he became involved in that year were new friends, acquaintances of only a short time.

Tkachev's interest in student affairs may have been stimulated by a young lady who at some time during these years began to call herself his common-law wife. Aleksandra Dmitrievna Dementeva was by all accounts an extraordinary person.[11] Born to a family of poor petty bourgeois in approximately 1850, she was orphaned as a child and given as ward apparently to several different families successively. None of the relationships was particularly happy. She attended gymnasium in St. Petersburg, but regulations prohibited the enrollment of women in the university. She became involved in the movement for women's rights and interested in teaching; she may have met Tkachev through one of his sisters. Dementeva impressed everyone who knew her with her charm, poise, vitality, and intelligence. She was to play an important role in the Nechaevist case and in Tkachev's life.

By 1868 the basic ingredients of the Nechaev affair were already assembled in St. Petersburg. The student rebellion was still rumbling, but it could explode, as indeed it later did, on the basis of any small incident. Radical young men who had gone underground to protect themselves from the tsarist police had not forgotten their aims and were, in all probability, still in secret contact with each other. Tkachev

9. For example, the assistant editor of *Russkoe slovo*, at whose apartments (the police recorded) he attended a meeting on the student cause; Tkachev, *Sochineniia*, p. 13. He was probably acquainted with Feliks Volkhovskii, an erstwhile student, a budding poet, and a clerk in a radical Moscow bookstore. Cf. Sokolov, *Russkaia literatura i narodnichestvo*, p. 83.

10. Tkachev's common-law wife Dementeva knew of it; surely so did he. See the introductory speech of the prosecution in the Nechaevist case, in *Michel Bakounine et ses relations avec Sergej Nečaev, 1870-1872*, ed. Arthur Lehning, p. 293.

11. Kozmin interviewed her in Russia shortly before her death and wrote an interesting article about her; see B. P. Kozmin, "Okolo nechaevskogo dela: Pamiati A. D. Dementevoi-Tkachevoi," *Katorga i ssylka*, no. 6 (1923), pp. 55-63.

by now was well known in radical circles; as his biographer Kozmin later wrote, "amidst Russian legal literature of the sixties there is no other espousal of socialistic and revolutionary convictions so clear and so open."[12] Nechaev was the catalyst who brought the elements together and set them in action.

The son of a serf, Sergei Nechaev was born in the textile center of Ivanovo in 1847.[13] Beyond his early training he was primarily self-educated. He lacked the background of the *intelligent*, but he was able to pass examinations for a teacher's certificate. He seems first to have come to the capital city in 1866. By 1868 he had taken a position teaching catechism in the St. Sergius parochial school. On the side he gave lessons in Latin and enrolled as a free auditor at St. Petersburg University. His young sister moved to the capital too.

Nechaev was an unusually striking young man. The testimony of his contemporaries leaves little doubt that he was not highly educated, unable to write with style, not versed in modern foreign languages, ignorant of philosophical and for that matter of many other intellectual traditions, and scarcely possessed of a keen and logical mind. Yet all his friends attested to his hypnotic intensity, enormous energy, and the fanatical dedication with which he threw himself into the revolutionary cause. Prince Varlaam Cherkezov, later tried with the Nechaevists, wrote to a friend:

Nechaev in my eyes is a man not especially broadly or clearly educated, one who is neither capable of directing nor of being the champion of earnest and important political agitation. But he has *one* attribute—energy that approaches fanaticism, love for work in the people's cause, fanatical devotion to this cause. In this last attribute one must seek the influence that he exerted over a certain group of honorable people. To these people he gave nothing, neither help nor education—they were more educated than he—he set forth no program to them nor the circumstances of the popular cause. They knew this without him and better than he.

12. Kozmin, *Tkachev*, p. 99
13. The details of Nechaev's activity before 1868 are not entirely clear. Nechaev's father apparently became a worker away from the estate where he was born. Nechaev himself worked in a textile factory at an early age. He left Ivanovo for Moscow as early as 1865 and was probably teaching in St. Petersburg as early as 1866. He did not enroll as a "free auditor" at the university until two years later. There is some wonderful material in N. F. Belchikov, "S. G. Nechaev v s. Ivanove v 1860-e gody," *Katorga i ssylka*, no. 14 (1925), pp. 134-56. See also Kozmin, *Nechaev i nechaevtsy*, especially the biographical index, and the testimony of the Ametistov brothers on pp. 57-61. One of the most interesting accounts of Nechaev's activity in St. Petersburg is contained in Zemfir Ralli-Arbore, "Sergei Gennadevich Nechaev: Iz moikh vospominanii," *Byloe*, no. 7 (1906), p. 136; this article has been translated into French and reprinted in Lehning, *Michel Bakounine*, pp. 372-79.

Although he gave them nothing, he drew them toward the cause as an energetic and active person; if not an upright man, he seemed to them a representative of this cause, which they took up more clearly and further than he.[14]

The wife of one of the later associates of Nechaev said the same: "To me, Nechaev gave the impression of an intelligent, extremely energetic man, with his whole spirit limitlessly devoted to the cause. He produced the same impression on my husband and, doubtless, on everyone he met."[15] He made her ashamed, she said, that she was not so dedicated, that she had her own personal life and private interests. An older defendant in the Nechaevist case (a Moscow man named I. G. Pryzhov) told the court that he had "never encountered such energy as Nechaev has and could hardly imagine it."[16] The most famous of Nechaev's friends, the anarchist Mikhail Bakunin, whom the young Russian found and enchanted in Switzerland, was aware of the same dedication and energy in his young protégé; before their quarrel Bakunin wrote many letters to Herzen and his other friends about "Boy," who made temporary conquests of Ogarev and Herzen's daughter Natalie as well.[17]

But that was later. Tkachev knew Nechaev for only a few months in the winter of 1868-69. Nechaev apparently arrived in St. Petersburg in October and brought with him a letter of introduction from his friend Vladimir Orlov, who was a teacher in Ivanovo, to two brothers who were students: Evlampii Ametistov, who attended the university, and his brother Ivan, a student at the Medical-Surgical Academy.[18] Nechaev

---

14. Quoted in Max Nettlau, "Bakunin und die russische revolutionäre Bewegung in den Jahren 1868-1873," *Archiv für die Geschichte des Sozialismus und der Arbeiterbewegung* 5 (1915): 392.

15. A. I. Uspenskaia, "Vospominaniia shestidesiatnitsy," *Byloe*, no. 18 (1922), p. 33. Uspenskaia, who was the sister of Vera Zasulich, married P. G. Uspenskii who managed Cherkezov's bookstore in Moscow and participated in the murder of Ivanov. She was one of the rare participants in the Nechaevist matter who never lost her faith in Nechaev's honesty and devotion to the cause. See also Michael Confino, *Violence dans la violence: Le débat bakounine-nečaev*, p. 63.

16. Quoted in Kozmin, *Tkachev*, p. 156.

17. There are many references to Nechaev in Bakunin's letters to Herzen and Ogarev: see Michail Dragomanov, ed., *Michail Bakunins sozial-politischer Briefwechsel mit Alexander Iw. Herzen und Ogarjow*. See also Kozmin's article "Gertsen, Ogarev, i 'Molodaia Emigratsiia,'" in *Iz istorii revoliutsionnoi mysli v Rossii*, pp. 483-587. The relationship of Nechaev and Bakunin is surely the most well-researched episode in Nechaev's life. Recent excellent contributions include those of Arthur Lehning in *Michel Bakounine* and of Confino; both these volumes contain letters, documents, and other sources.

18. See the deposition of E. Ametistov, in Kozmin, *Nechaev i nechaevtsy*, pp. 60-61.

soon persuaded Evlampii to move into his quarters, rooms that were closer to the university than the brothers' previous lodgings. There Ivan dropped by almost daily. There they argued about Schopenhauer, Ivan later told police, and reported that Nechaev's understanding of philosophy was naïve, inadequate, and irritating.[19] There meetings of a radical student circle frequently took place, for the Ametistov brothers soon introduced Nechaev to their friends—a group of students mostly enrolled at the Medical-Surgical Academy and, like the Ametistov brothers, radical if not revolutionary in their outlook. Among them was a man named Zemfir Ralli-Arbore, a Romanian born in Bessarabia who had been associated with the Ishutin-Karakozov circle at the University of Moscow two years before. In December Orlov, Nechaev's friend from Ivanovo, joined them, having left his teaching job to come to St. Petersburg and continue his education, he said.[20]

In the circle to which the Ametistovs brought Nechaev and Orlov, Ralli-Arbore spoke of his experiences and found Nechaev a fascinated listener. One scholar has suggested that Nechaev developed a cult of Karakozov, so deep was his immersion in the revolutionary tradition.[21] Soon Nechaev borrowed Ralli-Arbore's copies of the *Bell* to read, for the circle had access to illegal literature, perhaps through the Cherkezov bookstore. They had smuggled copies of de Rochefort's radical journal *Lanterne* (then being published in Belgium after the anti-imperialist editor had been forbidden rights of publication in his native land). Together they read articles on Robert Owen from old copies of *Fatherland Notes*. At some time during the autumn months a young man from this or another circle was sent to Switzerland to make contact with émigré revolutionaries; although he did not meet Bakunin, he brought back a copy of *Narodnoe delo* (The People's Cause), the Bakuninist journal first published in the autumn of 1868. It made, according to Ralli-Arbore, a great impression on Nechaev who learned to know Bakunin through its pages. The circle moved on to Buonarroti's *Conspiracy of Equals*, the story of Babeuf's attempted revolution; the book was a rare one, published in 1828, but they had managed to find a copy, Ralli-Arbore later wrote. They read part of Louis Blanc's *History of the*

---

19. Deposition of I. Ametistov, ibid., pp. 57-58.
20. Ralli-Arbore, "Nechaev," pp. 136-37.
21. See the recent work by Pomper, "Nechaev and Tsaricide," pp. 129-30. In March 1869 when Tkachev was arrested police found in his rooms a narrative of the execution of Karakozov, written in the form of a conversation between two soldiers. See also the speech of the prosecution, in Lehning, *Michel Bakounine*, p. 292.

French Revolution, but the process was irritating since Nechaev knew no French and someone had to translate for him, word for word.[22]

According to Ralli-Arbore's account, Nechaev gulped it all down. The revolutionary writings made a great impression on the schoolteacher from Ivanovo. One scholar presents a fascinating picture of Nechaev, the inspired but heretofore isolated revolutionary, taking in the writings of Buonarroti, listening to the stories of the Karakozov trial, surrounded by students more knowledgeable than he, and caught up by energy and hatred.[23] The intensity of Nechaev's hatred was remarked soon by other friends; it was matched only by the intensity of his dedication.[24]

In the link between Tkachev and Ralli-Arbore's student circle lies the key to the Nechaevist affair. Tkachev was not present at these early student meetings; Ralli-Arbore's later descriptions make this certain.[25] At some time during the winter Evlampii Ametistov, by his later testimony, had approached Tkachev and several friends for money supposedly for the student cause, but this meeting was probably later, after the initial contact had been made. Most likely it was Nechaev who first drew Tkachev toward the student intrigue. How they met is uncertain. But it was Nechaev who introduced Orlov, the schoolteacher from Ivanovo, to Tkachev, probably in January 1869.[26] It was Nechaev who also spoke mysteriously to Ralli-Arbore of a secret organization, a mutual aid society that he knew of. Ralli-Arbore was interested. He later told the police:

---

22. Ralli-Arbore, "Nechaev," pp. 136-39; cf. Svatikov, pp. 184-86. It is not clear exactly which "circle" sent the messenger, I. I. Bochkarev, to Switzerland to contact Russian revolutionaries in exile; Varlaam Cherkezov told Nettlau that his own circle had done so, but Cherkezov may have been referring to the Smorgon Academy rather than the Nechaev group. See Kozmin, *Revoliutsionnoe podpole*, pp. 117, 150; Lehning, *Michel Bakounine*, p. xv; and B. Nikolaevskii, "Varlaam Nikolaevich Cherkezov (1846-1925)," *Katorga i ssylka*, no. 25 (1926), p. 224.

23. Nettlau, "Bakunin," p. 378.

24. Vera Zasulich later wrote that Nechaev's hatred was directed "not only against the government but against institutions, against all society, all educated classes, all these sons of aristocrats, rich and poor, conservative, liberal, and radical. Even toward the youth attracted to him, if he did not feel hatred, then at any rate he did not feel the slightest sympathy for them nor a shadow of pity and [instead he felt] much contempt." See her notes as edited by her sister and by Lev Deich in the article entitled "Nechaevskoe delo," in *Gruppa "Osvobozhdenie truda,"* ed. L. Deich, 2: 69. Cf. Confino, p. 64, especially note 96.

25. Ralli-Arbore gives lists of people who attended their circle in his description in "Nechaev," pp. 136-38. He himself never met Tkachev until 1869.

26. Speech for the prosecution, in Lehning, *Michel Bakounine*, p. 289. This information is based on Orlov's own deposition.

I remember that I asked him the aims of the society. He said that the purpose was extremely moral: the expansion of schools, the facilitating of student fellowship (his expression), the establishment of libraries and of Sunday and popular schools. He said that the society had existed for a long time and promised to introduce us to one of its members.[27]

That was after a meeting of Ralli-Arbore's circle at Nechaev's quarters. The next evening Orlov and Nechaev came to find Ralli-Arbore and invite him to meet Tkachev, whom he did not know. Ralli-Arbore concluded that he was to be initiated into a secret circle, and he was disappointed when, arriving at Tkachev's, he realized that far from being a long-established circle, the group of the evening had never met before.

If Ralli-Arbore was telling the truth when he wrote his memoir on Nechaev many years later, then this was the first meeting of Tkachev with student members of the Ralli-Arbore circle although Tkachev, Orlov, and Nechaev had certainly all met before. Ralli-Arbore remembered that Dementeva was there, as well as an older woman named Elizaveta Tomilova, whose children Nechaev tutored.[28] Tkachev's stated aim in holding the meeting was to discuss student demands and the possibility of attracting favorable publicity for them in the St. Petersburg press. Truly or falsely, V. I. Kovalevskii, one of many students who were present, reported that Tkachev's attitude towards outright student rioting was negative. Remembering his own experiences in 1861 Tkachev said he was sure nothing would come of such protest and that newspaper agitation would bear bigger fruit. He understood and sympathized with student hopes for funds and for freedom of assembly, he told his guests (according to Kovalevskii), but he was sure violent outbreaks would only lead to repression as they had before. Rather he suggested that arguments be transferred to the literary area, where journal articles might gain society's sympathy for the student cause.[29]

At the end of the meeting, Ralli-Arbore later reported, Tkachev and Nechaev called him aside and suggested that an effective organization of students be set up with representation from all the St. Petersburg institutions of higher learning. They proposed to form a committee to do so. They asked that Ralli-Arbore make contact with Moscow students as well.[30]

---

27. Deposition of Ralli-Arbore, in Kozmin, *Nechaev i nechaevtsy*, p. 81.

28. Ibid., p. 82. Ralli-Arbore later confirmed his account of this meeting in his memoir on Nechaev but he erred on its date. It is impossible that the meeting took place in February because early that month Nechaev left St. Petersburg; Orlov himself soon followed (Ralli-Arbore, "Nechaev," p. 138).

29. Svatikov, p. 192; cf. Kozmin, *Tkachev*, pp. 161-62.

30. Deposition of Ralli-Arbore, in Kozmin, *Nechaev i nechaevtsy*, p. 75. This

Disappointed in the blandness of the subjects discussed at Tkachev's, Ralli-Arbore reminded Orlov of his promise to introduce him to the inner circle of a secret society. Ralli-Arbore told the police that Orlov demurred. "When I and others reminded him of the day before, he became confused and with that the matter was closed, and we dispersed," Ralli-Arbore said later. "It was very obvious that Mr. Orlov had extended an invitation without authorization."[31]

Sometime in the early weeks of 1869, Orlov gave Ralli-Arbore the program of a secret society he later claimed he had received from Nechaev. Neither of them described the document in detail to the police although Ralli-Arbore said the society was based on circles of ten, each new member to initiate ten more. Neither of them mentioned Tkachev. It is uncertain but possible that this was the "Program of Revolutionary Actions" found much later by the police in the possession of a suspected Nechaevist in Moscow, but dating by its internal evidence from the winter of 1868-69.[32]

The "Program of Revolutionary Actions" advocated a political revolution, that is, the seizure of power, with a social revolution to follow. In order to prepare for the revolution the program declared it necessary to create revolutionary types in as large a number as possible.[33] By revolutionary types was meant men who "will be able to renounce all possessions, professional occupation, and family ties because family and occupations turn members away from their activities." The "Program" called for intense activity to set up a revolutionary organization of such people, an organization that must thereafter define its internal structure, its methods of recruitment, and various means of action such as distributing proclamations, creating funds, and establishing relations with European revolutionary organizations.

The "Program" suggested a schedule for accomplishments. Early

committee, which met at least once more and may have included several people from Ralli-Arbore's circle, could well have been the heart of the conspiracy. If so, it was the committee to which Nechaev referred (with great exaggeration) in describing the Russian revolutionary movement to Bakunin. In Ralli-Arbore's later writings he referred to it as a "committee to direct the student movement," supposedly towards revolutionary ends. See Ralli-Arbore, "Nechaev," p. 138.

31. Deposition of Ralli-Arbore, in Kozmin, *Nechaev i nechaevtsy*, p. 75.

32. This program with quantities of other revealing documents was found in the Cherkezov bookstore in the possession of Felix Volkhovskii in Moscow in November 1869 (speech of the prosecution, in Lehning, *Michel Bakounine*, pp. 290-91). Orlov had probably given it to him. Orlov seems to have given another copy to an Ivanovo friend named Ivan Florinskii (ibid., p. 294). The "Program of Revolutionary Actions" was published in *Pravitelstvennyi Vestnik;* it is discussed in detail in Kozmin, *Tkachev*, pp. 145-50, and in Confino, pp. 43-51.

33. Confino, p. 43.

1869 was to see recruitment in capital and university cities with agitation among the poor of these cities. After May action was to extend to the provinces, with propaganda directed towards students in provincial cities and also towards the poor. By September the members of the organization who had remained in the major cities (those who ranked as specialists in social questions and natural sciences)[34] would devise a "Catechism" obligatory for members, defining rules of conduct and establishing the structure of the organization. The following month members were to meet in St. Petersburg to approve the "Catechism" and fix the date for insurrection, which the "Program" anticipated as February 19, 1870, the ninth anniversary of the emancipation proclamation. During the winter of 1869-70, systematic revolutionary activity would begin.

Authorship of the "Program of Revolutionary Actions" has never been definitely ascertained. All scholars, and indeed all contemporaries who knew of it, have believed that Nechaev at least had a hand in its composition, a fact borne out by the recent scholarly suggestions that Nechaev's actions after March 1869 were governed by the schedule here set forth.[35] Tkachev's role in the writing is uncertain; historians have been unable to determine whether he actually had a hand in drawing up the plans, whether Nechaev prepared them himself, or whether they were the result of consultation among members of a larger circle, including Ralli-Arbore and his friends.[36] The document was never found in Tkachev's possession, but Tkachev was always a cautious man. He must, at least, have known it. Orlov seems to have been the main distributor of the "Program" in Russia. That Nechaev knew the document is beyond doubt; he probably showed it to Bakunin when he left Russia and went to Switzerland in March 1869.[37]

For by February Nechaev was becoming restless and discouraged in St. Petersburg and eager to turn his efforts elsewhere in accordance with the revolutionary plan. In January student agitation had moved into high gear; indeed this was probably what inspired Nechaev and his friends to set down their plans. There had been a brief flare-up at the Medical-Surgical Academy in November when the newly appointed government inspector, the officer in charge of overseeing student conduct, had expelled a student for reasons deemed inappropriate by his fellows. Colonel Smirnov was a disciplinarian; the students hated

---

34. Ibid., p. 45.
35. Ibid., pp. 45-46; the same suggestion is made by Lehning in regard to other participants in the conspiracy in *Michel Bakounine*, p. xvi.
36. See Confino, p. 43 (note 61).
37. Nettlau, "Bakunin," p. 384.

him for his strictness on minor matters like smoking, long hair, and inappropriate clothing. After one meeting, however, the protest had subsided; perhaps the academy students remembered they were well off in comparison with their fellows at the university.[38]

However, shortly after Christmas student protests began again. Meeting after meeting was held to consider how best to demand changes in university regulations. Interest snowballed. According to one of Nechaev's reports to Tomilova, a meeting to consider the establishment of student corporate organizations attracted nearly four hundred students. Debate became heated when students divided on the issue of working through petitions and open meetings or concentrating in smaller circles. Students collected books to set up a library and considered projects to raise funds through handicraft artels. Once they sponsored a benefit concert for fund-raising purposes. In February they sent Ralli-Arbore and L. P. Nikiforov to Moscow to spread the word about their hopes and actions; Ralli-Arbore admitted later that many of the groups they met had revolutionary political intentions.[39] Nechaev and Orlov attended all the meetings they could; Tkachev was sometimes there. Nechaev spoke often and sometimes acted as chairman. Once he circulated a petition in favor of setting up a student fund; Evlampii Ametistov later said he signed it because Nechaev told him that only signators would be eligible to draw on the lending money.[40] At another meeting Nechaev collected a list of signatures that later mysteriously fell into the hands of the Third Section. At least one observer blamed Nechaev's naïve foolishness for many subsequent arrests.[41]

During the student meetings Nechaev, Orlov, and Ralli-Arbore's circle sought to politicize the student movement and to direct it against the government as well as against the educational administrations. Tkachev surely encouraged them although he did not directly participate. None of the witnesses at the Nechaevist trial admitted it outright, but Ralli-Arbore said as much in some memoirs written in 1906.[42]

38. Svatikov, p. 183.
39. This account of the student movement is drawn primarily from Ralli-Arbore's detailed report in his depositions in Kozmin, *Nechaev i nechaevtsy*, pp. 71-82. See also Ralli-Arbore, "Nechaev," pp. 136-40, and Zasulich, "Nechaevskoe delo," pp. 29-31.
40. Deposition of E. Ametistov, in Kozmin, *Nechaev i nechaevtsy*, p. 63. E. Ametistov confirms some of the events Ralli-Arbore mentions in his account of the student meetings.
41. Svatikov, p. 191. Zasulich describes this episode in "Nechaevskoe delo," p. 32. See Kozmin's interesting note about the great secrecy with which this list was protected by the Third Section (*Nechaev i nechaevtsy*, p. 188 [note 9]).
42. Ralli-Arbore, "Nechaev," p. 138.

Other students were aware that Nechaev had his own aims. Rumors circulated that Nechaev believed the student movement needed direction.[43]

By February, after a month of heated debate, Nechaev must have sensed that it was not working. Of course he made some friends. There was Tomilova, whose children he tutored, and Vera Zasulich, who lived in the same building as Ralli-Arbore. Zasulich, who was later to become famous in her own right, was a girl of fifteen but already a robust adolescent, in Ralli-Arbore's words. Ralli-Arbore introduced her to Nechaev who soon declared his love for her with more than his usual intensity. Wise beyond her years, Zasulich rebuffed him; he was not one for tender relationships, she wrote later.[44] But converts were few, and many students shied away. The reception they gave to Nechaev and Orlov was generally cool. Nikiforov, Ralli-Arbore's friend, later remembered a meeting at which Nechaev attempted to speak about women's rights and was hooted down; the students preferred to talk about their own immediate problems.[45] Nechaev may have felt out of his element among the educated intelligentsia. Zasulich later wrote that he "was not a product of our world, he was not a product of the intelligentsia; he was a stranger among us."[46] Whatever the cause Nechaev's leadership was not accepted by most students at all. His influence among them was confined to a few. After a month he probably realized it.[47]

At the end of January Nechaev first attracted the attention of the Third Section. He was attending a student meeting when rumors of a police raid circulated. Students attempted to flee, but the police simply waited outside and took down names at the door, Nechaev's among

43. Svatikov, pp. 186-87. Student hostility is evident in the rumor circulating in January 1869 that Nechaev was actually an agent-provocateur. See IU. Steklov, "Zapiska S. Serebrennikova o Nechaeve," *Katorga i ssylka*, no. 112 (1934), p. 16.

44. Vera Zasulich, "Vospominaniia V. I. Zasulich," *Byloe*, no. 14 (1919), pp. 96-97.

45. Kozmin, *Nechaev i nechaevtsy*, p. 80.

46. Zasulich, "Nechaevskoe delo," p. 69; see also Confino, pp. 31-32. Lev Deich in his summary of viewpoints on Nechaev disagrees with Zasulich about Nechaev's alienation from the educated group ("Nechaevskoe delo," pp. 76-77). Zasulich was not one of Nechaev's greatest partisans. When her sister once wrote that Nechaev had composed some poetry, Zasulich's response was "How can he write poetry? He can hardly write." See Uspenskaia, "Vospominaniia shestidesiatnitsy," p. 35.

47. Svatikov, pp. 193-94; see also Ralli-Arbore's deposition, in Kozmin, *Nechaev i nechaevtsy*, p. 71. Confino has an interesting discussion of Nechaev's position in the world of intellectuals; he suggests that Nechaev took up certain ideas and actions because of being frustrated in his efforts to sway the students (Confino, pp. 32-33).

them.[48] Early in February Nechaev appeared at his young sister's rooms in Tomilova's home and said he had been summoned to appear before the police. He returned to Tomilova's the same evening with word that the dreaded Third Section had commanded his appearance the following day. Leaving the apartment he shared with Evlampii Ametistov the next morning, he repeated his destination to his friends.

The next day Vera Zasulich arrived at Tomilova's in a state of distress. She had received a letter by the city postal service. "Going across the bridge," it read,

I met a carriage in which some arrested men were being transported; from it someone threw me a wad of paper, and I recognized the voice of the man dear to me. *If you are an honest man, deliver this;* this I hasten to fulfill and in your turn I beg you, as honest people, to destroy my note this minute so that they will not recognize me by my handwriting.[49]

The signature was simply "A Student." The enclosed note from Nechaev was written in red pencil on a smudged piece of paper. It read: "They are taking me to prison; do not lose energy, friends-comrades, intercede for me! We will meet again, God willing."[50]

Tomilova and Nechaev's sister—still a child according to Ralli-Arbore[51]—were frantic. They investigated possible alternatives, attempting to find Nechaev in the hands of the police or the Third Section. They spoke to a number of high officials, including the chief of the gendarmerie, all of whom denied knowledge of Nechaev's arrest. For the next few weeks the matter remained a mystery. Rumors circulated about Nechaev's secret exile or about some dramatic escape. He was seen here and there: at a railroad station, in Moscow, with Orlov—for Orlov had left St. Petersburg without telling anyone where he was going. Since Tkachev did not frequently appear at student meetings, the conspiracy to politicize the student movement had lost its two leading figures.

But Tkachev still had a role to play, a role he had probably undertaken in accordance with the Nechaev-Orlov plans. He had to acquire a printing press, and in February he and Dementeva set about doing so.

48. Kozmin, *Nechaev i nechaevtsy*, p. 43, as confirmed by Pomper, "Nechaev and Tsaricide," p. 136; Pomper found evidence in Russian archives that Nechaev had been called to appear before the St. Petersburg chief of police to explain his behavior at a student meeting of January 28, 1869. The net was obviously tightening.
49. Svatikov, pp. 194-95.
50. Ibid., p. 195.
51. Lehning, *Michel Bakounine*, p. 376. Orlov was said to be in love with her. Cf. Nettlau, "Bakunin," p. 377.

She was due to inherit some money (a dowry of 15,000 rubles) when she married or came of age. For reasons that remain obscure, Tkachev and his beloved decided not to marry each other; instead they opted to find a fictitious husband for Dementeva so that she could claim her inheritance. Tkachev asked Orlov before the latter left St. Petersburg, but Orlov demurred.[52] His passport had expired, he said; actually he had fallen in love with Nechaev's young sister. But in late February he wrote Tkachev from Moscow. He had located a young man willing to enter into fictitious marriage with Dementeva, one Nikolai Nikolaev. Tkachev and Dementeva went to Moscow to find him. But the scheme did not work. Nikolaev was even younger than Dementeva, and in spite of his petition to the bishop of Moscow he was unable to get the proper church sanction to marry under age.[53]

Chastened, Tkachev and Dementeva returned to St. Petersburg. Here they were luckier. A young man named S. I. Serebrennikov, an acquaintance of Nechaev's, was about to leave for Europe; he offered them a press for two hundred rubles down, which Tkachev could afford. Dementeva purchased the press with his money in her own name. It was then around the beginning of March.

The mystery of Nechaev's whereabouts was solved when Orlov returned to St. Petersburg early in March and persuaded Tomilova to give him some money for Nechaev. He was ready with a story of arrests, escapes, travels, and daring deeds. Actually Nechaev had never been arrested at all. He had used that particular bit of mystification to arouse support and sympathy. Instead he had left St. Petersburg, traveled to Moscow, then Odessa, then Moscow again. On March 4 he had borrowed the passport of Nikolaev, Dementeva's potential husband, and fled abroad. Hearing Orlov's fictionalized version, Tomilova came up with the money he needed. Orlov rewarded her with some letters of commendation that ultimately led to her arrest after a police search.[54]

Nechaev had left Russia, and Tkachev never saw him again. Perhaps the escape had been planned by all of them; history will probably never know.

When the student rioting broke out in mid-March of 1869, it was not instigated by any conspiracy. Indeed Tkachev, Orlov, and their friends were caught unprepared. The "Program of Revolutionary Actions" did not call for outbreaks among the students. Rather the student movement was to be used to recruit revolutionaries, and riots,

---

52. Speech for the prosecution, in Lehning, *Michel Bakounine*, pp. 280, 289.

53. Ibid., p. 289. The letter addressed by Nikolaev to the bishop of Moscow was later found in a search of Dementeva's quarters (ibid., p. 293).

54. Ibid., p. 290.

if anything, would impede the effort. But the students were aroused, and little was needed to push them into insubordination. A professor at the Medical-Surgical Academy lost a student's examination and not only did not apologize but spoke to the student "with impertinence."[55] The student petitioned to be excused from the exam, but the petition was denied and he was given a failing grade. Irritated friends organized protest meetings. Although tacit approval had been given the student to present a petition in his own behalf, Smirnov, the government inspector, prohibited the meeting at which such a petition was to be circulated. The students met in spite of his order. In the rapid course of events they elected and sent delegates to contact students at the university and the Technological Institute. They besieged Smirnov in his office, causing his indecorous flight to a professor's laboratory where they followed him, sat all night on the doorstep, and released him the next morning only when the professor personally escorted him through their ranks after making a plea in his behalf.[56] They sent protests of their grievances to the administration, refused to attend lectures, and continued forbidden meetings.

The following day a series of arrests began, apparently at Smirnov's request. Student protests were of no avail. On the night of March 13 Ralli-Arbore was arrested at his rooms. Tkachev was spending the night at Ralli-Arbore's apartment; he was not arrested then because evidently the police did not suspect revolutionary conspiracy but only student riots.[57] The following day and night police swarmed through the student sections. The governor-general of St. Petersburg himself directed them. The number of arrests was never officially revealed.

Once the rioting broke out, Tkachev determined his course of action. He had always argued that the student cause could only succeed if their case was brought before the public and found support there. Accordingly he wrote a brief proclamation entitled "To Society:"

We, the students of the Medical Academy, University, Technological Institute, Agricultural Academy, desire:

---

55. Svatikov, p. 197. V. IA. Iakovlev, *Aktivnoe narodnichestvo semidesiatykh godov*, pp. 132-33, says one of the factors in the riots was the disciplinary measures taken when a student failed to raise his hat to Smirnov, the government inspector at the Medical-Surgical Academy. Delightfully, M. N. Katkov called the whole thing a "Polish intrigue" (Iakovlev, *Aktivnoe narodnichestvo*, p. 133).

56. Svatikov, p. 197.

57. Apparently Tkachev and Ralli-Arbore had attended a meeting together. Zasulich confirms that the riots were not anticipated by the revolutionaries and they had made no plans either to take advantage of them or to go into hiding (Zasulich, "Nechaevskoe delo," pp. 38-39).

1. That we may be given the right to maintain a fund, that is, to aid our poor comrades.

2. That we may be given the right to deliberate about our own affairs in the halls of our educational institutions; and

3. That the humiliating police surveillance that stamps us with a shameful brand of slavery at the school bench may be removed from us.

The administration answers our demands with closed scholarly institutions, illegal arrests, and exiles.

We appeal to society. Society must support us because our cause is its cause. Remaining indifferent to our protest, it forges the chains of slavery for its own neck.

Our protest is solid and unanimous, and we are ready to suffer in exile and in prisons rather than be suffocated and morally deformed in our academies and universities.[58]

Dementeva printed the proclamation in forty copies on the press she had acquired. On the night of March 20 she mailed copies to the leading St. Petersburg newspapers, left some examples at Cherkezov's bookstore, and scattered the rest in the streets near the institutions of higher learning.[59]

In spite of the relatively mild tone of the proclamation, police reaction was immediate and violent. Later observers suggested that the Third Section was alarmed because the document was printed; no illegal press had been found operating in St. Petersburg since the early years of the Great Reforms.[60] It took only a few days for the gendarmerie to trace the press previously owned by Serebrennikov, who had already left the country. They discovered his negotiations with Dementeva and her relationship with Tkachev. The two of them were arrested on March 26.

Tkachev's active role in the Nechaevist case was over. He had no further contact with Nechaev and performed no further deeds for the cause of revolution, for he spent the next four years in prison. Nechaev's further actions had a bearing on Tkachev's case only insofar as they led to revelation of the conspiracy, for Tkachev's arrest had been based only on the proclamation he and Dementeva prepared.

Nechaev's activities following his trip abroad in March 1869 have been often analyzed and are relatively well documented. From Switzerland he sent inflammatory letters back to his friends in St. Petersburg, directly causing the arrest of several of his friends. Similar communica-

---

58. This proclamation has been reprinted in Iakovlev, *Aktivnoe narodnichestvo*, p. 134; Dragomanov, *Bakunins Briefwechsel*, p. 341; Svatikov, p. 207; Lehning, *Michel Bakounine*, pp. 467-68; and elsewhere.

59. By her own testimony. See speech for the prosecution, in Lehning, *Michel Bakounine*, p. 293.

60. Kozmin, *Tkachev*, p. 167; Svatikov, p. 207.

tions to Orlov threw suspicion on the latter. The letters, quoted at length by Max Nettlau, a historian of Bakuninism, represent indiscretion bordering on betrayal.[61] Later they were supplemented by a series of proclamations smuggled from abroad and also seized by police. In Switzerland, together with his new patron Bakunin, Nechaev wrote a "Catechism" for his revolutionary organization, probably the document anticipated in the "Program of Revolutionary Actions." Returning to Russia in August, he organized a society in Moscow called the People's Justice (*Narodnaia rasprava*), basing its structure and bylaws on the "Catechism" mentioned above. Orlov became a member; so did several of Tkachev's Moscow friends. The Cherkezov bookstore, Moscow branch, was a point of distribution for literature. Nechaev's notorious murder of the student Ivan Ivanov occurred in November 1869. Having accused Ivanov of being a spy—although probably he did not even believe that himself—Nechaev persuaded four other members of the society to aid him in the crime. Thereafter Nechaev fled to St. Petersburg and thence abroad. His activities there, particularly his friendship and break with Bakunin, have been amply investigated by recent scholars. He was extradited, convicted of murder, and imprisoned in 1872. He died in prison ten years later.

It was the murder of Ivanov, quickly discovered and solved by the police, that gave away the conspiracy of the People's Justice and caused the arrest of many of its members. Literally dozens of documents, including the "Catechism" and the "Program of Revolutionary Actions" (the latter never before known to the police), were discovered in searches conducted among Nechaev's Moscow colleagues.[62] But it was Ralli-Arbore who revealed the St. Petersburg conspiracy; it was he who convinced the police that the deeds of autumn 1869 derived from plans made in the capital city earlier in the year.

Ralli-Arbore had been arrested at the time of the student riots in March, temporarily released, and almost immediately arrested again. From the beginning he spoke more freely with the police than any other defendant in the Nechaevist case.[63] He described meetings, documents, and petitions, told of journeys, popular schools, and artels,

---

61. Nettlau, "Bakunin," p. 385. A special file of these communications was kept by the Third Section (Kozmin, *Nechaev i nechaevtsy*, p. 5).

62. A particularly lucrative find was made at Uspenskii's; see the list in the speech for the prosecution, in Lehning, *Michel Bakounine*, pp. 280-81.

63. These depositions make fascinating reading; they are included in Kozmin, *Nechaev i nechaevtsy*, pp. 71-83. Ralli-Arbore later admitted to a friend in Zurich some of the things that he had said; see M. P. Sazhin, "Russkie v Tsiurike (1870-1873 gg.)," *Katorga i ssylka*, no. 95 (1932), p. 57. Nettlau, "Bakunin," p. 417, notes the confusion resulting from Ralli-Arbore's frequent chronological errors.

and named places, dates, and people. At one time he volunteered a list of all the students he knew. He described the politics of each and freely revealed addresses and whereabouts. He spoke about revolutionary matters almost as easily as about student demands, describing the illegal literature he had read and the pictures of Herzen that decorated certain walls. He talked of fund-raising activities and named students who had secretly traveled to the provinces. His objective was clear. "My openness will be my guarantee in my case," he stated in his first deposition.[64] Exonerating himself of all blame, he pretended in the case of the students to have attempted to dissuade them from protest and action. In the case of the conspirators he said they had deceived him from start to finish.

I walked hand in hand with them, considering them honest, noble people, and if occasionally also unreasonable then only so in words not in deeds, and I thought that they, like me, were striving to lessen the grief and crimes in society, not to rouse it to terrorism as only now has become clear to me.[65]

Ralli-Arbore became more loquacious as the months wore on, desisting from his revelations only when they might have brought suspicion on himself; he never quite brought himself to reveal the exact goal of Nechaev's program and he maintained that he did not associate closely with Orlov and Nechaev, whom he said he "knew very slightly, for the former conducted himself very secretively and the latter disappeared shortly after I got to know him."[66] Ralli-Arbore was of great use to the Third Section, and the police appreciated his help. "Of the persons involved in the inquiry. . . ," one report read,

Ralli alone from the very beginning gave completely truthful testimony, not only not denying other people's testimony but serving to correct certain less sincere persons. Ralli's sincerity there is no cause to doubt. . . . Ralli personally is an honest and innocent young man and expresses his undisguised repentance at the role he played in the student disorders.[67]

Ralli-Arbore's loquaciousness paid off when he was released on bail in March 1870. He never stood trial. The next year he emigrated to Europe.

Unlike Ralli-Arbore, Tkachev denied everything.[68] In his depositions he stated that he did not know Nechaev and barely knew Orlov at all. Orlov had come to see him several times but discoursed at such length on popular schools and artels, which Tkachev said he found a

---

64. Kozmin, *Nechaev i nechaevtsy*, p. 74.
65. Ibid., p. 73.
66. Ibid.
67. Ibid., p. 190.
68. Speech for the prosecution, in Lehning, *Michel Bakounine*, pp. 291-92.

waste of time, that Tkachev got bored and cut their conversations short. He said he had never organized a circle and had not written the proclamation "To Society," which he read later in the *Police Gazette*. He did not know that Dementeva printed the proclamation. Anxious to save himself, he once smuggled a note to the cell next to his own that housed Nikiforov, Ralli-Arbore's friend, also arrested in the Nechaev affair. Tkachev requested that Nikiforov deny ever having seen him at a student meeting. Nikiforov, who had never met Tkachev, did his best in an interesting confrontation the police arranged among Orlov, Ralli-Arbore, and himself. "I was fully satisfied," Nikiforov wrote later, "as I thought I had succeeded in exonerating Tkachev and in proving the couple independent of the students in this movement. But of course, this was only how it seemed to me!"[69]

Dementeva also began by denying any knowledge of "To Society," perhaps at Tkachev's instruction. Soon after she changed her mind. She admitted printing and distributing the proclamation, but she insisted that she wrote it herself at the suggestion of the student Serebrennikov, now safely abroad where he became Nechaev's good friend.[70]

Ralli-Arbore's testimony implicated dozens of students as well as Tkachev, who was already in prison, and Orlov, who was promptly arrested (June 1869). The police investigation into Ivanov's murder revealed documents and membership lists from the People's Justice, the Moscow society founded by Nechaev in autumn 1869.[71] Nechaev's propensity for sending incendiary letters through the mail and proclamations via courier across the border played its part. More than one hundred and fifty people were arrested in connection with one or another phase of Nechaev's activity. The list of defendants in the Nechaevist trial, held finally in July 1871, was narrowed to a total of eighty-four, the others having been sent into administrative exile or freed (like Vera Zasulich and the Ametistov brothers) for lack of sufficient evidence.[72] Only a handful of the accused were associated with Nechaev in early 1869; most of them were members of the People's Justice later. The first group of eleven to be tried included Tkachev, Dementeva, Orlov, Tomilova, and Nikolaev, Dementeva's one-time possible husband who had taken part in the murder itself.

The trial of the Nechaevists finally took place without Nechaev

---

69. Nikiforov, "Moi tiurmy," pp. 187-88.

70. Speech for the prosecution, in Lehning, *Michel Bakounine*, pp. 292-93.

71. Ibid., pp. 280-81.

72. These statistics are given in ibid., p. 279, and in an interesting report of the Ministry of Justice found in the files of the Third Section and dealing with reasons for prosecuting, dropping charges, or continuing investigations on each of many defendants (Kozmin, *Nechaev i nechaevtsy*, pt. 1).

in July 1871. The courtroom was open to the public, and the atmosphere one of excitement. According to Third Section reporters who faithfully followed events from the floor and took notes for their files, the galleries were full of young people: students, artillery officers, young women. As many as two hundred spectators were on hand for some sessions. The Third Section observers viewed the situation with alarm in light of the presence of known nihilists in the audience. One girl fainted in the gallery during a grisly description of Ivanov's death. On the whole the crowd was sympathetic to the defendants. The Third Section observers noted the pride and daring with which the accused spoke and grumbled because the president of the court let the defendants make speeches about everything from social reconstruction and women's rights to the miserable details of student life.[73] Testimony was printed in the *Government Herald* and summarized in other newspapers as well.[74] Certain proclamations were regarded as so incendiary, however, that they were read by the court behind closed doors and not officially released for publication.[75]

In the act of accusation read before the court the prosecution summarized the student riots, the investigation, and the documents uncovered in various searches.[76] Evidence against each defendant was presented and analyzed separately. In each case the defendant's own statements were summarized and then scrutinized carefully in light of other testimony and evidence.

In Tkachev's case it was easy for the prosecution to disprove his disclaimer of acquaintance with Nechaev. Too many other witnesses had seen Nechaev at a meeting at Tkachev's and seen Orlov and Dementeva there as well. His story of needing money for a mutual assistance society was contradicted by Nikolaev and others to whom he mentioned his desire to purchase a printing press. To Nikolaev he had even spoken of writing a proclamation addressed to society, an incident Nikolaev passed on to the police.[77] There was no doubt in the minds of the prosecutors that Tkachev was deeply involved in the conspiracy; his name with Orlov's and Nechaev's stood at the top of the list.[78]

Dementeva and Tkachev turned out to be the defendants most

---

73. Kozmin, *Nechaev i nechaevtsy*, pp. 159, 161, 167, 169.
74. *Delo*, Tkachev's journal, requested permission to print the stenographic report, but permission was denied (Sokolov, p. 83).
75. Kozmin, *Nechaev i nechaevtsy*, p. 164.
76. This is the document often cited above, reprinted in Lehning, *Michel Bakounine*, pp. 279-301.
77. Ibid., pp. 299-301.
78. Ibid., p. 280.

popular with the crowd. Perhaps it was because they were free from the stigma of Ivanov's murder that hung over several of the defendants. Dementeva made a particularly vivid impression in her testimony; Russian women had seldom spoken with such freedom before their judges. Even the Third Section recognized it.

The whole conservative milieu, which here forms the great majority of the population, is permeated with strong indignation toward the originators of the secret society that is calling upon itself the most awful punishment of the law. It is impossible, however, to deny that among the young people there are also those who sympathize with certain of the accused, as for instance Dementeva, who has drawn their attention by the sympathy for the students warmly expressed on her part and by the cleverness of her answers to the Court's questions.[79]

Asked her name, Dementeva answered, "Aleksandra Dmitrievna Tkacheva," and then stopped as though correcting herself: "Oh, what am I saying. Dementeva!" She was reprimanded by the president:

Be good enough to refrain, accused Dementeva, from such indecorous conduct. You are summoned here in order that your fate may be decided. Of course your fate can be decided in a sense pleasant for you, but still you must refrain from indecorousnesses, from improper smiles, etc.[80]

The Third Section observer in the audience noted that Dementeva had lived with Tkachev as his common-law wife, and wrote: "What impudence this still young girl must have to declare before the court and even brag of her connection with Tkachev under the guise of a slip of the tongue, in order publicly to set forth the principles of civil marriage."[81]

But her speech to the court brought Dementeva even more admiration. She freely admitted that she had printed the proclamation "To Society" although she refused to answer the president when he asked her who gave her the original proclamation. She explained her reasons for printing and distributing it.

I had heard personally from the students, I had seen their meetings, been at them, and followed the affair from the beginning. They did not have the possibility of justifying themselves before society. The newspapers were forbidden to concern themselves with this question, and meanwhile the students had more than occasional need to say a word in their own defense, because [the police] arrested them and without trial sent tens of them out of Petersburg.[82]

Their desires, she said, were not political but purely administrative;

---

79. Kozmin, *Nechaev i nechaevtsy*, p. 172.
80. Ibid., p. 160.
81. Ibid.
82. Svatikov, p. 209.

they sought only the right to have meetings and to maintain a student fund. At the root of many troubles, as Dementeva saw it, lay the poverty and misery in which many students lived.

I was personally convinced that the poverty reigning among the students, and all those circumstances and conditions in which they are set when entering school, demand great closeness between students, in order that thusly they can support one another both in material and in moral respects.[83]

The need for a student fund Dementeva saw as a result of poverty and the unfair distribution of university stipends by the administration. Moreover, "the constant fear and danger of being deprived of a stipend evokes some sort of lackeydom in students; however, if they received assistance from a common fund, they would remain completely independent persons."[84] Some, she felt, were too proud, too ashamed of their poverty to beg help from the administration; dealing with their fellows might make the asking easier. She suggested that such a fund would require constant decision making and thus the right of meeting at academic locations.

Questioned about her search for a nominal husband, Dementeva turned the witness stand into a speaker's platform on women's rights.

By my own personal experience and by examples I have run across among my acquaintances I am convinced that the situation of educated women is much too difficult; that their labor is very thankless; they work from nine in the morning until nine in the evening and receive the most negligible reward. I consider the limited career fields open to women to be the cause of such a poor situation, because the main profession they can take up is teaching. The consequence of such limitation of professions is competition, which lowers pay to a minimum. True, there are a few women stenographers and accountants, but one must take the following into consideration: upon finishing the course of education and even frequently before finishing, the majority of needy girls are forced to remain without any means for subsistence because our institutes and other women's scholarly institutions do not offer us any practical knowledge, they prepare us only to be governesses and therefore, willy-nilly, we must become teachers, for to become stenographers or telegraphers, an additional one or two years in preparation is necessary. . . .[85]

The result of the lack of educational facilities and the lack of funds left women without alternatives.

Thus to this time women cannot attain to that labor where they could use their intellectual powers. . . . The most simple, easiest measure that could give women the possibility of taking up more profitable labor would be to present them with

---

83. Ibid.
84. Ibid.
85. Kozmin, "Okolo nechaevskogo dela," p. 58.

the possibility of acquiring a broader education and to teach various practical professions in the gymnasiums and institutes. But in spite of our universal and most convincing pleas that women be permitted to enter the university and academy, to this time we have been refused.[86]

After her day in court, Dementeva earned more than her share of attention.[87]

Tkachev, called on to testify the following day, made almost as strong an impression on the spectators. "During the interrogation," the Third Section reporter noted, "all persons making up the audience fully sympathized with those being judged, especially with Tkachev."[88]

Faced with Dementeva's admission that she had printed "To Society," Tkachev changed his testimony and admitted his authorship of the proclamation. Tkachev said he had written it to counteract certain fallacious rumors that had plagued society. In the words of the record published in the *Government Herald*, Tkachev affirmed that

after the closing of the Medical-Surgical Academy (the consequence of the presentation of certain demands by the students), in a certain part of society dark rumors began to be spread, as if the young participants did not at all need what they were asking about but, being unwitting tools in the hands of agitators, were playing no more than a game.[89]

The rumors were not new and not original, Tkachev said. In 1861, when students had been making similar demands for a fund and a corporate organization, fires had broken out in St. Petersburg and were blamed on the students; in 1866 the students were thought to be striving to destroy the existing order. Tkachev himself had watched such rumors harm the students' real cause. Certain students had come to him to ask him to write a journal article in their behalf; since such articles were forbidden to publication, he had decided to write the proclamation that Dementeva printed. The aim of the document was to demonstrate the honesty and importance of the students' stated demands and to show society that "society should regard the student movement with attention and not indifferently, for on it depends, to a certain degree, the future of society itself."[90] To quote Tkachev's speech as paraphrased by Svatikov from the *Government Herald:*

If living conditions in the higher academic institutions are such that they drive all the noble, unselfish motives out of the human character, if they manage to develop

---

86. Ibid., pp. 58-59.
87. As carefully noted by the Third Section observers (Kozmin, *Nechaev i nechaevtsy*, p. 169).
88. Ibid., p. 161.
89. Svatikov, p. 210.
90. Ibid.

selfishness, egotism, disuniting interests in the students, then these [students] can scarcely bring real benefits to society. In the students' declaration of their demands, Tkachev saw, perhaps, the unconscious proclamation of unselfish motives of the human character, although on a low stage of their development, in rudimental form, [motives] that with further development . . . should form one of the most noble, most humane motivations of human activity, that which we call the striving for the common welfare.[91]

Tkachev was saying that he saw the student demands not as a political issue but as moral concepts, dominated by the unselfish aim of human solidarity.

Called upon to account for his efforts to find Dementeva a nominal husband, Tkachev defended the institution of fictitious marriage. Such contracts were the result of familial, social, and governmental oppression of young girls, he said. Relationships entered into on a fictional basis retained their nominal character, that is, neither party misused his rights or took advantage of the other; rather the relationships were "based on mutual respect and trust." Such marriages were becoming increasingly common, he informed the court. He himself had been approached by two young women who asked him to arrange fictitious marriages for them. In an affirmation that shocked the Third Section, Tkachev clearly identified himself as one of the "so-called Petersburg nihilists."[92]

When the defendants were led from the courtroom, the spectators waved goodbye, especially to Tkachev who answered them "with a slight inclination of the head, touching the fingers of his right hand to his forehead," as carefully noted by the Third Section reporter.[93]

A few days after Tkachev's appearance on the stand his brother-in-law Annenskii testified in his behalf. Annenskii had been arrested late in 1869 but released shortly thereafter. He presented to the court a plan of his apartment where Tkachev lived, insisting that Tkachev could not have held meetings without his awareness.[94] V. D. Spasovich, a criminal lawyer who had resigned his teaching position in protest against infringements of student rights, represented Tkachev, who had once respectfully reviewed one of his books. The final summary for the defense left the courtroom respectful and excited.

Judgment was passed by the court on July 16. The galleries were full, crowded with young people, and the crowd was sympathetic. People called, "Young ones, don't be discouraged." Dementeva and her

---

91. Ibid., pp. 210-11; Kozmin, *Tkachev*, pp. 172-73.
92. Kozmin, *Nechaev i nechaevtsy*, p. 167.
93. Ibid., p. 162.
94. Ibid., p. 163; Annenskaia, p. 67.

friends read the newspapers and looked out of the windows, aware of the fond eyes of the crowd. Tkachev and Dementeva were both found guilty as charged. Both were sentenced to prison terms beyond the more than two years they had already served, he for one year and four months, she for four months. Both sentences were imposed because of the composition, printing, and distribution of the proclamation "To Society," "which includes in it offensive statements aimed at shaking public confidence in the structure of governmental institutions and justifying forbidden actions with the aim of fomenting disrespect for these structures and institutions."[95] Further reference was made by the court to Tkachev's writings, particularly to the foreword and notes to his translation of Becher's *The Worker Question* and to an unidentified article (apparently not Tkachev's own) scheduled by him for inclusion in the second volume of the *Ray*, which was confiscated before publication by the police.[96] No reference was made in the verdict to Tkachev's involvement in revolutionary conspiracy against the state. The court apparently found the accusation to be unproven.

Of the eighty-four Nechaevists brought to trial four who had aided in the murder of Ivanov were sentenced to hard labor, twenty-seven (including Tkachev and Dementeva) went to prison for various activities deemed illegal, two were exiled to Siberia, and the rest were freed under police surveillance.[97]

Tkachev went to prison and never saw Nechaev again. Their association covered a span of only a few months. No factual evidence testifies to their exact relationship. No eyewitness reported their conversations; no correspondence remains to indicate their mutual understanding. They never wrote of one another. The single documentary product of the Nechaev circle—the "Program of Revolutionary Actions"—is uncertain in origin; Tkachev may or may not have had a hand in its composition, and his proclamation "To Society" may or may not have been planned with the "Program" in mind. Speculation about Tkachev's relationship with Nechaev and the influence they exerted on one another must be based on other materials.

Viewing their friendship over the distance of years, it seems unlikely that the two were very close. The same gap that existed between the students and Nechaev[98] was even more apparent between Tkachev and the schoolteacher from Ivanovo. Tkachev was well educated, literate, well read and had trained himself in what Lavrov might call

95. Kozmin, *Tkachev*, p. 175.
96. Ibid., p. 171; *Russkii biograficheskii slovar*, 20: 598.
97. Iakovlev, *Aktivnoe narodnichestvo*, p. 147.
98. As detailed above; see Confino, pp. 31-33.

critical thinking. He was born to the intelligentsia and was never at home in any other milieu; he never propagandized among the peasantry nor taught among the workers as some of his contemporaries had. Nechaev was the opposite: born into a poor family, educated or self-educated haphazardly, he never acquired that discipline of mind Tkachev so admired. Over a long period of time they would have made a strange combination.

Yet their acquaintance was not lengthy, and Tkachev (like so many others) may have been initially impressed. His biographer Kozmin suggested that to Tkachev Nechaev must have seemed the embodiment of a man of the future with his energy, dedication, and will.[99] As a quiet and retiring person Tkachev must have admired those qualities. Nechaev's eagerness for action was also noteworthy. Tkachev had often deplored men unwilling to move—scholars in laboratories, philosophers in ivory towers—though of course he was an intellectual himself. With his willingness to act, his desire to risk everything for the revolutionary cause, Nechaev must have impressed the more conventional Russian critic. For Tkachev was cautious by nature and not a gambler at all.

The "Program of Revolutionary Actions" that emerged from the Nechaev circle contained some concepts that derived from Tkachev's work and others that did not. Some of the phrases—as for example the definition of a dedicated revolutionary—sounded like Tkachev. The "Program" provided a special niche for Tkachev, who was obviously one of the scholars whose place was in St. Petersburg where he (not Nechaev) was to produce the "Catechism" and rules for the new organization.[100] Tkachev had stated too that conspiracy was the best means for overthrowing a government, and the "Program" anticipated conspiracy on a mammoth scale. The use of political methods first derives from the whole conspiracy concept. Yet the "Program" also foresaw a peasant revolution that its authors believed would take place on February 19, 1870. Here Tkachev could not have agreed. He had no faith in the peasants's desire to rebel, as he had clearly stated in his early articles.[101] The popular revolution must have been Nechaev's idea. In spite of its statement that political revolution would precede social, the "Program" was vague and contradictory about how revolution would occur. It anticipated revolution of both sorts, possibly simultaneously, but it left the exact plan for rebellion to a future decision. To that extent it does not sound like Tkachev at all.

---

99. Kozmin, *Tkachev*, p. 160.
100. Confino, p. 45.
101. See chap. 6 above.

It is impossible to determine whether Tkachev's ideas coincided with Nechaev's because Nechaev's beliefs are impossible to define. Never possessing a clear-cut philosophy of his own, lacking the background on which to found a revolutionary ideology, Nechaev imbibed readings and ideas without caution or perspective. Kozmin wrote that he seemed an anarchist in his early years after his acquaintance with Bakunin in 1869.[102] B. Nikolaevskii assessed Nechaev as a Blanquist on the basis of his study of Robespierre and his acquaintance with certain Communards, one of whom became Tkachev's friend too.[103] Arthur Lehning has pointed out that Nechaev once urged the readers of *People's Justice* to consult Marx's *Communist Manifesto* for the answers to their revolutionary questions.[104] In short, as Ralli-Arbore insisted later, contradicting Nikolaevskii, Nechaev had no single revolutionary creed.[105] He absorbed them all and never assimilated them one to the other. He did not progress from one ideology to another because he retained elements of all of them at once. Michael Confino has most ably described the everything-and-anything of Nechaev's revolutionism. In his lack of political and moral principle (the *printsipialnost* so dear to Bakunin) Confino sees a major reason for the quarrel between Nechaev and his one-time patron.[106]

In the long run Tkachev was less concerned about *printsipialnost* than revolution, but he could not tolerate sloppy logic and disjointed eclecticism. But of course the two men never developed a long-term relationship. Later when Tkachev worked in Geneva on his own revolutionary journal he designed a tightly reasoned program that had little in common with the Nechaevist potpourri.

Meanwhile Nechaev drew from Tkachev as he drew from all his newly found friends and readings. Confino has pointed out features in the "Catechism," produced by Nechaev and Bakunin in 1869 that coincided with elements from Tkachev's "Men of the Future," 1868.[107] To most readers the entire tone of the two writings would seem different. Tkachev's "Men of the Future" were individualists, not automatons, dominated by devotion, not hatred, in spite of their rejection of conventional morality. But Nechaev's strange mind absorbed only their intriguing elements: their sacrifice, their dedication,

---

102. Kozmin, *Tkachev*, p. 152.

103. B. Nikolaevskii, "Pamiati poslednego 'iakobintsa'-semidesiatnika: Gaspar-Mikhail Turskii," *Katorga i ssylka*, no. 23 (1926), p. 217.

104. Lehning, *Michel Bakounine*, p. xxviii.

105. Nikolaevskii, "Pamiati," p. 217 (note 3).

106. Confino, pp. 29-31.

107. Ibid., pp. 48-50.

their intensity. The argument on authorship of the "Catechism" still rages and need not basically concern us here, but Nechaev's participation in formulating its ideas can hardly be doubted.[108] The Nechaevist hero—the obedient lieutenant, the cold-blooded murderer—was a perversion of the revolutionary heroes that Chernyshevskii and Tkachev described.

Nechaev's murder of Ivanov shocked many Russian radicals. N. K. Mikhaliovskii called Nechaev a "monster."[109] Humiliated and bitter, Bakunin soon broke with his young friend, calling him Jesuitical and Machiavellian.[110] Writing later B. Bogucharskii insisted with emphasis that the *nechaevshchina* "was merely an episode in the Russian revolutionary movement, completely isolated, not having as such any roots in the past movement and calling forth only a totally negative reaction among future generations of revolutionary youth."[111]

Yet some men were not shocked. In Russia Tkachev did not betray Nechaev after the murder; only those actually involved in the crime made full confessions. In Zurich in 1872 a movement was mounted to keep the Swiss government from extraditing Nechaev as a common murderer, on the grounds that his was a political crime.[112] Later

---

108. See the summary in ibid., p. 40. Arman Ross once claimed to have seen a copy of the "Catechism" written in Bakunin's hand (Lehning, *Michel Bakounine*, p. lxi). It is interesting that both Bakunin and Nechaev denied authorship of the "Catechism" (Confino, pp. 52-53) and most scholars interested in Bakunin would deny his participation too. Confino thinks the "Catechism" was written "in a primitive and vulgar manner" (p. 42); Kozmin called it a "very brilliant and talented work" (*Tkachev*, p. 194). In fact it is written in two different styles; the General Rules of Organization seem simple and ordinary; the Rules of Conduct of Revolutionaries, beginning with the phrase "The revolutionary is a man lost in advance," are handsomely and imaginatively constructed. It is highly possible, therefore, that Nechaev wrote the former and Bakunin the latter, always remembering that Bakunin wrote under the inspiration of his young "Boy."

109. Cf. Sokolov, p. 91; Kozmin, *Nechaev i nechaevtsy*, p. 3.

110. See his long letter to Nechaev in which he broke off their close relationship (Confino, pp. 135, 137).

111. Iakovlev, *Aktivnoe narodnichestvo*, p. 134. Zasulich, "Nechaevskoe delo," p. 70, believes that Nechaev demoralized the revolutionary movement. The Soviet scholar Galaktionov speaks of Nechaev's "unseemly role" in the revolutionary movement and sees him as a blackmailer and deceiver of honest revolutionary youth (Galaktionov and Nikandrov, *Ideologi russkogo narodnichestva*, pp. 106-7).

112. Some of these documents have been reprinted in Lehning, *Michel Bakounine*, pp. 159-68. It should be noted that the Nechaevists, especially those not involved in the Ivanov murder, gained more sympathy than Nechaev himself. Even Dostoevskii once said, "A *Nechaev* probably I could never become, but perhaps I could have been a *Nechaevist* . . . in the days of my youth" (quoted in Sokolov, p. 97; see also p. 81).

Nechaev smuggled notes from his prison cell to the organization called the People's Will, whose members considered plans to rescue him.

For others the process of evaluation took a long time. It was years later that Zasulich recognized that Nechaev had indeed been isolated among the young intelligentsia.[113] Varlaam Cherkezov later began to feel that Nechaev's role was only that of an activator and that the students had more to contribute as revolutionaries themselves.[114] Another student, looking back, concluded that Nechaev's carelessness with lists and letters was a manner of avenging himself on the intelligentsia, which was not responsive to his demands.[115]

Tkachev himself re-evaluated Nechaev. Removed from the influence of all that vitality, he too saw Nechaev in a different light. Reviewing Dostoevskii's novel *The Demons*, which was based on the Nechaev affair, he admitted that the murder of Ivanov was the deed of a mentally unbalanced man.[116] Nechaev was "sick," he wrote. He had been frustrated too long by his inability to realize his program and activate his ideals. It was not his own fault; Tkachev blamed society as a whole and the older generation in particular. But nevertheless the verdict stood. Murder of a colleague for his independence of mind was the deed not of a hero but of a sick man.

Tkachev gained little from his association with Nechaev. He had met a man of action, but his admiration was tempered when he realized where such action might lead. He had sympathized with the student revolutionaries and become a martyr to their cause. To the extent that he participated in the conspiracy he was discouraged by its failure. By 1871, confined to prison for another year and more, Tkachev must have viewed the world with a feeling of futility and bitterness. His experiences in the Nechaevist case lent him the impetus to leave his native land as soon as he was able.

Meanwhile, behind bars, he turned his attention back to his profession, devoting the tedious hours to some of his most intricate and serious critical reviews.

113. Zasulich, "Nechaevskoe delo," p. 69.
114. Nettlau, "Bakunin," p. 392.
115. This was Nechaev's friend Enisherlov; Svatikov, p. 191; cf. Confino, p. 73.
116. Tkachev, 3: 44.

8

Prison Interlude

For four years after his imprisonment in 1869 Tkachev languished in the notorious Peter-Paul fortress, isolated, his opponents later claimed, from the new currents of thought swirling outside prison gates. Yet tsarist prisons were seldom tyrannical by modern standards, and Tkachev's isolation was actually far from complete. His mother was in St. Petersburg and was probably permitted to visit her son. Tkachev's sister Annenskaia may have done so too, although in her writings she passed over further reference to her brother's plight as she and her husband continued on their own path. Among Tkachev's acquaintances most were in prison, in exile, or in hiding. Dementeva, his common-law wife, spent these years serving out her own sentence, but the two may have kept in touch by letter or through third parties. Most importantly Tkachev had his books. They were never denied to him; even the works of such flagrant radicals as Proudhon and Marx were always on hand. He may also have been permitted to continue his readings of the St. Petersburg journals although of course his own favorites (*Russian Word, Contemporary*) had been suppressed by the tsarist government. He was supplied (probably by his mother) with writing materials. The days must have seemed long and the years dreary, but he was not as isolated as his enemies believed.

Under the circumstances Tkachev's prison years were not wasted. Prison gave him time and indeed a kind of freedom. Released from the problems of earning a living that, according to some scholars, tortured many *raznochintsy* writers, Tkachev could read at his own pace and write what he chose. To his disappointment the censors denied him the right to publish; instead a number of his articles, obviously intended for publication, were seized in their final form by prison authorities and turned over to the secret police. Kozmin discovered some of them years later in the archives of the Third Section.[1] Many others were probably destroyed. The pages of the *Cause*, Tkachev's regular outlet for publication, do not reveal any writings that can be identified as his. Prison authorities had learned a lesson in leniency from their bitter experiences with Chernyshevskii and Pisarev, both of whom had roused Russia's radical youth from their prison cells.

His prison years rank intellectually among the richest periods of Tkachev's career. He was older now and ready to press forward; he had time to concentrate on issues only touched upon in the past. The conflicts of individual and society, statism and anarchism, voluntarism and determinism, science and humanism, posed questions not easily answered, but Tkachev was obviously determined to try. He turned again to the West: he read Marx and Spencer, Girardin and Quinet, modifying some of his early premises, but never abandoning them. As before, his rejection or acceptance of any viewpoint was determined less by its inherent logic or by its convergence with his own previous statements than by his angry insistence that society must be changed, radically changed, and changed at once. Nevertheless these frequently inconsistent conclusions reached by Tkachev in his prison years represent his most sophisticated effort to comprehend the nature and relationship of man and society. He never again tried to force his own thoughts into such a totality. Later his interests were to narrow.

Considering Western society, its principles and functions, present and future, Tkachev leaned heavily on two contemporary Western writers whom he read and admired. He was swayed by Herbert Spencer, for whom he had previously expressed only scorn.[2] His reading of the *Principles of Biology* obviously impressed him. He never came so close to admitting that science might dictate the laws governing society as it revealed the laws of biological evolution. Influential too was Karl Marx. Tkachev read the first volume of *Capital* in its early German edition before it was published in Russian in 1872.[3] What impressed

---

1. See Kozmin's notes in Tkachev, 2: 440 (note 8), 442 (note 20), 443 (notes 27, 29, 34). One Soviet investigator has suggested that Tkachev smuggled a proclamation out of prison and that it was circulated among medical students during a demonstration in memory of Dobroliubov on November 16, 1871; this assertion remains unconfirmed. See *Shestidesiatye gody*, p. 426.

2. Tkachev, 5: 298-303.

3. His references to Marx's *Capital* date from August 1870; they appear in his unpublished articles on Herbert Spencer (ibid., 2: 148 [author's note]). *Das Kapital*

him most was Marx's description of the condition of the English working class, a description based on reports of parliamentary investigations. Tkachev cited Marx in his dour evaluation of capitalism, a totally evil social and economic system in his view. Marx was very useful to him in his attacks on his optimistic opponents. Never before or after did he loom so large in Tkachev's works.

For to this angry young critic Marx was clearly on the right track. Like most of his radical Russian contemporaries Tkachev deplored Western European society and those iniquitous, inequitable, capitalist-democratic institutions that many Russians of his generation hoped their fatherland would never inherit.[4] In his early writings he had often heaped scorn on the evils of the Western system, attacking the defenders of capitalism and the theorists of democracy, identifying them bitterly as bourgeois, as if the term were a kind of expletive. By 1870 he was ready to launch a full-fledged attack on Western capitalistic exploitation and to add a scathing assault on Western democratic pretenses. In the first instance he leaned on the writings of Marx; in the latter he turned for aid to Proudhon.

Tkachev began as always with economics. His basic perennial criticism of society was that it permitted such inequities of wealth as to starve the productive poor at the expense of the callous rich. His 1870 study "Sophist Statistics," a review of two compilations on European demography published in France,[5] involved basically an accusation of fraud: his theme was that the progress claimed by bourgeois analysts for capitalist countries in the West was actually non-existent and had been speciously documented by Western statisticians. Admitting that statistics ("the youngest sister of political economy")[6] were difficult to manipulate because numbers represented hard facts and not elastic speculations, Tkachev still felt that skillful compilers craftily deceived their readers through misrepresentations all the more effective because of the widespread faith in the incontrovertability of

---

was first published in Hamburg in 1867. An interesting history of its translation and reception in Russia can be found in Albert Resis, "*Das Kapital* Comes to Russia," *Slavic Review* 29, no. 2 (June 1970): 219-37.

4. This anticapitalism and the hopes of skipping over any capitalist development is one of the themes Walicki, *Controversy over Capitalism*, develops in his definition of populism.

5. These statistical studies were edited by Maurice Bloc and M. Legoyt. Unlike most of the books Tkachev considered in his reviews, they had not appeared in Russian. Tkachev's article is in Tkachev, 6: 5-104.

6. Ibid., p. 6. Statistics were held in high regard by Tkachev and many of his contemporaries as representing the most concrete, scientific basis for historical and other judgments.

numbers. He suggested that bourgeois deceivers distracted their readers by presenting quantities of useless material and by deliberately extending the patches of sunlight to obscure the darkness of shadows; that they grouped statistics artfully to present the most favorable impression; that they shamelessly slanted their interpretations; and that if necessary they hid certain facts or lied about others in spite of the danger of being found out.[7]

The major objects of Tkachev's irritation were those "sophists" who measured a country's wealth in terms of its national product and who identified increasing production with necessarily increasing prosperity. To this angry young egalitarian who studied Karl Marx[8] total national wealth meant little. The key to prosperity lay instead in the distribution of wealth; what share, he asked, actually went to the worker, what share to the entrepreneur? Tkachev saw little good in capitalism, which produced, he thought, ever greater economic inequities. The introduction of the machine inevitably led to a decline in wages if not at once (when factories were being constructed and the need for labor was great), then at least in the later stages of development (when expansion could be achieved only through improved technology and the demand for labor decreased). Contemporary Western Europe (particularly France and England) had achieved the latter stage; the introduction of technological improvements in existing factories had replaced the construction of new plants as the prime method of industrial expansion.[9] Tkachev was convinced that owing to the malevolent system of distributing wealth, "the richer the factory state of Western Europe becomes, the poorer the majority of its population grows."[10] Marx's descriptions of the plight of labor in England clearly confirmed his judgment.

Examining one by one the conclusions of his bourgeois statisticians in regard to population trends, Tkachev determined that contrary to their opinions statistics actually indicated that poverty in Europe was on the increase. He was forced to admit that an increase in population such as Western Europe seemed to be experiencing generally indicated rising prosperity, but he hastened to demonstrate that the rate of population growth was actually on the decline. No progressive increase in life expectancy could be postulated since the countries with the

7. Ibid., pp. 7-12.
8. Marx's examples demonstrate that increasing national wealth in England had not eliminated poverty (Karl Marx, *Capital*, pp. 707-18). Chernyshevskii had made the same point; see Walicki, pp. 18-19.
9. Tkachev, 6: 94-95.
10. Ibid., p. 102; cf. Marx, *Capital*, p. 707.

lowest standard of living could claim the longest-lived inhabitants—
Englishmen and Norwegians, whom Tkachev seemed to consider poor,
were known to live longer than supposedly rich Frenchmen. A lower
birth rate (as in industrialized countries) did not indicate prudence and
promise more wealth to go around but must rather be read as a sign of
the sexual impotence of the poor and the physical degeneration of the
working class.

These developments Tkachev pictured as delighting the hardhearted
bourgeoisie. Drawing from Marx the analogy of labor, living and dead,
he wrote:

Living human labor, as is known, is valued very cheaply on the market; but for
dead labor, the labor crystallized in money, credit papers, and etc., in a word, in
capital, a very high premium always exists. . . . Thus one can understand why of
the two related factors of production—labor and capital—the bourgeois values the
latter very highly and the former very little. From this it is clear that a statistic
revealing the tendency to degeneration of the popular masses does not frighten
[the bourgeois] but on the contrary pleases him. In his opinion the mass of living
labor should be limited not by the limits of the means for subsistence . . . but
by the bounds of the demands of capital.[11]

Tkachev reminded his reader that Malthus and other bourgeois economists considered excess labor "a burden, surplus ballast in the social
organism,"[12] a conclusion that ill fit his earlier contention that an
oversupply of labor kept wages low, surely a boon to any profit-seeking
entrepreneur.

Tkachev was sure that the inevitable poverty of the worker within
the capitalist system was necessarily accompanied by his moral and
mental degeneration. Drawing on Marx's description of English labor,
which he cited in his footnotes,[13] Tkachev contended that the ratio of
illegitimate births was highest in large cities although he was hard
pressed to explain the high ratio in the bucolic areas of Mecklenburg
and Bavaria.[14] Challenging the statisticians' opinion that crime was on
the wane, he pointed to flaws in the particular methods of statistical
compilation, such as the exclusion of crimes brought before certain
courts and the tabulation of numbers of convictions rather than accusa-
tions. Mental illness, suicide, and alcoholism Tkachev found to be
major urban problems; the high rate of idiocy in agricultural areas he

---

11. Tkachev, 6: 23; cf. Marx, *Capital*, pp. 339, 666-67.
12. Tkachev, 6: 24.
13. Ibid., p. 161; cf. Marx, *Capital*, pp. 489-90.
14. Tkachev suggested that the problem was only temporary and local. He
blamed what he regarded as the continuing tradition of *jus primae noctis* (Tkachev,
6:36).

managed to blame on the bourgeoisie, which deliberately encouraged agricultural poverty (apparently the cause of idiocy) for its own purposes. The further degeneration of the worker was attested by a death rate that, in spite of the breakthroughs of contemporary science, had remained constant or increased in Tkachev's view.[15]

The conclusion was inevitable: capitalism was not a progressive historical development measured in terms of human prosperity but a regressive one. For mankind it had dire consequences in that the poor were not getting richer but poorer.

Increasing the productivity of a country to the highest degree, it simultaneously decreases the means of subsistence of the majority of its population, discomfits [the population] with infertility, premature death, illnesses, physical weakness, corruption, poverty and finally casts it from its home, from its native villages and cities to far-off foreign lands.[16]

To measure the progress of society by any criterion but the physical well-being of man was inconceivable to Tkachev. The goal of human happiness, in his mind, was always based on physical welfare. His negative evaluation of so-called progress in Western Europe remained one of the constants of his world view.[17] He was convinced of the retrogressive, degenerative quality of Western European social and economic mores, an attitude he shared with many Russian radicals of his time.

Tkachev did not limit his criticism of the West to the effects of capitalism on the masses of population. With equal vigor and acerbity he attacked the governments—and indeed the principles of government —in the nations he so despised. In his condemnation of the sham institutions the bourgeoisie called democratic Tkachev did not stand alone; other men of his generation also read Proudhon and Pisarev and agreed with him.[18] But the young critic parted company with many of his radical contemporaries when he took his stand firmly for statism as opposed to anarchism, collectivism as opposed to individualism, and authority as opposed to freedom. Doing so, he laid a foundation for those violent Jacobin plans that later so antagonized his fellow revolutionaries.

The political speculation of his prison years Tkachev wove around the essays of the French liberal journalist Emile Girardin whom the scornful critic regarded as the bard, "the pure poet and philosopher" of

---

15. Ibid., pp. 42–58.
16. Ibid., p. 104; Marx considered emigration in the last chapter of *Capital*.
17. See chap. 5 above, pp. 83–84.
18. See the description in Walicki, pp. 82–84.

the bourgeoisie.[19] Girardin was an ardent supporter of individual liberty in the waning years of the Second Empire. "Liberty is the law of man," Tkachev read in *Pensées et maximes*, published in 1867, and "it is through the individual that humanity raises itself, and will raise itself—thus to elevate the individual is to elevate humanity."[20]

Tkachev responded only with cynicism. Individualism was a capitalistic concept. Freedom was nothing more than a necessity in capitalist society, deriving not from meaningful philosophical principles but from the empirical economic demands of bourgeois competition. Liberty was to capitalism, Tkachev thought, what authority had been to feudalism. "The freedom of capital," he wrote, "can be realized only in a society politically and civilly free."[21] Unwilling to admit of freedom as simply a necessary postulate to the selfish accumulation of wealth, the bourgeoisie had deliberately elevated liberty to the unchallengeable heights of a philosophical principle and had taught modern Western society to worship it like a god. Like Adam Smith who saw the spirit of competition as an innate, inevitable trait of mankind, like jurists who raised everyday laws to the status of absolute universalisms, bourgeois political theorists observed the immediate realities of everyday life and called them eternal necessities.

But Tkachev was sure that vast confusions would arise from the elevation of transitory empirical fact to the status of eternal abstract law. Any political philosophy claiming universality but based on particular observation would end by retaining the contradictions of "life itself" rather than by setting forth a logical, thoughtful, desirable new order.[22] Capitalists had trapped themselves without foreseeing the dangers inherent in basing their theories on life when life was seldom logical. Only later did they realize their mistake. For on the one hand freedom was necessary to the operation of the capitalist system: only the free circulation of capital, the negotiation of free labor agreements, the spirit of free competitive individualism could lead to accumulations of wealth. On the other hand that same freedom liberated the worker to use his newly won suffrage to make inroads against the economic system: he could insist on factory inspection, safety rules, or the regulation of wages and hours. The European bourgeoisie had grown

---

19. Tkachev, 2: 7. Tkachev had published one article (a first installment of his views) on Emile Girardin in *Delo* before his arrest; it was entitled "Bardy frantsuzskoi burzhuazii: Emil Zhirarden i ego filosofiia," reprinted in ibid., pp. 5-28. His second article, never published in his lifetime, is in ibid., pp. 29-68.

20. Emile de Girardin, *Pensées et maximes*, p. 31.

21. Tkachev, 2: 33.

22. Ibid., pp. 32-33, 66-67.

sorry it had ever insisted that freedom as a principle be extended throughout the capitalist world. Bourgeois theorists, Tkachev wrote, had become frightened of their own words. He cited Comte who found constitutionalism to have outlived its usefulness; Proudhon (whom he identified with the middle class) who cried that separation of powers had become a meaningless fraud; and Girardin who proposed direction by one powerful leader who supposedly would best represent majority interests.[23]

Girardin's ideal government, in spite of its strong leader, was not one of force. In the system he carefully worked out for the future, the ideal state was to fade into the background, leaving individuals on their own as much as possible. Each man would have perfect freedom. He might or might not pay his taxes; he was bound by no general laws (save a few that protected him physically); he was compelled by no general authority. The state would make no demands upon him beyond the obligation (which greatly irritated Tkachev) to carry an identity card. As Tkachev interpreted Girardin's system, the individual was to devise his own laws while the state refused either to aid or to restrain him.

But this was a dreadful abdication of responsibility. This was anarchism, Tkachev cried, and anarchism indeed was his description of Girardin's bourgeois utopia.[24] Tkachev had never been a friend of the anarchists. For all his admiration of Proudhon's description of the evils of contemporary society, the young Russian radical had attacked Proudhon's utopia on the familiar basis that it was too bourgeois.[25] Anarchy could only be successful, he wrote, when it could be based on social solidarity and harmony. Without the solidarity of human interests men would remain full of mutual antagonisms. The unconditional rule of freedom foreseen by the anarchists would act against some to the profit of others.[26]

The key to social solidarity lay rather in full human equality. Without such equality neither harmony nor anarchy could exist. Without equality anarchism would become oligarchy, competition become monopoly, juridical protection merely a cover-up for exploitation.

23. Ibid., pp. 36-37.
24. Ibid., pp. 46-47.
25. See ibid., 1: 90-100; also p. 438 (note 20). Rolf H. W. Theen has written an excellent article on Tkachev's attitudes towards anarchism and statism: "Seizure of Political Power as the Prologue to Social Revolution: The Political Ideas of P. N. Tkachev in the Early 1870's," *Canadian Slavic Studies* 4, no. 4 (Winter 1970): 670-98.
26. Tkachev, 2: 16-17.

Girardin and Proudhon never went far enough. Seeking that harmony with which anarchy would be compatible, Girardin nevertheless rejected and feared equality. He looked for harmony, Tkachev cried, in a confusion where harmony could never exist, for freedom ungoverned could only lead to chaos. Until such time as liberty became meaningful, until such time as equal individuals had created total harmony in society, government should never abdicate its rightful responsibility. The state should insure its citizens against war, disease, and poverty; it should not abandon them to cope with social chaos without protection. The members of society who would suffer most from extreme individualism (from the chaos of unmitigated liberty) were the weak. In a world of inequality they would be preyed upon by the strong. The state must not desert its poor. Rather it must play a constant positive role. It must devote its strength to the welfare of its poor citizens.[27]

On paper Tkachev never carefully devised a utopia of his own, but the outlines of the society he believed ideal became ever more clear. He sought unity rather than diversity, equality rather than freedom, a collective society rather than individualistic fragmentation. A bourgeois Girardin, he wrote, would call his ideal collective despotism.[28] Unlike Girardin Tkachev was never afraid of general compulsory laws, for in his future state the instruments of power would not be destroyed but instead would be put to use to support the weak. Anarchism might come later, but Tkachev knew it would take long years and hard work in the creation. The future state must work toward that absolute equality upon which anarchy could be based. Once individuals were equal, harmony would replace competition, and the ideal would be achieved. Tkachev could foresee it, but he concentrated in his works on the interim period, the collective despotism that would be the means to the end. What he himself called communism he equated with strong central government; what most of his Russian contemporaries called socialism they linked irrevocably with weak government or anarchy.

If his statistical studies and his analysis of Girardin led Tkachev to criticize the West with the aid of Marx and Proudhon, the three longest articles of his prison years—articles unpublished during his lifetime— revealed his continuing fascination with the broad questions that so disturbed his generation: the nature of the forces that move history, the definition and creation of progress, the relationship of man to nature and its laws. Reviewing in turn books by Edgar Quinet, a French

---

27. Ibid., pp. 47-49, 25-26.
28. Ibid., pp. 50-53.

radical; Herbert Spencer, the sociological Darwinist; and P. L. Lavrov, the Russian mathematician and philosopher, whose *Istoricheskie pisma* (Historical Letters) had created a sensation in the Russian press, Tkachev considered the nature of social man from three points of view: that of the poet, the biologist, and the philosopher.[29] If his answer to each of them was primarily antagonistic, his denials were conditioned by his own preconceived ideas. Attacking his enemies he drew on them and pulled his own forces closer together.

Tkachev began with Quinet, whose book *La création* appeared in 1870. *La création* was more than a popularization of the current theories of biological evolution as applied to social history; it came close to romanticizing. Following the revolution of 1848 and the establishment of the Empire by Napoleon III, Quinet like many French radicals had suffered a deep loss of faith in his own beliefs and in his own hopes for the future. As he explained to his readers he had deliberately retreated from the political world into the mountains of Switzerland where he retired into a softer and more benevolent nature. By the late 1860s he had been swept up in the excitement of his contemporaries for natural science—for the nature that surrounded and restored him. "I undertook," he cried in his introduction, "to make the contemporary revolution in natural history enter into the general domain of the human spirit, that is, to establish the rapports of the new conception of nature with history, arts, languages, letters, social economy and philosophy."[30] His own awakening—that moment when "that which had been instinct, presentiment, became light and truth"— exploded when he realized that "nature is explained by history, history by nature. Both harmonize into the same tissue."[31]

Surprisingly Tkachev, the cynic, could be sympathetic. He laid Quinet's romantic mood to his age, the destruction of his dreams, his search for quietude; it was natural, he thought, that the French philosopher (a fearless opponent of the Catholic Church) should turn to nature to restore himself. Tkachev seemed to understand. Entitling his article "Science in Poetry and Poetry in Science," he began by warmly approving Quinet's idea that art and poetry should draw on science, should reawaken interest in science through the breadth of their imaginative appeal, and should show to others the way to Quinet's new land of peace and quiet. Art, Quinet believed, could portray nature and imagine

---

29. These articles were respectively "Nauka v poezii i poeziia v nauke," ibid., pp. 69-118; "Zakon obshchestvennogo samosokhraneniia," ibid., pp. 119-65; and "Chto takoe partiia progressa," ibid., pp. 166-223.

30. Edgar Quinet, *La création*, p. i.

31. Ibid., pp. iii, iv.

past ages; the poetic intuition could expand and develop the new scientific hypotheses. Tkachev recapitulated some of Quinet's poetry of the earth and appeared to enjoy it. He liked the pictures of the world as a huge ocean teeming with microscopic life; the lush reproduction of so many minuscule forms; the durability of the small and inadaptability of the large. He was not above drawing a social lesson from Quinet's descriptions as he paraphrased them.

> The giants appear on the scene of life, make a lot of noise, and quickly disappear; only the little Lilliputians remain unchanged and eternal rulers of the world.
> Beginning to create, [nature] turns above all not to the infinitely large, not to the aid of the giant, but to the endlessly small, to the microscopic work of the Lilliputian. In reforming a type it chooses not the aristocrat of organic forms but some sort of *raznochinets*, taken from goodness knows where. Eternity and unending rule over the world it grants not to this proud and arbitrary aristocracy but to the dark, unnoticed, disdained plebeian.[32]

Tkachev, the realist, seemed to delight in the idea that man learned from the bear and the deer and the bird, instinctively following "another nature." Although he noted that these hypotheses were based on poetic intuition and remained unproven by scientific investigation, he lauded Quinet as an exquisite popularizer, an intelligent and gifted poet with a keen sense of suffering.[33] His only real disagreement with Quinet's plea that poetry take up scientific subjects lay in the area of civic poetry, which the Russian critic considered not only sentimental and irritating (lacking both thought and energy, he said) but often dangerous, since the civic muse could too easily sell herself to blood and despotism.[34] For Tkachev, to paraphrase his title, science in poetry was on the whole an excellent innovation.

Not so, however, poetry in science, for the meddling poet aspiring to scientific conclusions relied so heavily on intuition that his conclusions were often fallacious, his presumptions inaccurate, and his analogies illogical. Quinet was a case in point. The Frenchman aroused Tkachev's greatest wrath by his insistence that Darwinian laws of nature's history were applicable as well to the history of man in society. Tkachev denied outright that any such analogy was valid. History might have its laws, but they were not nature's laws. Moreover, man (unlike lower organic life) always had the power to change them.

---

32. Tkachev, 2: 83, 84-85.
33. Ibid., pp. 90-91.
34. Ibid., p. 75. Tkachev here specifically mentions Nekrasov; he had in mind Nekrasov's conservative civic poems of 1866, probably written in the hopes that the editor could dissuade the government from closing down *Contemporary*. Unlike some of his contemporaries Tkachev later forgave Nekrasov and wrote of him glowingly after his death. Cf. ibid., p. 442 (note 23), and Sokolov, pp. 174-77.

Civil history and civil society have their laws, establishing a certain connection, certain relationships between people, their deeds, their thoughts. If man did not have a psychic apparatus by which he constantly can agitate and change these relationships, then, of course, we could apply the same attributes to the laws of human social life and to the laws of human history as to the laws of nature; and then a truly similar analogy could be found between these two categories of laws. But how do you strip from man this psychic apparatus, this, to express it in vulgar language, self-determining will?[35]

To Tkachev the conviction of the immutability of history's laws could only lead to fatalism. Attacking Quinet, he pointed out that the older man obviously believed in freedom of personality, in individual development of mind and spirit, in man's free will to create his own life style. Nothing in Quinet's multicolored view of human nature was fatalistic; nothing had led him to a pessimistic view of man or his potential. But Tkachev believed the logical application of Quinet's immutable law to human development could leave no room for such human variation or individual heroism; it would give man no possibility of altering what existed according to his own desires. Tkachev took hope from his conviction that man could change the laws of social relationships and historical progression. He berated the French "poet" for not understanding the dichotomy between a history predetermined by immutable scientific rules and history created by men and their heroes. Quinet's view illogically combined the two.

Furiously Tkachev attacked Quinet's Darwinian theories as applied to human society. The young Russian insisted that none of the laws of biological evolution, perfectly applicable in the science from which they derived, could pertain to mankind. In nature everything was progress because natural progress was history itself. No one could assign to nature some goal against which progress might be measured. Man understood a priori that nature, in spite of its occasional perversions, was always basically progressive. In human history, on the other hand, one could and must seek a universal goal toward which mankind eternally strove. To Tkachev the goal was axiomatic; it was clearly happiness. By this criterion must historical progress be measured, for change in man's history did not represent progress per se. By this criterion man must judge his past, his present, and his future, whereas (lacking knowledge of its goals) man had no right to pass judgment upon nature. Tkachev vented his fury on historians unwilling to pass judgments upon man and his deeds: such a historian was "a bad human being and even worse citizen. Servility and faintheartedness are disgracefully concealed under the veil of his *historical impartiality*."[36]

---

35. Tkachev, 2: 93.
36. Ibid., p. 97.

If nature progressed inevitably, man did not, for civil society had about it nothing inevitable or immutable. Unlike nature man must consciously work to move forward.

The laws of nature cannot demand more from living creatures than merely simple *adaptation* to the given conditions of life, which do not depend at all on the will of living creatures. On the contrary, the laws of civic development lay on man the obligation not only to adapt himself but constantly to strive to change and better these conditions.[37]

To Quinet's conviction that the biological laws of atavism could apply also to human affairs—that is, that after a period of rapid progress a period of regress naturally appeared—Tkachev replied furiously that it need not be so. No rule or cause for atavism had yet, he claimed, been discovered in nature, and the phenomenon was accidental in its social manifestation. Quinet clearly warned against revolution because of the probability of subsequent reversion; Tkachev necessarily took the opposite stand. He could never accept an argument that revolution might be futile or, worse, destructive beyond its capacity to rebuild.

To all of Quinet's other analogies Tkachev angrily set forth his objections. Society is not like an organism, he cried. In the first place society's parts are in no wise linked together as the parts of an individual organism; rather its segments are involved in continual struggle where those of the organism are unified. In the organism differentiation of functions is equated with progress; in society the differentiation of labor that once distinguished man's history has been terminated by the leveling power of the machine, a Marxist concept Tkachev seized upon with pleasure.[38] In nature more perfect forms prevail, and indeed victory is a simple criterion of perfection. In society victory does not indicate perfection, judged by the criterion of man's happiness: Tkachev cited the victories of Assyria over Jerusalem, taking Assyria to represent the society least beneficial to man—despotic tyranny, militarism, slavery—as against the fraternal, peace loving, patriarchal, and communistic society of the Jews.[39]

What fascinated Tkachev most was the frequently drawn analogy between the struggle for existence in nature and that in human society. On the one hand, he saw some justice in the analogy; on the other, it led (he claimed) only to monstrous conclusions. In nature, Tkachev believed, the struggle for existence was a primeval principle: the beginning of organic life, the key to its history, the immutable and necessary

37. Ibid., p. 101.
38. Ibid., p. 104; cf. Marx, *Capital*, pp. 430-40.
39. Tkachev, 2: 106.

condition of organic progress. Struggle for existence stimulated the organism to adapt and led it toward the perfection that conditioned its progress. In society although a struggle existed, it had no analogous significance. It was not primeval but a simple product of environment. It did not lead to perfection of social organization but merely to certain economic changes. Victory in the struggle designated not progress toward the goal of man's happiness but only economic development.

The struggle for wealth, Tkachev thought, was not a natural law but the irrational man-made rule of an economic system inaugurated by fallible human beings. If it conditioned economic progress in the sense of perfecting methods of production or abetting the accumulation of capital in certain hands, these developments still did not create social progress, man's happiness, or a perfect social organization. In nature the struggle for existence perfected the organism; in society it impeded perfection. Indeed, intense struggle for existence was the mark of a backward society.

Economic progress and consequently civilization too develop first where the struggle for subsistence has ended, where people have stopped fighting among each other entirely or have begun to fight not for subsistence but for riches, that is, more correctly, for capital.[40]

The whole organism-society analogy reeked of the poetic to Tkachev, and while poetry could use science, science could not tolerate intuitive artistry. Tkachev concluded that Quinet did not sufficiently separate poetry and science; in his confusion of the two he succeeded only in perverting the latter.

The problem of applying laws of the organic world to man in society dominated Tkachev's second long article written during his prison years, a review of what he called the "Laws of Reproduction" based on Herbert Spencer's *Principles of Biology* (1864). Spencer propounded at length the dichotomy between individual and species or, more exactly, the conflict between the individual's growth and the development of those functions (fertility in particular) necessary to carry on the race. To Spencer the two stood in opposition. Each organism must expend its food either for its own special development or for the process of reproduction; the one led to its individual prosperity, the other to the multiplication of the species. Should nourishment be concentrated on the development of the individual's particular traits, fertility would so regress as to lead to the numerical decline of the species, or perhaps, Tkachev suggested, to its extinction. On the other hand, if all subsistence were devoted to replenishment of the

40. Ibid., pp. 113-14.

species (reproduction), the individuum would degenerate into nothing more than a reproductive organ. As Tkachev put it succinctly, "The fertility of an organism stands in inverse relationship to its [individual] growth and the complexity of its structure."[41]

In Spencerian biological theory this dichotomy was modified by the struggle for existence. The struggle for food of the highly developed individual was eased by his higher intellectual capacity; while the less developed members of the species were fighting fruitlessly for the means to subsist, the more intelligent individual learned how to find what he needed. This efficient expenditure of intelligence kept the highly developed individual from dying out, for it provided him with enough food to keep himself and his reproductive system operating. Thus the struggle for existence urged the organism toward perfection, provided for expenditures for reproduction as well as for individual perfection, and eliminated the antagonism between species and individual. Harmony became not only possible but inevitable as perfection and progress continued.

Tkachev, the man who attacked Quinet's efforts to construct rules for society based on Darwin's biological laws, was suddenly ready to accept a great deal of Spencer and apply it to mankind. Like many of his contemporaries he was obviously impressed with Spencer's science and erudition. What is more, this young radical had frequently before sacrificed logic to necessity, and in this case the lessons he sought to teach could be derived from some of Spencer's premises. As he had done in the past he drew an arbitrary line between those scientific laws he felt actually pertained to man and those he believed applied only to lower species.[42] He went more than part way along the path Spencer traveled. "All these laws," he wrote, "it goes without saying, are completely and unconditionally applicable to the reproduction of people as well."[43] He went on:

---

41. Ibid., p. 123. Tkachev's long consideration of Spencer was apparently originally prepared in three installments, none of which was published during his lifetime. The first installment, an article of little interest that is restricted to summarizing Spencer's viewpoints rather than presenting Tkachev's, has recently been published in Tkachev, *Sochineniia*, pp. 570-601. The second has apparently been lost. The third, an interesting discussion of Spencer's ideas in their sociological ramifications, was selected for publication by the astute Kozmin; it appears in Tkachev, 2: 119-65, and forms the basis for the analysis herein.
42. See above, chap. 5, p. 96.
43. Tkachev, 2: 130.

That the laws of reproduction to which all living organisms have been subject, beginning from the first vesicle to the multicelled tree, from the rhizopod to the highest species of mammal, must also be the laws of human reproduction—this the most desperate and even the most ignorant spiritualist could hardly doubt.[44]

But if Tkachev accepted many of Spencer's premises without question, he objected to almost all of Spencer's conclusions. He urged caution on his readers; they should not accept unproven hypotheses from "dilettante" biologists although they should always agree to indisputable facts. Tkachev drew the line between hypothesis and fact exactly where he chose to do so. The position of man, he thought, was comparable to that of a lower organism in terms of reproductive and individual capacities, but the results of this similar situation were not for man what they were for lesser beings. Biological laws applied to man only part way.

In the Spencerian framework as modified by Tkachev there was indeed a conflict between the expenditure of foodstuffs on individual personality and on racial reproduction. The individual Tkachev identified with uniqueness, intellectual superiority, a low fertility rate, and progress in the sense of scientific and scholarly advancement.[45] The species or race Tkachev associated like Spencer with reproduction and regeneration; he linked race with fertility, the masses of population, and collectivism, in the sense that energy was expended on preserving the entire race rather than on the excessive development of any one of its members.

Echoing the Malthusian concept that the fertility of man exceeded the means available for his subsistence, Tkachev agreed that a struggle for existence was bound to ensue. Fighting for the means to survive, a few strong individuals would prevail over the weak and manage to provide for themselves.

At this point Tkachev's views clearly diverged from Spencer's. Spencer proposed a theory of automatic approach to equilibrium in a cyclical pattern. He believed that as the elite few devoted most sustenance to their traits of individuality, they would not have strength left to assume the burden of propagating the race. Soon population would decrease, and surplus food would become available. This in turn would permit more expenditure of energy on reproduction, and fertility would recur. But the resulting population growth would cause new

---

44. Ibid., p. 131.
45. On other occasions he identified the individual with the rich and the species with the poor.

food shortages, reactivate the struggle for existence, bring about the victory of a new intellectual, infertile elite, and set the cycle on its way again. Although equilibrium would never be attained, it would constantly be approached.

Tkachev objected on several bases. He disliked any theory that pitted an intellectual elite against the gray illiterate masses (the individual versus the species) and tipped the scales in favor of the former, the elite that proved itself most fit. He objected to any theory whereby human progress could be presumed to take care of itself: Spencer's assumption of constantly approached equilibrium was the sine qua non of the theory of progress, he complained.[46] Tkachev believed that harmony could be attained only through the conscious intervention of man.

More fundamentally he disliked the whole progressive evaluation of the struggle for existence. Looking around him with the aid of Marx, Tkachev had to admit that such a struggle existed and that some of Spencer's laws seemed to be functioning. The poor were fertile, and the birth rate among the rich was low.[47] But the analogy stopped there. The decline in population was not resulting in prosperity; it was not increasing the food available for the individual or for society, poor or rich. Society, then, did not function like nature. In nature the struggle for subsistence was a measure of organic strength, but in society it only indicated legal power. It was limited in society by juridical rules that deprived it of its natural progressive character. In society the struggle for subsistence was a struggle for wealth or capital.[48] It might stimulate what the bourgeoisie would call economic progress, but it did not (as in nature) stimulate either race or individual towards perfection.

Thus the victor in the struggle for capital was not ordinarily the individual with the greatest capacity and highest development. Intelligent, capable individuals did not always win. Instead the high development of some individuals had a deleterious effect on society as a whole, for the more complex physiological system demanded more food and more production in general. Like many of his radical contemporaries, Tkachev felt wealth existed in a limited quantity that must be divided among all living men. The more the intellectuals consumed, the less was left for the common, simple race. The worker suffered and bore the burden. Tkachev rejected Spencer's suggestion that the demand for produce necessarily evoked a demand for labor, which in turn automatically raised wages and increased prosperity for the working classes. He contended instead that "intellectual and economic progress, increasing

46. Tkachev, 2: 136.
47. Ibid., p. 132; cf. Marx, *Capital*, pp. 706, 708.
48. Tkachev, 2: 139-41.

expenditures on individuality, do not ease for society the possibility of satisfying its demands, for just as before and even more so it must strain its labor power to exhaustion, to breakdown."[49] Demand would not, he believed, rise beyond technology's capacity to respond.

Tkachev's theory presented a gloomy picture indeed. The unhealthy pressure exerted by the superior individualists would cause the degeneration of the working class. What the worker would adapt to was the machine. Tkachev drew again on Marx.[50] The machine demanded ever less education and little physical strength, causing a general decrease in workers' pay. It needed only the weak, the children, the women. Weak workers would want less.

With the constantly increasing sum of society's demands the exhaustion of laboring power will continue, and consequently the race of workers as before will degenerate, dulling intellectually, weakening physically; the circle of demands on workers will become more and more limited, beggardom and poverty will increase more and more.[51]

But the worker would not die out, permitting mankind to renew itself, as Spencer proposed. Rather he would increase in fertility as he weakened in strength because the machine demanded many weak hands. Strength would not pay, but the bearing of children would. Tkachev cited Marx who had dourly predicted in *Capital* that the premium on child labor would cause rapid reproduction and early marriages, a situation that, Marx wrote, "calls to mind the boundless reproduction of animals individually weak and constantly hunted down."[52] Tkachev came close to paraphrasing.

Because [the worker's] direct profit will lie exactly in strengthening the genus at the expense of his individuality, there is no doubt that over several generations this race of workers will degenerate into beings who will be very little like their ancestors and in whom, perhaps, our descendants will not want to see people equal with themselves. They will be, probably, weak beings with the bones and muscles of children, small of growth, completely undeveloped psychically, beings in whom of all the organs of the body, only the organs of reproduction will be well developed: they will reproduce as rapidly as they will rapidly die.[53]

Tkachev went back to Spencer to find a suitable biological example of an organism for which lack of food led to increased fertility. By the kind of analogy he himself often deplored, the worker became the insect of society, reproducing by the millions but dying just as fast.

---

49. Ibid., p. 150.
50. Marx, *Capital*, pp. 431-58, 702-8.
51. Tkachev, 2: 151.
52. Marx, *Capital*, p. 706.
53. Tkachev, 2: 154.

Tkachev was reminded of the same old lesson about progress: progress indeed would not bring about the results the bourgeoisie predicted.

In the future it will become more difficult for the working population to acquire the means for subsistence than it was previously and than it is now. The antagonism between individuality and the species will be resolved here by the regress of individuality, but the race will gain nothing from this regress because although the fertility of the individual will not decrease (at least to any significant degree), the death rate nevertheless will not decrease either and will grow even more rapidly; the number of mature individuals will decrease considerably although the number of children will, perhaps, increase. Society, viewed as a whole, as usual will have to strain working power to the point of extreme exhaustion to satisfy its demands, and the result [of this excessive strain] will be, as we have shown, the degeneration of the working classes, which will lead in the long run to the complete degradation of man, to the weakening of his physical organization, to the deadening of his intellectual capacities, in short, to his transformation into some sort of animal *sui generis*, an animal that most recent naturalists probably would find it difficult to identify in the same race as *homo*.[54]

While the worker degenerated, the intellectual who had developed through excessive feeding of his individuality would hardly become an admirable person nor lead society toward admirable goals. The traits demanded of him for maintaining himself and acquiring adequate means of subsistence for his costly demands were not in the long run advanced mentality or high moral quality. Rather they emphasized selfishness and egotism, competitiveness and hatred of his fellows. The man with the strongly developed moral sense would not adapt and would die out; he would become less fertile and his type would not renew itself. The survivors would be the most fit only in terms of the capitalistic ethic. They would contribute to society only their own antisocial aims, and eventually they would show the way to anarchy, to Tkachev the inevitable result of total individualism. A struggle that in nature led to organic progress and perfection, in society led to social regression, disorganization, and the degradation of the human personality.

In human society we note the same [natural] antagonism between species and individuality and the same struggle for existence, which strives to reconcile this antagonism. But as a consequence of the special character of this struggle, the harmonious reconciliation of the two opposite principles (species and individuality) takes place only for a small number of individuals, among whom this reconciliation is attained at the expense of the distortion, the degradation of the character of the human personality, and the disorganization of the social union.[55]

Society, in Tkachev's interpretation of Spencer, was indeed heading for disaster.

---

54. Ibid., pp. 155-56.
55. Ibid., p. 160.

Tkachev had a solution. Since the struggle for existence was not a perfecting process but a harmful one, it must be eliminated. Indeed its removal Tkachev saw as the first requisite of what he called social self-preservation, that is, the maintenance of species and individuality in some form of harmony. To eliminate the need for struggle while at the same time providing that subsistence essential to equilibrium he would ascertain that man's demands were fully met. He proposed a twofold operation: increase however possible the fund of foodstuffs and materials available to the human race and at the same time control and regulate human demands. Toward the first end, he had a comprehensive suggestion. It was sufficient, he said, "to unite people's individual forces into a collective force,"[56] a kind of social union of producers, dedicated to increasing material goods in an efficient labor combine. For controlling demand, he insisted on social regulation: an equable division of the means of subsistence and refusal to let any given individual have more than his share.

Did that not, however, emphasize the collective over the individual and in its own way restrict the development of individuality, of the human personality? As between collective despotism and individual freedom, principles that he viewed as irreconcilable, Tkachev clearly had made his choice. People say, he argued

that there will be no progress, that the individual not stimulated by struggle will not improve himself. But this is unjust. Controlling the development of individuality, society always can not only limit it but improve it. For the support of the improved individual, a large mass of means of subsistence is demanded—but this deficit is immediately equated by lowered fertility. The perfected individuality, in its turn, reveals itself not only in demanding more but also in producing more than before. Consequently lowered fertility will begin again to rise though it will not attain previous norms. Then society can provoke new improvement in the psychic organization of man, after which follows a new decline of fertility, then new increase in the means of subsistence, and so on. The species and the individuality will be constantly in a mobile equilibrium, and this will secure to society eternal progress, eternal improvement of individuality without the extinction of the race, without regress of fertility. The highest law of social self-preservation lies in this harmonious conciliation of the species with individuality by means of peaceful regulation of various things by the collective force of all and not by means of struggle of each with the other. With observance of this law, neither the fall of the social union nor the degeneration of individuality nor the extinction of the race is conceivable. On the contrary its inevitable consequences will be: the progress of society, the progress of individuality, the progress of the race.[57]

But this is just what Spencer sought. Spencer believed society could

<hr />

56. Ibid., p. 164.

57. Ibid., p. 165. Tkachev like Spencer viewed individuality and community as antagonistic principles; to others among his contemporaries (from Herzen to Mikhailovskii) they could in some wise be combined. See Walicki, p. 45.

reach biological equilibrium by itself, by its natural progression, through a process akin to the struggle for existence and survival of the fittest in nature. Tkachev was convinced Spencer's method would lead to disaster; although he did not say so outright, it called forth all the traits of contemporary man that Tkachev found most antipathetic. For struggle and competition Tkachev substituted a system of sharply controlled social equality more consistent with his own ideals. He accepted Spencer's premises and agreed with Spencer's aims. Only the process of moving from the one to the other evoked his irritation.

Clearly Tkachev appreciated Spencer's application of nature's laws to human society far more than he approved of Quinet's efforts along the same lines. Beyond a few flippant phrases he did not subject Spencer to the driving scorn he heaped upon Quinet. Gone was the sarcasm of his earlier review of Spencer's works. Perhaps in prison the young Russian had read Mikhailovskii, who was much intrigued by the Spencerian framework.[58] He may have become aware of the interest other contemporaries were demonstrating in the entire Spencerian concept of progress through increasing heterogeneity.[59] At any rate Tkachev swallowed much of Spencer's argument and adopted many of Spencer's analogies. The English "dilettante biologist" earned from Tkachev a degree of admiration the young Russian seldom expressed for anyone.

Not so another writer whose speculations on the nature of man and his society had left even more of a mark on Tkachev's contemporaries. P. L. Lavrov's definition of progress was indeed far from that of Herbert Spencer. The Russian mathematician-turned-sociologist viewed the world in a perspective contrary to that of the English sociologist dabbling in science. In his angry condemnations of Lavrov's ideas—condemnations that were to continue for a lifetime and dissolve their brief collaboration—Tkachev was demonstrating his affinity for the pseudoscientific method of Spencer as compared to the pseudophilosophical approach of his compatriot. He stood firm for the scientistic, realistic, materialist affirmations of his entire generation.

Lavrov's *Historical Letters* had exploded over Russia's radical youth like fireworks over a dark night. Published serially in 1868 and 1869 in the journal *Nedelia* (Week), where Tkachev certainly read them, the *Letters* became a sensation even before they appeared in book form in 1870. The time for a change in direction was ripe. Many of Russia's

58. James H. Billington, *Mikhailovsky and Russian Populism*, pp. 30 ff; Walicki, pp. 70-71. Like Tkachev, Mikhailovskii yielded to Spencer's constructions but disliked the concept of the struggle for survival as an automatic means to progress.

59. See for example Peter Lavrov, *Historical Letters*, trans. with an introduction and ed. James P. Scanlan, pp. 105-7.

young people, discouraged by the failure of their secret conspiracies, repulsed by an amoral Nechaev, sought spiritual regeneration along with new revolutionary methods.[60] Devoured avidly by radicals of all ages, the *Letters* turned the course of Russian thought in a new direction. Lavrov led his followers down a new path, and for a few years the quiet professor of mathematics was the idol of a large party among revolutionary youth.

Indeed Lavrov rejected many of the premises Tkachev and his generation had espoused. Turning away from Pisarev's mechanistic materialism he adopted what he called a subjective method, a method of evaluation based not on scientific objectivity but on morality and ethics, justice and humanitarianism. He wrote about good and evil rather than physics and physiology, denying that certain types of knowledge could ever be objective, insisting that men inserted their own ideals, their unconscious emotions into their pictures of the past and the future. He called for truth and justice as criteria in judgments even though truth might be variously interpreted by the judges. He was sure that human thought and will could effectively drive the wheels of history, taking his stand on the side of those who recognized progress as intellectual achievement and the accumulation of knowledge. Intellectual development provided him with the key to human history, and among intellectuals Lavrov isolated superior individuals, born and trained to think more critically than other men. These were his critically thinking individuals; he was sure they could become a social force. Lavrov's ideal was a rational civilization, and the youth of Russia saw itself in the role of critically thinking man. Thoughtful and speculative by nature, Lavrov inspired a revolutionary group that struggled to bring enlightenment to the peasantry, that attempted to educate the people toward that broad sociopolitical revolution he anticipated.[61] His stance against historical materialism and for the educated elite has led recent Marxist historians to judge his influence deleterious and the seventies a period of retrogression from the materialistic trends that went before.[62] Tkachev would surely have agreed.

In almost all these regards Tkachev bitterly took his stand against

---

60. On this point see Sokolov, pp. 79-81.

61. Walicki and other writers have called attention to the differences between Lavrov's views and those of Mikhailovskii; Walicki sees Lavrov as an enlightener and rationalist, Mikhailovskii as a more "backward-looking utopian in his image of the peasantry" (Walicki, pp. 31-35, 56-63, elsewhere).

62. See Kozmin, *Iz istorii*, pp. 682-700; Malinin in *Filosofiia revoliutsionnogo narodnichestva* calls the new outlook idealism coming into its own and terms the 1870s an epoch of reaction.

the older man. Doing so, as his own opponents later remarked, he maintained the stance of the sixties in the face of a new outlook. The mammoth article "What Is the Party of Progress?" written in September 1870 was his first effort to argue down Lavrov's views. It was never printed, but their continuing polemics reached scandalous public proportions in years to come.

The leading question that Lavrov's strange little book posed to Tkachev was the problem of what progress really meant. How is progress defined, he asked, or can it be defined at all? What is the party of progress, and of what should its program consist? Lavrov had insisted that progress could only be defined subjectively since the term involved highly personal concepts of good and bad. Tkachev was convinced that objective criteria might be set in defining the word and that progress could be mathematically measured by specific tests.[63]

The young critic was ready with his definition. The three elements of progress were movement, direction, and goal. Arbitrarily he insisted that the isolation of two of the three elements would provide a sufficient standard by which progress could be defined.

This analysis shows that the criterion for progress not only can but always must be objective, that in each order of phenomena thought of as progressive, there can be only *one* progress and *one* criterion for evaluating it, that this criterion is not *thought up* by man, that this progress is not created by the power of human *imagination*, but that one and the other are studied and revealed in the objective movement of observed phenomena.[64]

Tkachev began with nature; his study of Spencer stood him in good stead. The English sociologist had defined progress in the animal world, and the Russian radical applauded. The Spencerian criteria for evaluating natural progress—the increasing complexity and heterogeneity of organisms—Tkachev found to be objective and scientific, not merely the opinion of their author, but premised on empirically observed fact. Movement and its direction were clear. Life, Tkachev pompously pronounced, was progress; death was stagnation.[65] The growth of the organism from simple embryo to fetus to newborn to complex maturity clearly epitomized nature's direction in all organisms. However, progress implied a goal, as Tkachev and Lavrov agreed; but could a goal be imputed to nature? Lavrov had said no; in his Quinet review Tkachev had agreed. But now he reversed himself. Man had long labored under anthropomorphic delusions concerning nature. But once

---

63. Tkachev, 2: 171-72.
64. Ibid., p. 180.
65. Ibid., p. 187.

this humanizing of the inhuman was discarded by more sophisticated thinkers, the goal of nature—while man could never understand it— could be deduced from the movement of nature itself. Tkachev was certain

that a subjective measurement of progress could exist only until the human mind emerged from the immature anthropomorphic period of thinking, only while it conceived the idea of goal in general (of this essential, immutable element of the concept of progress) as endowed with the attributes of *human goal*, created and defined by a moving or changing object. But once the human mind has emerged from this immature period of thought, it does not imagine and does not attribute to nature its own goals but seeks them in the very process of change of the phenomena. . . . The idea of progress proposes evaluation of a given movement from the point of view of the goal of the movement itself, and not from the point of view of goals outside the observed movement, and not from the point of view of the moral or any kind of subjective ideals of the observer.[66]

Spencer's objective, careful, scientific methods represented his greatest contribution to modern thought, Tkachev wrote, and from his conclusions the existence of goals in nature could be deduced. Where Spencer went wrong was not in imputing progress to nature but rather in assuming that the same type of movement (from uniformity to differentiation) was common to man and animal, to society and organisms.

But what about man's progress: could it so readily be defined? Lavrov claimed that no absolute definition could exist, that each man projected his own meaning into progress, based on his own conceptions of where the world should be going. Lavrov found Spencer (along with most historians and scholars) to be subjective in setting the goal of human happiness as a criterion for progress. Indeed the Russian scholar himself had espoused the utilitarian ethic and saw nothing wrong with such subjectivity.[67] Although Tkachev agreed that the concept of happiness necessarily depended on subjective criteria, he was certain that a better definition of progress could be formulated.

We know there is movement in history, Tkachev wrote, and virtually let it go at that. Direction he found harder to determine, and he admitted that historical investigators did not agree as to its nature. Most modern thinkers clung to the optimistic hope that history was traveling in a straight line toward a better future. Others sensed some sort of rhythmic movement. Tkachev himself felt that the facts spoke more for cyclical development than for any other pattern.[68] At any

---

66. Ibid., p. 180.
67. Lavrov, *Historical Letters*, pp. 11-16.
68. Tkachev, 2: 190-91; Malinin seems wrong in including Tkachev among those who criticized this cyclical theory of development as espoused by Vico and Machiavelli. See Malinin, p. 220.

rate, clear conclusions as the to nature of history's direction were impossible to reach.

If some movement was certain but its direction remained unclear, could an absolute, objective goal for human society be determined? Tkachev was certain it could. Everyone agreed that society's goal should be man's happiness, but he out-of-hand rejected that utilitarian concept as too subjective, too varied, and incapable of objective scientific analysis, a pragmatic reason indeed for disqualifying a concept so substantive. For the same reason—for its indefiniteness and subjectivity —Tkachev declined to countenance the goals that seemed imperative to Lavrov: the development of the individual personality, physically, intellectually, and morally; the fulfillment of social justice and truth.

Tkachev's own definition of progress lay rather in his familiar materialistic concept of society's goals. Each human being, attempting to satisfy his needs just as the organism seeks to fulfill its demands in nature, should have whatever was necessary for his satisfaction. Attaining such universal fulfillment of physical demands was clearly the goal of the social complex. Tkachev coupled to it the same stipulation he advanced in his article on Spencer and insisted that demand must be controlled so that each individual's needs might become the same as everyone else's; so that nobody might become richer than anyone else; so that all men's physical and psychic organisms would seek and receive exactly the same fulfillment.[69] Society must insist on social unity, on the complete harmony of equal individual interests. It would be difficult to attain: "Perhaps to attain such full unity of life's goals never will be possible, but it is always possible to draw somewhat near it. The status of this rapprochement should serve *in one regard* as a measure of historical progress."[70]

Harmonizing and equalizing individual interests, society would regulate the balance between fertility and individuality that Spencer had taught Tkachev to respect.

Society can only *fully* attain its goals when it: first, unites the life goals of all its members, that is, sets them in completely identical conditions of nourishment and further activity, reduces to one social denominator, to one common level, all the chaotic divergencies of individualities produced by regressive historical movement; secondly, [when it will] bring means into harmony with demands, that is, will develop in its members only those demands that can be satisfied by the given productivity of labor or can directly increase this productivity or lower the expenditure for support and development of individuality; and thirdly, when the greatest possible level of satisfaction will be guaranteed for all demands of everyone in equal

69. Tkachev, 2: 204.
70. Ibid.

measure (we say greatest possible level because the establishment of absolute harmony of means with demands is an ideal scarcely attainable).[71]

The equality Tkachev demanded far outstripped the juridical and economic equality he earlier emphasized; now he was insisting that equality of all men be "organic, physiological, conditioned by similarity of nourishment and communality of conditions of life."[72] He allowed no room for different expenditures of energy, for bulk, for age, much less for personality, occupation, or incentive. Indeed, in Tkachev's ideal society individuals were to be reduced to a fearful stage of absolute identity, each resembling the other in feature and form, each subsisting as the other, each bound to each in a collective that would come to dominate to the point of exterminating differences and regulating all individual demand. Nothing, of course, could be further from Lavrov's concept of society's goals as the multiform extension of truth, justice, and the human personality. No idea could be less compatible with the new tendency in radical thought to emphasize the individual, the subjective, the moral, and thoughtful nature of man.

By Tkachev's distinctive definition history again had not been progressive but regressive.[73] The centuries had increased rather than mitigated the differences between individuals. Primitive men were closer to each other and to Tkachev's ideal social equality than were modern capitalists. Savages were lucky: today the miserable poor were forced to stand apart and watch the opulent rich drink champagne. The only class of society Tkachev thought had steadily progressed was a tiny group of individuals, a miniscule educated minority that persisted in believing itself the salt of the earth, the key to man's progress. But its existence increased inequality by raising consumption for its own individuality; its formulae for man's goals were indefinite and vague; it refused even to give a name to the progressist banner it pretended to raise. Tkachev must have meant Lavrov himself.[74]

What, then, should be the program of a party of progress? To Tkachev the lines were clearly drawn. Such a party should support all measures that tended to harmonize society's demands with the means for satisfying them; support all institutions that strove to equalize individuals; and support what he called collective rights over private rights, phraseology drawn from his legal days.[75] It should aid "negative-progressive" elements, such as proletarian organizations or societies

---

71. Ibid., pp. 205-6.
72. Ibid., p. 207.
73. Ibid., p. 204.
74. Ibid., pp. 217-20.
75. Ibid., pp. 208-9.

for popular education. It should combat to the death anything that accentuated the difference between groups or individuals, such "positive-regressive" functions as class-restricted educational opportunities.[76]

Tkachev ended with a warning to his readers. It was easy, he told them, to set time as a criterion, to be convinced that progress must have occurred simply because yesterday is past and today is present and the future is yet to come. Thus developing forms may seem progressive for their time but prove regressive on more careful analysis. Tkachev disagreed with Lavrov when the latter contended that elements once progressive could become harmful with the centuries (family, nationality, church, and state); rather he insisted on judging them permanently regressive on the basis of their eventual evil effect. The reader should beware and apply criteria with care. Nor should he seek laws of direction in history (they will lead him to fatalism) or specific goals in nature (teleological naturalism).[77] He must, indeed, not confuse natural progress with social progress, which in turn differs from the isolated progress of a handful of individuals. Each merited its own careful analysis on the basis of motion, direction, and goal.

For all its familiar demand for equality, its mistrust of intellectualism, and its pessimism about man's historical development, Tkachev's article on the *Historical Letters* stands unique among his early works. The vehemence of his reaction against Lavrov drove him to upend several of his own previous commitments, seemingly for the sake of battle. Arguing furiously with his opponent, he was willing to compromise himself. In opposing Lavrov, Tkachev became truly a polemicist.

For in many ways Tkachev did not really disagree with Lavrov's premises in spite of what he wrote. Lavrov thought too that natural sciences were less important than sociology,[78] that man's deeds must be subjected to judgment and not viewed with objective impartiality like the process of nature,[79] that little progress had actually been made throughout history, and that at a terrible cost,[80] that men's "grinding concern for their daily bread" inhibited their other potentially constructive activities.[81] It was Lavrov's contention that objectivity in evaluation was impossible to come by, that men judged on the basis of preconceived notions, that truth itself was difficult to define.[82] Tkachev

---

76. Ibid., pp. 210-12.
77. Ibid., p. 197.
78. Lavrov, *Historical Letters*, First Letter.
79. Ibid., pp. 85, 101.
80. Ibid., Fourth Letter.
81. Ibid., p. 120.
82. Ibid., p. 101.

had often written in a similar vein, deploring the abstract absolutes of
idealists and insisting that man made his judgments in a strictly environmental context. Attacking Lavrov, he changed his mind: now he
asserted that there were absolute, unconditional, and immutable criteria
for identifying truth.

> . . . and such a criterion there is, and this is not a phantom, not a dream, this
> criterion is *palpability* [*ochevidnost*], not in that vulgar meaning of the word in
> which it is often used in common life, meaning simple subjective belief in the
> correctness, that is, in the truth of this or that—but in that more exact sense by
> which *palpable* means something that each subject—whatever its general personal
> outlook—considers for itself unconditionally convincing, that is, true. The identity
> of our physical and consequently also psychic organization makes possible the
> existence of such *somethings*. These *somethings* we have a right to consider true
> *unto themselves* because they are true not only for me or for you but for all people
> in general.[83]

The argument is a mixture of absolute and relative definitions, an
argument extraordinary for Tkachev. He seems to be saying that men,
somehow freed from environmental differences, share such an intuitive
sense of "palpability" as to permit the definition of truth on the basis
of their common conviction. He went further, insisting that men could
rise above themselves to construct a *Weltanschauung* valid in time and
space, infallible, and objective. Through such an objective view of the
world must history be evaluated. Indeed if it could not, if the march of
history (which he once said was sparked by freak and accident) had no
timeless significance, then life itself was inconceivable.[84] If Lavrov
could not find universal, constant, and objective criteria for evaluating
progress, then he was "playing with words and playing a dangerous
game besides."[85]

For all the impression that Marx left on this young Russian critic,
it was not Marx who altered his approach. Tkachev read *Capital* for its
critique of Western society, finding there a stunning verification of his
own dislike of the competitive ethics and impoverishing economics of
the capitalist system. Like many of his contemporaries he did not
immediately glean the significance of Marx's historical determinism as it
was expressed briefly here and there in the first German edition of the
book.[86] He did not comment on the revolutionary potential, or lack of

83. Tkachev, 2: 173-74; in some ways this corresponds with the leap into faith
suggested by Lavrov's Fifteenth Letter.
84. Tkachev, 2: 185-86.
85. Ibid., p. 173.
86. In the preface to *Capital* Marx speaks of the "natural laws of capitalist
production" and the "tendencies working with iron necessity towards inevitable
results." "The country that is more developed industrially," he writes, "only shows

it in Russia, that such determinism suggested. He recognized that later when he went to Europe, discovered more about Marx, and reacted negatively.[87] Meanwhile he used Marx's work as a statistical compilation to re-enforce his vision of Western misery.

Instead it was Spencer who turned the tide. Tkachev was impressed as never before with the closeness of science and society. He accepted Spencer's analysis of social patterns, proposing only a few variations and some hopes for avoiding their destructive course. Spencer's pseudo-scientific approach—that objectivity that the keener Lavrov called subjective—Tkachev obviously condoned. Spencer led him closer to the scientific method, to science's analogies, and science's conclusions. He used Spencer's methods to attack Lavrov. Even utilitarianism was unacceptable. It was simply not scientific and objective enough; its goals could not be dissected or defined by scientific means.

Tkachev's objection to Lavrov began with his instinctive dislike of Lavrov's unscientific subjectivism. Lavrov wanted to talk philosophy; that was foreign to Tkachev and to his contemporaries of the 1860s. He detested the Kantian overtones of Lavrov's plea for the primacy of morality in a suffering world. Lavrov's elitist intellectual attitudes were apparent to all his readers and infuriating to Tkachev, who had always disliked effete intellectualism. The terrible cost of intellectual progress to the common man was a theme Tkachev had himself explored; Lavrov thought progress was worth it, and Tkachev did not.

But Tkachev had another clear motive in attacking the older man. Anticipating the conclusions of Soviet scholars, he was afraid that Lavrov's moral subjectivism coupled with the careful development of critical thought would lead young Russians away from their immediate revolutionary tasks. The rationalist, intellectual development Lavrov sought impressed the impatient Tkachev with its overtones of cautious education and slow enlightenment. Lavrov himself had expressed similar fear although he attempted to disprove it and to set forth his own concern for vigorous, positive action. Tkachev was not deceived. And if subjectivism led away from activism. if it threatened to return

---

to the less developed the image of its own future" (*Capital*, p. 13). Resis, p. 236, points out that the revolutionary implications of the book were lost on many Russian readers who had voluntarist views on social change. They could not accept Marxist determinism and until the 1880s did not view Marx as applying to Russia at all; for this reason the censor permitted the publication of *Capital* in 1872. Walicki, pp. 137-38, agrees, adding that the populists could not accept Marx's view of capitalism as progressive; they accepted only his statistics on capitalism's cruelty.

87. Tkachev's polemics with Marx and Engels are discussed in chaps. 9 and 12 below. See also my article "Tkachev and the Marxists."

Russia to the path of Herzen and his generation, Tkachev automatically stood opposed.

On a more positive scale Tkachev gained a great deal from his prison encounters. He had known the evils of Western society, but with the aid of Marx he now set them in their place. There was obviously no progress under capitalism; society had regressed from earlier times. What the bourgeoisie called freedom was a sham, and the total freedom it hoped for was dangerous. Society ran the risk of subjecting its poor to infinite misery, even—as Tkachev read from Spencer—of reducing them to the status of vast, buzzing clouds of stunted fruitflies. Not even Lavrov's critically thinking individuals could avoid a dreadful fate, for their cry for individualism would destroy anything like morality and the social conscience.

For the first time in print Tkachev proposed his own solution. In opposition to most of his comrades, he concluded that equality must be the driving principle of the future; that to avoid the doom he read in Spencer, man must be forced into a status no higher than that of his fellow man so his needs could be defined by those of his neighbors. The state emerged in Tkachev's writings as a tool whereby the poor might better themselves and the rich might be forced to descend to the level of the poor. Tkachev saw in anarchism not freedom but cruelty: the epitome of competition and the abandonment of the needy to fend for themselves. His proposition of a collective despotism he thought would ensure security and perhaps even happiness to the weak. The abdication of the state from its responsibilities could only justly occur when men had been forced into rigid equality. Only equality could provide the basis for social harmony and eliminate that vicious competitive struggle Spencer postulated as inevitable. But Lavrov's critically thinking man and Mikhailovskii's creative personality would have to become universal or not exist at all. Tkachev could not spare them the privilege they demanded at the expense of the productive worker.

To some extent Tkachev's proposals reflected his early distrust of the superintellectual who thought human history revolved around himself as an individual. Beyond that they foretold his later plans for a violently enforced dictatorship that would bring about social revolution.

9

Lavrov and Engels

The year 1873 marked a giant change in the life of Petr Tkachev and opened for him opportunities that had never existed before. Had he not emigrated from Russia his name might never have been recorded in history as a synonym for revolutionary Jacobinism, as it was often called, and he might never have taken his place alongside Lavrov and Bakunin as a major theorist of revolutionary action. Breathing the freer air of those very nations whose social and economic institutions he purported to despise, he could finally put pen to paper without inhibition and produce plans that had heretofore been confined to dreams and intimations. In 1873 and 1874 he made contact with the Russian émigré colonies in Switzerland and London as well as with the European radicals whom he had known through the underground grapevine in his homeland. If he found enemies, he found friends too; they all led him to formulate his own revolutionary plans. Between 1873 and the last months of 1875 when he started his own journal with a group of émigrés in Geneva, Tkachev once and for all set forth the plans for revolution for which he was known and remembered. For the young Russian revolutionary, not yet thirty, these were crucial years indeed.

The first step was to get out of prison. Some time late in 1872, having served out his sentence, Tkachev was released and sent into administrative exile (that is, exile imposed upon him by police officials rather than by the courts of law) in his home village near Velikie Luki. Within a few months he was joined there by Dementeva who had been

186

released from prison a year earlier and whose own sentence in exile expired in January 1873. For almost a year the two of them lived together, apparently on the family estates.

Dementeva had come into her own and into the public eye. The daring of her actions in 1869 and the courage of her testimony during the trial of Nechaevists gave her some notoriety. After she had completed the four-month prison term imposed by the court—a term served by the young girl in the Litovsk fortress—Dementeva had been sent into exile in Nizhni-Novgorod by administrative order. The action of the Third Section in commanding her to further grief after her legal atonement for her crime was condemned in the diary of A. V. Nikitenko, one-time censor for the tsar and Russia's nineteenth-century Pepys. To Nikitenko the extra sentence stood in violation of the Russian system of justice. He testified to Dementeva's charm and reputation.

By the testimony of prison guards she conducted herself in exemplary fashion, and generally this girl is beautiful unto herself—beautifully educated, gentle, and in general of orderly behavior. At the time of the trial itself, she moved everyone to sympathy with her. It would seem that, having undergone the punishment set for her, she should by now be purged and be set free.[1]

Obviously a woman of strong convictions, Dementeva was not about to retire to a life of embroidery, wherever she was sent. The "Center for Readings in Socialism" that she set up in her rooms in Nizhni-Novgorod came to the attention of the police.[2] In the autumn of 1872 she was transferred to the quieter city of Kaluga where again her quarters became a rallying place for the young intelligentsia. Fortunately N. V. Shelgunov, the radical writer and critic long associated with Blagosvetlov, was in exile there too. He and his wife became Dementeva's closest friends.[3] When she was released from her exile and left Kaluga to return to Velikie Luki and Tkachev, she left the Shelgunovs a romantic note, surely part of the reason that an admiring Kozmin saw in her the reincarnation of Vera Pavlovna, Chernyshevskii's heroine in *What Is to Be Done?*

Wherever I am, whatever happens to me, one memory of you will remind me how one should love all the downtrodden and humiliated, the poor and the hungry. To

1. Aleksandr Vasilevich Nikitenko, *Zapiski i dnevnik*, 2: 448.
2. These and following facts about Dementeva's career are taken from Kozmin's biographical article, "Okolo nechaevskogo dela."
3. M. L. N——n, "N. V. Shelgunov v Kaluge: Po neizdannym dokumentum," *Golos minuvshego*, no. 11 (1915), pp. 261-62; N. V. Shelgunov, L. P. Shelgunov, M. L. Mikhailov, *Vospominaniia*, 2: 225-30.

the battle for them I will give my whole life, my freedom, my personal joys, but if nevertheless I am not able to do anything for them, do not abandon me with words too cruel; I wish for much, but perhaps my ability will not suffice.[4]

In the village Tkachev and Dementeva lived a quiet and isolated life for almost a year. It is possible (but not likely) that they were married; Kozmin was unable to find any confirming evidence, and Dementeva kept her own, not Tkachev's, name. Tkachev was writing again. Even before his final release from prison the authorities had relented and permitted him to publish; half a dozen of his critical reviews had appeared in the *Cause* in 1872 although they were printed over pseudonyms. In 1873 between January and October he published in almost every issue of that journal.[5] It was not unusual for him to have several long articles appearing in serial form at the same time.

Whatever his sufferings in prison Tkachev's psyche had borne the blows more stalwartly than Pisarev's. After four long years behind bars he did not emerge emasculated or afraid. But time had not stood still. Plunging again into the protestations and polemics of the St. Petersburg journals, Tkachev must have been aware that a change of direction had occurred in Russian radical thought. He was out of step with the new trend. He disliked it from the beginning; he continued to dislike it for the rest of his life.

Populism has proved impossible clearly to define for people who embraced its causes and for historians looking back at them. The controversy over definition has led scholars to include under the populist rubric a panorama of thinkers ranging in time from Herzen to Victor Chernov, in belief from Pisarev to Sofia Perovskaia.[6] Nor can the essence of populism be isolated at any given moment in time, for each of its leaders held a set of beliefs different from each of the others. N. K. Mikhailovskii, whose populism has been considered classic or pure,[7] believed in the power and intuition of the peasantry. His genre of populism took a romantic line.

Oh, if I could drown in that grey rough mass of the people, dissolve irrevocably, preserving only that spark of truth and ideal which I succeeded in acquiring for the sake of that same people. Oh, if only all of you readers were to come to the same decision, especially those whose light burned brighter than mine and without soot. What a great illumination there would be, and what a great historical occasion it would make, unparalleled in history![8]

---

4. Shelgunov, Shelgunov, and Mikhailov, 2: 483; cf. Kozmin, "Okolo nechaevskogo dela," p. 57.
5. See the listing in Tkachev, 4: 452.
6. See the discussion below, pp. 307-8.
7. Cf. Walicki, pp. 26-27.
8. Quoted in Billington, p. 94. Richard Pipes, "*Narodnichestvo:* A Semantic

Lavrov's populism, based on the spread of knowledge and propaganda by critically thinking individuals, was more rational; Lavrov has been called an enlightener.[9] To Marxist scholars both new leaders have seemed to represent a step backward: Mikhailovskii for his hopes of returning to a simple preindustrial life, Lavrov for his interpretation of history in subjective terms and his call for a Kantian moral imperative. The young men of 1870 followed eagerly along. Tkachev was an exception. He detested Lavrov for his ivory-tower elitist intellectualism and Mikhailovskii for his idolization of the anti-intellectual simple country rube. It must have hurt Tkachev to watch the journal of populism, *Fatherland Notes*, overtake and surpass Blagosvetlov's *Cause* in popularity with the younger generation.[10]

A change in popular sentiment occurred too in regard to revolutionary methods. Perhaps in reaction against Nechaev the young generation abandoned those secret conspiracies that Tkachev admired, that Ogarev once condoned, and to which Chernyshevskii may have belonged. They spoke now of education and propaganda that could in the long run inspire the peasant to act on his own. To the new generation the greatest task was (as Lavrov had suggested) to prepare themselves first so that they might slowly spread knowledge about them. Educational circles, distributing legal and illegal books, took the place of conspiratorial plotting; immediate revolution was abandoned for propaganda among the peasantry.[11] The change from political action to social, from revolution to enlightenment, from action to propaganda was apparent even to men who were involved themselves.[12] Tkachev was not imperceptive in his own later analysis; he once referred to himself as a man of the old (conspiratorial) style as compared to the propagandists of the new.[13]

Inquiry," *Slavic Review* 23, no. 3 (September 1964): 458, defines one era of populism by this kind of effort to submerge the intellectual into the peasant tradition.

9. Walicki, pp. 34-35. Walicki presents a detailed analysis of the many differences among populist leaders (including Lavrov, Mikhailovskii, Bakunin, and Tkachev) on important issues. For another excellent treatment see N. V. Briullova-Shaskolskaia, "Lavrov i Mikhailovskii," published in the collection *P. L. Lavrov: Stati, vospominaniia, materialy* (Petrograd, 1922), pp. 404-19.

10. Sokolov, pp. 104-5.

11. The most famous among these circles is the Chaikovskii group. See note 17 below.

12. One of the best contemporary summaries of the Russian revolutionary movement was written by A. Kh. Khristoforov in the Bakuninist journal *Obshchee delo* in 1886; he clearly distinguished the old forms from the new. This article was reprinted by Lemke in "Materialy dlia biografii P. N. Tkacheva," pp. 156-72; the author of the unsigned article was identified by Kozmin in Tkachev, 3: 462 (note 59).

13. Tkachev, 3: 403; Lemke, "Materialy dlia biografii," pp. 166-67.

In the polemics that arose between them, Lavrov represented the ideas of the seventies and Tkachev stood for those of the preceding decade. Kozmin's interpretation that Lavrov represented the old gentry intelligentsia and Tkachev the new *raznochintsy* does not explain Lavrov's popularity among the *raznochintsy* after 1868. Other Marxist scholars disagree with Kozmin.[14] But clearly Tkachev was out of step. Lavrov, the older man, represented the new; Tkachev, the younger, stood for the old. *Historical Letters*, which Tkachev had so violently attacked in his unpublished review, led the way to a change of mood.

In 1870 Lavrov fled to Europe, invited to Paris by Herzen who died, however, before his guest's arrival.[15] Moderate by nature, the one-time mathematician found his views shifting rapidly to the left during the Paris Commune. He offered his enthusiastic aid to the young government and actually journeyed to Brussels and London in a futile search for outside support. After the defeat of the Commune, he found his way to Zurich, a center for Russian exiles. The loss of Paris had discouraged and depressed him, much as the French revolution twenty-three years before had affected Herzen. The Bakuninist colony at first welcomed Lavrov and offered collaboration, but their master was indignant at Lavrov's cautious approach to revolution, his intellectual-ism, and perhaps his neo-Kantian moral code.[16]

Lavrov was not long isolated. He was soon contacted in Zurich by a delegation from the Chaikovskii Circle, that most famous of propagandist and teaching circles that shared Lavrov's hopes of creating a critically thinking intelligentsia and claimed as associates such young Russian radicals as Dmitrii Klements, Sergei Kravchinskii, the youthful Plekhanov, and the scientist N. M. Morozov.[17]

14. Kozmin's provocative analysis of the Tkachev-Lavrov polemic in terms of attitudes, backgrounds, and personalities may be found in "Tkachev i Lavrov: Stolknovenie dvukh techenii russkoi revoliutsionnoi mysli 70-kh godov," published in the collection of his articles entitled *Ot deviatnadtsatogo fevralia k pervomu marta*, pp. 107-58. Cf. Boris Sammilevich Itenberg, *Dvizhenie revoliutsionnogo narodnichestva*, p. 211.

15. The following biographical material is drawn from Scanlan's introduction to Lavrov's *Historical Letters*.

16. This episode is described in Mikhail Bakunin, *Gosudarstvennost i anarkhii, 1873*, vol. 3 of the *Archives Bakounine*, in the introductory essay by Arthur Lehning, pp. xv-xviii. See also Zemfir Ralli-Arbore, "Mikhail Aleksandrovich Bakunin: Iz moikh vospominanii," *Minuvshie gody*, no. 10 (1908), pp. 142-69.

17. There are many good studies of the Chaikovskii Circle; one interesting volume is Nikolai Alekseevich Troitskii's *Bolshoe obshchestvo propagandy 1871-1874 gg.: Tak nazyvaemye chaikovtsy*. The *Chaikovtsy* began as a group dedicated to enlightenment; they printed and distributed literature for the use of intelligentsia circles. Later they changed to become propagandists among the workers and

The *Chaikovtsy* suggested that Lavrov found an émigré journal devoted to the revolutionary hopes of Russia's new generation, a journal printed in the free air of Switzerland that might (like Herzen's famous *Bell*) be smuggled back to Russia for illegal distribution. The result was *Vpered!* (Forward!), which became a well-known Russian émigré publication in its time.

Efforts at involving the Bakuninists were doomed to failure once Lavrov showed them his editorial program.[18] Undaunted, Lavrov with the encouragement of his Russian friends published the first issue in Zurich on August 1, 1873, and therein printed his plan for revolution. Leaving aside its "cry from afar" approach ("We are everywhere: in the circle of emigrants, torn from their motherland . . . in the ravaged village, in the sunny provincial town, in the bazaar, the fair, the metropolitan square. . . . We are far from you, we are among you. . . ."),[19] the program clearly represented revolutionary gradualism. Lavrov envisaged a long period of preparation before successful revolution became possible; from his later writings it is clear that he believed unpreparedness to have caused the downfall of the Paris Commune. Furthermore he was certain that only history itself could finally set the proper hour and call forth the great human effort. No use, he believed, in making a revolution at the wrong historical moment and thereafter watching it inevitably fail. Men must wait on history, but in the meantime each educated young Russian should read and study and, when he was ready, propagandize among the people: "To prepare the success of the popular revolution when it becomes necessary, when it is called forth by the course of historical events and the actions of the government—such is the first goal of activity."[20]

Some of Lavrov's own ardent followers found the journal inspiring. For more radical Russians the process of waiting for history was not good enough. Indeed, *Forward!* (for all its immediate readership) did not mark an upsurge in Lavrov's popularity and influence but rather the opposite; his following shortly disintegrated, discouraged by their leader's attitude and bewildered by their inability to follow his advice.

---

peasants. See Martin A. Miller, "Ideological Conflicts in Russian Populism: The Revolutionary Manifestoes of the Chaikovsky Circle, 1869-1874," *Slavic Review* 29, no. 1 (March 1970): 1-21.

18. Bakunin, *Gosudarstvennost i anarkhii*, p. xvi; the Bakuninists eventually made some reluctant overtures, but Lavrov was wise enough to proceed on his own.

19. Petr Lavrovich Lavrov, *Izbrannye sochineniia na sotsialno-politicheskie temy*, 2:22.

20. Ibid., pp. 35-36.

In Zurich the Bakuninists expressed such hostility that Lavrov soon came to lock his shutters at night in fear of assassination.[21] Among his *Chaikovtsy* supporters the reaction to his program was one of great disappointment. "Why should we have a *Vestnik Evropa* [Messenger of Europe, one of Russia's leading moderate-liberal journals] abroad when it already exists in Petersburg?" one of them is reported to have asked.[22] .Immediate measures were undertaken to strengthen the journal's policy. Probably on his own initiative Lavrov invited Mikhailovskii to join him on *Forward!*, but Mikhailovskii (associated with the legal journal *Fatherland Notes*) refused.[23] The *Chaikovtsy* sent one of their members, a young man named M. V. Kuprianov, to Zurich to negotiate with Lavrov in the autumn of 1873.[24] Probably exceeding the authority delegated to him, Kuprianov returned to Russia and went straight to Velikie Luki. There in great secrecy he persuaded Tkachev—whose reputation as a critic on *Russian Word* still stood him in good stead with the young revolutionaries—to travel to Switzerland and to join Lavrov on *Forward!*'s editorial staff.

In his own later words Lavrov welcomed "with pleasure the collaboration of this talented writer."[25] In the second (autumn) issue of *Forward!* he officially announced the association and printed a letter written by Tkachev (although not identified with his name) entitled simply "From Velikie Luki";[26] a more alert secret police might indeed have foreseen Tkachev's escape. The letter must have pleased the Chaikovskii group, for it set a far more activist tone than did Lavrov's original program. Concerned with the state's less than feeble efforts to solve the peasant problem, Tkachev saw a crisis developing in which the police were acting like incompetent fools. "Young people from among the educated classes are trying to draw close to the simple people," he wrote, anticipating the mass movement to the peasantry in

21. Lavrov, *Historical Letters*, p. 53.
22. Quoted in Itenberg, *Dvizhenie revoliutsionnogo narodnichestva*, p. 202.
23. Ibid., pp. 202-3.
24. B. Nikolaevskii, "Materialy i dokumenty: Tkachev i Lavrov," *Na chuzhoi storone*, no. 10 (1925), pp. 187-88. The Chaikovskii Circle, arguing between Lavrov's enlightenment and Bakunin's propagandizing, decided to send a delegate to Switzerland to consult with both revolutionary leaders. Owing to his neutrality, Klements was selected. But instead, for reasons that are uncertain, Kuprianov made the trip. He never even saw the Bakuninists; he only went to Lavrov with whom he made an agreement about distributing *Vpered!* in Russia. His trip to Velikie Luki and the hiring of Tkachev may thus have been at Lavrov's instigation. See Miller, "Ideological Conflicts," p. 14.
25. Petr Lavrovich Lavrov, *Narodniki-propagandisty 1873-1878 gg.*, pp. 74-75.
26. Ibid., p. 75; Tkachev, 3: 49-54.

the summer of 1874, "and with this aim [they] join the workers in the factories, the workers' artels, the local clerks, and so on."[27] The result was the throne's loss not only of its control but its convictions. The state was weakening, Tkachev was sure.

Now the youth must become conscious of his strength. Police persecutions and administrative pursuit must not deter him; on the contrary, they must hearten and renew him; above all the cowardly quaverings of tsarism, growing senile, are clearly expressed in them. This is the swan song. . . . The government itself has recognized that the soil is prepared . . . it is fertilized by century-long sufferings of the people, it is watered by [the people's] blood, sweat, and tears. The seed sown into it will not die; only sowers are needed. Let them get quickly to work. Now their labor will not be in vain—all promises an abundant harvest! It is only necessary not to let the propitious moment escape.[28]

If Lavrov's propitious moment was always somehow around the corner, awaiting the call of history, Tkachev's equally clearly was always now.

In December 1873 Tkachev made good his word. In the company of Kuprianov and several others, he left Russia never to return. Details of the journey are lacking. Tkachev had a propensity for secrecy and never did record his personal reactions and emotions. He did not even tell Dementeva of his plans. Once he was safely across the border, he wrote her a note from Königsberg, apologetic and guilty in tone, afraid perhaps that she would resent his lack of confidence. He suggested that some day she might join him.[29] In 1879 after much red tape and many interviews, Dementeva received official permission to leave Russia, only on the condition that she would promise never to return. Tkachev's revolutionary work was nearly done when the lovers were reunited in Geneva.[30] Dementeva's earlier influence might have earned them a warmer place among the considerable colony of émigrés (French, Russian, and Polish) who sought shelter there.

Tkachev's motives in accepting the offer to work with Lavrov have remained a mystery to historians. His hostility toward the older man, clearly expressed in his vituperative unpublished review of the *Historical Letters*, casts doubt on the sincerity of his proposed collaboration.

---

27. Tkachev, 3: 52.

28. Ibid., p. 54.

29. This letter has been reprinted (in photocopy) in Weeks, *First Bolshevik*, following p. 166. Weeks was unaware that Dementeva actually did join Tkachev some time later. One of Tkachev's early colleagues in the Russian legal press had actually commented on Tkachev's propensity to keep things to himself (Suvorov, "Zapiski o proshlom," p. 144).

30. The date is confirmed in Kozmin, *Nechaev i nechaevtsy*, p. 201. Dementeva later told Kozmin that this was the happiest period of her life (Kozmin, "Okolo nechaevskogo dela," p. 62).

He may somehow have thought he could change Lavrov's views. It is more likely that he hoped *Forward!* would become a sounding board for his own opinions.[31] One Soviet historian suggests that much of the move can be credited to Kuprianov, who was an unusually persuasive young man.[32] Tkachev's own dislike of Velikie Luki suggests the possibility that he was so glad to leave that little persuasion was necessary; he may long have dreamed of the time when he could circulate freely among the cosmopolitans of Europe and put pen to paper with a freedom his homeland would never allow. J. M. Meijer has suggested that Tkachev was still uncertain of his own mind, that the young Russian was not only willing to explore Lavrov's revolutionary philosophy, but that shortly after he arrived in Switzerland he visited Bakunin (then in Italy) supposedly for a firsthand account of the old anarchist's path to revolt.[33] Evidence of the Bakunin interview (supposedly at Locarno, December 1873) does not come from Bakunin himself but from a statement made orally by the unreliable Ralli-Arbore to a Bakunin biographer; Ralli-Arbore's closeness to Bakunin at the time is debatable, owing to the latter's animosity towards Ralli-Arbore's friend Nechaev.[34] Surely Tkachev admired Bakunin, but his own viewpoints had long led him in another direction. It is unlikely that he came to Europe to shop around.

As for Tkackev himself he claimed he agreed to collaborate with Lavrov purely out of altruistic concern for the Russian revolutionary movement. He was aware of the attacks on the first issue of *Forward!*, he later reported, and feared that the journal would collapse—or that if it continued, it would not truly represent the views of the young revolutionaries and would lead to drastic schisms in their ranks. He claimed to respect the editor's literary talent and his vast knowledge of mathematics, philosophy, and history, but he thought Lavrov ill informed "in the area of those practical questions, those vital interests that concern and motivate our youth."[35] "I considered it my obligation to accept the invitation extended to me," he wrote, "to leave exile, and

---

31. This was suggested later by Khristoforov in the obituary republished by Lemke, "Materialy dlia biografii," p. 163.

32. Nikolaevskii, "Materialy i dokumenty," pp. 187-88.

33. Meijer, *Knowledge and Revolution*, pp. 149-50. Ralli-Arbore's actual words to Nettlau suggested that it was Tkachev who was trying to convert his older colleague. Bakunin would hear nothing of it (Max Nettlau, *The Life of Michael Bakounine*, vol. 3, pt. 2, note 2719-56).

34. Ralli-Arbore was not welcomed by Bakunin because of his association with Nechaev, with whom the older revolutionary had just painfully broken his connections (Lehning, *Michel Bakounine*, p. lxiv).

35. Tkachev, 3: 56.

to enter into direct relationship with the editorship of *Forward!* "[36]
Such altruism is only part of the story. More logical is the theory
that Tkachev was bored and irritated in his isolated life and that he had
secret hopes of making Lavrov's journal into a vehicle for his own ideas,
ideas more definitely formulated at the time than Meijer believes.

Tkachev arrived in Zurich in December 1873, shortly after the
publication of the second (autumn) issue of the journal he was sent to
improve. He stayed in Switzerland only a few months, but there is
little doubt that he took advantage of the time. Surely he made contact
with the Russian émigré colony, now divided into hostile camps between supporters of Bakunin and Lavrov. Possibly he got in touch too
with the French Communards, many of whom had settled in Geneva,
encouraged by the prospect of living in a French-speaking country. He
might have stayed in Switzerland, but in March 1874 Lavrov moved
Forward! to London, and Tkachev accompanied him there.

Lavrov had become discouraged with the factionalism among
Russian émigrés at Zurich and with the series of hostile encounters
("episodes") that indicated to him that the émigré ideology was becoming "distorted little by little."[37] A good many Lavrovists had left
Zurich the previous summer when the tsar had ordered home the
considerable colony of women university students.[38] Lavrov was
sensitive to his lack of support. Moving to London he saw a chance for
a fresh start. Unfortunately before the publication of the third issue of
his journal a bitter quarrel developed between the editor and his newly
hired assistant, and the London collaboration of the two terminated
within a few weeks.

Tkachev's quarrel with Lavrov was based not only on their long
term irreconcilable ideological differences but on a conflict over the
editorship of *Forward!* All indications are that Tkachev had expected—
and now demanded—a role in formulating the journal's editorial policy
and in determining what should and what should not be printed.
Lavrov wrote later that an article Tkachev had composed for the new
(third) issue had proved so distressing to certain of his colleagues that
he decided not to print it. Tkachev bitterly complained and made, in
Lavrov's words, "such demands regarding influence on the general
conduct of editorial matters as rapidly revealed the complete impossibility of [our] working together."[39] While Tkachev admitted that

---

36. Ibid.
37. Lavrov, *Narodniki-propagandisty*, p. 74.
38. Ibid. Cf. Meijer, whose subject is the revolutionary beliefs and activities of
this considerable female colony in exile.
39. Lavrov, *Narodniki-propagandisty*, p. 75.

Lavrov had been cordial to him and welcomed his partnership when he arrived in Zurich, he wrote later that he was surprised to discover the journal's editorial policy to be so clearly a one-man operation, concentrated strictly in Lavrov's hands. Indeed it was clear as day, he said, that on any journal editorial responsibility should be divided equally between all participants.[40] Not personal ambition but the revolution came first.

Tkachev's radical disapproval of Lavrov's politics led him to insist on a role in formulating journal policy. But he found no support among Lavrov's editorial staff. After the initial disagreement he tried to persuade Lavrov's fellow workers to rebel with him, but they remained loyal to their editor.[41] Tkachev chose his course. Before he officially severed the relationship he wrote a long letter to Lavrov explaining his own revolutionary aims and his editor's revolutionary errors. The document represents Tkachev's first free statement of his own revolutionary beliefs, a statement uninhibited by the rigors of censorship or the demands of the legal Russian press.

Lavrov, Tkachev wrote, was out of touch and sympathy with the young radical generation. He had never really been one of them. The attack was particularly cruel because it made the most of Lavrov's age, his fifty years to Tkachev's twenty-nine. Tkachev may have remembered Chernyshevskii's disagreements with Herzen when he wrote:

> He is by age a man of another generation, the generation of the forties, the generation of fathers; the generation of the "children," the generation of the *new youth* that was born under the influence of social conditions directly preceding the serfdom reform and entered the scene with such an uproar in the beginning of the sixties—this generation he does not know, and if he knows it he knows it theoretically, so to speak, through rumors and through books.[42]

Lavrov's past stood against him, the angry young rebel wrote. He accused the older man of having avoided involvement in revolutionary action, a matter of some truth if applied to Lavrov's younger years. At the peak of the agitation in 1860s, Tkachev wrote, Lavrov only philosophized. He associated with hated people on hated journals. Tkachev boldly accused him of publishing in government periodicals and writing for *Fatherland Notes* when that journal was polemicizing with *Contemporary;* he forgot that he himself had published in the government press and once written for the conservative Dostoevskii

---

40. Tkachev, 3: 59. Weeks, p. 52, misrepresents this episode by inserting the word *should* in a quotation otherwise accurate and making it seem that Tkachev was arguing for, not against, one-man editorship.

41. Tkachev, 3: 61.

42. Ibid., p. 56.

brothers. Setting himself as a spokesman for the intelligentsia and refusing to admit that young radicals had turned to Lavrov's leadership, Tkachev insisted the Lavrov's knowledge was too abstract for revolutionary youth. He was conditioned by metaphysical philosophy; he could never change into an activist. "The *old man*," he wrote nastily, "tells in the *new one*,"[43] ignoring Lavrov's active role in support of the Paris Commune. The philosopher had in vain donned the clothing of the revolutionary wolf. Lavrov, wrote Tkachev, was two faced: one face was that of the metaphysician who believed in evolutionary progress, the other that of the "radical revolutionary" who edited *Forward!* But the second face was a deceptive mask, for when the editor wrote of revolution it was not revolution at all. In words that were designed to hurt, Tkachev berated him: "You very clearly do not *believe* in the revolution and do not *wish* its success."[44]

What Lavrov meant by revolution was really peaceful progress. He was reverting to his old hopes, his old beliefs in continual progress created by educated, knowledgeable, critically thinking men. The long, slow process of educating the majority to "consciousness and understanding" was not revolution at all. Lavrov was confusing the minds of young Russians, diverting them from their revolutionary path, putting off their revolutionary deeds. His journal was doing more harm than good and playing into the counterrevolutionary hands of the notorious Third Section. Under his tutelage youths were losing faith in themselves and in their ability to make revolution.

For he was creating not revolutionaries but civilized men. The long process of education he advocated would not make revolution at all. The way of Lavrov's majority was toward slow evolution, toward peaceful progress, but not toward action.

The people of the real revolution—this is the stormy element, destroying and breaking everything in its path, acting always unaccountably and unconsciously. The people of *your* revolution—this is the civilized man, fully aware of his own situation, acting consciously and expediently, answering for his deeds, well understanding *what* he wants, understanding his true needs and his rights, the man of principles, the man of ideas.[45]

But such men, wrote Tkachev, do not believe in violence and bloodshed. Such men choose the path of compromise and reform—like Lassalle, dreaming of a way to a new society along the peaceful road of universal suffrage. Education does not make revolutionaries at all.

---

43. Ibid., p. 62.
44. Ibid., p. 63.
45. Ibid., p. 65.

Tkachev included in the category of peaceful evolutionists the proponents of the "German" program of the International (the newly formed
Social Democrats) and the Western labor movement in general, statements that probably inspired Friedrich Engels to enter the argument
later on.

In fury Tkachev attacked Lavrov's conviction that the revolution
must wait until the proper historical moment. The historical moment
is always now when men create it. Environment makes revolutionaries;
oppressed peoples are *always* ready to rebel. "The people are *always*
ready for revolution," he cried to Lavrov. "They always *can*, they
always *want* to create a revolution; they are always ready for it."[46]
Tkachev seemed on the surface to contradict himself, but the confusion
is only superficial. The way of the majority was the way of inertia, of
peaceful progress, of slow evolution; yet under the surface the people
were ready to break through their bonds into the violence of revolution. Only spontaneous action could bring them to rebel. Propaganda
and education were futile and self-defeating.

The tasks, then, of a revolutionary journal were far different in
Tkachev's mind from Lavrov's concepts. A Russian journal should not
be dedicated to principles (even principles of revolution) or to philosophy or to generalities about the state of the world or to Western European problems. Rather it should be concrete and practical, concentrating on agitation and organization. Rather than diverting the Russian
youth with questions of theory, it should urge him to act; it should
serve as a practical weapon of struggle.

> In our veins, the veins of the revolutionaries, dear sir, there does not flow the
> blood that [flows] in the veins of philosophers-philistines. When we think—and we
> always think only of this—when we think of the shameful lack of rights in our
> country, about its bloodthirsty tyrants, soulless butchers, about those sufferings,
> about that infamy, those humiliations to which they subject [our country], when
> our gaze turns toward the Calvary of popular martyrdom—and it is not within our
> will to avert it from the spectacle—when we see before us this unhappy nation,
> glazed with blood, in a crown of thorns, nailed to the cross of slavery, oh, then we
> do not have it in our power to preserve that tranquillity becoming to philosophers.
> We do not want to speculate about those remote reasons that led [the people]
> to the cross, we do not want to say to it, as to the robber: "Having saved the
> others, save thyself, descend from the cross!" We do not want to wait while the
> crucified martyr "will come to understand and clearly become conscious" of *why*
> he uncomfortably hangs on the cross, *why* he is pounded with thorns, *for what
> reason* the nails are driven into his hands and legs, and *why* they cause him such
> sufferings. No, we want only *by whatever means and as soon as possible* to remove
> the sufferer from it.[47]

46. Ibid., pp. 66, 71.
47. Ibid., pp. 81-82.

Lavrov must have smiled from his sophisticated viewpoint, knowing
well that many revolutionaries who were fanatical in their antireligious
crusades would have found the analogy amusing.

Harking back to the familiar hero of Russian youth, Tkachev undertook to answer Chernyshevskii's famous query. "The question *what is
to be done* should no longer be put to us," he cried. "It is already
long since determined. *A revolution should be made.*"[48] The task of
Lavrov's journal should be to inspire organization, to call for agitation
so that the revolution might be made successfully.

But how? By what means? Tkachev's answer went far beyond
Lavrov's call for preparatory propaganda among the people. Making
the revolution, he suggested, should involve three methods: political
conspiracy against the state, direct agitation, and the propaganda
Lavrov proposed. Let us utilize all three, he cried, and stop our arguments as to which is most important. In addition to Lavrov's methods
Tkachev was calling for Bakunin's revolution through local agitation
and *bunty* (uprisings), and he was mixing in a measure of that conspiratorial seizure of power of which he himself became the strongest
émigré advocate. The three leaders of the Russian revolutionary émigrés,
Russia's revolutionary methodologists of the seventies, should combine
their forces and work for their goal together, each in his own manner.
Tkachev's letter to Lavrov anticipated his own journal in its suggestions
for common action. Indeed, Tkachev denied that revolution could be
accomplished by any one means alone, even by conspiracy, which he
favored.

. . . if we limit ourselves only to state conspiracy, then, although it is very easy
and convenient to make a revolution by means of this method, still this revolution
will have a state [*gosudarstvennyi*] and not a popular character; it will not permeate the bosom of popular life, it will not uplift nor agitate the lower classes of
society, it will disturb only its peak—to put it briefly—this will not be a popular
revolution at all.[49]

Although Tkachev advocated cooperation, the bitterness of his tone
suggests that he did not expect it: the difficulties of working with
Lavrov had already proved overwhelming. His pleas for cooperative
action in the future were often similarly negated by his furious attacks
on his contemporaries.

Certainly Tkachev did not anticipate benevolence in Lavrov's
response. His London friend M. P. Sazhin, who went by the pseudonym
Arman Ross, later found him duplicitous and pictured him smiling at
work in the *Forward!* editorial offices while he composed his slashing

48. Ibid., p. 85.
49. Ibid., footnote.

attack on Lavrov's policies during his free hours.[50] Reluctant to take responsibility for his attitudes in further face-to-face confrontation, Tkachev avoided Lavrov's probable annoyance as he had fled from Dementeva's possible rebukes a few months before. Rather than argue the issues out he one day awaited his editor's absence and secretively left his treatise on Lavrov's desk. Then in the company of Ross he left quickly for the railroad station to slip out of the country before his editor read his complaints. Ross tells the story of how the plan almost went awry: how Tkachev spotted Lavrov meeting the same boat train that he himself hoped to board, and how Petr had to duck and hide to avoid facing his still friendly editor before he sneaked out of town.[51] He managed his bit of deception without being caught.

From London Tkachev went to Paris. Ross, a follower of Bakunin, later published Tkachev's vitriolic attack on Lavrov under the title "The Tasks of Revolutionary Propaganda in Russia."[52] The open letter to the editor of Forward! by prearrangement prefaced with what Tkachev called a short personal explanation, evoked immediate comment among the Russian émigrés for its personal invective, its bitterness, its "merciless scorn and endless disrespect," reminiscent, it was said, of the violent sharpness of Pisarev's polemics.[53]

Tkachev stayed in France for a number of months in mid-1874. In Paris he reconsidered his position. Even before he read Lavrov's rebuttal in the pages of Forward! he recognized that without an outlet for publication he had given the editor a chance to have the last word. From Paris in June 1874 he wrote once more to his adversary.[54] Deprived now of printing facilities, Tkachev requested space in the pages of Lavrov's journal to explain his viewpoint in the interests of truth, as he put it. Always denying (as did Lavrov) any personal bitterness in their argument, he suggested that he contribute an article covering such topics as the kind of revolution that would be most effective in Russia, the means by which it could best be realized, and the type of agitation and propaganda necessary to its preparation. He awaited, he said, only a guarantee of publication before submitting the text. The

50. M. P. Sazhin (Arman Ross), Vospominaniia, 1860-1880 gg., p. 53.

51. Ibid.

52. This open letter has been republished in Tkachev, 3: 55-87.

53. Lemke, "Materialy dlia biografii," pp. 159-60. See also Deich, Russkaia revoliutsionnaia emigratsiia 70-kh godov, pp. 83-84, and N. A. Morozov, Povesti moei zhizni, 1:396.

54. This letter has been published by Nikolaevskii in "Materialy i dokumenty," pp. 191-93; see also Kozmin's note in Tkachev, 3: 453-55 (note 16).

guarantee never came. Perhaps somewhat chastened, Tkachev moved back to Switzerland. He was in Zurich at the end of 1874 and settled in Geneva the next year.[55]

Meanwhile Lavrov confirmed Tkachev's fears. His long article entitled "To the Russian Social-Revolutionary Youth," a response to Tkachev's attack, was printed in *Forward!* where it was more widely read than Tkachev's original open letter.[56] Lavrov went through Tkachev's complaints and argued his points one by one. His description of their quarrel increases our knowledge of Tkachev's ideas beyond the younger man's own written words and demonstrates clearly that by 1874 Tkachev had formulated his own revolutionary platform more positively than he himself had indicated in print.

The timing of the revolution was obviously central to the two men's polemic. Lavrov did not agree with Tkachev that the people were ready. He denied that they would respond with enthusiasm, that they would rally to the cries of the revolutionary minority, that radical youth could start a successful uprising at any time simply by calling the people to rebellious *bunty*. If the people were ready, why hadn't they made revolution yet? Why did Tkachev himself admit that the major task of organization still lay ahead? Disorganized people were by definition not ready to rebel. Tkachev's schemes for revolution at once represented no more than a "hurried call to a *bunt* of the unprepared people by unprepared agitators."[57] But revolutions unprepared in plan and theory had always ended in disaster. Lavrov's experiences in the Commune had taught him this lesson that Tkachev was unwilling to learn.

Premature revolution meant certain defeat. But on the other hand if Tkachev was right in thinking that the revolutionary moment was approaching, Lavrov could do nothing but applaud, and there was nothing to argue about at all. Lavrov himself was awaiting that historically correct moment without which the revolution would be doomed. Lavrov refused to hear of impatience.

You cannot wait? Weak-nerved cowards, you must wait, until you can arm yourselves, until you can rally together, until you can command the faith of the people!

---

55. Tkachev, 3: 459 (note 33). Akselrod dates his arrival in Geneva as spring 1875 (P. B. Akselrod, *Perezhitoe i peredumannoe*, p. 161).

56. The article has been reprinted in Lavrov, *Sochineniia*, 3: 335-72. Some of his supporters felt his tone was too mild. See the draft of a letter dated 1874 from members of an unidentified circle in Russia to Lavrov in regard to this polemic in *Revoliutsionnoe narodnichestvo 70-kh godov XIX veka*, ed. S. N. Valk et al., 1:172.

57. Lavrov, *Sochineniia*, 3: 342.

You do not *want* to wait? You do not want to? Correct? So from your revolutionary fidgetiness, from your baronial revolutionary fantasy, you throw the people's
future to the winds![58]

Lavrov knew from Tkachev's writings or oral statements that slogan
the younger man would later use on the masthead of his own journal:
"Now, for if not very soon, perhaps never." He was aware of Tkachev's
argument (not yet recorded in print) that the coming of capitalism to
Russia would diminish Russia's revolutionary potential by supplying
the tsar with a powerful class—the bourgeoisie—in his support. Lavrov
knew his Marx, and he denied Tkachev's theory. In Europe, he argued,
the very presence of the bourgeoisie had inspired the proletariat to
rebellion. Although he must have resented Tkachev's personal attacks
on him as an evolutionist, he admitted that the slow pace of peaceful
progress held its appeal; peaceful progress, Lavrov wrote, spreads
truth as the revolution spreads justice, and both must go hand in hand.

But the theme to which Lavrov returned again and again is that
Tkachev's revolution will not be made by the majority, that is, it will
not be a social revolution at all. Clearly Tkachev had not deceived him
by his contention that all revolutionary methods were essential to each
other; Lavrov saw the young radical as a conspirator before Tkachev
admitted it himself. He deplored the role Tkachev assigned to the
revolutionary minority, which Lavrov saw as voraciously thrusting
consciousness on the people, molding popular desire as the potter
manipulates pliable softened clay.[59] He detested Tkachev's idea that
the revolution should be political, that is aimed at seizing power rather
than overturning society.

Whether the moment for the revolution has come or whether it has not come,
whether it will occur before the formation of a large bourgeoisie among us or after
that, the conditions of revolution remain one and the same. It must be popular, it
must be social, it must be produced by the people, it must be directed not only
against the government, not only with the aim of transferring power from certain
hands to others, but it must with the same blow overturn the economic bases of the
present social structure. Only such a revolution can be the goal for which Russian
youth should sacrifice without regret.[60]

Lavrov went further, for he knew Tkachev well. During their arguments he had made certain witnesses were present, witnesses who
would surely support his version of the battles. At the height of their
quarrels Tkachev had clearly recognized dictatorship by the revolutionary minority after the seizure of power as "not only possible but
but desirable, necessary." Seeking to change the program of *Forward!*

---

58. Ibid., p. 345.
59. Ibid., p. 342.
60. Ibid., p. 350.

to suit his own viewpoints, the angry rebel told Lavrov that the Lavrovist group should at least be ready to cooperate, to become fellow-travelers with the defenders of dictatorship, to work through the journal and toward the revolution together.

Lavrov had been shocked. This was a Jacobin theory, he said, and he refused it any endorsement on the pages of *Forward!* Like most revolutionary populists Lavrov was an anarchist who feared centralized government and regarded the state itself as a source of great evil. "State power, no matter in whose hands it rests, is hostile to the socialist structure of society," he wrote.[61] Dictatorship was wrong. History had proved repeatedly that absolute power could corrupt any man. The dictator repressed not only his enemies but those who dared to disagree, and a dictatorship—even a revolutionary dictatorship—only invited constant secret intriguing for power. The Lavrovists could never work with those who endorsed such a program: "We would only fight with them tomorrow, so we cannot walk with them today."[62] The strong moral strain that Lavrov himself had lent to the revolutionary movement led him to despise repression, the manipulation or deception of the people, and the rule by force of any minority, whatever its declared political aims.

Not so his new assistant. Tkachev was already a Jacobin, and Lavrov knew it. He had endorsed conspiracy, the seizure of state power, and subsequent dictatorship by a revolutionary minority. By April 1874 the totality of his revolutionary plans had been formulated. If his beliefs owed anything to the Geneva Communards, the debt was established before this time.

Lavrov's article brought the polemic to the attention of the Russian émigrés in Europe and established their pattern of hostility toward his antagonist, the violent and impatient Russian revolutionary. The vehemence of the argument also attracted notice from another social democrat, more famous than either of the polemicists but equally sharp of tongue. In the periodical *Der Volksstaat* (Leipzig) Friedrich Engels had been publishing a series of articles dealing with émigré literature. He wrote first about Polish émigré groups in Western Europe and then (June 1874) about the Communard exiles in London, like Geneva a haven for refugees.[63] Seeking further grist for his mill Engels turned to the Russian émigrés, their journals, and their squabbles. Tkachev and Lavrov presented an example too timely to be ignored.

The two articles on Russian émigrés that Engels published in

---

61. Ibid., p. 361. For a comparison with Tkachev's attitudes see Theen, "Seizure of Political Power."

62. Lavrov, *Sochineniia*, 3: 361.

63. Marx and Engels, *Werke*, 18: 521-35.

Volksstaat in October 1874 were little more than sarcastic attacks on the snipings and snarlings of young Tkachev and his ex-editor.[64] The historian A. Walicki has suggested that they be read in connection with Marx's recent battle with Bakunin in the now-defunct International, and in light of Engels's scorn for Nechaev, whose conquest of Bakunin had reached scandalous proportions and whose conspiratorial mystifications Engels found amusing but deplorable.[65] To Engels the Russians and their polemics were all a little bit comical, reminiscent of the caricatures and exaggerations of a comic opera. The Russian affinity for pseudonyms seemed ludicrous indeed to this Western European, and in his article he carefully avoided identifying Lavrov by name, referring to him only as Friend Peter. He found Lavrov eclectic in his ideas and disliked the editor's cautious habit of finding good and bad sides in everything, a criticism that Tkachev himself picked up in his later attacks on the older man.

But Engels reserved his finest scorn for Tkachev. Describing the bitter polemic and quoting freely from both sides, Engels chided Tkachev for his concept of democratic editing, treating him like a petulant child who had dared to attack a respected older scholar. To Engels Petr was "a green gymnasium pupil," childish and immature, and he deliberately addressed him in the second person familiar.[66] In sophisticated Germany Tkachev could have been laughed out of court for his "childish, tedious, contradictory views that constantly turn around in circles."[67] He used, Engels was convinced, "Bakunin language." If he were really eager for a revolution, he should stop being petulant, stop manufacturing arguments, and go ahead and make one. Tkachev's polemics Engels insultingly called bothersome twiddle-twaddle. However there was little of substance in his own articles. Engels's sarcasm represented a superficial if nasty attack.

To Tkachev's credit, his reply rose above petty invective. Although Engels's considerable reputation must have been known to the younger man, Petr did not recoil from the fray. His "Open Letter to Mr. Friedrich Engels," written in German, was published privately in Zurich within a few weeks.[68] The article was not without personal jibes, but it remains a classic defense of the populist position against that of the Marxists, of Tkachev's awareness of Russia's special situation and her necessarily special route to revolution.

64. Ibid., pp. 536-45.
65. Walicki, p. 193.
66. Marx and Engels, 18: 541.
67. Ibid., p. 542.
68. Reprinted in Tkachev, 3: 88-98.

Relying on what many historians have termed the hallmark of populism, the belief in Russia's special path in history, Tkachev contended that Engels erred in not recognizing the uniqueness of his country's situation. He lacked knowledge, Tkachev wrote in irritation; it is as if a Chinese had tried to explain German politics merely on the basis of having studied the German language, a reference to Engels's recent study of Russian.

The situation of our country is completely unique, it does not have anything in common with the situation of any country in Western Europe. The methods of struggle adopted in the latter are totally and completely unsuited to us. We need a very special revolutionary program that must differ from the German in the same degree as social-political conditions in Germany differ from those in Russia. To judge our program from a German point of view (i.e., from the point of view of the social conditions of the German people) would be as absurd as to view the German program from a Russian point of view.[69]

For Russia had no urban proletariat, no free press, no representative assemblies, no literate lower class, no highly developed bourgeoisie. It was not only illegal to publish revolutionary propaganda in Russia, but worse still it was futile because the peasants could not read it anyway. It was against the law even to mix with the lower (*chernyi*) classes. It would be foolish to use those revolutionary methods that Engels knew so well in the West. To set up an International for Russian workers would be (and he borrowed a phrase from Engels's attack on himself) a "childish dream."[70]

Nevertheless Tkachev believed a socialist revolution to be a strong and immediate possibility in Russia although this revolution would rest on different foundations from those of Engels's revolution in his familiar milieu. Turning again to a traditional populist thesis, Tkachev pointed out to his adversary that capitalism was less well established in Russia than in the West and the task of overthrowing it was thereby made simpler. "Our workers will face a struggle merely with *political power*—the *power of capital* among us still exists only in embryo," he wrote.[71]

Russia's second advantage over the West lay in the tradition of her peasantry. Again relying on a classic argument of populism, Tkachev contended that the people of Russia were instinctively collective minded. For a critic who had frequently attacked idealizers of the peasantry he presented his own rosy ideals. The people, he told Engels,

69. Ibid., p. 89.
70. Ibid., p. 90.
71. Ibid. Tkachev was arguing what Walicki has termed the "privilege of backwardness," p. 107.

in the majority (especially in the northern, central, north- and southeastern part of Russia) is permeated with the principles of communal ownership; it, if one may so express it, is communist by instinct, by tradition. The idea of collective ownership is so strongly ingrained in the whole world outlook of the Russian people that now, when the government is beginning to understand that this idea is incompatible with the principles of a "well-constructed" society and in the name of these principles seeks to introduce the idea of private ownership into popular consciousness and popular life, it can attain this only with the aid of bayonets and whips.[72]

Thus, Tkachev concluded righteously, in a tone that must greatly have irritated his antagonist, "It is clear that our people, in spite of their ignorance, stand much closer to socialism than the peoples of Western Europe, although the latter are more educated than they."[73]

Another great instinct of the Russian peasants set them ahead of Engels's West with respect to revolution. They were, Tkachev told the German socialist, instinctively revolutionary just as they were by intuition socialists. In spite of their apparent torpor, in spite of the lack of clear awareness of their own actions, the Russian people were ready to rebel.[74] Peasants refused to pay taxes, joined dissenting sects, robbed, stole, and sporadically broke out into rebellion.

Revolution, Tkachev cried, would be easy in Russia. Lacking capitalists, the state had little support. The clergy was weak, and the gentry class was neither economically nor politically powerful. The Russian government was (at least for the moment) impotent to defend itself.

Only from a distance does our government produce the impression of power. In reality its power is only illusory, imaginary. It has no roots in the economic life of the people, it does not embody the interests of any class. It crushes equally all social classes, and they all equally hate it. They endure the government; they obviously endure its barbaric despotism with complete equanimity. But this patience, this equanimity must not lead you to error. They are merely the product of an illusion: society created for itself an illusion of Russian governmental power and itself falls under the spell of this illusion.[75]

A few military actions, simultaneous uprisings here and there among the peasantry, and the revolution would be accomplished for no one would step forward to defend the tsar.

In this regard we have a greater chance for victory of the revolution than you do. . . . Our social form owes its existence to the state, a state that is hanging, so to speak, in the air, a state that has nothing in common with the existing social strata and the roots of which lie in the past, not in the present.[76]

---

72. Tkachev, 3: 90-91.
73. Ibid., p. 91.
74. Ibid.
75. Ibid., pp. 91-92.
76. Ibid., p. 92.

The special advantages of Russia were clear. Intuitively revolutionary, by instinct socialist, opposed by a government that represented only the sham face of power, the peasants could make revolution without awaiting and undergoing the long course of capitalist-bourgeois rule that the Marxists found necessary. Engels did not understand Russia at all.

Nor did Engels have any idea of how the revolution must be organized. Open struggle, Tkachev told him, was impossible in a country where no legal means for such struggle existed. Like the revolutionaries in Spain, Italy, and France—Tkachev reminded Engels that it could happen in Germany—Russians were forced into underground activity (by inference, pseudonyms). Worker organizations were out of the question where most toilers were isolated, impoverished peasants and where no historical precedent for trade unions existed. Western revolutionaries had had a simple task.

You and your friends did not create the International, but history created it; its first seeds are rooted as early as the Middle Ages; it is the inevitable consequence of all professional, cooperative, striking, credit, and other unions and associations in which the masses of European proletarians were already united long ago . . . and traces of which you seek in vain in Russia.[77]

Russia's advantages and disadvantages prescribed for her a separate course. Tkachev patiently explained to Engels two possible roads to revolution: Lavrov's hope that education and consciousness would eventually create a peasant revolutionary force and his own conviction that the time was favorable now and time was of the essence. Lavrov was wrong, he wrote; Russia could not wait. The young, daring, energetic people with whom he identified himself were convinced that "while we pursue the unattainable, our enemies will gather their forces, our embryonic bourgeoisie will be able in this time to strengthen itself to a stage sufficient to become an unshakable prop for the government."[78]

Tkachev openly berated Engels for his condescending attitude toward the Russian revolutionary émigrés. Engels should not attempt to denigrate Russians to his German readers, to shame them and sneer at them disrespectfully. Did he not understand that in doing so, he was serving the common enemy—the Russian tsarist state? Perceptively Tkachev recognized that Engels was moved by personal animosity toward Bakunin and the Russian anarchists who had so recently split and destroyed the Marxist International. Engels's attacks on Bakunin at the time of the quarrel were unfair, Tkachev told him; he had tried "to

77. Ibid., p. 94.
78. Ibid., p. 95.

vilify one of the greatest and most selfless representatives of that revolutionary epoch in which we live."[79] Engels had identified all Russians with his enemy Bakunin; his dislike of Lavrov stemmed from Lavrov's own defense of the old anarchist in previous years. In calling Tkachev a Bakuninist Engels was setting him "on the side of the man who dared to raise the banner of revolt against you and your friends and who from that time became your sworn enemy, became a nightmare—the bête noire of your apocalypse."[80] Engels's only friends among the Russians were those few émigrés who formed a Geneva section of the International. Tkachev did not hesitate to tell him that he had the limited viewpoint of a bureaucrat (*chinovnik*). Bakunin had every right to tell him, "physician, heal thyself."

Tkachev's defense of Bakunin and his endorsement of so many principles of populism make it likely that his attack on Engels was composed under the influence of (or perhaps in collaboration with) the Russian émigrés he met again on his return to Switzerland. He may have hoped to mend his fences after the attacks on Lavrov through a defense of Bakunin and the Russian emigration as a whole. His personal opinion of Bakunin had never been so favorable; his defense of the peasant's socialist and revolutionary intuition, a cornerstone of classic populism, had never been so strong.

Marx recognized the affinity. Before answering Tkachev's open letter Engels sent it on to his more famous colleague in London for an opinion, and the brief note Marx wrote in return read simply, "So stupid that Bakunin could have worked it out with him."[81] Marx urged Engels to reply so that the last word might not appear to give Tkachev the victory. In *Der Volksstaat* in the spring of 1875, serialized in five issues, Engels explored his differences with the young Russian radical. The more substantive of his articles, the last three, were reprinted in pamphlet form under the title *Soziales aus Russland* (1875), together with a special introduction written by Engels explaining the circumstances of the argument.[82]

Engels again sarcastically attacked the "green gymnasiumist" who had "tears of lost innocence in his eyes."[83] Quoting freely from

79. Ibid., p. 98.

80. Ibid.

81. Marx and Engels, 34: 5. The episode so impressed one Soviet scholar that he has reprinted Tkachev's article with the underlinings Marx made therein. G. Ginsberg, "Marks o Tkacheve," in *Gruppa "Osvobozhdenie truda,"* 4: 389-94.

82. Marx and Engels, 18: 546-67. The little volume *Soziales aus Russland* was published by Engels in Leipzig, 1875.

83. Marx and Engels, 18: 553.

Tkachev's letter, Engels (inaccurately) denied that he had indulged in vitriolic personal attacks, refused to acknowledge his antagonist in any way as a spokesman for Russian youth, and called Tkachev "a true Bakuninist" for his spirited defense of his Russian compatriot. The German activist repeated his accusation that Russian émigrés always talked a great game but never really did anything.

Yes, if only the Russian Mr. Bakunins really and earnestly were conspiring against the Russian government! If they, instead of lies and frauds against their co-conspirators who are real swindlers like Nechaev, this "typical representative of our present youth," according to Tkachev; instead of plots against the European worker movement like the Alliance, luckily revealed and thereby destroyed; if they, the "activists," as they boastfully call themselves, finally would just once accomplish one deed that would furnish proof that they really have an organization and that they are busying themselves with something other than trying to make a dozen! Instead, they cry out to the whole world: We are conspiring, we are conspiring! just like those operatic conspirators who bellow in chorus for four voices: Quiet! Quiet! Don't make any noise![84]

Admitting the "the first part of my answer refers for the most part to the Bakuninist type of literary battle that consists simply of hanging an outright load of direct lies on one's opponent,"[85] Engels continued in *Soziales aus Russland* with a more sober and substantive attack on Tkachev's premises. His argument revolved around his conviction that Russia could go no separate path and that to attain socialism she must necessarily pass through a stage of bourgeois government, capitalism, rising proletarian strength, and finally revolution. Socialist revolution could not (as Tkachev supposed) be imminent in Russia.

The Marxist attacked populism on fundamentals that Marx himself mitigated but to which Engels much more stubbornly adhered. The socialist revolution could not precede the capitalist. To Tkachev's argument that Russian upheaval would be easier because no strong bourgeoisie existed, Engels answered that a well-developed middle class was as essential to revolution as was the proletariat: ". . . a man who can say that this revolution will be easier to accomplish in a country because it possesses no *true* proletariat *but* also no bourgeoisie thereby proves only that he still has to learn the ABC of socialism."[86]

Impatient of Tkachev's contention that the Russian state "hangs in the air," Engels proceeded to identify a number of classes in Russia from which the government gleaned support. Among them were, of

---

84. Ibid., p. 554.
85. Ibid., p. 555. In his introduction to a later edition of *Soziales aus Russland*, Engels admitted he had been wrong to identify Tkachev as a Bakuninist (ibid., p. 63).
86. Ibid., p. 557.

course, the gentry but also all exploiters of the peasants including
kulaks, merchants, and middlemen as well as an industrial bourgeoisie
that Engels regarded as rapidly growing with Russia's railroad construction. He included the large army of civil servants he was sure stood
behind the tsar. He stood firm by the Marxist view of the state as
superstructure.

And if Mr. Tkachev assures us that the Russian state has "no roots in the economic
life of the people, it does not embody the interests of any kind of class," it hangs
"in the air," it is our opinion that it is not the Russian state that hangs in the air,
but much more Mr. Tkachev.[87]

If Tkachev believed that Russia would undergo a socialist revolution
such as Western European Marxists were seeking, to Engels it was out of
the question. Russia was in no wise unique; she was bound to travel the
path of the West through the economic stages the West had known.
Engels denied that Russians were any more naturally socialistic than
Europeans. The artel was not a purely Russian phenomenon for it
appeared in many areas under similar productive conditions. It was no
harbinger of socialism in Russia any more than in the West, and it
would disappear in Russia (as in other areas) when heavy industry
inevitably developed. The Russian peasant was not a uniquely intuitive
socialist, as the populists believed. The *obshchina* was once widespread
in Europe and over the world. It had not brought socialism to the West,
and it would not help the Russian revolutionaries realize their dreams.
Indeed, the primitive socialism of the communes, isolated as they were
one from another, would never give birth to modern socialism but
rather would serve as "the organic basis for *oriental despotism*," as in
India; tsardom, not socialism, was the necessary and logical product of
Russia's communal system.[88] Engels had studied the commune, and he
pointed out to his young adversary that the *obshchina* did not represent
pure cooperation. On the contrary, each family traditionally received
land to cultivate on its own. He concluded that the Russian commune
had long passed its flowering. The only way to preserve the communal
agriculture life was to bring about a proletarian revolution in Europe.
The victorious proletariat would aid the commune in prolonging its
existence. Far from seeing the Russian peasant as close to socialism
Engels found him in dire need of help even to preserve what little he
had.

To Tkachev's contention that the Russian peasant was instinctively
revolutionary Engels answered with an equally certain negative. Reveal-

87. Ibid., p. 559.
88. Ibid., pp. 563-64.

ing a knowledge of Russian history unusual for a Western European of his day, he pointed out to his young antagonist that throughout their history of rebellions the peasants never attempted to destroy tsarism; even at the height of peasant revolution, under Pugachev, for example, they sought only to establish a pretender-tsar on the throne. Revolutionary aims and theory were equally beyond their ken. To speak of revolution as easy was ludicrous under the circumstances. No revolution was ever easy to accomplish. Should revolution in Russia have been the exception, it would long since have been accomplished; Engels bolstered his point with a telling list of Russian peasant revolutions that had ended in failure.[89]

Closely following the line he and his collaborator had devised, Engels contended that if revolution should come to Russia, it would not be a socialist revolution but would rather establish bourgeois constitutionalism and capitalism, following the pattern Marx had set down on the basis of his study of England. Russia could not violate the rules. Her revolution might be progressive, but it would not be socialist. To become a socialist country she would have to abandon her peasant tradition and travel the long road Marx had analyzed in the West. Tkachev was wrong, Engels wrote; peasant socialism could go nowhere and peasant revolution was fruitless.

Tkachev never answered Engels's letter. He may actually have felt uncertain of his grounds, for he had always contended that the intelligentsia must demonstrate revolution to the peasant and that peasant "instinct" was not to be idealized. He did not take up his polemic with the Marxists again until he was able to attack them in a journal of his own.

The argument had strayed into Marxism against populism instead of Tkachevism versus Lavrovism. Tkachev brought it back to its original topic with a jolt. Completing his plans for a periodical in which he would continue his arguments with his ex-editor, he turned back to the legal Russian press and in September and December 1875 published an attack on Lavrov's philosophical ideals every bit as vehement as his critique of the older man's revolutionism. For Lavrov's treatise *Experiment in the History of Thought* had been serialized in the Russian journal *Znanie* (Knowledge). Tkachev seized his opportunity to review it for the *Cause*, and his critique, entitled "The Role of Thought in History," tore into Lavrov's subjective sociology almost paragraph by paragraph.[90]

Lavrov's subjective method and his critically thinking man bore the

89. Ibid., p. 566.
90. Tkachev's review is reprinted in Tkachev, 3: 176-218.

brunt of Tkachev's savage attack as they had in his earlier unpublished review. To Tkachev the subjective method was a screen for the typically Russian effort to reconcile the contradictory, to merge the actual with the possible, the emotional with the intellectual, objective truth with subjective moral convictions. "From the objective point of view it is impossible," Tkachev aped Lavrov as saying, in what the younger man viewed as the ludicrous Russian insistence on seeing all sides of all questions ad infinitum (Engels's criticism and almost in Engels's words), "but on the other hand, from the subjective. . . ."[91] Lavrov and his school, he wrote, never did really define their subjective method; perhaps they themselves did not know quite what they were talking about. For himself objective truth was gained through scientific observation of the world around him while subjective truth, whatever that was, was deduced from moral convictions, aesthetic tastes, and other personal inclinations. Objective truth was obtained by the intellectual process while subjective truth was by definition emotional and psychological in nature.

To investigate a subject by the subjective method means to sort out, analyze, judge, and so on, that subject from the point of view of the particular state of my emotions. . . . To investigate a subject by the objective method means to investigate it however it is (that is, how it presents itself to my mind) without any regard for the state of my emotions.[92]

By his subjective method Lavrov thought easily to resolve those problems that Tkachev himself had not yet solved. Tkachev groaned at the formula: objectively the universe might have its predetermined course, but subjectively man had freedom. This semantic paradox constituted no answer at all.

Just tell me, what mind other than the Russian mind, inclined toward the reconciliation of everything possible and even of the completely impossible, could think up such a solution to one of the most fundamental questions of man's world outlook?[93]

Sneering at the view that history was objectively predetermined but could be subjectively changed by man, Tkachev set forth an argument that has its peculiar interest.

History is a series of necessary causes and effects, and from whatever point of view the individual regards the historical process—whether from the subjective or the objective—he inevitably arrives at the conviction that to understand this process otherwise is impossible, psychically and logically. But such an understanding of the historical process does not contradict but, on the contrary, fully accords with

91. Ibid., p. 191.
92. Ibid., p. 190.
93. Ibid., p. 191.

another one of the individual's convictions—the conviction that he, the individual, as a necessary product of given causes, is a major mover [*deiatel*] of this process. Being on the one hand a consequence of the previous links in the world chain of causes and effects, on the other hand he plays the role of a cause for later links. Since our individual is shaped not only by events and conditions of social history preceding him but also by many other events and conditions not within the realm of "public history," then obviously his activity in this realm often leads to such consequences as cannot be explained only by the facts and conditions of previous history. Thus the individual constantly brings into the process of development of social life much that is not only conditioned by but even definitely contradicts both preceding historical premises and the given conditions of society. On this purely objective fact is based our subjective consciousness that we, individuals, can influence the course and development of the historical process, that we are not completely blind, suffering tools in this process, but on the contrary are active and independent movers.[94]

Thus man, a product of the historical past, acting in accordance with it and his personal environment, produces the future or at least thinks he does.

Tkachev identified subjectivism with medievalism because of Lavrov's philosophical attempt to fit his beliefs into some single grandiose scheme. Phenomena of nature in medieval times, he told his readers, were not studied scientifically or objectively but were viewed through the rosy haze of some previously designed subjective doctrine. The criterion of truth was not objective exactness, trueness or falseness to reality, but was based instead on subjective contentions about the morality or immorality, the desirability or undesirability of certain phenomena. Social scientists, he was sorry to say, had not risen above such medieval, subjective, moral judgments; like Lavrov they were by nature idealists and metaphysicians, interested not in discovering the scientific laws governing society but rather fitting facts into a network of subjective concepts, viewing history as the unfolding of good or evil, recreating cause and effect out of their own subjective ideals. Tkachev did not approve. History could be scientifically analyzed even though Lavrov refused to believe so. Tkachev cited Buckle as one who, not altogether successfully, had attempted to view history objectively and scientifically. Lavrov's contention that history did not repeat itself and therefore could not be studied objectively was firmly rejected by his young critic. Tkachev believed that even if events were not exactly reproduced in future times, relationships in juridical and economic life were often repeated in the same patterns.

Furiously Tkachev attacked Lavrov's critically thinking man and his role in history. Who, he demanded of Lavrov, was this admirable ideal,

---

94. Ibid., pp. 192-93.

this analytical genius, if not a scholar? And who, indeed, could call himself scholar but one who knew and analyzed the world by objective, not subjective means? Yet Lavrov idealized his critical thinker as a hero of subjective thinking. How, demanded Tkachev in bitter satire, could the scientist-scholar play the subjective game, create everyman's ideal of culture, define justice, morality, and progress? The critical positivist had no place in Lavrov's subjective world.

More important still was whether critical thought (that is, by Tkachev's definition, scholarship) was an important force in human history and played that major role in creating progress that Lavrov and his followers presumed. The role of thought in history, to quote Tkachev's title, depended on the degree of stimulation intellectual considerations exerted on men's actions and on the actual role of thinking people in the social organism. With his usual vehemence Tkachev again disagreed with Lavrov. The young critic was convinced that ideas were unimportant in the activity-producing process and that intellectuals in particular were psychically unable to translate ideas into reality. The capacity to convert one's hopes and one's thoughts into action progressively diminished for any man as he carefully, intellectually considered his chances of success. When one was young, when one's enthusiasms carried one in leaps across the cold stone walls of reality, one was better off.

Before, when . . . you had a desire to finish something, this desire, not discovering any impediments in your mind, which was unaccustomed to reasoning, was rapidly realized. Speaking in the language of the scholar: between the inclination motivating in you a desire to act and the occurrence of action, there were no or almost no intermediary steps. With the development of your mental capacity, with the increased fund of your "idea" experience, the interval between the beginning of the act (inclination) and its end (action) lengthened more and more, and simultaneously the probability of the inevitable sequence of the latter (the action) after the former (the inclination) decreased. The impulse, not finding itself immediately satisfied in action, gradually evaporated into abstract thought.[95]

Only the impulsive young, only the uneducated could act without excessive consideration. The inclination to passivity was the fate of the entire older thinking class. Tkachev sadly concluded that

the influence of thought on human action is inversely proportional to the development in a man of his intellectual side as compared with his affective side; the more highly developed the former, the more suppressed is the second, and the more meager is the role of thought in the active life of people, and consequently the weaker also its influence on the general course of human affairs.[96]

---

95. Ibid., p. 212.
96. Ibid., p. 213.

Thus intellectualism, which he had recognized as effete even in his *Russian Word* days, was actually an impediment to any cause demanding action. The critically thinking individual so admired by Lavrov would waste his energy on abstract speculation and seldom if ever be moved to the deed.

Tkachev attacked Lavrov's conviction that critical thought might be turned to action when it was based on strong moral conviction; in the younger man's view critical thought turned to matters of morals was not critical at all, for the scholar then abandoned his objective stance and threw his scholarship aside in favor of subjective emotionalism. To Tkachev just this kind of uncritical thought played a far greater role in the essential content of history than the kind of scholarship an objective intellectual might be expected to produce. More people were motivated to action by personal emotions and personal interests than by intellectual, scholarly conclusions. If civilization had changed, Tkachev doggedly lectured his opponent, the cause of such change should be sought not in scholarly outlooks but in those economic relationships that dominated man's personal interests and thus "create a soil favorable to transforming knowledge into conviction and conviction into deed."[97]

Not moral doctrines, not critical thought move history; they do not comprise its essential content; its content is defined purely by individual impulses, by scarcely intellectualized, almost instinctive demands; and these individual impulses, these little-thought-out demands are conditioned, in their turn, by the economic interests of that environment in which they arise and develop. They comprise the nerve of social life, the spirit of history; on them the historian should concentrate all his attention.[98]

Lavrov should step to the background—his theories, his philosophies, his science could not move the world forward because they were not transmutable to deeds. Indeed, Tkachev snarled, Lavrov was a typical Russian scholar who spent so much effort on the trees he lost sight of the forest, who insisted on beginning all discussions with Creation itself, who polemicized and intellectualized, confused his sciences, insisted on reconciling all blacks with all whites, became a dilettante, and in his efforts to create a grand totality, to fuse everything into one, was unable to come to any decision. He was a typical Russian *intelligent.*

We constantly hesitate, not only when it comes to transforming words into deeds, when it comes to choosing between this or that course of action, but even when it comes to choosing between this or that form of thought. Thus in our heads scraps

---

97. Ibid., p. 214.
98. Ibid., p. 217.

of the most obviously contradictory world outlooks live very peacefully and calmly in harmony. In order to avoid the necessity of choosing, which is difficult for us, we always try to compromise. . . . "The Experiment in the History of Thought" is no exception in this regard as the essential points of the world view of any thinking man are touched upon in it, and on each point a compromising-evasive answer is given in the end; thus it can be seen as a typical example of our contemporary thought or, to put it better, of those of our intellectual traits that are defined by our beloved formula: "On the one hand, it is impossible not to agree although, on the other, one must realize. . . ."[99]

It was a bitter condemnation, to accuse Lavrov of having no convictions, of standing forever in the middle of the road. Tkachev had pitted his cry for action against Lavrov's demand for reason and thoughtfulness. The young man despised the old, not just for his approach to revolution but for his way of thinking and living. Antagonistic personalities added fuel to the flame of intellectual disagreement.

His attack on Lavrov's rationalism again demonstrated that Tkachev held no illusions about achieving social revolution through education and persuasion. Rationalism had no place in the peasant's orientation. Chernyshevskii and Herzen had favored enlightenment and studied the peasantry, but they were wise enough to separate the two; they did not insist that the peasant become educated and submerge his intuition in knowledge. Bakunin rejected scholarship in favor of instinct and intuition. Tkachev leaned more heavily on the intelligentsia's capacity to plan consciously for revolution although he hoped for aid from the peasant's spontaneous, unreasoned reactions. But from the start he saw the illusion of Lavrov's plans to enlighten the peasant and argue him into action. The plans might eventually work, but they would take too much time.

Moving abroad into new revolutionary acquaintanceships, Tkachev was driven by a sense of urgency. Time lay at the basis of his disagreements with Lavrov and his polemics with Engels as well. Clearly Tkachev accepted the Marxian analysis that Russia was moving toward capitalism. Clearly he rejected Engels's contention that capitalism was a progressive phenomenon; instead he was alarmed at its coming. Like the populists he hoped Russia might avoid the evils of Western society. He was convinced that a capitalist-oriented tsardom would be harder to overthrow because of the support it would receive from a powerful bourgeoisie. That made time of the essence. Only a revolution could stop capitalistic development, so the revolution must be made at once.

The elements of Tkachev's revolutionary program grew from his analysis of the social, economic, and political forces in his native land.

---

99. Ibid., pp. 185-86.

Although he agreed with the arguments of some of the populists, he maintained a more realistic view of the peasantry's capacities than Lavrov, Bakunin, or Mikhailovskii. In the sense of N. V. Berdiaev's definition of populism as putting one's faith in the peasantry,[100] Tkachev was hardly a populist at all.

He might have found more friends among his Russian colleagues had his analysis not called for independent revolutionary action on the part of conscious, dedicated revolutionaries, virtually eliminating the peasant from consideration and changing the nature of the revolution from a broad, social to a narrow, political movement. The populists of 1875 did not endorse political conspiracy nor the forceful use of governmental power. They had moved over into the democratic camp. Thus it was not just the scathing violence of Tkachev's attacks that caused his enemies to reject his pleas for unity in the revolutionary movement. It was their fundamental disagreement with his analysis of Russia and his resultant choice of revolutionary methods. His early polemics with Lavrov and Engels only set the stage for future hostilities.

But by 1874 Tkachev had clearly enunciated what he wanted and where he was heading.

---

100. N. Berdiaev, *Istoki i smysl russkogo kommunizma*, p. 48.

10

Intelligentsia, Peasantry, and Philosophy

Tkachev's decision to become an expatriate did not end his deep concern with his homeland. Unlike Bakunin he maintained close ties. From prison, from exile at Velikie Luki, and above all from wherever he lived in Europe he sent a stream of articles back to St. Petersburg where Blagosvetlov faithfully published them in the *Cause*, that characterless journal termed by the editor himself as "neither fish nor meat."[1] Tkachev began writing again in 1871 when prison authorities became more lenient and agreed to send his articles, after scrutiny by the prison censors, for publication in Blagosvetlov's journal. Kozmin has identified six such essays published in 1872, primarily in the early and late months of the year.[2] From exile in Velikie Luki in 1873 Tkachev intensified his efforts, at least in the first half of the year when he published in every issue, some of his articles running to as many as five installments. After his flight abroad his pen temporarily lost its inspiration, and in the years 1874 through 1876 only two long Tkachev articles appeared in the *Cause*, supplemented by a series of very short and vitriolic attacks on people and causes he particularly detested.[3] In 1877, a year when his revolutionary commitments in

1. Quoted in Kozmin, *Tkachev*, p. 49.
2. Kozmin lists these writings of Tkachev in Tkachev, 4: 449-54.
3. For the most part these attacks struck out at what he called the "new formation of *pochvenniki*," certain populists who reminded Tkachev of the earlier Slavophiles and came in equally for his disrespect (ibid., p. 5). He wrote as well several articles on education, attacking Tolstoy's suggestions that the peasantry should select their own classroom subject matter and be permitted greater freedom

Geneva diminished, he began to work harder. His articles in this year and the several following were long and diverse in their subject matter. By 1880 he was through, and his many pseudonyms (P. Nikitin, P. N., P. N. Niunov, Vse Tot-zhe) faded from the pages of the *Cause*, the final installment of his last article having appeared in August 1880, probably as composed early that year.[4]

In subject matter too Tkachev returned again and again to his native land. His interest in the squabbles of the international revolutionary set never led him to abandon Russia. Gone (except for a few articles) were the critiques of strictly Western writers, philosophers, and economists. His greatest efforts centered around four major topics. The first was philosophy, for he became concerned about the adoption by the classic populists of some new concepts he regarded as neo-Kantian. The second area was literary criticism; following the tradition of Russian radical thought he set down criteria for judging novels and literary works. The third was his generation; he devoted many pages to somewhat naïve attempts at social psychology and group analysis. Finally came the peasantry, its mores and its traditions, including Tkachev's analysis of communal life and its effects. Tkachev's pen remained sharp and his condemnations devastating, but his articles lacked his youthful attempt to construct a systematic philosophy of the universe. Sometimes he dealt in broader, quieter tones with the same problems he raised in his much more radical writings in Geneva. Still his ties with Russia remained strong and his interest in her concerns dominated his work.

Tkachev had moved into the field of literary criticism by the back door. Trained (such as he was) in law, interested primarily in economics and what was coming to be called sociology, he had taken up criticism

---

in the schoolroom; "To Teach the People or to Be Taught by the People" was one of his angry titles. Unlike Tolstoy he favored the Germanic system of education with its strictness and intellectual discipline. He believed Tolstoy's system would result in the perpetuation of such evils as mysticism and superstition in the countryside. Because of his educational theories Tkachev lumped the "philosopher of Yasnaia Poliana" with the "Dostoevskii crowd" for their idealization of peasant instinct. See ibid., pp. 5-15, 32-58.

4. Ibid., p. 454. G. Prokhorov in his short essay entitled "P. N. Tkachev ob izdatelskoi i literaturnoi deiatelnosti G. E. Blagosvetlova" in *Shestidesiatye gody*, pp. 220-21, identifies the pseudonym Zhane (the French Jean) as Tkachev's and suggests that perhaps Tkachev also wrote under the pseudonym Grachioli. Although his dates seem persuasive, other evidence is not; the article he publishes does not seem to be written in Tkachev's usual style, and it was not like Tkachev to adopt foreign-language pseudonyms.

as a remunerative profession and as a vehicle for getting his ideas across to Russia's expanding reading public. He had only the slightest background in aesthetics and philosophy, and he was probably self-educated in the field of letters, literary styles, and art history. Yet he wrote on all these matters. More carefully than his predecessors—Belinskii and Chernyshevskii, Dobroliubov and Pisarev—he considered the criteria for literary criticism and the techniques of writing.

His first statement about the function of the literary critic dates from a review he wrote for *Library for Reading* as early as 1864.[5] Here Tkachev began by isolating the elements of "artistry," by which he meant reproduction of reality, and "tendentiousness," by which he meant the particular view of the world that the author, consciously or unconsciously, hoped to impress on the minds of his readers. Of these factors, he found tendentiousness more important and was convinced that it was increasing in the novels of his time. Tendentious novels were outselling purely artistic works in France, Germany, and even Russia, he wrote, an improvement he regarded as a sign of maturity and depth, of a "new phase in the development of social thought."[6]

By 1868 Tkachev was insisting that all great literature must be tendentious and have a didactic purpose, a utilitarian viewpoint long advocated by the Russian realistic critics. Artistic production was unthinkable without the insertion of the author's viewpoints. The author should not just call attention to particular social problems but

define as much as possible in what form life can and must satisfy these [social] demands. Here is the tendentious, didactic side of each living fictional work that does not intend to be restricted merely to landscapes but has in mind some sort of more or less serious, thoughtful goals. This didactic, tendentious side, in our opinion, is also the most important and essential.[7]

The literary critic played an important role in the didactic process. For each work, Tkachev wrote, he must above all explain; he must "try to catch the idea and the purpose, and if this purpose is harmful in its influence on intellectual and moral development of the readers he must mercilessly unmask all its harmfulness and show all its absurdity."[8]

Insisting like his predecessors that the literary critic must aim to teach, Tkachev demanded that in method he proceed scientifically. Criticism called for objectivity, and the critic must relate to a literary work as the naturalist relates to nature. He should begin, Tkachev wrote, by making himself knowledgeable in the fields of sociology and

5. Tkachev, "Geroi perekhodnoi epokhi."
6. Ibid., p. 4.
7. Tkachev, 1: 314.
8. Ibid., p. 317.

psychology, particularly that psychology "that utilizes the objective method of natural sciences, that draws its conclusions not from *self-view* and *self-consciousness* but from exact data of physiology, anatomy, anthropology, etc."[9] Tkachev hoped that with this concrete knowledge the critic would approximate the scientist rather than the artist.[10]

For Tkachev rejected aesthetics as a basis for literary criticism. To him artistic judgment was personal, subjective, and conditioned by the physiology, environment, and intellectual development of the individual involved. One and the same object, Tkachev observed, "frequently produces completely opposite aesthetic impressions not only on different people but even on one and the same man in various years of his life, in different moments of his spiritual mood."[11] Artistry and beauty could not be judged scientifically.

The question of artistic truth can be solved by no means other than on the basis of purely subjective, completely arbitrary impressions; the personal convictions of the critic can be subject to no objective verification. A critic who does not have any realistic foundation under his feet is plunged headlong into the vast sea of subjectivism; instead of realistic, objective facts he is forced to deal with elusive, unconscious internal sensations; there can be no talk of exact observations, logical conclusions, and proofs here; unconscious aphorisms, the sole *ultima ratio* of which is the personal taste of the critic, are substituted for them.[12]

Such a critic could be no scientist, no realist, and therefore no good.

The realistic critic, as opposed to critics who concentrated on aesthetic evaluation, could set objective criteria for his judgments. Tkachev enumerated several tests: realism of reproduction, psychological realism, social realism, and contemporary significance.

---

9. Ibid., 6: 314.

10. Tkachev's views on the relationship of science and art were expressed in an article never published during his lifetime; it was suppressed by the censor in 1872. He identified science with intellect and art with emotion. The artistic mind therefore stood forever below the critical mind, the artist below the scientist. To Tkachev the death of poetry would hail the advance of civilization, because science was, as he put it, the art of the higher intellect. See ibid., pp. 324-25, 345-48. Some of these thoughts had already been expressed by Pisarev.

11. P. N. Tkachev, "Printsipy i zadachi realnoi kritiki," in his *Izbrannye literaturno-kriticheskie stati*, p. 77.

12. Ibid., p. 71. Tkachev thought the music critic's job was much easier. Harmony, he believed, could be clearly defined on an objective basis in terms of tonal relationships. Thereby would the critic make his judgment. Fortunately Tkachev was unacquainted with the twelve-tone scale. Tkachev once suggested that a critic had an obligation to influence his readers' perception in all fields and might occasionally be permitted aesthetic criticism to educate his readers in art, but he dropped this idea and did not bring it up again (ibid., p. 73).

Realistic reproduction Tkachev called "truth to life" (*zhiznennaia pravda*) in some articles and "artistic truth" (*khudozhestvennaia pravda*) in others. Tkachev's ideal of reproduction was something close to photography. The author must reproduce the reality around him with scientific exactness. Although Tkachev admired the phrase of his favorite critic Dobroliubov when Dobroliubov spoke of the "truth of the author's images," he felt that even Dobroliubov had allowed writers unpardonable leeway in regard to realistic reproduction and had thus sometimes fallen into metaphysics in his judgments.[13] Camera clarity was the test.

But the realistic critic must ask for more: he must judge an author for his portrait of character and his descriptions of social environment. As to the former, Tkachev believed that psychologically accurate character evaluation was fraught with almost insurmountable difficulties. He regarded psychology as a semiscience at best, suffering from inexact, problematical conclusions and from a "more or less subjective character." "The science of 'the human spirit,' of 'human character,'" he wrote, "is in such a youthful state that it can give us no direction in this regard."[14]

In the evaluation of characters from a psychological point of view, it is difficult and even almost impossible for the critic to maintain himself on a strictly realistic, objective base. Willy-nilly he is constantly forced to turn for aid to the purely subjective method, a method reigning in our time in psychology, and consequently to plunge into an area of more or less arbitrary opinions and purely personal considerations.[15]

Tkachev did insist on one criterion: the critic must demand that authors unify character traits into a whole person. The author must present the entire man rather than one element in his make-up. Tkachev was thinking of Dostoevskii, who had (he believed) removed his work from reality by exaggerating, coloring, and distorting the abnormal until it became the overpowering force in all of his characters.[16] Tkachev himself never liked uniqueness in characters. He preferred typical persons, probably for their didactic usefulness.[17]

As to social realism, Tkachev required the critic to consider the author's selection of subject. "Is the reproduced reality," he asked,

---

13. Tkachev, 2: 365.
14. Tkachev, *Izbrannye Literaturno-kriticheskie stati*, p. 65.
15. Ibid., pp. 65-66.
16. Tkachev, 4: 59-60.
17. An interesting article on Tkachev's use of the typical is V. M. Senkevich's "Tipisheskoe v realisticheskom iskusstve: K voprosu o tipicheskom v estetike P. N. Tkacheva," in *Teoriia i istoriia russkoi literatury*, Uchenye zapiski Moskovskogo gosudarstvennogo pedagogicheskogo instituta, vol. 190.

true in its characters and relationships of life? What kind of social significance have these characters and this relationship? By what conditions of social life were they generated? By dint of exactly what historical causes were the social conditions that engendered them formed?[18]

The critic must be ready to answer these and other questions. Indeed he must be able to analyze society, set forth its history, and recognize its types.[19]

Finally realism laid upon an author the responsibility for directing his camera lens toward men and matters of significance to society. An accurate description of a flower was not enough.

A writer can very truly as regards psychology and very clearly as regards form present to us this or that human character, very exactly, vividly, and realistically describe this or that phenomenon of nature (for example the sunrise or sunset, a mountain, a rivulet, etc.), one or another human emotion; but if the characters and emotions described thus are unimportant and insignificant unto themselves, if they do not play any essential role in the common structure of social life, [if they] are not the direct expressions of this or that social interest, are not provoked by this or that inclination of social thought, then realist criticism recognizes the literary talent of this writer as insignificant and superficial.[20]

Realism demanded an important subject and one with significance in the contemporary world. "Once they lose the significance of the contemporary," Tkachev wrote of literary works in general, "they will not have any meaning at all."[21] An ideal author must teach not for other times but for his own.

Tkachev sometimes added another element to his list of criteria for realistic critics: this was what he called "fantasy," by which he meant imaginative plot and story development in works of fiction. Although fantasy should take second place to social significance (as it often did in Tkachev's reviews), it was an important element in novels and tales. Tkachev furiously denounced its weak development among Russian authors, particularly criticizing Dostoevskii.[22] The great author, whom the young critic considered "one of the first class artists of our times,"[23] leaned too heavily on psychology as opposed to plot in his literary creations. From his many reviews it becomes clear that Tkachev himself preferred novels filled with intrigues and complications.

Thus realism demanded, and its critics must seek, a true-to-life style, psychological accuracy, truthful social descriptions, and important themes and characters. Tkachev returned over and over to his

18. Tkachev, *Izbrannye Literaturno-kriticheskie stati*, p. 62.
19. Tkachev, 2: 365.
20. Ibid.
21. Ibid., 3: 144.
22. Ibid., pp. 13-14.
23. Ibid., 4: 59.

insistence that the novel (for he felt fiction was the best means for conveying the convictions of an author to the greatest number of people) be didactic, that the author and his critic never forget the clear call to present a point of view. The author's world outlook should shine through the actions and speeches of his characters although it might and should be subtly conveyed; the critic should reveal it to those who may have missed the point. One could not teach if one had nothing to teach, and Tkachev clearly favored authors with a cause. Do not present all sides of the question, Tkachev told his writers; think in black and white, and remember that black and white have nothing in common.

Now it is constantly necessary on every favorable occasion to remember the fading elements of *difference*, to refurbish the worn-down boundaries of *oppositeness*, otherwise in the near future we will be threatened with the danger of losing all consciousness of the different essences of black and white, true and false, that is, the danger of finally going intellectually and morally blind.[24]

Tkachev always insisted that realism as a literary style and mood was far superior to any other school of writing. In a long article written in 1875 called "Empiricist Novelists and Metaphysical Novelists,"[25] he rejected as invalid and worthless both the romantic (metaphysical) and naturalist (empirical) fictional styles. The romantic or aesthetic school that descended from Pushkin (who "clothed his delightful muse in the *pomeshchik*'s cap")[26] Tkachev saw as conditioned by serfdom and setting artistic value above social truth. Naturalism (identified with Emile Zola and Gleb Uspenskii) he condemned as lacking in "tendentiousness."[27] Photographic truth was not truth enough, he insisted, for photography lost itself in details and did not distinguish between the important and the insignificant. It presented no conclusions and no generalizations, thus remaining passive, unimaginative, and meaningless. Uspenskii's works in particular Tkachev found characterized by poverty of characters, poverty of imagination, no knowledge of psychology, and reflective of the author's "very insufficient intellectual development."[28] Tkachev missed the point in his reading of the naturalists. The lessons that they taught shone through their works strong and clear, but his own didactic demands called for presentation of the author's point of view in a less subtle, more argumentative manner.

Tkachev's insistence on the unique validity of social realism and tendentiousness set him in the camp with those Russian critics he had

24. Ibid., 6: 298.
25. This article is published in ibid., 3: 99-175.
26. Ibid., 2: 226.
27. Cf. ibid., pp. 99-105.
28. Ibid., pp. 229-32.

most admired in his generation. In the words of one Soviet scholar, his criteria for realistic criticism and by implication for all realist writers reveal "the militant nature of the author striving primarily for social action."[29] The concepts he expressed were scarcely original and by his own admission drew on works that had been published before. In a further sense they anticipated the future. Had Tkachev had his way socialist realism would surely have maintained an advantageous hold over literary production as it one day was to do, so vehement were his condemnations of any other approach.[30]

Tkachev's attitude towards classical philosophy was always negative. In his early articles he frequently attacked idealists and metaphysicians.[31] In the last years of his life he published several essays on new philosophical trends, including "On the Benefit of Philosophy," 1877, "The Wells of Wisdom of Russian Philosophers," 1878, and a long study of utilitarianism published in 1880.[32] In none of these essays did the Russian critic find cause to change his negative views.

Tkachev's dislike of philosophy grew from the utilitarian demand that all men's thoughts and deeds be devoted to bettering the world in practical ways. Philosophy, he wrote (with exceptionally heavy sarcasm), had its uses. It might keep one from becoming bored by providing inoffensive intellectual gymnastics.[33] Occasional amateur philosophizing might save one from the grubby embarrassments of everyday life.[34] But above all, philosophy was useful as an escape from

---

29. M. M. Klevenskii, "P. N. Tkachev kak literaturnyi kritik" *Sovremennyi mir*, nos. 7-8 (1916), p. 2.

30. Space does not permit analysis of Tkachev's criticism of various Russian and Western writers here. Suffice it to say he had one of the sharpest pens of the sharp pens Russia produced. Of the "Golden Age" Russian novelists, earning for themselves and their country an eternal place in the literary sun, he had little good to say. Turgenev was always sweet, unable to rouse emotionalism, and inhibited by his aesthetics and landlordism (Tkachev, 2: 227). Tolstoy Tkachev regarded as a man of no talent, a writer famous only because of careful public relations; in 1878 Tkachev reviewed *Anna Karenina* under the title "Parlor Art" (ibid., 4: 453; see also Klevenskii, p. 17). His running argument with Dostoevskii once led him to accuse this great novelist of "creative bankruptcy" (Tkachev, 3: 13).

31. See chaps. 3, 4 above.

32. None of these articles was included in Kozmin's collection. "O polze filosofii" appeared in *Delo*, no. 5 (1877), pp. 66-95; "Kladezi mudrosti rossiskikh filosofov" in ibid., no. 10 (1878), pp. 1-30, and no. 11 (1878), pp. 123-66; "Utilitarnyi printsip nravstvennoi filosofii" in ibid., no. 1 (1880); and "Utilitarnyi printsip nravstvennoi filosofii" (second article) in ibid., no. 7 (1880), pp. 1-22, and no. 8 (1880), pp. 317-41.

33. Tkachev, "O polze filosofii," pp. 72, 93.

34. Ibid., pp. 73-75. Tkachev puts this in amusing anecdotal form.

the agonies of the real world, a distraction from the problems of men on earth.[35]

Carefully, without expressing outright hostility—a ploy that led one historian to suppose him ambivalent toward his subject[36]—Tkachev set up a straw man vulnerable to his attack. Tongue-in-cheek, he quoted and paraphrased contemporary philosophers about their aims and considerations. They speculated, he wrote, on "the life of the spirit."[37] They attempted to "explain the inexplicable and comprehend the incomprehensible, to reveal the beginning of all beginnings, the cause of all causes, to understand the essence of things, to unravel the secret of the world."[38] They sought to develop "the unification of individual inclinations and activities into one common will and harmonious activity of all society, humanity, and through it, the world" or to define the "bond and unity of things outside the limit of time and space."[39] He delighted in letting philosophers drown in the vast sea of their own definitions. No wonder that in Tkachev's eyes they failed to attain their stated goals. His attitude toward the sweeping pretensions of philosophers often served to keep him from considering their specific principles seriously.

Clearly Tkachev wanted philosophy to come down to earth. He sought a philosophy that would divorce itself from metaphysics, reject pure abstractions, and concentrate on humanity and human needs.[40] He could tolerate speculative constructions only when they began with concrete phenomena and then only when they stopped before they climbed into the thin air of the fantastic, the stratosphere remote from reality. He once suggested that philosophers might as well abandon their generalizing to scientists, who were more competent at it. He sought a philosophy so stated as to be comprehensible to ordinary people instead of just to geniuses and insisted that philosophers constantly submit their speculations to the down-to-earth judgment of what he called "healthy sense."[41] He wanted an effective philosophy that, in spite of its speculative nature, would be of social value and could demonstrate its usefulness to humanity. Unfortunately philosophy, defined in his terms, was patently unable to do so without completely abandoning its premises and aims.

---

35. Ibid., pp. 94-95.
36. Malinin, *Filosofiia revoliutsionnogo narodnichestva*, pp. 82-83.
37. Tkachev, "O polze filosofii," p. 71.
38. Tkachev, "Kladezi mudrosti," no. 10, p. 11.
39. Tkachev, "O polze filosofii," pp. 76, 87.
40. Malinin, p. 83.
41. Tkachev, "O polze filosofii," pp. 83-84, 88-89; "Kladezi mudrosti," no. 1, p. 20.

Tkachev did not hesitate to attack all manner of philosophers for their inability to attain his (and sometimes their own) goals. Metaphysics remained his bête noire, and his condemnation of new trends in philosophy often consisted in identifying them with the old metaphysical tradition. Among the greatest nineteenth-century philosophers, he particularly deplored Hegel, who, he wrote, had attempted to construct a philosophy of nature, deducing nature from an absolute spirit; doing so Hegel reduced "all the rich multiformity" of nature into his "narrow, fantastic system."[42] The dialectic Tkachev rejected as mystification, as many Soviet scholars have pointed out.[43] He concluded that

we do not have and cannot have the slightest reasonable basis nor the slightest actual reason to concern ourselves with Hegelian philosophy. This philosophy does not have at the present time any but purely historical significance.[44]

His estimate of Schopenhauer was equally negative.[45]

Considering other new trends in philosophy Tkachev in each instance found elements of idealism creeping into philosophical concepts, elements he rejected as not useful, not beneficial, and often even harmful in terms of their practical consequences. Such was the case in his analysis of the "empirocriticists," those followers of Ernst Mach and Richard Avenarius who were beginning to write in the late 1870s. Tkachev's article, called "The Wells of Wisdom of Russian Philosophers," was basically an attack on V. V. Lesevich (later a founder of one of Russia's leading populist journals) who was a positivist and a disciple of Mach. Tkachev had read in the orginal Avenarius's *Philosophie als Denken der Welt gemäss dem Prinzip des kleinsten Kraftmasses*, published in Leipzig in 1876. The critic accused the "empirocriticists" of blending positivism with neo-Kantianism, and of adding to their pseudoscientific philosophy certain a priori elements that Tkachev considered metaphysical. The philosophy of Avenarius was unable to fit all of science into one higher universal concept for it "pursues the same shadows as the metaphysicians pursue."[46] Tkachev objected to Lesevich's division of thought into ordinary and scientific categories. Knowledge and understanding, he wrote, are interdependent; it is impossible to understand anything about which you have no objective

42. Quoted in Malinin, p. 50.
43. For example ibid., pp. 49, 123; Galaktionov and Nikandrov, *Ideologi russkogo narodnichestva*, p. 117; Kozmin in Tkachev, 3: 473 (note 136); Georgii Valentinovich Plekhanov, *Sochineniia*, 2:43.
44. Quoted in Malinin, pp. 49-50.
45. Ibid., p. 51; cf. Tkachev, "Kladezi mudrosti," no. 11, pp. 137, 144-46, and "O polze filosofii," p. 91.
46. Tkachev, "Kladezi mudrosti," no. 11, p. 152.

knowledge.[47] No philosophy, he wrote, could unify people as Lesevich hoped, for intellectual differences between people were conditioned "not so much by physiological differences, not so much by errors in emotional perception, as by so-to-speak moral-social differences."[48] He decried what he termed the Russian philosopher's idealism. "Truth!" he cried. "What is truth? Does truth not have the slightest relationship to existing social orders?"[49]

Other philosophies came in for criticism in the same vein. By 1877 Tkachev had decided that Spencer's law of development was meta-physical and abstract although he continued to use it in some of his own analyses.[50] He wrote that the French historian Hippolyte Taine had "attempted to link the conclusions and observations of experi-mental psychology with idealistic mysticism";[51] Tkachev always believed psychology must be founded firmly on a physiological base or lose its dubious position as any kind of science at all. Even in utilitarianism the Russian critic now found certain "remnants of moldy metaphysics," and he accused the utilitarians of designing their philosophy to justify a certain empirical morality, namely the happiness of that social group "on which our personal prosperity depends."[52] The Comtean positivists he denounced because he said their philosophical treatment of science really was no philosophy at all.[53]

Philosophy had failed to attain the dual goal Tkachev had set for it. It had formed no adequate abstract system embracing all reality and it had conceived no principle useful to people, by inference a revolution-ary guide. Philosophy had not demonstrated the power "to raise itself above the fatal contradictions of life, to emerge from the enchanted circle of its antithesis, to carry harmonious unity into the disorderly chaos of everyday humdrum relationships."[54] The Soviet historian Malinin's contention that "Tkachev in general did not reject the right of philosophy to be an instrument of understanding the world"[55] may be literally correct. However, Tkachev so constructed his definitions that

47. Ibid., no. 10, pp. 28-29, and no. 11, pp. 124-25; cf. Galaktionov and Nikandrov, pp. 117-18.
48. Tkachev "O polze filosofii," p. 79; see also idem, "Kladezi mudrosti," no. 10, pp. 22-24.
49. Quoted in Malinin, p. 91.
50. Tkachev, "O polze filosofii," pp. 84-85.
51. Cf. Malinin, p. 210.
52. Quoted in ibid., pp. 160-61.
53. Tkachev, "O polze filosofii," p. 93 (footnote).
54. Quoted in Malinin, p. 71.
55. Ibid., pp. 82-83.

philosophy would have little chance to fulfill the tasks he demanded of it. Surely no philosophy that he examined ever came close. Tkachev's attitude thus remained implacably negative, as many scholars have pointed out.[56]

Among Russian writers of his times Tkachev was not the first to insist on the unique characteristics of his own generation and to attempt to set his colleagues in clear relief against the past. The generation gap fascinated contemporary writers. The men of the sixties seldom tired of social self-analysis and generation self-concern. Tkachev's works demonstrated two themes: his often expressed conviction of economic-oriented environmentalism and his burning desire to discover the relationship of men toward their revolutionary goals. The two concepts often stood in conflict in his bifurcated view; for all his environmentalism Tkachev was never quite sure whether men were driven by their pocketbooks or their ideals. He tried on most occasions to merge the two as motivating forces.

In accordance with his environmentalist convictions Tkachev analyzed the outlooks of the Russian intelligentsia on the basis of the Russian economy. He began with the generation of the twenties although he touched upon it lightly; his own times interested him more. Philosophy, literature, and the world views he found were conditioned by serfdom, Russia's predominant economic and social phenomenon. Because the landed gentry constituted the leading social class in Russia, literature necessarily developed what Tkachev called a "salon character."[57] Social thought remained fickle and superficial. The Decembrist revolution, Tkachev wrote, was bound to fail for it lacked deep roots—such was always, he wrote, the "fate of ideas not emerging from and not based on the economic conditions of that environment that develops and disseminates them."[58]

Tkachev saw a change in Russia's economic situation by the 1840s. Serfdom, he wrote, was beginning to become less profitable. Productiv-

56. For example, Galaktionov and Nikandrov, pp. 116-17; see also A. L Reuel, "Sotsialno-politicheskie vozzrenie P. N. Tkacheva," Nauchnye zapiski Moskovskogo finansovogo instituta, no. 8, p. 241; Kozmin, Iz istorii, p. 373; and Tkachev, Sochineniia, 1: 63, 88.

57. Tkachev, 2: 269-70.

58. Ibid., p. 269. Soviet writers have castigated Tkachev for his failure to "evaluate Decembrism as a most important stage in the development of the Russian liberation movement"; this is the viewpoint expressed in an essay on Delo's critics (Blagosvetlov, Zaitsev, and Tkachev) in Istoriia russkoi kritiki, ed. B. P. Gorodetskii, A. Lavretskii, and B. S. Meilakh, 2: 256.

ity of the land was decreasing, credit disintegrating, and the gentry falling into debt because of its lowered income.[59] The economic position of the gentry was becoming insecure, and this insecurity was of course reflected in ideals and ideas. Insecurity drove most men of the forties into rigidity and lethargy; yet it caused a small minority to question the institution of serfdom and the entire social system.

The fossilized gentry of the old generation Tkachev considered in one of the last of his writings, an article entitled "Rotten Roots," which appeared in the *Cause* in 1880.[60] Reviewing some stories by a novelist named V. Krestovskii, he identified the less educated, less secure, less intelligent majority of the upper and middle gentry groups as political and social conservatives. Tkachev had nothing good to say for them. They remained frozen, petrified, and interested only in pre-serving the old way of life against encroachments by the new. Their outlooks were petty, and they lacked curiosity about anything outside of their own families and immediate environment. They feared life; they asked only to be left alone, vegetating in lethargy, avoiding move-ment—people who live in a grave, Tkachev called them.[61] To emerge from their coffins to breathe free air would demand the expenditure of energy; they preferred inactivity and sought only to rot in peace. These pre-emancipation noblemen played games as a substitute for living, were dominated by petty egotism in their relations even to each other, and deliberately raised their children to be drones. If among these children rebellious spirits should occasionally develop (perhaps from exposure to education or to a dynamic outsider), they were unable to break away. They instinctively or even consciously knew that without roots, however rotted, they could not exist.

The major tragedy of their situation lay in the not only material but the moral-psychological impossibility for these adapted, cultured people to tear themselves away from their nurturing and nourishing rotten roots. The roots gave them poison instead of healthy food; they felt and understood this, but at the same time, they felt and understood that there is and can be no antidote against this poison for them.[62]

The rare child who broke away could do no more than become a prostitute, a nun, or a monk. Their roots remained forever rotten. They could be no more than egotists, selfish, blind, and unsympathetic—occasionally beasts of prey, robber men of business, heroes of the bourgeoisie.

Tkachev was more interested in the other breeds: those rare men of

59. Tkachev, 2: 268.
60. Ibid., 4: 350-412.
61. Ibid., p. 363.
62. Ibid., p. 404.

the forties who developed doubts in the system and began hesitantly to question. These particular "fathers"--gentry of sensitivity, intelligence, education, and usually wealth—were caught in a torturing dilemma. On the one hand they were beginning to develop ideals that challenged serfdom as an institution; on the other, they were unable and unwilling to reject serfdom's *obrok*, that annual usurious payment that kept them alive. Their high ideals could not be reconciled with the reality of their pocketbooks. Thus the few liberal men of the forties by nature were never activists. They could not afford to apply their ideals to reality, so instead they developed what Tkachev called elusive idealism, deliberately removing their speculations from the mundane matters of serfdom in the world around them.[63] They suffered in their efforts to close their eyes to actuality. Many of them turned to intricate, psychological self-analysis. Others became lazy, timid, fainthearted, flabby, apathetic, and weakminded. "To think—this is dangerous; to act, to live— this is also dangerous; the only thing without danger is to lie on one's side, and they turn into Oblomovs," Tkachev wrote stingingly, referring to the title character in Goncharov's widely read novel.[64] Their egotism contributed to their self-indulgence, to the "sick development of self-love."[65] Concentrating upon themselves in an unreal world they suffered from "Russian grief" (*Russkaia toska*), a direct relation to English spleen and German *Weltschmerz*. They suffered from the intense melancholia of the man who was superfluous, who found no place for himself in the world around him, and this melancholia "was manifested among our fathers in an oppressive consciousness of their own nullity, ignorance of where their activity comes from and on what it is based, and swaying from side to side."[66] They were tragic and comic, buffeted between these poles by circumstances around them. They repented of their sins and delusions, but their mental paralysis deprived them of the ability to act.

In spite of his obvious disgust at their sterility and weakness, his scorn for their apathy and incapacity for positive action, Tkachev did not see the generation of the fathers as all bad. The men of the forties at least were gentle, and on one occasion the young critic actually contrasted their sensitive perceptions and deep emotions positively with the voluptuousness and casual passions of some men of his own generation.[67] He seemed sometimes willing to forgive them for much of their foolishness because it resulted from the environment in which they

63. Ibid., 2: 245.
64. Ibid., 3: 19.
65. Ibid., p. 22.
66. Ibid., p. 25.
67. Ibid., 2: 346-47.

lived. They could not help themselves, he seemed to be saying.[68] Their withdrawal from real life—into self-examination, idealism, egotism, and melancholia--resulted from guilt and from their inability to match their ideals to reality, a favorite Tkachevian theme.

Like the fathers of the forties the children of the sixties were products of their environment. The abolition of serfdom, although it had little effect on very wealthy landowners, made the middle and poorer gentry truly economically superfluous. Deprived of the serf labor on which their fathers' existence had been founded, left without function on their impoverished estates, the children were forced to seek new livelihood. By Tkachev's theory they were simultaneously forced to reformulate their ideals and to find some outlook on life that would correspond to their new economic status.

When the logical development of vital social relationships introduces new orders in place of the old, then usually (and this is a logical necessity) the development and extension of a world view very negatively relating to these old orders precedes the final abolition of the latter and the establishment of the [new]. . . . Thus among the children . . . grew a new world view, alien, hostile to the fathers' viewpoints, a world view very clear and definite, foreign to the "elusive idealism" of the so-called people of the forties.[69]

Fortunately the new generation had some advantages. Firstly, it was exposed to an exciting and challenging intellectual rebirth that Tkachev on several occasions referred to as a "renaissance." Secondly, the Great Reforms opened new economic opportunities: young people were needed as doctors, lawyers, writers, professionals of many sorts, as businessmen or civil servants. But even set in new social conditions, exposed to new ideas, and faced with new economic realities the children were plagued by their inheritance. The advantages were countered by the sickly melancholia their fathers left them. We are all, Tkachev wrote, mostly copies of our fathers and of their fathers before them.

Although the conditions under which the "children" developed were different from those under which the "fathers" developed, they were not so different as to paralyze in the children the habits inherited from their parents, [the habits] of intellectual inactivity, weakness of will, and loss of individuality of character. On the contrary, all the elements of our social life that enhance the development of such qualities continued to exist and flourish in the period of the children's growth as they have existed and flourished among us from time immemorial.[70]

Witness for instance the way the children reacted to the intellectual excitements of the 1860s.

68. Ibid., 3: 19-20.
69. Ibid., 2: 243-45.
70. Ibid., p. 243.

Now imagine that life set the people who inherited a [passive] intellect from their ancestors into conditions completely different from the conditions in which their fathers had vegetated, and that these [new] conditions suggested to them new ideas foreign to their fathers'—ideas fully harmonizing with their new life interests. Of course because of the critical impotence of their minds they will very rapidly and easily adopt these ideas—and owing to the harmony of the latter with their real, practical interests, there will appear among them a burning demand, completely unknown to their fathers, to solidify the adopted idea into a cause. The trait, inherited from the fathers, of being content with a very meager supply of intellectual material, [a trait] inevitably leading to intellectual one-sidedness, will compel them to adhere to the newly adopted idea with all the powers of their empty souls. Outside of it, except for it, no other ideas will exist for them, [they will have] no other intellectual interests, especially at first when the idea has not yet lost its originality, not yet become one of those vulgar, soiled, public things on which all base their meager spiritual values, from which all construct their slim intellectual culture.[71]

Thus the children of the sixties made crusades of their new findings, embraced new ideas with special excitement, and permitted their ideas to possess them body and soul.

For some children—those of the "first formation," in Tkachev's term—inheritance eventually triumphed over the spirit of the new world. Basically uncertain of themselves, they soon began to question whether their new ideas were correct. They were prone to misgivings and distrusts. Critically unprepared to dissect their ideal and to evaluate it objectively, they fell into their fathers' habits of expressing themselves in debate rather than in deed. In theory as daring as Columbus, Tkachev wrote, they were in practice unable to act. They were made impotent by their conviction of their own impotency. Their "delicate feelings," as Tkachev sarcastically dubbed their emotional sufferings, could only tremble before the need for indelicate actions.[72]

Some children of the first formation lapsed back to the traits of their fathers; they became cautious, abstract, indecisive, self-analytical. These Russian men eternally moralized and overreasoned.

Moralizing is our national weakness. People not used to broad activity, constantly occupied with microscopic considerations [and] with petty personal interests, people who lead primarily a *vegetable life* cannot help but be moralizers. In moralizing all of their intellectual life will be exhausted.[73]

Some men simply became dullards. Tkachev once compared the Russian character to the landscape: the unendingly even steppes, the unendingly dull forests unbroken by the drama of mountain peaks.[74]

---

71. Ibid., 4: 111-12.
72. Ibid., 2: 246-47.
73. Ibid., p. 329.
74. Ibid.

For others the conflict of new and old was torture. Some (and Tkachev referred to several characters created by Gleb Uspenskii) turned to drunkenness and debauchery—a "turn to dust," as Tkachev put it. For others the agony was such as to drive them to suicide; Tkachev had in mind Nezhdanov in Turgenev's *Virgin Soil*.

The children of Tkachev's second formation differed from those of the first in that they were able more successfully to set their inheritance behind them. These were the radical men of the sixties, the intelligentsia of Tkachev's youth. Exposed to the excitement of new ideas, these second formation children preferred thought to emotion, critical analysis to blind acceptance. They were scholarly, rational beings, people of keen, hard thinking. Lack of emotionalism was not an affectation but a fact of their nature, an essence of their character. They were incapable of ordinary love, of tenderness, of jealousy, "that inevitable accompaniment of powerful love."[75] They were disciplined, objective, calm, and realistic. Their preference was for action rather than passivity. Like the people of the future they were energetic, clear minded, and ready to work for a cause.

The traits of their inheritance—traits that so confused the children of the first formation—were for the most part cast aside. Tkachev mentioned their tendency toward physical weakness of mind, conditioned by long disuse of their brains, which tired too easily. Beyond that they knew inward harmony and spiritual peace. True, the firmness of their convictions sometimes bred the evils of egotism; Tkachev cited a prosperous Russian in one of the novelist I. A. Kushchevskii's tales.[76] True, their incapacity for emotion could lead to callousness and inability to understand the emotions of anyone else. Tkachev, who loved to categorize, divided them into "speculative-abstract" and "egotistical-selfish" personality types and declared that he preferred the latter.[77] The men of the second formation were not perfect but they were better off than their older brothers described above; better off except for the future. Sadly the older Tkachev, a decade removed from his youth, watched his contemporaries disintegrate and saw his hopes destroyed. To his great discouragement the men of the sixties were never able to live up to what he thought to be their potential. By 1877 most of the men of the second formation had abandoned the burning ideals of their youth.

In that year Tkachev reviewed *Virgin Soil* and evaluated Turgenev's

---

75. Ibid., p. 272.
76. Ibid., p. 307; the novel was *Nikolai Negorov ili blagopoluchnyi rossiianin*, by I. A. Kushchevskii.
77. Tkachev, 2: 319.

new man, the "even-tempered soul," as Tkachev called him.[78] He was a man of noble aims but in maturity he had become convinced that they could best be attained through small deeds. In working legally, slowly, and quietly he had found a harmonious equilibrium of spirit. The answer to the dilemma of hopes pitted against reality lay in a pragmatic solution. The man of the sixties, a decade older, had become an agronomist, an earnest civil servant (convinced that the greatest benefit of humanity was served by railroad construction), a cattle breeder, a hospital technician, a worker in an artel. Without losing his conviction that he must serve society, he had tempered the means by which this service could best be accomplished. He had compromised his burning ideals and become a practical man. The arena of his work had been adjusted downwards. He settled for less than his hopes and deluded himself into thinking he was accomplishing more.

To Tkachev the potential heroes had become waxen knights in miniature size. The "waxen traits of their souls" had protected them from disillusionment. But they had refused to carry the torch that life had handed them. Tkachev was agonized.

The holy spark of human emotion rapidly dies out amid the stifling atmosphere of the "kingdom of darkness," and the "kingdom of darkness" again sinks into impenetrable dusk while here and there again a new little spark of salvation is lit, perhaps just as short-lived as the first. And only these short-lived little sparks heat and light [the kingdom]. Use them! Do not let them go out! This flame is the flame of truth and humanity; it scourges everything evil, inhumane, it drives away the darkness and shows people the direct, open road to the kindom of "lightness and good."[79]

Even the hero of Turgenev's novel—the educated peasant Solomin, the even-tempered man of Tkachev's title—was no hero in Tkachev's grand tradition but merely a man who lived by small deeds instead of great ones. Tkachev never embraced hopes that a better world might be created by evolution or by small acts; he viewed with despair a generation that seemed intent on trying to forego revolution for peaceful progress.

But for some men of the sixties, fate held an even more cruel destiny. Those who held firm to their ideals suffered tortures of frustration when society forbade them to make their dreams a reality. Tkachev in part blamed their parents. The fathers had raised their children to accept new ideas and then refused them the right to put their ideas into action.

From the wax they thought to mold figures destined for thought! How inapt!

---

78. This review is reprinted in ibid., 4: 87-155.
79. Ibid., p. 148.

But this is still not all: having allowed these figures to think, to wish, to create spendid ideals, they did not grant them the slightest opportunity to realize their wishes, to transform theory into practice, the ideal into reality. Their ideals were caulked inside their heads; if they were sometimes permitted to fly out, then it was only in the form of the same abstract idea. Eternally to carry in the mind an idea that is never transformed into the deed, that is, [never] reaches the last phase of development of any thought, this is in itself torture, deeply tormenting torture.[80]

Energetic and keyed to action, the young men did not have the resources to adopt their fathers' solution and abandon reality altogether. Instead their frustrations forced them toward emotional illness. Their early education extolling intellectualism over and above the simple joys of childhood and their inherited weakness of intellect only compounded their agonies.[81] Even external conditions were conducive to mental illness: the earning of one's own living with one's own hands demanded physical strength and called for "masculinity" from children whose inheritance left them without these ingredients. All these circumstances forced the "thinking proletariat" into a manhood that trembled between health and sickness.

In this psychic and economic environment Dosteovskii set his novel *Demons*, and Tkachev, reviewing it, claimed that Dostoevskii should here have sought out the causes for the madman ravings of his demented characters. In a review article he entitled "Sick People" Tkachev analyzed all Dostoevskii's major characters as mentally ill, pushed toward their fates by inheritance, environment, and education. Although he criticized the famous novelist for not helping his readers understand the ravings of his lunatics and for not explaining their insanity ("The [maniacal] idea for the author remains unto itself and the man unto himself, and between the ravings and the raver there is not the slightest connection"),[82] Tkachev did not deny the presence of madness. Surprisingly, because Dostoevskii's maddest man was clearly drawn after Nechaev, he considered Verkhovenskii to be "sick."

Like the other hopefuls of the sixties, Verkhovenskii had been frustrated in turning his dreams into reality.

The end result of thought is expedient action; in action it finds its highest manifestation and its verification and its material for further development. Thoughts not crowned with actions, *passive thoughts*, very frequently give birth to and become *sick thoughts*.[83]

---

80. Ibid., 3: 30.
81. Ibid., p. 31.
82. Ibid., p. 38.
83. Ibid., p. 44. Pisarev once said something similar; Lenin quoted him in "What Is to Be Done?" See V. I. Lenin, *Selected Works in Three Volumes*, 1: 239, 835 (note 156); cf. Pisarev, *Selected Essays*, pp. 100-101.

The process was the more devastating for those (like the men of Tkachev's generation, according to his own analysis) who valued their ideals more highly than life itself.

It is still all right when these inactive sick thoughts are no more than transitory episodes in the intellectual life of a man, if he does not assign them any essential significance, if he takes to them without enthusiasm and takes leave of them without pain; then it is very easy for him to free himself from them—they themselves even free themselves. . . . But their influence on the psychic organism of a man has completely different repercussions if they comprise, so to speak, the basic fund of his world outlook, if they are closely interlaced and threaded through the finest threads of that fabric from which his whole intellectual life is cut, if they play in him the role of ruling, predominant factors; in this case it is hard, almost impossible, for a man to break with them, to forget them.[84]

The pressures upon such a man might become too great for his beleaguered mind to conquer.

. . . A thought that does not find its legal outlet in *reality*, that is forced eternally to struggle like a caged bird within the tight cage of the human brain, that never can tear itself to freedom and fly around the world, rousing people with its song—such, if it can be so expressed, a powerless and impotent thought almost inevitably must lead to a very serious disorder in the intellectual functions of a man.[85]

In 1873 Nechaev seemed such a man to Tkachev. Petr was sympathetic toward the young revolutionary, as portrayed with less sympathy by Dostoevskii, but this "sick man" scarcely emerged a hero or a saint. He was tortured, possessed by the demons Dostoevskii imagined, substituting for his unsatisfied hopes the fantastic, the insane. Clearly Tkachev did not condone Nechaev's murder of his coconspirator. If he did not react with the horror demonstrated by many of his young contemporaries, he nevertheless regarded the act as one inspired by insanity. The analysis of Nechaev as a sick man indicates that Tkachev had not yet carried his own revolutionary ethic to such an extreme. He may actually have emerged from his prison experience with bitterness toward the violent young man whose cause had indirectly sent him there. More likely, he identified with Nechaev's frustrations; the man who believed in action, condemned to Velikie Luki in administrative exile, must have felt as frustrated as the "children" he described.

His evaluation of Nechaev is the most significant point in Tkachev's portrait of the men of his times. Unfortunately the other portraits were muddled in color and texture. Having drawn his examples from numerous stories and novels Tkachev was unable to merge the many characters and several periods into any clearly typical man. His dates

---

84. Tkachev, 3: 44.
85. Ibid.

are uncertain, his generations blurred. One personality blends too easily into another, leaving his reader unsure of which he found typical and which he admired. The environmental psychology Tkachev was trying to practice called for an extraordinary feat of legerdemain, especially when he restricted his examples of the generation gap to characters in the novels and stories he reviewed.

Tkachev's view of his favorite *raznochintsy*, the new men of the sixties, ended with disappointment and pessimism. His one-time men of the future had either abandoned their ideals to become "even-tempered souls" or clung to them to become emotionally unstable. Four of Tkachev's long articles analyzing his generation appeared before the "crazy summer" of 1874, during the period of Lavrov's greatest influence among Russian radical youth. His gloomy review of *Virgin Soil* appeared in 1877 just when he was trying and failing to rouse another revolutionary effort, just before young radicals, discouraged by their inability to rouse such an effort among the peasantry, turned again to conspiratorial action and violence. Tkachev must have sensed that these were years of limbo for Russian revolutionism. However fervently he sounded the tocsin from abroad, the great cause, the great heroes, the great generation must have seemed lost.

Tkachev's evaluation of the peasant in terms of his potential for revolution and his instinct for communism is difficult to assess from his writings because of the author's apparent ambivalence. On the one hand he occasionally lauded both these traits of the peasantry and found them deeply rooted in Russian tradition. On the other he shrank back from his generalizations and proposed so many exceptions and uncertainties in peasant responses as to cast grave doubt on his faith in his own conclusions.

As ever Tkachev wrote as a literary critic. He began with his usual acerbic attack on the manner in which the peasant was portrayed in Russian literature. In his mammoth article "The Peasant in the Salons of Contemporary Novelists," published in the *Cause* in four installments during 1879, he advanced the theme he had stated before: the peasant was seldom treated with honesty, seldom viewed objectively as a full, whole man. Sometimes he was viewed as subhuman; sometimes he emerged recreated in the image of the *intelligent*. Sometimes he was elevated to a pedestal on the basis of certain mystical ideals. He was distorted into the personification of virtue, the embodiment of love, peace, patience, devotion, foolishness, simplicity, ignorance, or Mother Russia. Neither Westerners (Tkachev mentioned Turgenev) nor Slavo-

philes (Dostoevskii) were interested in him for himself; rather they used
him to justify their own viewpoints.[86]

Tkachev again was particularly critical of those writers who painted
the contemporary peasant in rosy tones. In 1876 in several articles in
the *Cause* he made free to attack the populists of *Fatherland Notes* and
Nedelia (Week). Comparing N. K. Mikhailovskii and his colleagues with
the old *pochvenniki* who published their bucolic tales in the Dostoevskii
journals of the early sixties, Tkachev castigated the idealists who saw
village people as pure and devout. The irrational was not necessarily
moral, he wrote, and knowledge not always the corruption of good.[87]
Each of the populists had his own moral concept of the peasantry,
Tkachev growled. To Dostoevskii the village stood for Orthodoxy; to
Mikhailovskii the "Russian people" was a total *profession de foi.*[88]
Others found the peasant patriarchal, moral, virtuous, the bearer of
culture; to Boborykin, Tkachev's own ex-editor, the village was no more
than pure confusion.[89] These new progressives, as they dared to call
themselves, had inherited the Slavophile concept of holy peasant and
consecrated earth and were convinced that peasant life had only been
perverted by the formulae, legalisms, and aridness of Western thought—
by the Western propensity for the realistic, the rational, and the scientific. An article in the *Week* claiming that Russian literature had been
sucked of its vitality by professionalism, remoteness, and foreign
influences Tkachev saw as rehabilitating the thought of the Slavophile
Kireevskii brothers.[90] The "healthy part of society," he wrote, had
always stood on the side of the Westerners. Those "false patriots" who
saw everything Russian as glorious and everything Western as crass he
rejected out of hand.[91] If he was indeed a populist at all, this angry
critic had nothing but scorn for his bedfellows.

To his pleasure, Tkachev wrote, he discerned in recent articles a
more scientific and objective approach to peasant life. Descriptive
research on language, dress, and mores in the village was beginning to
reveal the peasant as he actually existed. Writers went to the countryside, visiting towns and fairs, trying to discover what this strange sub-
culture was really like. Analytical sociologists were dissecting family
and social relationships; others were studying peasant psychology and

---

86. See chap. 6 above.
87. Tkachev, 4: 16-31.
88. Ibid., p. 22.
89. Ibid., pp. 23-24.
90. Ibid., p. 9.
91. Ibid., pp. 324-25.

the inner man.[92] Research was, Tkachev thought, not yet adequate, but a beginning had been made. So far no writer had delved deep enough to determine the particular characteristics that made the Russian peasant unique.

For Tkachev's peasant was as distinctive and unique as the gentle *paysan* portrayed by Russian novelists. In accordance with the critic's principles of environmentalism he viewed the peasantry as cast in a special mold by the traditional ways of village life. In particular the peasant was shaped by the principle of communal living. It was the *mir* that determined the traits of the peasant's character, his socialistic outlook, and even his attitude toward revolution.

The commune as an institution embodied the form of social organization Tkachev had admired in his discussions of Spencer and Quinet.[93] For in the peasant commune, society ruled over the individual, and the individual existed for the collective alone. The peasant, Tkachev wrote,

strives . . . to submit the individual to the social. . . . The family and personal interests are so closely merged and interlaced with the *mir*, [with] common interests, that in the majority of cases it is difficult even to define where the one ends and the others begin.[94]

In Tkachev's rosy picture the *mir* and the peasant were intertwined and devoted to each other. The *mir* protected and sheltered each family within it. It found a special place for women, although Tkachev had to admit that members of the weaker sex were not permitted to participate in communal decisions. For his part the peasant fit into the *mir*; he and his family never maintained independence as a unit unto themselves. He was always devoted to his community: "His personal, family interests and his *mir* interests are so closely and so firmly interlaced that he by necessity must hold the latter almost as close to his heart as he holds the former."[95] No single individual in the village escaped the pervading influence and protectiveness of his commune.

This principle of community, this absorbing social system molded the peasant's psyche and distinguished him forever from men of the outside world. Tkachev took a stand against the educated intelligentsia when he wrote:

The kingdom of cultured people is primarily a kingdom of anarchy, of mutually opposed, antagonistic, individual interests and strivings. To this kingdom the *"mir* people"* . . . really present sharp exceptions, fresh sparkling pinpoints against the general dark background.[96]

92. Ibid., p. 215.
93. See chap. 8 above.
94. Tkachev, 4: 225.
95. Ibid., p. 239.
96. Ibid., p. 240.

Molded by their commune, the peasants developed egalitarian, altruistic, and benevolent views toward their fellow man. In the commune, Tkachev wrote, each lived the life of all, and all lived the life of each brother. The people of the village shared their joys and sorrows with each other. Their only goals were to aid their neighbor in his need, to lighten his burdens, to help in life's great struggles. They protected him as they protected their *mir*, for they would defend it against incursions, stand for it against outsiders, sacrifice for it, and kill for it should that become necessary.[97] In this mood of harmony and altruism, in this eternal consciousness that the whole is more than the individual and society more than its parts, the peasant lived his dedicated life. He knew no other way.

Nobody ever denied and will never deny the undebatable fact that a social structure of life built on the principles of equality and communal solidarity permits the development of humane, altruistic feelings in people to a comparatively greater degree than a social structure based on the principles of competition, individualistic isolation, on the principles of conflict of personal interests.[98]

Like other elements of his character the peasant's revolutionism was conditioned by the communal way of life. In his arguments with Lavrov and Engels as well as in certain early articles in the *Cause* Tkachev had claimed that the peasant was ready to rebel; he could be moved to action by the intelligentsia, particularly if he were convinced that his cause would succeed. Left to himself, unstimulated by external forces, the peasant was unable to initiate revolutionary action. Tkachev had an explanation for this quiescent outlook of the Russian peasantry: the *mir* was, he wrote, of a passive nature. Fundamentally, he admitted, it was conservative in tone; it preserved tradition and stability, progressing or regressing "only when some sort of external jolt pushed it out of its stable equilibrium."[99] In his discussions of Spencer he had anticipated just such an equilibrium in the future harmonious society. But the ideal passive nature of the commune obviously conditioned the peasant's attitudes and made him less eager for revolution and change.

Tkachev had to admit of some flaws. The commune was not perfect. Gleb Uspenskii, whose tales he reviewed, had discovered some problems. People unable to work were not permitted to belong to the *mir* and were often heartlessly cast out. Poverty existed where there should be plenty. Moral swinishness occasionally broke into the circle of altruism. Some of the egotism and selfishness of the capitalist world seeped through cracks in the village walls. Solidarity was corrupted by

97. Ibid., pp. 276-87.
98. Ibid., p. 260.
99. Ibid., p. 330.

competition through the practice of allocating lands to individuals and households for their use.[100] Tkachev was sure this duality evolved out of constant struggles for existence. Bring prosperity to the countryside, he hinted, and the peasant would live in harmony without fear.

Deviations from the principles of community could be traced through the history of the *obshchina* itself. Tkachev delved back in time. The Russian commune, he wrote, had its identical counterpart in the West, a point Engels had once made to him. Any differences really reflected the chronological age of the one as compared to that of the other; they did not represent essential disparity in nature. All communes (and Tkachev had done his homework in the Scandinavian, Indian, German, and English traditions) originally featured not only common ownership but the common tilling of all lands. All of them (at a pace determined by factors ranging from climate to conquest) gradually disintegrated; the centuries had seen the communal principle in retreat.[101]

Tkachev believed the troubles of the commune developed out of external not internal problems. The early Sumerian military communes, he wrote, lost their essential nature under pressure of foreign invasion. The same fate shattered the pure communistic tradition in Russia when in the ninth century the Ruriki superimposed an upper class above the egalitarian members of the *mir*, expropriated communal lands, and imposed such high taxes as to destroy communal prosperity. Violently Tkachev attacked those idealizers of Russia's peaceful origins who felt that the Varangians made no more than superficial changes in early Russian civilizations.[102] The destruction of the harmonious communal way of life could hardly be termed an insignificant episode in history.

When the screws tightened on the commune, its members began a desperate struggle for survival. As arable land became scarce and valuable owing to princely seizures, the commune was forced to supervise the division of land between desperately quarreling households. Periodic reapportionments became necessary and competitive. Individual working of lands replaced communal labor. The *obshchina* was forced to restrict the freedom of its members, for flight impeded the crucial collection of taxes. It increased its directional powers; it developed fiscal and police authority. By the end of the seventeenth century the commune had proved itself unable to protect the peasant from poverty or to provide security against the outside world.

---

100. Ibid., p. 295.
101. Ibid., pp. 325-27.
102. Ibid., pp. 330-35.

The communal tradition lost and communal power destroyed, many peasants fled to seek protection from the powerful and the rich. The rich devised their own solution. Tkachev's version of the introduction of serfdom made this vital process seem like a measure legislated by the upper classes overnight in the most casual manner. Rejecting the economic theory that serfdom resulted directly from peasant indebtedness, he espoused the legalistic view: the upper classes enacted this daring solution of the labor problem for their own benefit. At first hesitant (as though ashamed of themselves, Tkachev wrote)[103] the high nobility by 1649 had finally tied the peasant to the land. In contrast to those historians who regarded serfdom as inevitable under the given socioeconomic conditions, Tkachev viewed it as unnecessary, as a kind of vast historical blunder, an evil deed perpetrated by a powerful interest group.

It was simply one of the greatest historical errors, costing Russia so dearly. Society has paid a high price for this mistake, and when finally it recognized this, when it was moved by a passionate irresistible wish to cleanse itself from this "historical sin," it was almost in the same economic situation in which serfdom had found it.[104]

For serfdom was economically debilitating for every class. The peasant obviously hated it; his continued flights converted him into a village tramp like the old *guliashchie liudi*. The small landowner sank into poverty in spite of the new labor supply. The rich suffered because agriculture remained technically in a primitive, low-productivity stage.[105]

Thus the promised land of communality with its security and its plenitude, its altruism and its social consciousness, fell victim to conquest and greed. In spite of his legalistic version of the coming of serfdom Tkachev seemed to feel that the commune was historically doomed to fall, just as eventually the feudal relationship between peasant and landowner was bound to disintegrate. Tkachev identified three basic elements of the economic structure in labor, immovable capital (primarily land), and movable capital (money, bonds, and so on). Drawing on Spencer, he advanced the idea that the process of history resolved itself into the progressive differentiation of these forces. The landlord-peasant evolved into two different entities although as a serf the peasant retained some of his ancient feudal property rights. Eventually movable capital arose as a new economic factor and began to

103. Ibid., pp. 342-43.
104. Ibid., p. 349.
105. Ibid., pp. 198-203.

devour the old landed assets, merging landowner into capitalist in a pattern that Spencer had suggested.[106]

Tkachev clearly anticipated the coming of capitalism to Russia. His acceptance of the view that Russia and Europe had hitherto traveled the same economic path set him apart from some of his contemporaries. He was sure that the pattern of the West was being generally recapitulated in Russian history. He saw his native land still on a lower stage of development, still in a transitional period during which neither movable nor immovable capital (neither money nor land) had the power to dominate the economy. Reiterating the opinions that had so irritated Engels, he insisted that in this transitional stage no powerful social class dominated in his native land. Landlords were weak, destroyed by the system of serfdom that had plunged them so deeply into debt. Capitalist interests were embryonic, for the process of differentiation of movable capital from immovable had barely begun. Even when it started, it seemed unlikely to Tkachev that a near-impotent father (the landlord) could produce a healthy capitalist child. That left labor.

Only the third factor of economic production, that factor represented by the "ignorant peasant," is thus revealed as the sole self-sufficient economic force. Only he alone, poorly or prosperously, lives on his own account, stands on his own feet, and not only does not draw any resources from the state budget but on the contrary himself provides its resources [which are] necessary for extended aid and support to the other factors of economic production.[107]

In Russia's transitional stage Spencerian differentiation and integration were not as far advanced as in the West. Peasant, land, and capital were only beginning to find parties of support such as had developed in the West.

The historical experience of Western Europe shows us that with the influence of the progressive dismemberment, the progressive differentiation and integration of the factors of economic production, social consciousness [and] social thought . . . also disintegrate, also become differentiated and integrated into two [or] three separate directions [and that] each direction [of social thought] always is based strictly on that economic factor, the interests of which it embodies.[108]

In Russia such parties were still embryonic in form, chaotic, not yet distinguished by clear programs, and not yet clearly separated one from another,[109] but Tkachev recognized them as harbingers of the coming capitalist system.

Russia's path lay toward capitalism, but Tkachev was sure there was

106. Ibid., p. 196.
107. Ibid., p. 203.
108. Ibid., p. 197.
109. Ibid., p. 198.

a way to save her. He believed in the power of men's wills in history; he had already advanced the theory of possible historical jumps.[110] We in Russia, he wrote,

can begin our history "with those primitive forms through which all peoples have passed in their historical development" and [still] never live through such economic evils as Western Europe is suffering. This is obvious even to a small immature child, but alas! it is certainly not obvious to our patriots although many of them are not only completely mature but long since overripe.[111]

The particularly revolutionary solution Tkachev proposed could of course not be specified in the legal Russian press.

Tkachev's idealization of the commune—for he surely idealized it in spite of his recognition of some of its failings—was based on his concept of the future communistic society. The commune came as close to what he sought as any institution in or out of Russia in Tkachev's time. To see it for what it was in this period of disintegration of the communal principle might mean to denigrate for his readers the fundamental principles of communism. To view the peasant as an ordinary man, uninfluenced by the *mir* or, worse, hostile to it, would undercut his contention that communist society would produce harmonious man and that environment forms the individual. Like the classic populists whom he continually attacked, Tkachev was caught on the horns of a dilemma. He solved his problem by donning the same rose-colored glasses he accused his opponents of wearing. The peasant who emerged from his writings was no more real that Mikhailovskii's peasant. The village was no more true to life than the village Dostoevskii portrayed. And in 1870 the commune itself was far more perverted from its origins than Tkachev was willing to admit.

Under the circumstances it seems that Tkachev deliberately evoked for his Russian readers a better peasant than he knew to exist. His own actual viewpoints, expressed in his Geneva journal after 1875, were more realistic. Here the peasant's revolutionism was restricted to local and destructive forms. Here the peasant's socialism was so slightly ingrained as to demand physical force to push him back to the communal way of life.[112] Tkachev's view of the peasant was far more pessimistic than the picture he painted for the legal Russian press. His feigned optimism was only his way of converting his readers to his own utopian vision of the future.

---

110. See chap. 5 above, pp. 90-91.

111. Tkachev, 4: 324-25. The quotation is from a study Tkachev was reviewing, a book by a man named Vasilchikov.

112. See chap. 11 below.

Tkachev's contributions to the legal Russian press were at an end. His essays right up to 1880 were distinguished by the acuity and acerbity through which he had made his reputation. He continued to attack his colleagues—novelists, essayists, and critics—as sharply and bitterly as any Russian journalist of his time.

The conclusions he reached were no longer optimistic. He analyzed Russian literature and found it and its critics wanting in terms of the standards he set, standards first espoused by Belinskii and the radical critics of his youth. He agonized over his own generation—the intelligentsia of the sixties—and recognized its failure to live up to what he considered its grand potential to be one of the severest disappointments in his own sad lifetime. He turned to philosophy in the hopes of setting men back on the right path, for the men of the seventies were flirting with ideas foreign to his own generation and contrary to his own beliefs. The balance sheet remained negative. Only in the peasant had Tkachev found hopes for the future, and even the peasant was not to be depended upon; Tkachev knew him better than he cared to say.

In his writings of these latter years Tkachev himself had taken on a kind of maturity; he had abandoned the optimistic ideals that had once marked his essays. Gone were his efforts to devise an answer to the problems of will and determinism; gone were his plans to set forth a philosophy that would explain progress or clarify history. Like the other men of his generation Tkachev had settled for somewhat less.

But in 1875, living abroad, he had not abandoned his hopes. He still believed that the spark of the revolutionary cause might be blown to a new flame, that the young intelligentsia could still be recruited for noble battle. In Switzerland he plunged into the greatest project of his life without realizing that it too would end in failure.

11

The *Tocsin*

For a few brief years after 1875 Tkachev busied himself with concerns more important to him and to history than his writings for the legal Russian press. He had fled abroad in 1873 and immediately embarked on polemics with his enemies, polemics that launched his career as a young, violent, and audacious revolutionary on the international scene. But his role in the polemics was negative; he could only attack. In his argument with Lavrov he felt the lack of a vehicle of his own, a journal on the pages of which he could freely express his own plans and beliefs. What was a long-cherished hope reached fruition two years later. In 1875 in company with some new-found friends Tkachev began his own revolutionary journal. Working with sympathetic collaborators on a publication of his own in the free air of Geneva—it may have been the dream that drove him away from his native land. In the pages of the *Nabat* (Tocsin), a name evoking yet more urgent summons than that of the famous *Bell*, Tkachev could pour forth his ideas in print with the collaboration of men who shared them.

In the *Tocsin* Tkachev's revolutionary plans reached their fullest expression. Here he clearly set forth those ideas that have caused him to be known as a Blanquist or, less accurately but more often, a Jacobin. Here he continued his running battle with Lavrov and took up arms against Bakunin's anarchists and Marx's social democrats as well. Here he made a handful of friends who stood by him for the rest of his brief lifetime. Here he made a name for himself, repugnant to many, attractive to a few, but written indelibly on the pages of the history of Russian revolutionary thought.

The circumstances surrounding the founding of the *Tocsin* and the formulation of its revolutionary program remain obscure. Neither Tkachev nor any of his colleagues on the new journal seems to have systematically preserved records of the agreements about financial arrangements, editorial responsibilities, and policy that must have preceded the *Tocsin*'s appearance. No notes have been discovered regarding the first contact established between the colony of Geneva Communards and the newly emigrated Russian critic; one of the Communards later said he had "conspiratorially" sought out Tkachev on the basis of his reputation,[1] but Tkachev too must have been searching for like-minded friends and supporters. Contact may well have been made during Tkachev's first brief stay in Switzerland from December 1873 to March 1874, perhaps through the Russian émigré colony. On the other hand it is possible that the Communards were first attracted to Tkachev through the summary of his ideas published by Lavrov after the two had quarreled. Perhaps Tkachev discovered the similarity of his views with theirs during his stay in Paris in the summer of 1874, a Paris that must still have been talking about some of the Commune's defenders.

Speculation is complicated by Tkachev's own penchant for secrecy. Through the year 1874 Tkachev was writing—he regularly published articles in the *Cause* in St. Petersburg—but even his whereabouts are uncertain. His stay in Paris after he left London lasted at least several months; beyond that it is only certain that he was back in Switzerland late that year. In spite of his relative security in Western Europe Tkachev never advertised his activities; travels, residences, and friendships were kept under wraps by this secretive young man. Still he demonstrated no urgency in returning to Geneva and getting to work; the *Tocsin* did not appear until two years after his first stay in Switzerland. At the time he quarreled with Lavrov he apparently had no plans for the future. If he met the Blanquist Communards, they could not have decided to work together before 1874.

The exact role played by Tkachev's Communard friends in the formulation of his final revolutionary program is more important and

---

1. This was the Polish émigré Gaspar Mikhail Turski; see Nikolaevskii, "Pamiati poslednego 'iakobintsa'-semidesiatnika," p. 219. Much of the material on which Nikolaevskii based this article (material on the whole quite favorable to Turski's points of view) is drawn from a correspondence between Turski and V. L. Burtsev in 1924 and 1925, preserved in the Hoover Institution archives, Stanford, California, B. Nicolaevsky collection, file 221, folder 2. Burtsev was seeking the files of *Nabat* from Turski, who apparently left them with a friend when he left Switzerland. The files disappeared, probably destroyed when Turski's friend died a short time later.

equally difficult to determine; indeed it has been a matter of debate among historians of Russian revolutionary thought. Tkachev's name is most frequently identified with that of Louis Auguste Blanqui, lifelong revolutionary, founder of Parisian secret societies, archadvocate of conspiracy, and mentor of a considerable faction among the Communards. Blanquism, which merged the influence of Babeuf and Buonarroti with the aura of the French Charbonnerie and its Italian prototype, was a considerable force in the Parisian underground and later even in the Third Republic's Chamber of Deputies. Tkachev probably first came to know it in Switzerland. He may indeed have heard Blanqui's name before he left Russia; the acquaintance of young Russian radicals with the works and deeds of their European counterparts is often startling in view of tsarist efforts to impede it. But Blanqui was no bookwriter, and those of his ideas that were committed to paper appeared only in his notes and in his newspapers, never widely circulated outside of Paris.[2] Even in France people knew less of Blanqui's theories than of his deeds, and the same probably held true in other countries. The elements of Blanquism hidden in Tkachev's works in the legal Russian press and the explicit expression of the *Tocsin*'s program made in almost the same words to Lavrov in 1874 were of Tkachev's own independent devising. But the followers of Blanqui whom he met in Geneva added something unique: they encouraged him to set his views into a system, they solidified his beliefs, they supported him and bore him out. Tkachev came into his own when he found their kind of reassurance.

Blanquism as encountered by Tkachev in Geneva was distinguished by a special character of its own. True, among Tkachev's new acquaintances were people who had known and worked with Blanqui in Paris. They included men whose commitment to the "Old Man," as Blanqui was called, and whose Communard experience had not distracted them from political and intellectual accomplishments—such were Edouard Vaillant, later elected to the Chamber of Deputies, and Elisée Reclus, famous scientist, geographer, and writer. But Vaillant and Reclus were contributors to the journal; they may have inspired Tkachev, but they did not formulate the *Tocsin*'s policy on any regular basis. Nor did the several other editorial employees—like the Russian P. G. Grigorev, of whom little is known—influence policy decisions. Instead Tkachev met Blanquism primarily secondhand through a man who worked closely with him and apparently provided the journal's financial support—an

---

2. The posthumous collection entitled *Critique sociale*, published in 1885, contained the clearest formulation of Blanqui's ideas produced in book form.

extremist of unsavory reputation and arrogant personality named Gaspar Mikhail Turski.

Several years younger than his new Russian colleague, Turski was a Polish émigré, ex-Communard, and one-time friend of Nechaev.[3] A man of noble and wealthy background, he first came to the attention of the Russian police during the Polish Revolution of 1863. He attended Kharkov University in the early 1860s and in 1866 or 1867 (after the Karakozov affair) he was exiled to northern Russia. In 1869 he escaped to Switzerland, but he soon found his way to Paris. There he fell in with a group of Polish exiles who were followers of Blanqui; Turski probably belonged to the Society of Seasons during the last year of the Liberal Empire. As French forces collapsed during the Prussian War, he joined the Polish Legion organized by Garibaldi. Eighteen seventy-one found him fighting on the barricades with the Paris Communards. He was one of many who escaped when Thiers's forces moved into Paris in May. He fled to Zurich, where he apparently became part of a Jacobin circle among the Russian and Polish émigrés there.[4] His instinct for conspiracy was cemented in a brief friendship with Nechaev in 1872 in Zurich, where the latter was hiding, hoping to escape arrest and extradition to Russia.[5] Some time in 1874 Turski apparently moved to Geneva and lived on the outskirts of the colony of Communards who settled there.

By all accounts, Turski was a man of strong personality and positive convictions. But for all his Parisian associations, Turski's Blanquism remained less an intellectual commitment than a call to action. Salted as it was with a dose of Nechaevism, with his personal drive for violence and terrorism, with his arrogance and elitism,[6] it became perverted in many measures away from Blanqui's original themes. In his association with Tkachev, Turski never maintained as firm a Blanquist stance as the young Russian himself. Their relationship on the *Tocsin*, therefore, was probably from the start uneasy. Prone to exaggeration, Turski later claimed that Tkachev had nothing to do with formulating the journal's program, a task he said the Jacobin colony had accomplished before

---

3. The information noted here is derived from the article by Nikolaevskii, "Pamiati poslednego 'iakobintsa'-semidesiatnika."

4. The existence of this circle has been asserted in ibid., pp. 215, 219-20.

5. See also Nettlau, "Bakunin," p. 412; Ralli-Arbore, "Nechaev"; Sazhin, *Vospominaniia 1860-1880-kh gg.*, pp. 62-74; and the many documents and reminiscences published in Lehning, *Michel Bakounine*.

6. For a negative view of Turski's character see Deich, *Russkaia emigratsiia*, p. 85.

Tkachev ever appeared.[7] Yet the young Russian had clearly stated his plans to Lavrov as early as 1874 before he and Turski embarked on the journal project.[8] Whoever moved first, it seems clear that the collaboration was born of necessity; Turski had the money, Tkachev had the ideas and the literary talent. In the early days it was clearly Tkachev who dominated. The program of the *Tocsin*, phrased in his own words, contained his unique blend of Blanquism with Russian populism and Western intellectualism. Turski's influence remained in the background until 1878. Then the two of them quarreled.

The first issue of the *Tocsin* appeared on December 1, 1875. As tradition demanded it contained the journal's revolutionary program.[9] The slogan on the first page was Tkachev's favorite; he had told it to Lavrov almost two years earlier. "Now," the masthead demanded, "or if not very soon, perhaps never." Tkachev's feeling for the urgency of revolution in Russia was devised from his estimate of his homeland's peculiar situation and unique needs. Blanqui had never been driven by the same compulsion to accomplish the revolution at once before time raced on and revolution became impossible.

The title article "Program of the Journal" was clearly written by Tkachev and based on his own analyses as expressed before in his polemics with Lavrov and Engels. The toll of the *Tocsin*, Tkachev claimed, cried urgency, but it symbolized more than that. The strident bell sounded not just for alarm but to call the population to a peak of dedicated, community self-sacrifice. The opening paragraphs of the new journal contained an urgent plea for unity, Tkachev's theme, not Turski's. Tkachev had said something similar to Lavrov.

With the glow of a fire when the sound of the tocsin peals out, each man abandons his home and speeds to the blaze to save the property and life of his neighbor; the abstract idea of the solidarity of human interests emerges here in all its real force and simplicity. Each feels that only by saving the property of another can he save his own. Personal enmity, petty trivial squabbles—all is forgotten in the face of the common danger. Enemies stand side by side and act as one. Everything that is petty, squabbling in man fades into the background; his most elevated, most noble motives move forward. Thus only abject cowards, only weak egotists remain deaf to the sound of the tocsin.

Thus those moments when it rings out are usually the best moments in national life although these are moments of the greatest popular calamity.

7. Nikolaevskii, "Pamiati paslednego 'iakobintsa'-semidesiatnika," pp. 219-20. It is actually uncertain how close Turski was to the Blanquist émigré colony. His own statements should be taken with a grain of salt.

8. See chap. 9 above, pp. 196-203.

9. The journal's program has been reprinted in Tkachev, 3: 219-31.

We are now living through such moments.
The time has come to strike the tocsin.[10]

Urgency, the driving pressure of time—Tkachev had explained it to Engels and he told his readers again. As "bourgeois progress" (or capitalism) developed, Russia's economy and social structure would change. A powerful bourgeoisie would replace the weak gentry as the most influential social class. The state would become stronger as it drew increasing support from the new capitalists. Thereby the revolution would become more difficult to accomplish. Today we are strong, Tkachev cried in the new journal, and our enemies are weak. "Today [the state] is absolutely absurd and absurdly absolute. Tomorrow it will become constitutionally moderate, prudently bourgeois."[11] What Tkachev called economic progress would lend new life to the government, tender it new vigor and new power, and produce new and more potent enemies to the revolution.

Capitalism would in addition destroy that unique communal spirit that gave Russia such an advantage in achieving the socialist idea.

Look! The fire of "economic progress" already has touched the basic roots of our national life. Under its influence the old forms of our social life are already being destroyed, the very *"principle of the commune"* is being annihilated, the principle that must lie as a cornerstone of that future social structure about which we all dream.[12]

Tkachev admitted that he agreed with Engels.[13] The *obshchina* and its spirit were being undermined although the Russian saw the development as retarding the revolutionary cause and the German as abetting it. If capitalism were permitted to expand and to devour Russia's social tradition, the *obshchina* and its communality would disappear. In a later article Tkachev made it clear that artels would of course suffer the same fate.[14]

Time, then, was of the essence. Time dictated Tkachev's Jacobin plans as it had not those of Buonarroti and did not those of Blanqui. The program of the *Tocsin* screamed of time.

It is time, it is time to take up the real cause. . . . We cannot for a moment forget that our immediate goal is the revolution, revolution not in the far-off future, not "sometime," but right now, close to us in the present. We must not forget that, deviating from this goal, allowing various delays and procrastinations, we will become traitors to our people. "Its blood falls on us and our children!" Our own

10. Ibid., p. 219.
11. Ibid., p. 220.
12. Ibid., p. 219.
13. See chap. 9 above, p. 210.
14. Tkachev, 3: 272.

children will curse us as traitors to the people's cause, as apostates from their principles, as conscious accomplices and colleagues of the nations' hangmen.[15]

Time pushed Tkachev to action. It was a rare moment in history, he cried to his readers. To let it slip meant to "postpone the possibility of social revolution for a long time—perhaps forever."[16] If Tkachev's new friends contributed cohesive elements to his revolutionary program, he surely added the element of time to theirs.

How, then, should revolutionaries react, what should be their aims? Tkachev insisted that they concentrate on practical methods for struggling against the autocracy, on a definition of immediate goals, ending their maunderings about the far-off future. They should abandon their procrastinations and stop putting the revolution off. Even in this first program, Tkachev bitterly attacked Lavrov's Utopian fallacies and Lavrov's reliance on long-term propaganda to bring about the successful uprising.

At a time when [youth], filled with power and faith, throws itself into the cause and wants as rapidly as possible to tear from the people the chains set upon it, they say to [youth]: "wait, do not touch, first *propagandize*, inspire, preach, and then later raze." Anarchy as the closest immediate goal of the revolution, propaganda as the practical means for realizing it, and finally organization without discipline, hierarchy, and submissiveness—is all this not a fantastic Utopia, not childish dreams?[17]

In the *Tocsin*'s program, Tkachev admitted that anarchy was, after all, the Utopia men should seek. The anarchy he endorsed was no bourgeois creation but represented rather that social harmony, with its total identification of one man's desires with those of his neighbor, he had sought in considering contemporary Western social thought. If Tkachev was ready to accept statelessness as an ideal, he continued to insist that it was unthinkable without the absolute fraternity and total equality of men. In order to establish his kind of anarchical society where men cease exploiting one another, in order to establish brotherhood and equality among people,

it is necessary in the first place to change the given conditions of social life, to destroy all those institutions that bring into the life of the people inequality, hostility, hatred, competition, and to lay the basis of institutions bringing into [social life] the opposite principles; in the second place, to change the very nature of man, to re-educate him.[18]

---

15. Ibid., pp. 237-38.
16. Ibid., p. 221.
17. Ibid., p. 222.
18. Ibid., pp. 223-24.

Tkachev had always thought it possible to remake human nature; his environmentalism had shown him the way.

But who could accomplish this revitalization of mankind, the institution of that equality, harmony, and peace that must necessarily precede the establishment of the stateless, free world? It was a task to discourage any man whose way was not lit by optimism and hope. Tkachev thought it could be done. It demanded, first of all, inspired leadership.

Of course, only people who understand it and sincerely strive for its solution can realize this great task, that is, people morally and intellectually developed, that is, a minority. This minority, in the light of its higher intellectual and moral development, always has and must have intellectual and moral power over the majority. Consequently, the revolutionaries are people of this minority, revolutionaries, embodying in themselves the better intellectual forces of society. . . .[19]

By the intervention of what his opponents were to call an elite the revolution would be accomplished.

Tkachev's revolutionary minority could not expect to complete the job on the basis of its prestige alone. Its first task was to change the nature of its power, to substitute for its present "purely moral, so to speak spiritual, character" such material strength as could successfully challenge the government's military forces.[20] Power was anathema to a Lavrov; it was essential to a Tkachev.

In this metamorphosis of powers lies the basic essence of any true revolution. Without it revolution is inconceivable. Intellectual force isolated from material force can create only so-called *peaceful progress*. On the other hand, any assault on the existing order of things not led and not disciplined by intellectual force can lead only to chaotic fermentation—a thoughtless, aimless, and in the long run always reactionary movement.[21]

Only the armed, militant intelligentsia could make revolution, Tkachev was saying. The scholarly, ivory-tower man, although he might be conscious of revolutionary aims, never had the potency to create the real uprising.

Revolution demanded material power. How, then, could such power be acquired in Russia by an intellectual, morally superior revolutionary minority? Tkachev's answer was clear: since armed force in Russia was presently concentrated in the hands of the government, the minority must seize the government and take to itself the government's material strength. "In other words, the immediate, direct aim of the revolution must consist in nothing else but acquiring governmental

19. Ibid., p. 224.
20. Ibid.
21. Ibid.

power and transforming the present *conservative* state into a *revolutionary* state."[22]

Even in his first program Tkachev made it clear that the seizure of power was not the ultimate aim of the revolution. The overthrow of the government could not be considered the revolution itself. The seizure of power, he wrote,

is only [the revolution's] prelude. The revolution will be realized by the revolutionary state that, on the one hand, fights and destroys the conservative and reactionary elements of society, abolishes all those institutions that impede the establishment of equality and brotherhood; on the other hand, introduces into the way of life institutions favorable to their development.[23]

Tkachev's statism had not diminished; the state had its uses, and he proposed to take all possible advantage of them.

After the seizure of the government the revolution would be brought about by force. The revolutionaries would utilize the state and its coercive power to effect the revolution itself. The *Tocsin*'s program recognized that the revolutionary state could not expect to achieve its goals without violence. Some of the changes Tkachev anticipated he termed revolutionary-destructive, and others revolutionary-constructive. The former involved elimination of all institutions deemed foreign to the revolutionary objectives. Destructive change was characterized by the use of powerful weapons.

The essence of the former is struggle and consequently *force*. The struggle can be conducted with success only by combining the following conditions: centralization, strict discipline, speed, decisiveness, and unity in actions. Any concessions, any hesitations, any compromises, variations, decentralization of the fighting forces weakens their energy, paralyzes their action, deprives the struggle of all chances for victory.[24]

Revolutionary-constructive actions were different.

Revolutionary-constructive activity, although it must go hand in hand with destructive activity, must still by its very character operate on completely opposite principles. If the former primarily operates on material power, then the second does so on moral force; the first has above all in mind rapidity and unity of actions, the second, durability and practicability of changes introduced into life. The first is realized by force, the second by conviction; the *ultima ratio* on one is victory, *ultima ratio* of the other is the people's will, popular intelligence [*razum*].[25]

Here, under "constructive activity," Tkachev listed the spreading of education, the raising of moral ideals, the realistically cautious steps

22. Ibid.
23. Ibid., p. 225.
24. Ibid.
25. Ibid., pp. 225-26.

that might be taken to establish a popular, representative assembly. Construction demanded less discipline and less bloodshed than destructive action. Tkachev even found a place for Lavrov's propagandizing, an activity impossible to promote under the tsarist regime.

We realize . . . that without propaganda the social revolution cannot be realized, cannot be brought to life. But we affirm . . . that propaganda can only be effective, expedient, can only bring about the results expected from it when material power, when political power lies in the hands of the revolutionary party.[26]

Propaganda, reconstruction, and re-education could only take place *after* the revolutionaries have seized the government. Tkachev specifically listed the nature of the reforms toward which his revolutionary government would strive. There would be, to begin with, a remodeling of the *obshchina*, turning it back toward its ancient policy of common ownership of tools and common labor on the land, abolishing the contemporary practice of allocating land to families and individuals for private exploitation. Means of production would be expropriated and turned to public use. The revolutionaries would strive to end competition and substitute the principle of brotherly love and solidarity while they worked to end inequalities and to renovate public education in the spirit of love, equality, and brotherhood.[27] Tkachev's program demanded that fundamental of so many nineteenth-century revolutionary plans, the "gradual elimination of the existing family, which is based on the principle of subordination of women, slavery of children, and the egotistic arbitrariness of men."[28] Finally, he promised the development of communal self-government simultaneously with the gradual weakening of the centralized state, a suggestion that had not previously characterized his views on government at all.

The program of the *Tocsin* contained one more major point in Tkachev's system, a measure anticipated in many of his previous writings. He could not help but consider the character of the revolutionary party and its organizational principles. Conspiracy, he made clear, was the best method of attaining the immediate goal, that is, the overthrow of the tsarist government. But conspiracy dictated militant organization, both before and after the seizure of power. Autonomous, decentralized, federalized groups were impotent and vulnerable; Tkachev went so far as to identify them with the bourgeois principles of individualism, personality, and egotism, as opposed to the socialist principles of totality, collectiveness, and the submission of individual

26. Ibid., p. 226.
27. Ibid., p. 227.
28. Ibid.

parts to the whole.[29] The revolution must be directed by one vital body, acting by one common plan, subservient to one common leadership—an organization based on "centralization of power and decentralization of revolutionary functions."[30] Conspiracy demanded, of course, secrecy. Legalism and openness Tkachev rejected out of hand. Legal forms were dead forms, he insisted; real revolution must be secretly won.

In the conspiracy against the state the people must not be forgotten. "The successful attainment of our goal," Tkachev announced (in the tone of an afterthought), "is unrealizable without the direct and indirect support of the people."[31] Even before the seizure of power he planned to encourage the organization of *bunty,* the local, self-sufficient, spontaneous outbursts of revolution among the peasantry, long advocated by Bakunin. He anticipated a division of functions: the conspirators would seize power from above while the *bunty* enforced revolution from below. As he had told Lavrov, there was room for everyone in the revolutionary struggle. Bakuninists could immediately aid in the fray; Lavrovists would have their tasks later.

The *Tocsin*'s program ended with the insistence that Russia was indeed unique, as Tkachev had contended to Engels.

The major materials for the development and explanation [of the revolutionary movement] we will draw from our Russian life; these conditions are so unique that they create a completely special situation for the Russian revolutionary party among the ranks of the revolutionary parties of Western Europe, place it in a more or less exclusive relationship toward people, society, and government. To see in these relationships a complete analogy with the relationships existing in the West (as some do) is not to understand that radical difference that exists between the economic and political conditions of a society only now beginning to take its first steps along the path of bourgeois progress and a society that has attained the highest culminative point of this progress.[32]

Rejecting a common membership, common leadership, or the changing of Russia's immediate aims, Tkachev still suggested that Russian revolutionaries closely coordinate their affairs with those of Western European parties and especially with Polish revolutionary groups.

The program of the *Tocsin* raised many questions about Tkachev's own convictions, both in terms of the fuller explanation of some of its points and in regard to possible sources of Tkachev's ideas. Tkachev himself (often under attack from other Russian émigré publications)

---

29. Ibid., pp. 227-28.
30. Ibid., p. 228.
31. Ibid., p. 229.
32. Ibid., pp. 229-30.

explained and enlarged on his program in subsequent issues of the journal in a series of articles, identified by Kozmin, which appeared sporadically from 1876 to 1878. The major questions and issues, although always interrelated, may be considered separately as to sources and significance.

THE MAKERS OF REVOLUTION

Tkachev's concept of the intellectually and morally developed minority that was to seize power and thereafter retain control of the state during the revolution's dictatorial period demands careful consideration, for it is this phrase that has earned him the term *elitist* from adversaries and scholars alike.[33] The presence of some sort of revolutionary elite is of course necessary to any plans for secret conspiracy, since conspiracy by nature is the work of a few and cannot be revealed to nor shared in by the passive majority. However, the phrase "intellectually and morally superior" has elitist overtones beyond the terms previously employed by Tkachev. Tkachev never carefully set down the exact qualifications for his revolutionary leaders. In later issues of the *Tocsin* he modified the phraseology of the original program. His own concept of a good revolutionary seems to have been based more on dedication and heroism than social or intellectual distinction.

Indeed the concept of an intellectual elite was totally in opposition to Tkachev's earlier statements. Intellectual superiority he had always rated as characteristic of the effete and the impotent.[34] Even in the same *Tocsin* program in which he first used the elitist phrase he had sneered at the inability of intellectuals to lead a revolution.[35] He had always derided Lavrov's "critically thinking individual" as a revolutionary leader; his review of the *Experiment in the History of Thought*, in which he set the intellectual at the opposite pole from the activist and harangued the former for his inability to act decisively, appeared by coincidence in the *Cause* during the same month when the *Tocsin*'s program was published.[36] His own "People of the Future" resembled Chernyshevskii's dedicated elite far more than Pisarev's intellectually oriented "thinking proletariat." Indeed if Tkachev held hopes for the *raznochinnaia* intelligentsia it was not because of the keenness of their critical abilities, which he came seriously to doubt, but because of their practicality and their ability to act. To this Russian elitist activism stood at the opposite pole from intellectualism. Even "morality" had

---

33. Cf. Venturi, *Roots of Revolution*, pp. 426-27.
34. Tkachev, 3: 224.
35. Ibid.
36. See chap. 9, pp. 214-15.

never sufficed to define the revolutionary temper unless by morality Tkachev had in mind dedication, sacrifice, and devotion to the cause.

His new Blanquist friends could scarcely have suggested intellectual superiority as a condition for the ideal revolutionary without going against the grain of their own inclinations and backgrounds. Blanqui had drawn on Buonarroti and on the example of the Carbonari in putting together his revolutionary organizations in Paris.[37] His conspirators could hardly have been considered intellectuals: the Blanquist secret organizations probably contained more actual laborers than the other revolutionary parties of his day. The Old Man himself was fond of calling them déclassés, referring to members of modern urban society who had rejected their class origins, a social category not unlike that of *raznochintsy*.[38] The Blanquists were never as conscious of social origins in mobile Paris as was Tkachev in rigid Russia. Blanqui himself, a journalist by profession, on at least one occasion insisted that he was a proletarian and often considered intellectuals as déclassés.[39] In the secretive, semi-Masonic ritual of initiation into Blanqui's revolutionary organizations, intellectualism played no role.[40] Rather Blanqui's men, associates of Tkachev's new colleagues, were an assemblage of what Buonarroti had called "wise and devoted men," a phrase more accurately descriptive of Chernyshevskii's characters in *What Is to Be Done?* or of Tkachev's own men of the future than of any intellectually and morally well-developed faction.

It is tempting to believe that the whole elitist phraseology sprang from Turski. Turski had little commitment to Blanqui's philosophy; he was a Blanquist only by adoption and less involved with the Parisian-style organization than were Tkachev's other colleagues. His support of Blanqui had not kept him from becoming a dedicated Nechaevist and a disciple of Robespierre.[41] According to contemporaries Turski was endowed with arrogance and egotism, which they found annoying.[42]

---

37. Cf. Venturi, pp. 398, 777 (note 26). Tkachev may well have known Buonarroti's work on the Conspiracy of Equals since Ralli-Arbore and his student circle possessed a copy of this book immediately before the Nechaev affair. Buonarroti termed his conspirators "wise and devoted men"; he sometimes substituted "wise and courageous" or "wise and vigorous." Cf. Arthur Lehning, *From Buonarroti to Bakunin*, p. 83.

38. See Alan B. Spitzer, *The Revolutionary Theories of Louis Auguste Blanqui*, pp. 162-65; Boris Isaakovich Gorev, *Ogiust Blanki*, p. 92.

39. Gorev, *Ogiust Blanki*, pp. 89-90.

40. Louis Auguste Blanqui, *Izbrannye proizvedeniia*, includes description of the Blanquist rituals and oaths, pp. 115-24.

41. Venturi, pp. 779-80 (note 81).

42. Deich, *Russkaia emigratsiia*, p. 85.

Surely it was Turski who, next to Tkachev, most intimately influenced the pages of the *Tocsin*. The phrase "intellectual and moral superiority" could easily bear his personal stamp, for it hardly carried Tkachev's.

The elitist overtones of the *Tocsin*'s program irritated some of Tkachev's critics, and it is interesting that he himself changed his tone in future articles. Accused by a number of anarchists of drawing his leaders only from the privileged environment, the educated elite, Tkachev quickly denied the charge, seemingly retreating from his own original words. The revolutionary minority, he wrote, would be drawn from many classes: from the peasantry, from the petty bourgeoisie, from the intelligentsia.[43] Education would not provide a standard for admission, and the minority would not be exclusively intellectual. Tkachev excluded only two social groups from among his revolutionaries: the elite class of gentry (by which he meant the wealthy; his own origins lay in the poor stratum of the gentry class) and—even more vehemently—the bourgeoisie, against whose "progress" the revolution must be directed. The bourgeoisie, he wrote, could never be revolutionary; if certain members of the class temporarily joined the cause, they would only be "revolutionaries by misunderstanding."[44] The concept demonstrated how far Tkachev stood from the Blanquists when he asserted the uniqueness of the Russian situation. In Paris Blanqui particularly welcomed the bourgeoisie into his revolutionary clubs; "thank God for the bourgeoisie," he once wrote.[45] His dislike of capitalism never caused him to eject a so-called wise and dedicated man from the revolutionary ranks because of his social background. Tkachev never saw it that way.

Polemicizing with his antagonists, Tkachev denied their contention that his revolution would be antipopular. Among the conspirators would stand members of the people itself. Tkachev insisted that what he had first called intellectually and morally developed revolutionaries would not really be superior in social origin and education but rather in dedication and something Lenin later termed consciousness—an insight into the importance of the cause and a knowledge of its goals.[46] Education would not be essential, he wrote. The revolutionary who emerged from Tkachev's reassessment was not so remote from the man he had

---

43. Tkachev, 3: 248.

44. Ibid., p. 249.

45. Blanqui, *Izbrannye proizvedeniia*, p. 166. Blanqui thought the bourgeoisie could provide other classes with leadership. There is an interesting discussion in Gorev, *Ogiust Blanki*, pp. 89-90.

46. This analogy was actually made by the perceptive Akselrod, *Perezhitoe i peredumannoe*, p. 198.

envisioned before: the man distinguished by dedication, willingness to sacrifice, and an understanding of revolution born of some supraeducational wisdom. Tkachev quietly dropped the phrase "intellectually and morally developed" and never used it in his *Tocsin* writings again.

Whatever the social and intellectual backgrounds of his revolutionary minority, Tkachev never satisfied his opponents in his definition of the minority's relationship to the people both in the conspiratorial and the postrevolutionary periods. His neglect of popular, social revolution as an element in his schemes drew him more criticism than any other facet of his plans. "Do you really think you can push the people around this way?" Pavel Axelrod, the young expatriate Bakuninist (soon to become one of the first handful of Russian Marxists) remembered asking one of Tkachev's colleagues.[47] The anarchists accused the *Tocsin* of a haughty attitude toward the people, of arrogance, of seeking revolution without popular support, of advocating revolution only from above. They echoed Lavrov's insistence that the revolution must be social and not strictly political in nature.[48] Both Bakunin and Lavrov had considered the intelligentsia to be potential revolutionary leaders but not so much makers of the revolution as inspirers of the people in its cause. For Bakunin young men and women were to become agitators, arouse the peasantry to those spontaneous local rebellions he called *bunty*, and coordinate *bunty* so as to broaden the revolution throughout the land. For Lavrov critically thinking men, having first educated themselves, would spread propaganda among the majority, educating it to a level (perhaps not quite to their own) of understanding that would cause it to rebel. In Tkachev's early plans, insofar as they can be read through the censor's constant threat, the intelligentsia would play a role of encouragement and inspiration among peasants otherwise reluctant to take a chance. But in the *Tocsin*'s program the majority was relegated to one brief paragraph near the end, in which (perhaps as a sop) Tkachev admitted that conspiracy could not succeed without the direct or indirect support of the people.[49]

Tkachev's insistence that revolution be made by a minority grew out of his feeling of urgency and his realistic estimate of the revolutionary potential of the Russian peasantry. The conviction that the peasantry was capable of fomenting successful revolution—a conviction shared by tsar and revolutionary alike—Tkachev regarded as an illusion.

47. Ibid.
48. See above, chap. 9.
49. Tkachev, 3: 229.

The peasant was revolutionary in potentiality, he was "*ready* for revolution," Tkachev wrote, playing with the words he had first used to Engels.[50] However, the peasantry was not revolutionary-active in the sense of instigating rebellion. The trouble was, Tkachev told his readers, that the peasant world was steeped in conservatism and tradition. Even the communistic *obshchina* was hidebound by its own past and by no means a revolutionary organization, as Tkachev noted in his special study. It was stagnant, stale; it was bowed down by inertia; it would move only when pushed or driven. "In it there is nothing that can move it forward or backward; all its elements are in steady equilibrium."[51] Awareness of his poverty and the misery of his life was not enough to turn a peasant away from his past and lead him to active revolt. Action based on rational decision, Tkachev wrote, was reserved to "people standing on a very high stage of intellectual and moral development; people used to living the intellectual life, used to formulating all their actions on purely intellectual motives,"[52] a description that comes close to negating the Tkachevian view of intellectual impotence. But the peasant could not shake tradition and rebel because his emotional attachment to his old ways was stronger than his intellectual capacity to look to the new.

Nevertheless, the peasant was ready for revolution in the sense that he might well be moved to action by some outside force. Tkachev considered two methods. The Bakuninist call to *bunty*, he thought, might be successful. Peasant passions might be aroused by agitation, and the peasant might be led to a "paroxysm of delirium" in which he would take up the axe against society in strength lent by passion. But Tkachev was not sure. The peasant was by nature passionless, phlegmatic, and bred with a slave instinct for accepting his lot that even agitators would not easily overcome.[53] Bakunin's plans could easily founder on the rock of the peasant's nature. Tkachev was more certain of his second scheme. The peasant would become a revolutionary, he wrote, if he were convinced in advance that his actions were bound to be victorious. The best way to move him to rebel was to demonstrate to him the actual impotence of the government he had been taught to fear. Convince the peasant that the state really "hangs in the air," in Tkachev's earlier phrase, and he would recognize its weakness in the face of his own strength. In other words, "*We (that is, the revolutionary minority), we must first shatter, weaken, destroy the political structure*

---

50. Ibid., p. 242.
51. Ibid., p. 263.
52. Ibid., p. 243.
53. Ibid.

that oppresses him—the conservative, exploiting, autocratic state.[54]
Once the government was deposed by the revolutionary conspiracy the
peasant would rise and join in battle. Years before Tkachev had urged
the intelligentsia to demonstrate to the peasant that he was more
powerful than he thought.[55] Until then Bakunin's plans were probably
no more than delusions and dreams.

His negative evaluation of the Russian peasant as revolutionary was
clearly Tkachev's own assessment based on his studies and reviews for
the legal Russian press. Tkachev soon recognized the similarity of his
conclusions to those of Blanqui who, discouraged by the failure of the
Commune to spread to the provinces and mourning the peasants'
refusal to rise to revolution in 1848, had come to believe that most
Frenchmen were not revolutionaries. The convergence of their ideas delighted the young Russian. In the same issue of the *Tocsin* in which he
revealed the illusion of peasant revolutionism Tkachev printed a short
report on a series of readings sponsored in Geneva by the Swiss section
of the International.[56] Of all the speakers he was most impressed with
Elisée Reclus, whom he had probably met before in the *Tocsin*'s
formative days. A one-time colleague of Kropotkin on an anarchist
French journal and (unlike Tkachev) an admirer of Bakunin, Reclus
discussed geographical and social divisions of the population in France
and came to the conclusion that peasant owners (who loved their
possessions), the agricultural proletarians (who hoped to become
peasant owners), the priests, bureaucrats, aristocrats, and even the
majority of workers in France were not revolution-minded. Proletarians, Reclus reported, were far too oppressed by their miserable living
conditions to devote themselves to other concerns: "No revolutionary
propaganda in their environment can count on success."[57] Tkachev had
made the same point before in regard to the Russian peasants. Reclus
saw only small, privileged groups of workers as revolutionary by inclination; he shared Blanqui's intuitive feeling for the Paris mob. The same
situation, Tkachev wrote in his review of the lecture, applied throughout Europe; he might have added in Russia as well. Reclus and Blanqui
joined in Tkachev's insistence on minority revolution rather than social
upheaval simply because they too believed the latter impossible to
attain. Tkachev's admiration for Reclus, first publicly expressed here,
seems never to have varied.

54. Ibid., p. 244.
55. See above, chap. 6, pp. 111-13.
56. Tkachev, 3: 258-61; see also James Guillaume, *L'Internationale: Documents et souvenirs*, 4: 8.
57. Tkachev, 3: 261.

Skillfully making use of his many proofs, surrounding himself with figures and facts, the lecturer developed and proved his thesis with such convincing clarity that all [the other] childish argument flew into dust before it.[58]

THE METHODS OF REVOLUTION

The necessary concomitant to the peasant's refusal to become a revolutionary was that somebody would have to make revolution for him. Because no other social class of Russia (or of the West) was intuitively revolutionary and there was no time left for education or lengthy polemical preparation, the natural answer was that revolution must be made on behalf of the people by the revolutionary minority. But this minority was small, its forces spiritual (in Tkachev's word) rather than physical. Since it could not hope to defeat the tsarist army in the field, it must proceed by another plan: it must overthrow the tsarist government and seize the reins of state power by means of secret, politically oriented conspiracy.

The method of conspiracy was dear to Tkachev's heart. He never seriously in writing considered any other except as an adjunct. As early as 1866 he had endorsed conspiratorial methods as the most potentially successful means of revolution, and there is no evidence that he ever thereafter changed his mind.[59] Tkachev was the product of a Russia (as he insisted to Engels) in which oppositional political activity was not legally tolerated. He matured in the 1860s, a decade when conspiracy was the form of operation accepted by antigovernment groups and when underground circles were a prime modus operandi. Pisarev had been associated with such an illegal group; the association resulted in his imprisonment. Chernyshevskii's name was linked with the early Land and Freedom organization in St. Petersburg.[60] Even the frequently romantic Ogarev had urged young Russians to turn to conspiracy against the state.[61] In his years in Russia Tkachev had certainly himself operated within secret, illegal circles. By 1875 he was aware of the past existence of many of them, including Land and Freedom and Ishutin's student organization (Moscow).[62] Indeed secrecy can become a facet of psychology, deeply engrained in a man who was trained to it and who by his natural reserve preferred to operate quietly and alone. Tkachev's own penchant for secrecy, whether or not it was necessary, led him to slip out of Russia without telling even his common-law wife;

---

58. Ibid., p. 260.
59. See above, chap. 4, pp. 70-71.
60. Venturi, pp. 251, 171; Pisarev, pp. 141-47.
61. Ogarev, *Izbrannye proizvedeniia*, 1: 527-28.
62. Tkachev, 3: 395-420.

sneak out of England without facing his adversary-editor; and conceal his movements around Europe as though he were constantly faced with the threat of imprisonment and extradition.

By nature and upbringing a secretive conspirator, Tkachev found re-enforcement elsewhere. Scholars have suggested that he studied the Conspiracy of Equals in Buonarroti's published description dating from 1835.[63] Yet the conspiracy of 1793 could hardly have served as a model for Tkachev's plans in that the followers of Babeuf publicized their activities with the aim of rousing popular support; Buonarroti did not turn to secrecy until years later, probably under the influence of the Carbonari.[64] The Blanquist model, carried to Tkachev by the Geneva Communards, more positively re-enforced the young Russian's convictions. Blanqui began his active political life with involvement in conspiratorial societies dedicated to armed insurrection, and so he was to end it.[65] Blanqui's reputation with the revolutionaries in Paris rested primarily on his gifts as an organizer and forger of militant plans. Tkachev admired and respected his example. More immediately his colleague Turski passed on the conspiratorial arts as he had learned them. At Kharkov University during the 1860s Turski became acquainted with the conspiratorial mood of student organizations there. He learned more from his experience with the Paris Commune. Turski's acquaintance with Nechaev was even closer than Tkachev's and his approval of Nechaev's methods surpassed Tkachev's tempered evaluation. As the major link between Tkachev and the Blanquists, Turski encouraged the Russian editor's own inclinations and added a tone of his own.

If conspiracy was the form the revolution should take and secrecy was the key to successful conspiracy, then the disciplined party became the cornerstone on which revolution must be constructed. Tkachev always insisted that the revolutionary party "act by one common plan, subservient to one common leadership."[66] Individualism, diversity, and decentralization would inevitably give the secret away and spoil the game. An unorganized revolutionary party, an undisciplined host, could be no more than "an unhappy Penelope, destroying each night with her own hands everything that she had worked by day."[67] Only

63. Buonarroti's account of the conspiracy was known to Ralli-Arbore and his circle, so it may be presumed Tkachev read it too. Venturi suggests the indebtedness, p. 398.

64. Lehning, *From Buonarroti to Bakunin*, p. 68.

65. Spitzer's biography of Blanqui emphasizes Blanqui's role as an activist.

66. Tkachev, 3: 228.

67. Ibid., p. 286.

militant, taut, centralized, hierarchical organization could successfully seize power and provide the basis for the government that must make the revolution. Tkachev was fond of the same army analogy that Blanqui often used in describing his forces.

Tkachev drew on the Russian example to prove his point. In a long article printed in *Tocsin* in 1878, he insisted that the history of Russian revolutionary movements had demonstrated that only conspiratorial, secretive methods could attain success.[68] His heroes were the Decembrists and the Petrashevskii Circle; he exaggerated the force and purpose of both almost beyond recognition. He referred to the secret student organizations of his own youth: the organization Hell [Ad] and the Nechaev conspiracy, about which a number of his factual statements were exaggerated and inaccurate. True, he admitted, these movements had failed—if indeed they had ever actually attempted—to unseat the tsar, but they demonstrated their worth, Tkachev believed, in that the captured members of the organizations did not turn informer and many eluded capture at all. On the other hand such revolutionary movements as the Going-to-the-People fiasco of 1874, a particular small society founded in Moscow in 1875 by some ex-Zurich students, and the Chaikovskii Circle (Tkachev's benefactor in his escape from Russia, here called reactionary) asked for trouble through the loose and undisciplined nature of their organizations. In a time of crisis many members were arrested and the societies easily disintegrated under pressure. On the basis of his historical survey Tkachev concluded that decentralization and federation of revolutionary parties would lead to dramatic failure and to personal insecurity for their members. On the other hand militant organizations provided greater force and disgorged fewer victims to the investigating police. Aware that he was out of step with the new times, Tkachev urged revolutionaries to return to the conspiratorial methods of the sixties, to the "old type of well-tested centralized organization. In it lies their power; in it their salvation."[69] He proposed that the Bakuninists and Lavrovists abandon their easy-going revolutionary ways and join him in a hierarchical, centralized force. The plan fell notoriously short of success in spite of Tkachev's urgent pleas for unity.

In 1878 in his article on the importance of secrecy in revolution Tkachev tersely announced the formation of a new secret organization to be called the Society of Popular Liberation.[70] At a future and

68. Ibid., pp. 382-404.
69. Ibid., p. 403. Tkachev's account indicates that he never knew how Ralli-Arbore turned informer in regard to the Nechaev conspiracy.
70. Ibid., p. 404.

unspecified date a statute of the society was issued in pamphlet form.[71] Although this statute was probably composed by Turski, not Tkachev, it seems certain that Tkachev was aware of its contents and that it met at least his tacit approval.

In view of the political oppression and economic exploitation of the people of Russia, the statute read, the society was constituted "with the aim of rapidly overthrowing the monarchy, fully destroying any exploitation of the people, and proclaiming their natural rights based on political and economic equality."[72]

The regulation demanded full secrecy. Members were to be known only to the "Committee," the organization's mysterious leadership. The Committee alone admitted them to membership; withdrawal was permitted only with Committee approval. The leadership kept in communication with the members through a network of agents. Members were instructed to keep in touch with these agents and report regularly to them, especially as to their own immediate location. The "Instruction to Members," a separate document, outlined specific obligations.[73] Members were to relay to agents (and thus to the Committee) information as to activities of local administrative, judicial, and police authorities, about any troop movements in their assigned area, about the situation in prisons, the mood of young people, and the temper of the workers (peasants were not mentioned). They were to distribute books and literature as instructed and whenever possible influence local authorities in whatever direction they might be commanded to do so. One of their duties was to inform the Committee's local agent about any revolutionary circles they discovered in their districts. Indeed the members of the new organization resembled a revolutionary-oriented secret police, and their duties closely approximated those of traditional spies. Secrecy was emphasized in the statute again and again. No member should reveal his membership in the society to anyone under any circumstances, except, of course, when instructed to do so. The penalty for betrayal was, melodramatically, death, surely reminiscent of the student Ivanov's demise at the hands of Nechaev.

Several elements of the society's operations deserve special attention for their apparent variance from Tkachev's personal code. The most important is clearly the murder clause. In its penalties for betrayal the Society of Popular Liberation resembled not Blanqui's organizations

71. This statute has been published by E. Kusheva, "Iz istorii 'Obshchestva narodnogo osvobozhdeniia," *Katorga i ssylka*, no. 4 (77) (1931), pp. 56-57.

72. Ibid., p. 56.

73. Ibid., pp. 57-61.

but Nechaev's views. The provisions of the notorious revolutionary "Catechism" that Nechaev and Bakunin composed, as well as Nechaev's premeditated murder of Ivanov, anticipated the society's command. Tkachev had not approved of Nechaev's methods; in his analysis of Dostoevskii's *Demons* he had found Nechaev and his friends to be psychologically ill. In Geneva Turski apparently persuaded him to endorse what he had once rejected, for Turski represented not just a link with the Blanquists but—even more—a tie with Nechaev and his actions. Luckily the society's murder clause remained a dead letter. At least one member is known to have withdrawn at his own request without suffering any drastic consequences for his change of heart.[74]

A second element arising both in the society's statute and in its purported activities might also be traced to Nechaev's influence. "Mystification" was secrecy carried too far, and just such mystification to the point of deception was Nechaev's trademark in his relationships with the student community in St. Petersburg and later with Bakunin in Switzerland. On the society's documents mysterious numbers represented a code or perhaps nothing at all. Mysterious persons, identified by initials, were reported expelled from the society for mysterious misdeeds; the first such expulsions were announced in the same issue of the *Tocsin* that reported the society's formation.[75] Tkachev had his penchant for secrecy, but the mystifying byplay took on the foolishness of a childish game. The hand of Turski was probably more closely involved.

Never had Tkachev come closer to a public endorsement of Nechaevism. The "Program of Revolutionary Actions" of 1868-69 had advanced concepts he had not entirely condoned, such as the conviction that a peasant rebellion could be fomented by the revolutionary intelligentsia at work in the countryside. The giant, nationwide conspiratorial organization the society now envisioned was not necessarily equipped to promulgate the deed Tkachev saw as its goal: the overthrow of the tsarist government. A taut circle of St. Petersburg conspirators would have been better suited to the task Tkachev had in mind. Nevertheless under Turski's influence he moved back to the Nechaevist plan; the society closely resembled in structure the organization Tkachev and Nechaev had attempted to set up six years before.

Thus through Turski (although with Tkachev's tacit approval) the Society of Popular Liberation derived its nature from Nechaev's tradition as much as from the pattern set by Blanqui's Parisian organiza-

---

74. Ibid., p. 35.
75. Ibid., p. 40.

THE *TOCSIN* 269

tions. The Blanquist pattern did not always prevail, not only owing to the imposition of Nechaev's influence but owing to differences in the French and Russian experiences. Like the *Tocsin*'s, Blanqui's organizations were based on centralization, hierarchical structure, and discipline. Blanqui had learned from Buonarroti—the Buonarroti of the Carbonari of 1830 rather than of the Conspiracy of 1793. The organization of Blanqui's Society of the Seasons and the Society of Families was structurally more complex than Tkachev's and Turski's plan for individual operators and contact agents. Mystification found outlet in Blanqui's plans in the neo-Masonic ritualistic practices adopted, particularly during initiation;[76] there is no evidence that Tkachev and Turski copied these rituals at all. Blanqui's demands for secrecy were equally rigorous and even more difficult to enforce. Members of his organizations knew each other; they met together with considerable frequency in each other's apartments or in certain Paris cafes, most of them known to the French police.[77] Secrecy was a grave problem for Blanqui, and eventually the Blanquists abandoned it as a principle and came out into the open. Tkachev and Turski ran into trouble too. Their own role in founding the secret Society of Popular Liberation could hardly be doubted by potential members. The identity of the secret leadership was thereby at once revealed. In their efforts to attract members Tkachev and Turski published accounts of heroic deeds by individuals in Russia by no means consistent with their demand for concealment.[78] Indeed the very idea of publicly announcing the formation of a secret society was contradictory to say the least. The need for support outdistanced the need for discretion.

Blanqui's considerations in forming his societies differed from those of the Geneva Jacobins and the societies themselves reflected the diversity. Blanqui pulled around him not so much an organization to manipulate a palace coup d'état as one successfully to man the familiar Parisian barricades. His men constituted an army that was to operate on a detailed, preordained battle plan.[79] Resolute men, capable of shooting a straight shot, bred to the barricades and knowledgeable in their construction, formed the center of Blanqui's corps. Although Tkachev

76. Blanqui, *Izbrannye proizvedeniia*, pp. 115-24.
77. Spitzer, p. 159; cf. Maurice Dommanget, *Les idées politiques et sociales d'Auguste Blanqui*, pp. 351-58.
78. Cf. Kusheva, p. 35 (note 3).
79. Blanqui's detailed plans for the military capture of Paris have been published by Georges Bourgin under the title "Instruction d'une prise d'armes," *Archiv für die Geschichte des Sozialismus und der Arbeiterbewegung* 15 (1930): 270-300.

referred to his party as an army, he meant not a group possessing military skill so much as a group trained in military discipline and obedience. If he dreamed of an armed force, winning one after another the streets of St. Petersburg as the Russian tsar (like the French kings of 1789, 1830, and 1848) fell or fled, he never wrote such plans or they have not been preserved to us. The conspiratorial activities of the Society of Popular Liberation were not even to be concentrated in St. Petersburg where the tsar lived. It is difficult to imagine how the society might have proceeded.

Tkachev's method of revolution aroused as much enmity among his émigré contemporaries as the elitist nature of the minority party. Political revolution was regarded by most Russian radicals of 1875 only as one facet of social revolution, as the result of a popular upheaval that would overthrow society and topple government along with it. Tkachev's view was directly the opposite. Political revolution was to him a necessary precursor of social upheaval. Social upheaval resulted from the overthrow of government instead of vice versa. Tkachev agreed with Blanqui, who insisted that political power was essential to successful social revolution, for only government's force could destroy the "conspiracy of capital" and the "black army of the clergy," to say nothing of providing constructive social advances.[80] This whole statist power-oriented plan was anathema to the contemporary Russian anarchists. From Marx to Bakunin socialist revolutionaries had insisted that revolution must be made by the people. Tkachev's *Tocsin* was the only important Russian journal of the day that advocated political instead of social revolution, and the policy caused his isolation from the other Russian émigré groups.

AFTER THE REVOLUTION: DICTATORSHIP

Given Tkachev's premises, the demand for a temporary dictatorship following the political seizure of power was logical enough. According to the program of the *Tocsin*, constructive and destructive tasks awaited the power instruments that would belong to the revolutionaries once the coup d'état was achieved.[81] Blanqui used the same phrases.[82] The revolution must destroy its enemies, a task that demanded physical force and in which it could afford to show no mercy. In achieving this goal the revolutionaries could count on help from below, for the lethargic peasants, convinced now of the revolution's success, would take up the axe and the people would become spontaneous leaders in

---

80. Blanqui, *Izbrannye proizvedeniia*, pp. 226-30.
81. Tkachev, 3: 225.
82. Spitzer, pp. 177 ff.

the destruction of the exploiters, landlords, and government officials for whom they bore long, simmering hatred. Yet Tkachev recognized the limits of this hatred: the peasantry was immersed in its concept of the tsar as father, in its adulation of the Orthodox church.[83] Dictatorship must stand firm and act fast in its destruction of those undesirable elements in peasant life that the peasant himself looked upon with pleasure. The peasant, steeped in conservatism, bred under the traditional, passive, patriarchal influence of the *mir*, would not do the job thoroughly enough, and the destruction of counterrevolution could not completely be left to him, for all his profound grievances.

In terms of the constructive work of the revolution the majority could surely not be relied upon. Left to itself it would soon retreat into the ways of life it had always known. It had, Tkachev was saying, little desire for a new order; rather it preferred to carry on the old ways, destroying only those superficial evils of which it was keenly conscious. Force would be necessary to move the peasant in his own behalf; power must necessarily be applied to set his life in a new mold.

Do you seriously think that in order to recreate certain private, family, and social relationships—relationships developing for centuries and supported by all the habits, instincts, and sympathies of the people, that for this mere moral influence is sufficient? Mere spiritual power? Do you imagine that the power of conviction means more than the power of routine?[84]

Revolution having been made on its behalf, the majority would have to be compelled to a better world. The newly seized government would have to force the peasantry to change its way of life "according to its true needs, according to the ideal of the best, most just common life."[85] The power of dictatorship was necessary not only to destroy the revolution's enemies but to construct the new society.

The revolutionary minority, having liberated the people from the oppressive yoke of fear and horror of the powers that be, opens to [the people] the possibility of manifesting its destructive revolutionary power, and, operating on this power, skillfully directing it toward destroying the immediate enemies of the revolution, it destroys the fortresses preserved by [the state] and deprives them of any means of resistance and opposition. Then, using its own power and its authority, it introduces new progressive-communistic elements into the conditions of popular life; moves this life from its century-old stagnation; animates its stiff and cramped forms. . . . *The revolutionary minority, benefiting from the destructive-revolutionary force of the people, destroys the enemies of the revolution and, basing itself*

---

83. Tkachev, 3: 312-13; he brought up these points in one of his attacks on Bakunin.
84. Ibid., p. 254.
85. Ibid., p. 252.

on the common spirit of the positive popular ideal (that is: the conservative powers of the people) lays the basis for a new reasonable order of social life.[86]

Thus Tkachev admitted that what he had extolled to Engels as the "instinctive communism" of the peasantry would not suffice. He was forced to agree (with G. V. Plekhanov and Engels, among others)[87] that the forces of individualism had advanced so far in his native land as to make any peasant communistic instinct unreliable at best.

Dictatorship, then, was the only method of bringing about the vast social equality that the peasant did not want but which, in Tkachev's view, he should have. The conservative nature of the peasantry would be not a help but a hindrance.

The [peasant's] social ideal is the self-governing *obshchina*, submission of the individual to the *mir*, the right of private usage but not private ownership of the land, mutual responsibility, brotherly solidarity of all members of the commune—in a word, an ideal with clearly expressed communist overtones. Of course, it is still very far to full communism from the forms of life conditioning this ideal; communism is hidden in them, so to speak, in the kernel, in the germ. This kernel can expand, but it can also be smothered.[88]

If the peasant was a communist, he was passively communistic and he could only be expected to support the revolution passively if at all.

Because of the *obshchina*'s conservative nature Tkachev rejected the anarchist hope that this peasant commune would immediately become the core of the new government. Until most peasants were permeated by revolutionary principles the *obshchina* and local government were bound to remain conservative. Thus any decentralization would lead to a reaction, to a counterrevolution, to the revolution's defeat.[89] To be revolutionary the government must be highly centralized. To introduce the social revolution it must possess power. Tkachev was not taking an extreme position, he wrote; for even the maintenance of simple public services (postal services, regulation of weights and measures, education) demanded that any government have the power to enforce its laws.

His anarchist enemies could not see things his way. But the idea of dictatorship had never frightened Tkachev as it did his more democratic colleagues. Much of Tkachev's thinking before 1875 led him to accept and endorse undemocratic means to his egalitarian ends. He had harangued against the sham externals of that democracy that benefited only the rich. He had written of the need for the social whole to rule

---

86. Ibid., pp. 266-67.
87. See Plekhanov, *Sochineniia*, 2: 148-49; also above, chap. 9, pp. 210-11.
88. Tkachev, 3: 263
89. Ibid., p. 255.

over its parts to the point of what he called "collective dictatorship."
His dislike of anarchism and his statist inclinations, re-enforced by his
legal training and his respect for the force of law, divorced him from
anarchistic fears of centralized, concentrated force. Rejecting anarchism
as bourgeois, he contended that the state in itself was not evil. The evil
lay in the purposes to which the tsars had put it. Tkachev saw government as potentially constructive, a tool for enforcing reforms, a means
for achieving social equality, an institution for protecting the weak and
the poor. In his early writings he clearly foresaw the state's acting to
coerce society to a better future. "Why do you fear the word *state*?"
he cried in *Tocsin* to his anarchist critics. "To fear words is a sign of
childishness."[90]

Tkachev's own conclusions were re-enforced from many sides.
Revolutionary dictatorships were nothing new although they took
different forms among different advocates. Robespierre had been a
revolutionary dictator although he was less dictator by principle than
expediency; Tkachev must have heard much of Robespierre from
Turski, who was a follower of the Robespierre cult. Buonarroti, whom
Tkachev probably knew before his escape abroad, had elevated Robespierre's expedient means of governing to the status of theory; he
endorsed dictatorship by the conspirators and he once wished that
Robespierre could return to life and lead the Conspiracy of Equals
toward its hoped-for victory.[91] Marx's dictatorship was to be that of a
class, as exercised through its vanguard. Blanqui insisted that the dictatorial leaders (probably a triumvirate) were to be elected by the
entire Paris population; the Old Man's laconic phrase to describe the
government of France during its transitional period was a "dictatorship
of Paris," a dictatorship by the men he knew and trusted.[92] If Tkachev
had once endorsed a transitional government elected by limited suffrage
such as Blanqui anticipated, he had come by 1875 to feel that even
semidemocratic measures might defeat the revolution. In the end his
dictatorship had one of the narrowest bases of all.

For in Tkachev's revolutionary government (as in Buonarroti's)
control would rest exclusively in the hands of that same unrepresenta-
tive minority that had seized power in the first place. His dictatorship
was one of conspirators rather than popular favorites, cities, or classes.
No good revolutionary, he wrote, would let power slip through his victorious hands (like the French republicans in 1848) simply by turning

90. Ibid., p. 253.
91. Lehning, *From Buonarroti to Bakunin*, p. 81.
92. Blanqui, *Izbrannye proizvedeniia*, p. 231; Gorev, *Ogiust Blanki*, pp. 94-95;
Dommanget, pp. 170-73.

his fate over to popular judgment.[93] The minority must take on the responsibility of creating the social revolution by dictatorial means. Countering claims by the Bakuninists that no minority entrusted with power would long remain true to the people's welfare, Tkachev insisted that his men of revolution would never betray the cause. Power could not corrupt honest men, he wrote.[94] Robespierre—and it is Tkachev's rare reference to any of the men of the French Revolution whose contributions his colleagues so hotly debated—Robespierre in power remained true to his aims. Once committed, a revolutionary, in the image of a "man of the future," forgot his egotism and sacrificed everything for the great cause. "The personal element," Tkachev wrote, "never plays and never can play any important role."[95] If all men were not perfect and a few succumbed to the temptations of power, this percentage of failure was inevitable and would characterize men until they became angels. Tkachev insisted that his selfless dictators, the minority who made the revolution, could and must be trusted with the powers they themselves had seized.

As to the tasks of the revolutionary dictatorship Tkachev was somewhat more explicit than many of his contemporaries. Certain basic social reforms should be enacted. The legal basis for certain antiegalitarian institutions must be destroyed. The dictators would begin a program of popular education in the spirit of brotherhood, aid the *obshchina* in its climb toward pure communism, and otherwise prepare the ground for a future when man would equal man and harmony would reign. Like Blanqui Tkachev set for his dictators both negative and positive goals. Unlike Blanqui he anticipated the use of force in achieving them. For Blanqui's instructions to his dictators in Paris were hesitant and cautious compared to the radical Russian's. The French revolutionary seemed concerned that the conspirators keep the wheels of society turning smoothly and instruct everyone to stay at his post. Blanqui had great faith in the efficacy of education. Education and communism to him went hand in hand.

The moon will fall to the earth sooner than one will establish a system of communality without the inevitable element—education. It would be as difficult for us to breathe without air as for [communism] to exist without education, which is its air and its conductor. Between education and communism such a close tie exists that the one cannot take a step without the other, neither forward nor backward.[96]

93. Tkachev, 3: 372.
94. Ibid., p. 251.
95. Ibid., p. 283.
96. Blanqui, *Izbrannye proizvedeniia*, p. 223.

He was convinced that an educated people would automatically turn to communism as its ideal form of life. Although Tkachev set education as a task for the dictatorship, he never believed it would be enough. To the Old Man communism was inevitable once people learned about it; to Tkachev education represented Lavrov's way and would not in itself suffice. The popular masses would have to be coerced into accepting their happy fate.

The dictatorship of Tkachev's conspirators would last a long time, he explained. People who had read the *Tocsin*'s program were wrong to believe that Tkachev's statism anticipated the legislation of revolution by decree. He had been misunderstood, he complained; he did not believe that the minority could perform their task simply by changing the laws. The social revolution would take time even if the revolutionaries possessed all the powers of a government in arms. Tkachev may have read Buonarroti before he wrote:

They do not understand . . . that the social revolution, that the construction anew of all our economic, juridical, all our social, private, family relations, all our viewpoints and understandings, our ideals and our morality, that such a revolution will not be accomplished in one or even two years, that it will demand the work of a whole generation, that it appears not *ex abrupto* but is prepared and brought to life slowly, gradually, step by step. Never did we, socialist-revolutionaries, deceive ourselves on this account, never did we imagine that it would suffice for us to seize power in our hands and the next day we would make all society happy, establish communality of possessions, organize common labor for the common benefit, destroy the family, uproot from their foundations all the durable shameful egotistical instincts and habits of people, recreate all their emotions and thoughts, beat down their ingrained prejudices and superstitions and so on.[97]

Tkachev's dictatorship, like that of Karl Marx, was unlimited in time; a lot had to be accomplished. Blanqui restricted his Parisian leaders, sometimes to a year, sometimes ten, sometimes as many as seventy.[98]

Tkachev and Blanqui were both hazy in their plans for ending the dictatorship once the need for it was past. Neither man trusted democracy, Blanqui out of his bitter experience in the days of 1848, Tkachev from his estimate of the conservative nature of the peasantry. But both men anticipated instituting democratic forms once the need for force was over. Tkachev only mentioned the possibility once when he spoke of the cautious institution of what he called a "land assembly." Blanqui spoke of elections once the people were properly educated.

To both of them, obviously, future programs could wait. What was vital was the revolution itself. Most important was getting there and, to Tkachev, getting there as soon as possible.

---

97. Tkachev, 3: 280.
98. Blanqui, *Critique sociale*, 1: 183, 207-9; 2: 154.

AFTER DICTATORSHIP: COMMUNISM

"The final goal of social revolution is the victory of communism," Tkachev wrote in the *Tocsin*.[99] Yet in the pages of his journal Tkachev never described communism in any detail. Like Marx and Blanqui, he left only hints of Utopia. To discover what he had in mind, his readers would have had to open the files of the Russian secret police and delve into the writings, not yet published, of his prison years.

In the *Tocsin* he clearly envisaged a final Utopia without compulsion. Under communism there would be no need for police, prisons, armies, governments, and courts of law. Like Buonarroti, Tkachev found the key to communism in economic equality. He had always been an economic determinist and an egalitarian; the two put together determined his vision of the future society. True, he had written, egalitarianism entailed the end to the competitive spirit among men and thus the remaking of human psychology. That would follow automatically when men found themselves equal, one to the other. Blanqui had a different vision: he saw communism as a kind of moral perfection, revolution as an exalted, religious crusade, and the victory of revolution as spiritual inspiration.[100] Tkachev derived little interest from such ideals. Instead he set the equal division of wealth at the foundation of the new society, expecting man's attitudes to follow after the partitioning of his possessions.

But pure communism and pure anarchism seemed to Tkachev to be a long way off. He did not often consider his Utopia in his *Tocsin* writings. Beyond a passing suggestion that the dictatorship work to strengthen local responsibilities, he was no more certain than Marx as to how the state might be induced to wither away. To a great extent Tkachev in the *Tocsin* became a technician of revolution. Getting there assured success; tactics made the difference. Such concentration on methods rather than goals was typical of Blanqui, but Lavrov and Bakunin could be accused of it too.

His few years as the editor of his own journal demonstrated that Tkachev stood in close but not perfect affinity to the followers of Blanqui. Like Blanqui he doubted the revolutionary capacity of the majority; he advocated conspiracy as a revolutionary method; he demanded secrecy and discipline as essential to conspiracy's success; and he anticipated a period of dictatorship following the seizure of

---

99. Tkachev, 3: 264.

100. Blanqui, *Critique sociale*, 1: 173, 189, 198; Gorev, *Ogiust Blanki*, p. 102; Dommanget, pp. 127-28, 131; see this interesting idea as suggested by Sylvain Molinier, *Blanqui*, pp. 30-31.

power, during which time the dictators would secure to the revolution its permanent goals. Tkachev's program differed from Blanqui's in many details: in the nature of the minority, the preparations for conspiracy, the extent of secrecy, the path of the dictatorship. The differences derived from differences in personalities, outlooks, and experiences. Blanqui's vision of revolution sprang from his faith in the influence of ideas on men in history; Tkachev was too much of a materialist. Blanqui was an old hand at secret societies and Tkachev much more of a novice. France was, after all, different from Russia and more sophisticated in her revolutionary tradition.

Elements of elitism and Nechaevism crept into Tkachev's programs, probably through the influence of Turski who was less of a Blanquist than he claimed. But if Turski swayed Tkachev (as Nechaev had once influenced Bakunin), he did not succeed in subverting Tkachev's permanent commitment to Blanqui's view of revolution nor Chernyshevskii's portrait of the elite; Tkachev poured into the pages of the *Tocsin* many of his own old ideas. Indeed Tkachev's program for revolutionary action had been formulated before he quarreled with Lavrov and probably before he met the Blanquist Communards in Geneva. He had not abandoned the conclusions he reached when he was writing for the legal Russian press. The Blanquists provided the final cement for a program that was very much his own. Franco Venturi has rightly contended that Tkachev was a Russian Jacobin before he became a European Blanquist.[101]

Among the revolutionary tactics endorsed by his Russian contemporaries—compared to Lavrov's dreams of educating the peasantry and Bakunin's hopes for spontaneous peasant rebellion—Tkachev's plans were the most practical and realistic. For all their uncertainties and question marks, they surpassed the plans of his rivals in their vigor, immediacy, and logic. Tkachev set his program forth in the *Tocsin* and elaborated on it again and again. Given his premises (more realistic than those of Bakunin or Lavrov), his program of conspiracy, seizure of power, and the forcing of social change upon a population he knew to be reluctant made logical sense. His proposals set him on a par with his older Russian antagonists, Bakunin and Lavrov, as a leading revolutionary strategist of his times. None of the three men succeeded in his plans to bring revolution to Russia, but when it did come, revolution appeared not as Bakunin or Lavrov but as Tkachev would have had it.

101. Venturi, p. 403.

12

Last Days

Tkachev was never successful in his revolutionary efforts. By all standards, including his own, he must be judged to have failed in what he most wanted to accomplish. After 1877 it must have been clear even to him that he was not achieving what he set out to do. His friends were few, his influence limited, his journal restricted, and his hopes, on the whole, unfulfilled. He could not foresee how soon he would die in obscurity and poverty. But when he moved away from the *Tocsin*, he must have realized that the high tide of his life was ebbing and that his future could not be expected to live up to his past.

For one thing, Tkachev failed in his stated aim to add vital strength to the Russian revolutionary movement by uniting its quarrelsome factions. In spite of his bitterness and his sharpness of tongue, there is little doubt that he sought such unity. He was wise enough to realize that the cause divided could not succeed. He had once almost sacrificed his independence to the united front. When he first arrived abroad, the Russian émigrés seemed to view him with respect and to value his opinions; it was only after the founding of the *Tocsin* that they turned away. A. Khristoforov, writing Tkachev's obituary in the Geneva journal *Common Cause*, remembered that early in 1875, before the *Tocsin* first appeared, a group of émigrés approached Tkachev with the aim of founding a jointly run, antiautocratic journal. Although Tkachev refused to join the staff—perhaps plans for his own journal were already under way—he read the proposed program of the new periodical and made suggestions to its authors. Khristoforov indicated that the founders of the journal, which finally began publication as the *Common*

Cause in 1877, gladly sought Tkachev's aid, and many conversations and negotiations took place before Tkachev made his refusal final. On the whole, Khristoforov reported, Tkachev's attitude indicated that he would not have been averse to conditional cooperation.[1]

After the founding of the *Tocsin*, Tkachev continued his pleas for unity and cohesion among the Russian émigré groups. The very title of the journal, as he had explained, symbolized the cooperation of men, summoned by the alarm, ready to sacrifice for one another and work together selflessly for the cause of one and all. Social revolution was the goal of all émigré factions, and disagreements among them centered merely about which path would lead most directly to their common ends.[2] Tkachev argued that factionalism was dangerous to the revolution and debilitating to the Russian radicals. He hoped that conspiracy, "buntism," and propaganda might all be coordinated in the revolution's service; they were not, he wrote, mutually exclusive. The seizure of power by conspirators could only benefit other revolutionary groups. "We fraternally hold out our hand," he cried.[3]

In the name of our love for the suffering people, in the name of our hatred for their tyrants, in the name of the liberation of the masses from the chains oppressing them, finally in the name of our unhappy comrades languishing in exile, in prisons, in Siberia, in penal servitude, comrades for whom only we can open the doors of darkness, we exhort them to rally into one friendly, close union, to merge into one common revolutionary organization![4]

Unfortunately Tkachev's own attitudes stood in the way of such cooperation and made joint activity unlikely at best. Much too early in its existence the *Tocsin* took on a highly polemical tone. Tkachev and his violent friend Turski attacked group after group of revolutionaries who disagreed with them, and attacked with such bitterness that to suggest that they turn the other cheek was asking more than Christian charity might expect. In many instances Tkachev took on the aspect of a pure polemicist, one who would argue simply for the sake of defeating his opponent. His first onslaughts against the ways of Lavrov and Bakunin began as early as 1876 in the second issue of *Tocsin*. Other revolutionary groups came in for their share of invective, from the Marxist International to the German social democrats to the nationalist Ukrainian socialist émigrés. Tkachev's cries for unity foundered on the rock of his own bigotry.

---

1. This incident was related by Khristoforov in Tkachev's obituary. See Lemke, "Materialy dlia biografii," p. 163.
2. Tkachev, 3: 289.
3. Ibid., p. 291.
4. Ibid., pp. 291-92.

He began with the anarchists, and his running battle with Bakunin indeed took up more pages than his attacks on all his other antagonists combined. Tkachev still occasionally expressed respect for the Grand Old Man of the Russian revolutionists; he had once argued Bakunin's part with Engels himself. But in the first three issues of *Tocsin* for 1876 he published an angry analysis of Bakunin's *Statism and Anarchy*, a book that had appeared in 1873 and for all its lack of coherence had been taken to heart by most members of the émigré Russian colonies.[5] Tkachev singled out for his anger Bakunin's views on thought, instinct, and popular ideals, and he identified the aging anarchist's posture with those many pseudo-Slavophile attitudes that he, Tkachev, had often denigrated in the legal Russian press.

Bakunin, Tkachev claimed, confused realities and ideals in the program he had advanced. Quoting liberally, the young Russian detailed Bakunin's inept phrases—indeed writing was scarcely Bakunin's forte and his language frequently lacked exactness of expression. It was Bakunin's conviction that an idea must always arise from the life around it, from the social milieu in which it was developed, a concept not far from Tkachev's own environmentalistic conclusion expressed many years before. What caused Tkachev's angry reaction was Bakunin's claim that having been born of social conditions, no idea could reverse itself to the extent of changing them; thus no idea could basically influence social life. Tkachev might have agreed; in his attacks on Lavrov he vehemently denied the "Role of Thought in History," to use his own title. Here as polemicist he took the opposite view: the cause gave birth to its effect, but the effect could still evoke reaction in the cause. Springing from society, ideas could still influence their source. Tkachev accused Bakunin of evolutionism and "Hegelianism," referring to the anarchist's conviction that human beings cannot by thought and will change society.[6]

Indeed Bakunin's undervaluation of the role of thought in history irritated Tkachev just as much as Lavrov's opposite view. To Bakunin's contention that instinctive popular strivings, conscious or unconscious, could change the course of the world where intelligence had no such hopes, Tkachev reacted with cold fury. He would not give preference to instinct over reason. "Tell us then, God willing," he cried to his adversary, "why the popular ideal should be more clearly expressed in the 'murky waters' of instinct than in the 'luminous world' of thought?"[7]

---

5. The article was entitled "Anarkhiia mysli," and it appears in ibid., pp. 303-37.
6. Ibid., p. 310.
7. Ibid., p. 311.

Bakunin's equation of the common people with potent instinct and the intelligentsia with impotent reason evoked all the ambivalence of Tkachev's attitudes towards both groups. For all his defense of the peasant's communist instinct to Engels, he continually attacked those populists who held faith in "popular genius," a phrase covering all the intuitive and instinctive facets of the peasant's orientation, including his communism. For all his defense of Westernism and its educated intelligence, he could equally support and deny the potency of intellect in determining historical trends.

Angrily Tkachev pointed out to Bakunin that the peasant retained many intuitive drives that outweighed his instinct for communism and that Bakunin himself would reject. If the popular ideal included fatalism, faith in the tsar, patriarchy, religiosity, and submissiveness, then Bakunin should not encourage its development.[8] Tkachev sneered at the thought that young people could live among the peasantry and correct its erroneous traditional ideas; re-educating emotions, redesigning habits, rehabilitating feelings, and rechanneling ancient instincts was no easy job. He was sure that Bakuninists would fail in their effort to spur the peasantry to *bunty*. Bakunin deceived himself; the peasantry was not revolutionary, it did not believe what Bakunin thought it believed: "On the contrary, its social world outlook, the forms of social life it has worked out, personal and family relations—everything goes at odds with your anarchy."[9]

In spite of his admission of Bakunin's great talent and the great influence on the direction of thought of revolutionary youth that *Statism and Anarchy* had in Russia, Tkachev reviewed the book unfavorably. It was careless, illogical, "some sort of chaotic disorder"[10] — not an unfair criticism. It was European, not Russian, for it dealt with such problems of Western diplomacy and politics as should not concern socialist revolutionaries. It contained fallacious analogies and definitions. It stooped to foolishness in the generalization that Slavs and Romanic peoples were born anarchists as Germans were innately statists.

Who does not know that all these broad generalizations, which arbitrarily select one or another feature from popular life and make it into a characteristic of a people, [which] place all its multiform traits and inclinations under one uniform image, attaching the label to a whole nation . . . that all these fantastic generalizations are related to the area of pure poesy and rhetoric, that this is no more than a metaphor.[11]

---

8. Ibid., pp. 312-13.
9. Ibid., p. 317.
10. Ibid., p. 306.
11. Ibid., p. 307; cf. chap. 5 above, p. 86.

Tkachev wrote this, conveniently forgetting that he had not long before defined German character in similar generalizations of his own.

Besides Bakunin, other anarchists came in for Tkachev's criticism on the basis of their writings and beliefs. He chided them for their fear of the "state," confident that they were confusing evil uses of government with the institution itself. He accused them of compromising by endorsing the independent commune, self-administration, and common accord. Government was government, he wrote, whether local or centralized. Decentralizing government did not mean ending it—rather than nongovernment (*bezvlastie*) the anarchists were really talking about multigovernment (*mnogovlastie*).[12] Local traditions solidified in local government would only institutionalize provincial conservatism. In a tour de force article entitled "The Anarchistic State" Tkachev made fun of anarchists (and particularly Lavrov whose press in this case published the project under attack) for planning the public administration of certain services that they contradictorily hoped to maintain while simultaneously doing away with government.[13] He insulted the anarchists by telling them that their plans were not communistic but transitional and differed only slightly from the program he himself proposed. If he once consoled Bakunin's followers with the left-handed compliment that they were more revolutionary in temperament than Lavrov, he constantly berated them for working to destroy the unity of the revolutionary cause and for preferring a bourgeois, federalist, democratic organizational structure to the necessary tight, disciplined party.[14]

After reading Tkachev's *Tocsin* Engels reversed himself and realized that Tkachev was surely no Bakuninist. G. V. Plekhanov, writing later as a social democrat, associated Tkachev with Bakunin too. Polemicizing with Lev Tikhomirov, who in his definition had become a Blanquist, this "first Russian Marxist" compared Tkachev with the anarchists Tkachev so frequently attacked.

Not setting out on the rocky road of the dialectic, [Tkachev] did not make the false logical steps peculiar to Bakunin. . . . He was more logical than Bakunin in the sense that he held to his arguments more consistently, drew from them more logical conclusions. All the trouble lay in the fact that not only these arguments but even the point of view where he stood in working them out were beneath Bakunin's, for the simple reason that they were nothing other than simplified Bakuninism, Bakuninism divested of any attempt to create a philosophy of Russian history and substituting some kind of attempts at revolutionary anathema.[15]

12. Ibid., p. 255.
13. This article has been reprinted in ibid., pp. 338-59.
14. Ibid., pp. 387-88.
15. Plekhanov, *Sochineniia*, 2: 143.

Plekhanov erroneously believed that Tkachev agreed with Bakunin on the "sociopolitical situation of our fatherland" and saw Russia through the prism of the peasant's communist inclinations. Plekhanov had not read the *Tocsin* carefully enough to realize that Tkachev did not really believe in instinctive communism at all. He was more correct when he wrote that both Tkachev and Bakunin thought that Russia could find her own special historical path.[16]

If Tkachev's arguments with the anarchists took up more space in the *Tocsin* than his other polemics, it was probably because the anarchist group in Geneva was the most active set among the Russian émigrés. Any reading of the journal, however, makes it clear that Lavrov, not Bakunin, remained Tkachev's evil demon, the cause of his most vehement reactions and most pathological hatred. For all his attacks Tkachev retained certain respect for Bakunin, but the same can scarcely be said for his attitude toward Lavrov. Indeed, in one article he stated outright that the *Forward!* group was infinitely more harmful than the anarchists. His hostility toward his ex-editor knew no bounds.

Tkachev opened broadsides on Lavrov in 1876, beginning in response to Lavrov's article "To the Russian Revolutionary Youth," Lavrov's answer to Tkachev's own earlier open letter.[17] Tkachev was steeped in scorn. Lavrov he accused of complete confusion, of double-mindedness, of being full of phraseology that made no sense, of eclectic chaos and contradiction.[18] Revolution made by the people as educated by the conscious minority would never occur, for such attempts at education were doomed. Lavrov did not know real revolution, for he believed not in violence but in peaceful progress. "He knows that everything is moving towards the better," Tkachev wrote angrily, "that today is better than yesterday and that tomorrow will be better than today,"[19] that society had no alternative but gradually to perfect itself. Why then, Tkachev asked bitterly, have a revolution at all? Why not just wait? Lavrov he saw as divided.

The goddess of progress and the devil of revolution are dividing his soul into parts. He definitely does not know which of them to listen to, which of them to believe. Among other things, as a well-educated man he obviously gives preference in all important matters to the goddess over the devil. In order to stop up the devil's mouth, he is ready to tolerate the necessity of revolutionary propaganda, of revolutionary agitation, and revolutionary organization. But tolerating all this, he still

---

16. Plekhanov, interestingly, believed that anarchism had outlived its day but that Blanquism still had a future. See ibid., p. 153.
17. Tkachev attacked Lavrov along with Bakunin in "Anarkhiia mysli," Tkachev, 3: 303-37.
18. Ibid., pp. 323-24.
19. Ibid., p. 332.

pours the holy oil of the optimistic theory of progress into revolutionary formulae in order to please the goddess. The demand of revolutionary propaganda is shuffled over by the more modest demand of "explaining the phenomena," broadening and strengthening the truths of worker socialism, "revealing basic causes of social evil." And the most revolutionary organization becomes in the long run a simple tool, a method for more successful "explanation," "broadening," unifying and revelation of significant truths. The evil devil demands blood, force, murders, destruction. The sentimental goddess goes into indescribable horror at such vandalistic demands. Listening to the devil, the author falls into revolutionary ecstasy . . . but the goddess is after all, you see, the victor.[20]

From all this conflict Lavrov emerged as an antirevolutionary. He tried to permeate and demoralize the revolutionary spirit of Russian youth. "That is why we consider this philosophy of villainy and compromise, this philosophy of progress masked by revolution to be even more harmful for the success of the revolutionary cause than is the thoughtless, silly philosophy of anarchy."[21]

Tkachev found much to complain about in his attacks on the Lavrovists. He called them waiters—those who were willing to play the waiting game, those who for reasons based on their analysis of history would postpone the revolution until some other day.[22] He disliked their reliance on propaganda as an agitational technique, for propagandizing revolution meant time, meant waiting, meant involving too many people for revolutionary effectiveness. He resented their refusal to construct a secret, militant organization, their refusal to admit the need for power and force, their insistence on freedom of personality and freedom of action within the revolutionary vanguard. He called them reactionary, a term that must have hurt, for in Tkachev's mind they were holding back the future instead of pushing faster forward. His attacks came thick and fast: "Is Social Revolution in Russia Possible at the Present Time?" 1876; "Revolutionaries-Reactionaries," 1876; "On the Eve and Just after the Revolution," 1876-77.[23] Once Tkachev found a gleam of hope even in the Lavrovists, but his sarcastic reaction indicated not pleasure but continuing hostility. In Lavrov's pamphlet entitled *The State Element in the Future Society*, published in 1876, Tkachev rightfully found indications that the older man was ready to accept the idea of a minority revolution, the need for a disciplined organization, and even the continuing influence (be it only moral and spiritual) of the minority after the revolution was accomplished. Tkachev was gleeful. *"We went against the tide,"* he cried, "but ob-

20. Ibid., pp. 335-36.
21. Ibid., p. 337.
22. Ibid., p. 271.
23. Ibid., pp. 276-84, 269-75, 360-81.

viously this tide has turned."[24] One Soviet author has suggested that
Tkachev did indeed influence Lavrov to a greater extent than Lavrov
himself admitted.[25]

The *Tocsin* attacks extended to groups other than the anarchists
and the propagandists. Particularly in the article "Revolutionaries-
Reactionaries" Tkachev continued his broadsides against Engels's social
democrats. After all, the social democrats were reactionaries too, by his
standards, in that they (like the Lavrovists) could only anticipate
revolution in Russia some time in the far-off future when the proletariat was strong enough and its organizations powerful enough to
effect revolutionary change. In the West, Tkachev wrote, it took
centuries; in Russia such a revolution might be a hundred or perhaps a
thousand years in the future.

. . . when bourgeois progress finally succeeds in equating conditions of village
industry to conditions of urban factories, there is no doubt that then the present
organization of Western European urban proletariat will be broadened to the village
proletariat. But even in Western Europe this will take a long time, and with us, the
Russians, even longer.[26]

The social democrats, like the Lavrovists, were playing the waiting
game. Tkachev could not wait.

They understand that under present economic and political conditions of Russia,
a correct and in any way reasonable organization of workers' groups is absolutely
inconceivable. But this does not disturb them. Why, then they will wait. They do
not lack patience! The people's grief, the people's tears, are not their grief, are not
their tears! Why should they compromise themselves in risky enterprises? They
want to act only when it is a sure thing. It is impossible to act now as a sure thing.
We, all the revolutionaries, understand this very well, and they understand it as well
as we do. But we are not afraid of a risk. Neither we nor the people have anything
to regret, anything to lose![27]

He suggested that if the social democratic reactionaries wanted to
hasten the revolution, they had better join forces with the bourgeoisie
and aid it in its progress, for only thus would be formed the proletariat
that was essential to their revolutionary plots.

Tkachev had, then, little respect for Marx's revolutionary plans.
He had even less for the late Marxist International, which he called
reactionary (in part for its degeneration into squabbling factions)
and revisionist (for its willingness to support legal social democratic

24. Ibid., p. 364.
25. Boris Isaakovich Gorev, "K voprosu o blankizme voobshche i russkom
blankizme v chastnosti," *Voinstvuiushchii materialist*, pp. 114-15.
26. Tkachev, 3: 272.
27. Ibid., p. 274.

parties).[28] He regarded the social democrats of Germany as particularly corrupt for their willingness to settle for legal status.[29]

Other groups came in for their share of invective. The anarchists centered around the journal *Rabotnik* (Worker), edited by Nikolai Zhukovskii, Tkachev found more confused and foolish than Bakunin himself ("O poor Russian revolutionary thought, to what impenetrable depths of self-contradiction, stupidity, and foolishness you have fallen!").[30] Zhukovskii personally he found a naïve and silly dreamer. He attacked the ex-Communard Lefrance who had written a book on anarchism in which he argued that dictatorship could result in nothing good, as good could never be born of evil.[31] He scorned the anonymous Ukrainian author (probably M. P. Dragomanov) of a pamphlet on socialism and religion in revolution.[32] He never minced words. Only for Elisée Reclus did he express lasting admiration.

Under the circumstances it is not surprising that Tkachev had few friends among the Russian émigrés in Switzerland. All sources indicate that he was despised by and isolated from most of his fellow countrymen. Lev Tikhomirov, a man of some Jacobin tendencies himself, suggested that the major impediment to Tkachev's popularity lay in the intelligentsia's continuing reaction against Nechaev and Tkachev's identification (particularly after his association with Turski) with Nechaev's principles.[33] Lev Deutsch, one of the Russians working on the Bakuninist journal *Obshchina* (Commune) in Geneva in the late seventies, echoed the opinion. Writing later of the high moral character of most of the émigré revolutionaries, Deutsch was convinced that

the enormous damage revealed not long ago that was caused to the revolutionary movement by the renowned Nechaev with his Machiavellian methods and the principles which he practiced, "the aim justifies the means," in great degree determined the reasons for our rejection of Tkachev's proposed organization. In our conviction the tasks Tkachev set forth and the organization he proposed were indissolubly tied with mystification, fraud, all kinds of unworthy measures, even secret murder and other crimes.[34]

Deutsch reported that his circles viewed the *Tocsin* not only with "extreme displeasure" but even "with horror." Similarly Sergei Krav-

28. Ibid., pp. 388-89.
29. Ibid., pp. 434-40.
30. Ibid., p. 322.
31. Ibid., pp. 259-60.
32. Ibid., pp. 405-24.
33. Lev Aleksandrovich Tikhomirov, *Russia, Political and Social*, 2: 160.
34. Deich, *Russkaia emigratsiia*, p. 84. Cf. Deich's statements in *Gruppa "Osvobozhdenie truda,"* 2: 70-73.

chinskii, another of the *Commune*'s editors and previously a member of the Chaikovskii Circle, disliked Tkachev's views although he had nothing against the group of ex-Communards in general.[35] Axelrod, at the time a devout Bakuninist, identified Tkachev with the Nechaevist viewpoint. "I will merely say here," he reported later, "that the rest of revolutionary emigration maintained almost no relations with Tkachev's group."[36] Even Tkachev's biography in the *Russian Biographical Dictionary* points up his personal isolation from the other emigrant groups.[37] Petr's sharp tongue led the *Tocsin* into continual conflict with other émigrés.

In all of the arguments and rebuttals, Tkachev's association with Turski did nothing to help him. Turski was rich; he lived a life far out of reach of the ordinary Russian émigrés. His 1872 association with Nechaev was well known in emigrant circles. The rumor that he had considered the assassination of several titled nationalist Polish leaders as a contribution to the Polish liberation cause contributed to his unsavory reputation. Deutsch wrote of Turski that among Russian emigrants he was regarded as "unclean," both as a revolutionary and as a private man.[38] On the whole, Axelrod's judgment was accurate:

The *Tocsin* did not have any marked influence on the Russian emigration in general or the Geneva emigration in particular. The circle of the *Tocsin* was isolated, and other emigrants stayed away from it and did not maintain any contact with it.[39]

Tkachev was not completely isolated, for he developed a circle of his own. It was not a Russian circle but a French óne, centering around those Parisian ex-Communards he had come to respect and admire. Among them was Elisée Reclus, always Tkachev's favorite. Edouard Vaillant, technically the London correspondent for the *Tocsin*, served as liaison between the Communards of Geneva and the larger group that had settled in the English capital. Vaillant was a civil engineer, physicist, and Commune minister of education who after the amnesty of 1880 was to become leader of the Blanquists in the French Chamber of Deputies. There were others besides Turski—French, or infrequently Russian, like P. V. Grigorev who acted as the *Tocsin*'s editor when Tkachev was away.[40]

35. See Vera Spiridovna Ostashkina, *Dalekoe i nedavnee*, p. 57; Deich, *Russkaia emigratsiia*, p. 4.

36. Akselrod, p. 163.

37. *Russkii biograficheskii slovar*, 20: 599.

38. Deich, *Russkaia emigratsiia*, p. 85.

39. Akselrod, p. 199.

40. Some of the other Blanquists associated with the *Tocsin* included Ernest Granger, F. Cournet, and Emile Eudes. Certain other names I have been unable to identify further; they include Z. Schultz, P. T. Grezko, B. Limanowski, Lakiev, and

Two others cut through the wall of hostility among Russian émigrés and found Tkachev to their liking. One was Vera Figner, whose later memoirs were to attest to her talents. Politically she may not have agreed with Tkachev, but her relationship with him confirmed his sister's earlier judgment that in person he could be gentle and kind. His bark was worse than his bite. He and Figner used to go for walks together in the lovely Swiss countryside.

In Geneva, on a vacation from school, I met Tkachev who had recently emigrated there from exile in Pskov province. He and I soon became involved in discussion on political themes. His dedicated Jacobinism sickened us, and when he later tried to carry out business-like discussions with the "Frichists" about revolutionary activities in Russia, he had no success. The first issues of *Tocsin* not only evoked no sympathy but appeared laughable to us. Despite his political theories, we considered him in no way to be a really serious figure in the revolutionary movement—his personality made no impression. However, he was very cheerful and a pleasant debater, with whom one could carry on a discussion in a comradely fashion. I always felt personally cheerful and comfortable in his company. We often spent our time boating on Lake Geneva, hiking along the shore in the evening, or sometimes matching wits and playing little games with each other.[41]

A second friend was the young scientist N. A. Morozov who came to Geneva shortly after 1874 and returned to Russia some years later to write for the journal of the People's Will, the terrorist organization. For a time Morozov, once a member of the Chaikovskii Circle, was thinking of joining the staff of *Worker*, an anarchist émigré publication. His own experiences in the Going-to-the-People fiasco caused him to agree with Tkachev as to the impossibility of successfully propagandizing the peasantry to revolution. Morozov liked Tkachev; he reported with pleasure of his Geneva evenings with Tkachev and Dementeva, with whom he was particularly enchanted. Tkachev he identified with Pisarev as a one-time idol of Russian youth. He was "full of enthusiasm," he wrote, "for this talented man."[42] After he returned to Russia, he never denied his friendship with the *Tocsin*'s extremist editor.

If Tkachev's beliefs had isolated him from most Russian émigrés in

Grakch. It should be noted that the *Tocsin* remained a peripheral project to many of the important Frenchmen listed. Vaillant lived primarily in London; Elisée Reclus was friendly with a vast colony of émigrés and in 1878 published a journal with his friend Petr Kropotkin. The commitment of many of these men to Tkachev's project was secondary for them though important to him.

41. Quoted in Weeks, *First Bolshevik*, p. 56. The "Frichists" were a group of Russian women students in Zurich. Figner knew Tkachev only during his early years in Europe, for she returned to Russia in December 1875, was arrested after the assassination of the tsar in 1881, and thereafter was tried and imprisoned until after the turn of the century.

42. Morozov, *Povesti moei zhizni*, 1: 402-3, 469.

Switzerland, his influence in Russia itself was even more restricted. In his homeland, wrote Axelrod,

the group of Geneva Jacobins did not acquire influence in the revolutionary environment and did not have any kind of serious connections, if one does not count connection with certain out-of-step individuals who sympathized with *Tocsin*.[43]

Soviet scholars have unearthed one organized Jacobin group in Russia in the 1870s, that which centered around P. G. Zaichnevskii, the erstwhile author of *Young Russia* a decade before. Later living in exile in Orel, Zaichnevskii had inspired a group of young women toward the aims of conspiracy and political seizure of power. Among them were Elena Rossikova, Galina Cherniavskaia, Maria Oshanina, and Maria Lavrova.[44] Individual members of this young female circle may occasionally have read the *Tocsin* or achieved some sort of contact with Tkachev. Kozmin expertly disproves the existence of any more systematic contacts, for Zaichnevskii's group had dispersed (when he himself left Orel) before Tkachev and the *Tocsin* made any efforts to set up a Russian organization.[45] The Soviet scholar V. A. Tvardovskaia has affirmed that Tkachev did not inspire a single important circle within his homeland.[46] Khristoforov related how a handful of *Tocsin* supporters, traveling secretly to Russia, returned astonished at their indifferent reception.[47] With the formation of the People's Will in 1879 many of the Russian activists found another outlet for their activities; Maria Oshanina, for example, went to St. Petersburg where she became an ardent supporter of the terrorist organization.

As to the Society for Popular Liberation, there is little doubt that it was more of a fraud than a failure. Observers occasionally accused Tkachev of deliberate mystification, the old Nechaevist technique, in the society's strange and secret ways; the organization was once reported to the Third Section as pure mystification. Rumors of the organization's widespread influence in Russia appeared in the French socialist press, probably contributed by Turski (whose passion for the revolution consistently exceeded his passion for accuracy), only to be denied by less partisan observers.[48] Actually membership was so small as to question whether the organization was worth the paper its statutes

---

43. Akselrod, p. 199.

44. Ibid.: Deich, *Russkaia emigratsiia*, p. 85; M. R. Popov, "Iz moego revoliutsionnogo proshlogo," *Byloe* 5 (1907): 273-74.

45. Kozmin, *Iz istorii*, pp. 324-27.

46. V. A. Tvardovskaia, "Problema gosudarstva v ideologii narodovolchestva, 1879-83 gg.," *Istoricheskie zapiski* 74 (1963): 153.

47. Lemke, "Materialy dlia biografii," p. 164.

48. Kusheva, pp. 31, 33, 44-47.

were printed on. Deceived by the rash of instructions, statutes, proclamations, and claims, the Soviet scholar E. N. Kusheva went out of her
way to find Russians who were said to be Jacobins, who collected
copies of the *Tocsin*, or who actually belonged to the society. She
found only three card-carrying members.[49] Her speculations about
others were attacked point by point by M. F. Frolenko who remembered the people she was writing about. The society, Frolenko claimed,
simply did not exist.[50] A kinder verdict would have found it barely
breathing in the *Tocsin*'s Geneva headquarters. Even Tkachev seems
soon to have lost interest. If his lifetime aim was to unite Russian
revolutionaries into a tightly knit, disciplined, conspiratorial organization, he must surely be judged to have failed.

The question of Tkachev's influence in Russia has evoked considerable debate in another respect. In 1879 after a split in the revolutionary organization Land and Freedom, a new group was formed by a
number of members of the old. The notorious People's Will was in large
measure dedicated to disruption of the tsarist government by means of
terrorism. Scholarly argument has centered around Tkachev's possible
influence in turning the tide toward the new activism.

Tkachev himself, aware of the change in nature and goals among
Russian revolutionaries, remained unusually ambivalent. The truth is
that he did not endorse terrorism as a revolutionary method although
he greatly admired the courage of the new young terrorists and he
hesitated to discourage any course of action that renewed revolutionary
fervor. In 1878 in one of his now infrequent articles for the *Tocsin* he
welcomed the new wave of activism inaugurated by Vera Zasulich's
attempt on the life of the governor-general of St. Petersburg and Kravchinskii's successful effort against the head of the secret police. These
acts of terrorism proclaimed a new phase in the revolutionary movement, he wrote—perhaps its final stage. He rejoiced that the age of reaction, the age of peaceful propagandizing that had busied young Russians in the early 1870s had come to an end. Youth was turning "back
to our tradition" of the sixties, back to direct action.

To prepare, to develop, peacefully to propagandize, and to wait while the majority
of the people grow to understanding their rights and obligations, all these and
similar symbols of the revolutionary-reactionary programs of past years have

---

49. Ibid., p. 35.

50. M. Frolenko, "Obshchestvo narodnogo osvobozhdeniia," *Katorga i ssylka*,
no. 3 (88) (1932), pp. 81-100. It did have a few members; see A. V. Pribylev,
"Neskolko slov o dvukh predstaviteliakh gruppy 'Nabata,'" *Katorga i ssylka*,
nos. 84-85 (1931), pp. 105-11.

stopped satisfying the present mood of revolutionary youth. It strives to set forth now on a purely revolutionary path, and by its example, by its daring, to carry the people too along this road.[51]

Because they stood as David against Goliath, because their motives were of the highest moral order, assassination was justified, he told his readers; the terrorists were not simple murderers.

Yet Tkachev was not sure that terrorism would succeed. He could not believe that it would manage to bring about the collapse of tsarism.

. . . Recognizing fully all the great moral and agitational significance of such phenomena as [these executions], we nonetheless affirm that such executions and demonstrations should be viewed merely as one of the *methods* and certainly not as a *goal* and the main task of revolutionary activity. For the development of the revolutionary cause in Russia, it will be harmful to the highest degree if this *method* is turned into a *goal* as the widening of forbidden circles, going to the people, local *bunty*, and more or less partial revolutionary methods have been turned into goals before. Whoever forgets the goal for the means thereby draws further from realization of the goal.[52]

And again, more clearly:

We strive not for the destruction of one or another *individual* who embodies these or those functions of the present governmental power, we strive for the destruction of this very *power* itself, for the liberation of the people, not from the yoke of this or that servant of the given state, but from the state itself.[53]

Tkachev foresaw the results of the assassination of the tsar more accurately than did its perpetrators.

A little later he seemed to change his mind. Following the systematic blows the terrorists were delivering against the tsarist government, Tkachev let himself be carried away by the daring and courage of the young assassins. Suddenly it seemed to him that terror was the revolution, that the goal was attainable through assassination itself; that any action "toward *disorganization*, toward *terrorization* of the government" might indeed lead to its demise.[54] Obviously not knowing of the existence of the notorious Executive Committee, he lectured the young revolutionaries on the need for a strictly disciplined organization without which their movement might soon falter. But he had learned to have faith.

The revolution has begun, it began at the moment when we, the revolutionaries, having discarded the false path of peaceful propaganda, turned to direct revolution-

51. Tkachev, 3: 430.
52. Ibid., p. 432.
53. Ibid.
54. Ibid., p. 442.

ary action, expressed in a series of armed oppositions, demonstrations, *bunty*
. . . , executions of tsarist butchers, agents, and traitors. A revolution is not
accomplished in a day, in an hour.[55]

Tkachev's change in attitude may well reflect his colleagues' disapproval
of his original stance. His quarrels with Turski were probably based on
his refusal to recognize the efficacy of terrorism, a technique of violence closer to Turski's soul than to Tkachev's.

The new terrorists demonstrated a certain Tkachevian bent. Having
found themselves notoriously unsuccessful in rousing the peasant to
social rebellion, the young revolutionaries turned their attention from
social revolution to political, from propaganda to action.[56] On the
whole the People's Will shared Tkachev's concept of the Russian state
as weak, as "hanging in the air"; a similar expression was used by
Tikhomirov, the leading theoretician of the People's Will, who called
the Russian government "an iron colossus on clay legs."[57] This conviction of the state's weakness lay at the basis of the hopes of many
Narodovoltsy that the government could be frightened into concessions.[58] Nevertheless some members of the People's Will expressed
doubt (like Tkachev) that terror could change the broad social order.[59]
Others counted on strikes of assassination to stimulate a social revolution among the people as a whole.[60]

Additionally the members of the People's Will shared a sense of
urgency with Tkachev. "Now or never," one of them wrote, "that is
our dilemma."[61] The functions of the Executive Committee and its
demands upon members of the organization might well be regarded as
a move in the direction of a Tkachev-style authoritarian revolutionary
organization. Yet it should be remembered that the Executive Committee recruited volunteers for its assassin's chores, debated policies at
length before voting on and adopting them, and never maintained that
mystifying secrecy that characterized Tkachev's society.

The similarities of the new terrorism and the old Blanquism impressed Tkachev himself. He was not above claiming later that his

---

55. Ibid., p. 443.
56. Many historians have called attention to this change; cf. Malinin, *Filosofiia
revoliutsionnogo narodnichestva*, pp. 321-22; Walicki, *Controversy over Capitalism*,
p. 85. See also Plekhanov, *Sochineniia*, 2: 41; and Berdiaev, *Istoki i smysl russkogo
kommunizma*, p. 59.
57. Quoted in S. S. Volk, *Narodnaia volia 1879-1882 gg.*, p. 195.
58. Ibid., pp. 229-30.
59. This was S. M. Kravchinskii, as quoted in Walicki, p. 102.
60. Volk, pp. 229-30.
61. Ibid., p. 240.

influence had shown the light to the new generation of Russian revolutionaries. "We *first* in our times," he wrote,

indicated the inevitability of this fiasco [of the propaganda method], we *first* (in the émigré press, of course) called upon youth to abandon this harmful antirevolutionary path and again return to the tradition of direct revolutionary activity and a militant, centralized military organization. And our voice was not a voice crying in the wilderness. The basic principles of our program have become in our time . . . the basic principles of activity of all honest and sincere revolutionaries.[62]

A more careful analysis demonstrates that Tkachev exaggerated. Many aspects of the People's Will program were never carefully defined. Members disagreed radically among themselves and disagreed with Tkachev too. Never did they agree on what they anticipated would result from their acts of terror. Never did they agree on the kind of government they might find ideal: a temporary democratic government, a government set up by a constitutional assembly, or that kind of nongovernment that Bakuninists found more to their taste.[63] One of them once claimed that the membership as a whole believed less in the power of government than in the "power of the ideas of society," whatever that meant.[64] Their very conspiracy was dedicated not to the seizure of power but simply to effecting terroristic deeds. Within the organization the followers of Zaichnevskii constantly attempted to persuade the Executive Committee to endorse the principle of the seizure of power by conspiracy. Among them in particular were Maria Oshanina, E. D. Sergeeva, and Tikhomirov, the husband of the latter Jacobin lady. The members of the Executive Committee argued the point but refused the request. Only after the assassination failed to disrupt the government did the Executive Committee endorse in principle the seizure of power.[65] By then it was too late. Tkachev would have had different perspectives.

Whatever the viewpoints of the People's Will—and sometimes they are difficult to determine—cautious study indicates that they were not compiled through the intervention of Tkachev or the *Tocsin*. Most active members of the Executive Committee were hostile to or at best uninterested in Tkachev's political writings. Few of them ever saw the *Tocsin*, Morozov reported; Vera Figner said it was hardly distributed at all.[66] Only two or three copies were found in searches when People's

62. Tkachev, 3: 442.
63. Volk, pp. 202, 206-7.
64. Lemke, "Materialy dlia biografii," p. 168.
65. Volk, pp. 240-44.
66. Ibid., p. 239.

Will ringleaders were rounded up after the assassination of the tsar.[67] For those few who, like himself, had seen the early issues of Tkachev's journal, Morozov reported that the Jacobin viewpoints "called forth among the revolutionaries only sneers and scorn, even indignation."[68] As Tkachev's only close personal friend among the Executive Committee members, Morozov once described how he used his friendship with Tkachev to blackmail his horrified colleagues into publishing one of his articles they had at first rejected.[69]

Few members of the Executive Committee held Tkachev in more respect. The clique of lady Jacobins from Orel—particularly Oshanina and Sergeeva—had learned from Zaichnevskii, not Tkachev, as Kozmin has demonstrated. Sergeeva probably influenced her husband Tikhomirov; he did not cite Tkachev as an authority. Plekhanov remembered that A. D. Mikhailov, at first violent in his anti-Jacobin stance, later began to believe his earlier prejudice unfounded, but Tkachev personally did not seem to be responsible.[70]

The only close personal tie between the St. Petersburg terrorists and the *Tocsin* circle was provided by Morozov, Tkachev's long-term friend. In Geneva in the spring of 1880 Morozov contacted Tkachev and Turski. Together they worked out a draft agreement whereby the *Tocsin* would cease publication abroad, its typography and several of its staff (including Tkachev) would be moved to Petersburg, its benefactor (Turski) would supply all necessary funds, and a new journal would be published and distributed jointly by the Society for Popular Liberation and the People's Will. Clearly dubious of the acceptability of their proposal, the three contractors also wrote out an alternative agreement, calling only for general cooperation between the organizatons. They were wise to be uncertain; both suggestions were turned down by Tikhomirov, speaking for the Executive Committee.[71] Morozov clearly did not have the confidence of his Russian colleagues. After all, as early as 1879 the editors of the *People's Will* had begun to reject his articles.[72] He and Tkachev remained close in spite of the rebuff. "Your [personal] program coincides completely with mine," Tkachev

---

67. Ibid.
68. Ibid., p. 238.
69. Morozov, 2. 481-83.
70. Volk, pp. 238-39.
71. Turski and Tkachev attached to the agreement a proviso that the new journal *not* support constitutionalism or a *zemskii sobor*. This episode is analyzed by Vera Figner in Dmitrii Kuzmin, *Narodovolcheskaia zhurnalistika*, pp. 244-47, on the basis of Morozov's notes unearthed by S. N. Valk. Turski's claim that a written agreement was reached (Nikolaevskii, "Pamiati," pp. 224-25) exaggerates the results of the negotiations.
72. Volk, pp. 232-35.

wrote his friend later that year.[73] He could never truthfully say that of the Executive Committee.

Most contemporary observers agreed that Tkachev never exerted any influence at all over the terrorist movement. The Bakuninists on *Commune* (Geneva) considered Tkachev's claims to have done so as an obvious lie.[74] Axelrod, living in Switzerland, was convinced that the People's Will arose spontaneously in response to conditions in Russia and not on the basis of anyone's stated political philosophy.

If the centralized and terrorist-conspiratorial tendency at the end of the seventies began to reign among those revolutionaries who then organized themselves into the party the People's Will, this occurred gradually by empirical means, under the spontaneous influence of the course and conditions of our revolutionary movement, which had prepared a ground psychologically favorable to this tendency.[75]

Khristoforov, a Bakuninist, echoed Axelrod's contentions. Pointing up what he considered the breadth of the People's Will movement in comparison to Tkachev's narrow-minded, exclusive, and dogmatic revolutionary ideas, he saw the Russian organization as a reversion to the ideals of the sixties, not influenced by Tkachev at all.

That is why in spite of the similarity of the ideas of the *Tocsin* with the ideas of the People's Will party in major and effective measures, it is in our opinion impossible to assign to the *Tocsin* that decisive influence on the return of revolutionaries to the political aims of which Tkachev speaks. . . . [76]

Only Plekhanov and Deutsch disagreed. Plekhanov once claimed that the journal of the People's Will merely rewrote Tkachev's editorials, although he saw there the influence of Bakunin and Lavrov as well.[77] In his memoirs Deutsch contended that the *Tocsin*'s propaganda had turned the tide.

In view of the very great significance of the People's Will in the history of our country, one must recognize that Tkachev's preaching remained far from fruitless and that his activity was far from without consequence. On the contrary his ideas and methods were greatly successful, for several decades, yes, in essence they have not disappeared finally even now. . . . As often, history has done a grave injustice to Petr Nikitich; to this time, as far as I know, no one of the people writing about the party of the People's Will refers to the great importance that the ideas and plans of Tkachev had among its members. We will hope that with time he will be granted a just evaluation of his activity in the pages of an impartial history of the Russian liberation movement.[78]

---

73. Ibid., p. 239.
74. Deich, *Russkaia emigratsiia*, p. 86.
75. Akselrod, p. 199.
76. Lemke, "Materialy dlia biografii," p. 170.
77. Volk, p. 240. Volk denies the correctness of Plekhanov's assessment.
78. Deich, *Russkaia emigratsiia*, p. 87.

Caught up in the disciplined activism of the People's Will, Deutsch did not understand the difference between its individual acts of assassination and those plans for the actual seizure of power that were the key to Tkachev's hopes. More balanced viewpoints appeared over the years. Thus the author of Tkachev's biography in the *Russian Biographical Dictionary* recognized that the terrorists did not care for Tkachev although their own successes created the soil for the spread of his ideas.[79] The Soviet historian S. S. Volk in his careful analysis of the terrorist movement has written:

> The closeness of the *narodovoltsy* to Tkachev in the first place did not exclude a series of disagreements and in the second place was determined not so much by direct borrowing as by a similarity of viewpoints. A recognized similarity of viewpoints also played a certain role in the approach to the People's Will of P. L. Lavrov and N. K. Mikhailovskii.[80]

Bitter days awaited Petr Tkachev after 1878.

Not long after their Geneva reunion in 1879, he quarreled with Dementeva. She left him and struck out on her own, forbidden to return to her native land. Eventually she earned a medical degree at Montpellier University and came to make a specialty of surgical practice. In 1903 she received permission to return to her native land. She worked as a volunteer during the Russo-Japanese War and (then a woman in her fifties) was arrested for propagandizing among the troops. She never married. Her death came in 1923 in Russia.[81] Tkachev, the loner, must have felt more than ever alone after she left.

Following its first year of existence, Tkachev seems rapidly to have lost interest in the *Tocsin*. Perhaps he suffered more than he would admit from the hostile attitudes of the Russian émigré colony. His articles appeared in the journal with less and less frequency: in 1878 only one, in 1879 two. He spent increasing amounts of time in Paris; several young Russian radicals reported meeting him there in 1877. The journal itself degenerated. Tkachev quarreled with Turski about editorial policy, particularly about Turski's support of terrorism as a revolutionary technique. Frequently Turski himself left Geneva although he could not return to Paris until the Communards were officially amnestied. For some time Grigorev handled editorial tasks on the

---

79. *Russkii biograficheskii slovar*, 20: 599. Many other historians have expressed this and opposite viewpoints. Cf. Reuel, "Ekonomicheskie vzgliady P. N. Tkacheva," p. 144; Kozmin, *Iz istorii*, p. 403; Gorev, "K voprosu," p. 114; S. I. Mitskevich, "Russkie iakobintsy," *Proletarskaia revoliutsiia*, nos. 6-7 (1923), p. 18; and Malinin, *Filosofiia revoliutsionnogo narodnichestva*, pp. 321-22.

80. Volk, p. 240.

81. Kozmin, "Okolo nechaevskogo dela," pp. 62-63.

Tocsin, and later issues reflected his lack of interest in increasing numbers of errors and misprints.[82] Then Grigorev too found more compelling occupations, and one Molchanov took over as editor. Axelrod claimed that Molchanov was later exposed as a government agent and returned to Russia to join the staff of the *Novoe vremia* (New Times), a conservative journal.[83] In 1879 the *Tocsin* moved to London and then ceased to appear on a regular schedule. No issues at all were printed in the year 1880.

A few half-hearted attempts were made to keep the journal and its press alive. Khristoforov remembered that several *Tocsin* staff members later attempted to revive publication on a weekly basis. They solicited some articles from Tkachev, then living in Paris. However, according to Khristoforov, they felt the themes much weaker than his earlier materials and actually refused to print them.[84] Tkachev himself had a hand in publishing a collection of his *Tocsin* articles entitled *Anarchy of Thought: Collection of the Political Essays of P. N. Tkachev*. The volume was printed in London on the Tocsin Press, presumably acquired or moved there by Tkachev or by his friends in the émigré colony. A year later a second collection appeared, this time entitled *Orators-Buntists on the Russian Revolution: On the Theme: It Is Necessary Rapidly to Enter a Secret Organization without Which Political Struggle Is Impossible.*[85] In 1880, according to a statement printed in *Tocsin*, Tkachev attempted to transfer the press to St. Petersburg, hoping to found a new underground journal there.[86] In Soviet archives S. S. Volk has unearthed an article dealing with Poland that was probably written by Tkachev and that was intended for publication in his new journal, but instead was seized by police.[87] If Tkachev was there during the autumn he did not stay; arrested or threatened with arrest, he soon returned abroad.

As he turned his back on the greatest project of his lifetime, Tkachev could not help but pause and reflect. At some unspecified date (probably 1881) one of his acquaintances who worked on the *Common Cause* suggested that the *Tocsin* might be revived if it were changed from a polemicizing sharp-tongued journal of revolutionary theories

---

82. Lemke, "Materialy dlia biografii," p. 164.

83. Akselrod, p. 163.

84. Lemke, "Materialy dlia biografii," p. 171.

85. Tkachev, 4: 454.

86. *Nabat*, Year 5, no. 1 (June 20, 1881), p. 1; also *Russkii biograficheskii slovar*, 20: 599; and E. Zaleski, *Mouvements ouvrières et socialistes*, 1: 42.

87. Volk, p. 405. Kozmin, *Iz istorii*, pp. 371-72, states that Tkachev's trip was cancelled at the last moment when the press was confiscated by police.

into a biweekly propaganda sheet agitating for the overthrow of the
tsarist government. In response Tkachev wrote a long letter to the
Common Cause. It was his effort to justify—and perhaps to understand
—what had gone wrong. It seemed to him, he wrote,

the renewal of publication of the *Tocsin* abroad right now is not a real necessity. A
revolutionary journal is needed at the moment of weakening of practical revolutionary activity, at the moment of revolutionary stalemate and quiescence. At the
precise moment of open struggle the revolutionary party is going through now, it is
much more useful for all who have money and also physical and intellectual skills
to give for the revolution, to turn exclusively and completely to the organization of
efforts such as those that have distinguished recent days. To answer the gallows
with journal articles is extremely naïve. Now it is necessary to think not about the
structure of typography, nor about acquiring type, nor about setting the printed
pages. Of course, these moments of active struggle . . . will not be very long-lived.
The arrests of the majority of most energetic revolutionary activists will immediately produce a certain, although momentary, calm in revolutionary activity. Then
in this moment of quiescence not one but two or more revolutionary journals will
be necessary.[88]

The *Tocsin*, he was saying, was no longer needed, but his words hardly
reflected an optimistic view of the future.

Irritated at his antagonist's contention that the *Tocsin* had always
been superfluous, that it had been a "laughable comedy" from the
start, Tkachev firmly disagreed. In his outline of the journal's successful
fulfillment of its charges lay a clear definition of its failures.

The *Tocsin* completely fulfilled its task within the limits of possibility and fulfilled
it with complete success. . . . They reproach us for caring little about the distribution of the *Toçsin* in Russia, for not organizing our party in Russia, and so on.
But, in the first place, what could we accomplish toward this goal with the lack of
any definite material means and with that systematic, deliberate hostility the
anarchist and *Forward!* circles turned against the *Tocsin*. In the second place, and
this is most important: I never attached special importance to distributing the
Tocsin in Russia. The *Tocsin* was not an agitational revolutionary leaflet; its task
consisted strictly in returning revolutionaries to the sole practical and valid idea and
principle of revolutionary activity that they, under the influence of reaction, under
the interest of anarchistic and L[avrov]istic nonsense, had come to disown. . . .
It was enough merely that *certain* revolutionary activists were acquainted with its
program and its basic principles, that among them it aroused talk and argument,
enough to bring to mind the forgotten ideas of a small number of revolutionaries;
and thereafter revolutionary practice itself did not delay in recognizing the reason,
the practicality of these ideas and distributing them among the majority of revolutionaries. I am very glad to know that in Russia few have the *Tocsin* at hand, but
almost all the revolutionary circles know of its existence and its program, about its
principles.[89]

He was taking credit, of course, for the activism of the People's Will,

88. Lemke, "Materialy dlia biografii," pp. 165-66.
89. Ibid., pp. 164-65.

but he was defensive too in tone. For all Tkachev's bravado the *Tocsin*'s demise was clearly his defeat.

By 1880 Tkachev seems to have moved permanently to Paris. It was the year of the amnesty; the Communards flocked back to their homeland from exile in London and in Geneva. Blanqui himself was released from prison in the autumn of that year—a finally old Blanqui, never quite to recover his one-time vigor. Still his friends began a new journal, *Ni dieu, ni maître*, and Tkachev and Turski both worked on it. Tkachev's name was listed on the masthead as a Russian correspondent. To one of the journal's first issues he contributed a "Letter from Russia," describing the trials of the terrorist-revolutionaries whose spiritual father he believed himself to be.[90] In the same month (November 1880) he began publication in *Ni dieu, ni maître* of a French translation of Chernyshevskii's novel *What Is to Be Done?*, the work that had so inspired Russian youth of his own generation. Tkachev's preface extolled the author for his influence on the young men of the sixties.

Never did any writer have such influence on the intellectual development of his contemporaries. The most progressive part of Russian society considered him its leader. On the other hand, the reactionary part, the ruling classes, saw in him the basic cause of popular power and a source of the revolutionary movement that had already begun to agitate Russian society. Fearing his influence on youth, they trembled before this mind so clear, so logical, so enticing. . . . Russian youth found in *What Is to Be Done?* the practical solution of great moral and social questions. . . .[91]

The project was never finished; only one long installment of the novel appeared. The reaction of Tkachev's editors may well have been negative; the great inspiration of Russian teenagers in 1860 could have roused little interest in sophisticated Paris twenty years later.

Even when the new Blanquist journal ran into financial difficulties and publication had to be curtailed, Tkachev's name was kept on the masthead. But he did not again contribute to *Ni dieu, ni maître*. All indications are that he led a quiet life and deliberately withdrew from political activity. During his few years in Paris he never spoke at any of the Blanquist meetings, and if he attended any he stayed well in the background. His name was never listed among the contributors to Blanqui's campaigns and causes. So far had he sunk into obscurity that he does not seem to have been known to the Paris police.[92] If he ever met Blanqui in person, he made little impression on the Old Man and

---

90. Tkachev, 4: 415-18.
91. Ibid., pp. 413-14.
92. There is no file in the Archives de la préfecture de police under Tkachev's name; nor is he mentioned by name in the several files concerning Blanqui and the Blanquists.

was not mentioned in Blanqui's numerous notes and records.[93] In the summer of 1880 Blanqui had suffered a series of strokes that rendered him inactive; his followers carefully kept him out of the public eye.[94] The Old Man died in January 1881, and Tkachev was called to speak at his funeral as a representative of the Russian radical émigrés. Misdirected by the police (deliberately, they later contended), he and several other scheduled orators got lost in the large crowd at the cemetery and were never able to make their way to the graveside where ceremonies were held. Tkachev's projected brief funeral oration was later published in *Ni dieu, ni maître*. Blanqui, he claimed, would remain as much a part of the Russian revolutionary movement as he had long been of the French.

To him, to his ideas, to his unselfishness, to the clearness of his mind, his penetration, we are obligated in significant part for those successes the revolutionary party in Russia is achieving daily. . . . He is our teacher and molder in the great art of conspiratorial activity. . . . The great victim of all reactionary governments, he is the personification of the revolutionary idea.[95]

For a year and a half thereafter, Tkachev's life and actions remain obscure. He no longer published articles in the *Cause*. He may have earned his keep by working with a Russian radical woman—his old friend Anna Korvin-Krukovskaia, who had married a Communard named Jaclard—but other evidence makes this claim dubious at best.[96] His slender ties with the radical movement weakened, although on occasion his old colleagues remembered him and sought him out.[97] By 1881 he may already have been suffering the initial agonies of the disease that was shortly to end his life.

On November 30, 1882, the day of Louis Blanc's massive funeral, Tkachev was found roaming the streets of Paris in a state that suggested

---

93. Blanqui's papers are in the Bibliothèque nationale in Paris, placed there after his death by his secretary, E. Granger. They are filed among the *Nouvelles acquisitions françaises*, nos. 9578-98.

94. Cf. Archives de la préfecture de police, file BA 869, reports nos. 35, 36.

95. *Ni dieu, ni maître*, January 9, 1881.

96. *Deiateli revoliutsionnogo dvizheniia v Rossii*, 2: 1715. Anna Jaclard and her husband had both been involved in the Paris Commune. He was taken prisoner by French troops but escaped with her aid. In 1874 they returned to Russia to write for several radical journals. Jaclard went back to Paris in 1880 after the amnesty, but his wife lived for the most part in St. Petersburg, where her contact with Tkachev would have been only through correspondence. Any correspondence Tkachev supposedly was editing for her never appeared in print. Their close association cannot be documented.

97. Cf. V. Ia. Iakovlev, *Iz istorii politicheskoi borby v 70- i 80-kh godov*, p. 362.

mental incompetence.[98] He was arrested for his strange behavior and taken to a police station, where he was somehow recognized by an acquaintance, vouched for, and transferred to St. Anne's Asylum. There for several days he refused even to reveal his name. Some time later he communicated with an unspecified visiting relative. His illness was diagnosed as "paralysis of the brain." Whatever the scientific description, he suffered from a disease that destroyed his personality and gradually deprived him of all his faculties. A visitor who saw him shortly before his death said he was a living corpse, unable to speak or to recognize anyone near him. One writer has stated that Dementeva came to see him near the end.[99]

He died on January 4, 1886 (Western style). The funeral was held the following day although some of his friends had hoped to postpone it until more people could be notified. According to the obituary in the *Common Cause* the Russian emigration in Paris attended the services "almost in full force." The Blanquists were there: Elisée Reclus and Vaillant, who spoke on their behalf. Grigorev termed Tkachev "one of the outstanding activists of our tempestuous epoch, a clear thinker and a very talented writer of the terror," scarcely what Tkachev would have called himself.[100] In a great final irony Lavrov gave the main funeral oration. A man of sixty-two, destined to outlive his rival by another fourteen years, Lavrov insisted that "at the grave, all personal quarrels disappear, all party divisions become nothing, and we remember only the common struggle against the common enemy." Generously he confined his remarks to Tkachev's literary activity before 1874 when the two men had so bitterly quarreled.

His sparkling talent as a writer, his diversified knowledge, made him a valuable colleague in the publications that continued the work of Chernyshevskii, Dobroliubov, attacking political, economic, and literary banality in all spheres and preparing a broad movement of social-revolutionary apostles, which began in 1878 to move forth into the bloodier struggle. Tkachev's articles were read then by the youth in the schools and forced many young hearts to beat with hatred for tyranny and exploiters of the people.[101]

Of their effort to collaborate Lavrov only stated that it had not lasted long. Concluding, he cried out: "Eternal war on despotism! Inflexible struggle for the suffering classes of the people!"[102]

98. Lemke, "Materialy dlia biografii," p. 156; *Vestnik narodnoi voli* (Geneva), 5, pt. 2 (1886): 157.
99. Robert Payne, *The Fortress*, p. 203.
100. Lemke, "Materialy dlia biografii," p. 157.
101. Ibid., pp. 157-58.
102. Ibid., p. 158.

Two wreaths were laid on the grave, one from unidentified relatives and one from Tkachev's former colleagues on the *Tocsin*. The plot had been purchased only for five years, and the headstone was wooden, not stone. Tkachev's friends hoped to raise money for a more impressive memorial. They never did, and eventually the remains were transferred to a crypt.

A brief obituary, written by Lavrov, appeared in the émigré journal *Herald of the People's Will*, 1886. The longer and far more interesting document, frequently cited above, was Khristoforov's thoughtful analysis of Tkachev and his times published in the Bakuninist journal *Common Cause*. Khristoforov's history of the revolutionary movement was developed with perceptiveness and astuteness, considering its contemporary composition. It was the editor's contention that at the time of his illness Tkachev was moving into the seventies, farther from the exclusiveness that Khristoforov associated with the decade before. Thus the editor explained the "weakness" of Tkachev's last writings: they were the works of a man undergoing great intellectual ferment, a moral transformation that might have opened a new road and could have brought him closer to the spirit and the principles of the new times. Khristoforov was touchingly sympathetic.

Personally, to us, Tkachev always gave the impression of a man the personality of whom was far from exhausted in the political program of the *Tocsin;* it seemed to us that he was broader than this program, that it was not his last but only his first word. The sharp partisanship of his journalism did not keep him from discerning the good in those people whom he mercilessly persecuted as a writer. Thus, for instance, reacting against Dostoevskii for his political obscurantism, he was able to value the huge talent of this singular artist and was entranced by him. In conversations with friends he from time to time stated ideas much broader than those he set forth in the *Tocsin*, and when they asked him why then he did not express the same concept in print, he only shrugged his shoulders in answer, as if wanting to say, "What do you want? . . . they would not understand me. My thought would be misinterpreted." All this naturally evokes the proposition that not a small share of the frequent political paradoxes of the editor of the *Tocsin* must be laid to account of those exaggerations that are found in almost every activist who, entering on the road of political struggle, is devoting a significant part of his effort to the formation, enlargement and discipline of a party of his partisans.[103]

It is a strange requiem, to hope that a man was not what he seemed and that perhaps he might have changed. Yet they were surely among the kindest words that anyone had ever written of Petr Tkachev.

---

103. Ibid., p. 171.

13

Evaluation

Tkachev as a person is difficult to appraise owing to the lack of intimate materials. No radical leader of his generation left fewer memorabilia; no one of his competitors expressed himself so drily and impersonally in those published writings remaining to history. Tkachev had more than the usual penchant for privacy and secrecy. His natural inclination to keep to himself was reinforced by his isolation among Russian émigrés whose hostility led them to avoid social contact. The patterns of his thought are often elusive too. Although he expressed himself boldly and clearly, he contradicted himself, sometimes from month to month. His polemics against his enemies caused him to refute their ideas even when he shared them. Sometimes he deliberately adopted a stance not true to his own beliefs for purposes of propagandizing among his readers.

Tkachev was never a natural leader among men. Lacking the charisma and the aggressiveness that leadership demanded, he was not particularly popular among his contemporaries. Described as quiet by his acquaintances, he preferred to stay in the background while others made the speeches. Except for the Nechaev affair, when he threw off his discretion to purchase a printing press and publish a proclamation, he remained a cautious revolutionary. In Russia Tkachev was probably in touch with underground student communes, but he kept his name out of police records. Occasionally he sponsored a meeting or ventured out to one; undoubtedly he plotted and planned with his colleagues, particularly the student group around Nechaev. Still his own role in revolutionary action was for the most part confined to his acerbic writings. He did not change after he fled abroad. Few people remember seeing him at meetings; he apparently took little active part in organizations, legal or illegal. Outside of his usually anonymous writing he did nothing to attract the attention of the police.

In his writings Tkachev was bold; in his actions he was sometimes cowardly. History has recorded several instances when he fled rather than face an awkward situation, and there were undoubtedly many others. In spite of his early stance on feminism, a position that earned him sighs of admiration as a hero to young Russian women, Tkachev never seems to have made and maintained close relationships. No contemporary wrote that Tkachev was his best or even his close friend. His single recorded love affair ended in ashes. When he chronicled the negative effects of his generation's objective, intellectual orientation—that is, when he wrote of the inability of the men of the sixties to feel or to express deep emotional commitments—he may have been thinking sadly of himself.

Tkachev's contribution to history lay not in his deeds but in his words. His ideas—insofar as the work of a lifetime can be summarized—are best approached from three angles: the fundamental political, sociological, and philosophical principles he espoused; his analysis of contemporary society, based upon and intertwined with these basic principles; and his program for revolutionary tactics as conceived on the basis of his sociological evaluation.

The fundamental principles devised by Tkachev formed no cohesive system for they were in every case modified by his demand for social change to be accomplished through revolution. The Russian critic often tried to fit his viewpoints into a whole, but the revolutionary cause stood in his way. Revolution he viewed as a voluntary action of man, and its complementary conviction of man's freedom of action did not logically assimilate into the system he attempted to construct.

Thus Tkachev was basically a historical determinist and believed that history unrolled in accordance with certain basic laws. Recognizing that the essence of these laws had not yet been revealed, he blithely assigned to philosophy the task of seeking it out. He himself set forth certain negative assumptions. The course of history, he was sure, did not derive from any motive force of a spiritual nature as metaphysicians contended, nor did it unroll through men's attitudes or ideas. The laws of history were not identical with those of biological or geological evolution, although Tkachev's enthusiastic reading of Spencer caused him to admit the considerable influence of biological dictates on mankind. But to any principle fundamental to the historical order Tkachev found a major exception. Whatever the laws of history man had the power to break them, he wrote. Man was master of his fate and could change not just history but its rules. Tkachev's theory of historical jumps superimposed voluntarism on determinism. He was insisting that revolution could be successfully made. He could not accept the fatalism he found in the deterministic interpretation of history, but he was equally unable to visualize historical events as meaningless, as occurring without principle or direction. The insoluble contradiction in his sociological thought lies here.

Tkachev faced the same problem in regard to his conviction that all facets of human life—behavior, ideas, institutions—were directly or indirectly determined by economic considerations. His mechanistic interpretation of these relationships, which has caused Soviet scholars to deny his understanding of Marx, did not signify lack of depth or durability in his economic determinism. But here again Tkachev made exceptions to the rule. Thus truly great revolutionaries—"people of the future"—were dominated not by their pocketbooks but by their ideals. Should such men, economically impotent, desire to rebel, their revolution might overthrow a political system supported by a strong economic class, although generally government was always based on economic power. "Breaking the magic circle" countermanded Tkachev's economic determinism as "historical jumps" negated historical determinism. For the truth was that economic relationships altered but slowly over the generations, and Tkachev was impatient for change. Individuals oppressed by the economic order were by their weakness unlikely to change that order, but Tkachev was dedicated to revolution. Voluntarism had to prevail, for the revolution must not be denied the possibility of victory. Tkachev coped with the contradictions as best he could.

Tkachev's materialistic interpretation of history caused him to insist that human efforts and humanity's progress be evaluated strictly by measurable, objective standards. From the beginning he condemned the positivist theory of progress as ivory tower and overly intellectual, and he insisted that progress could not be measured by ideas or by scientific discoveries. In his younger years he had demanded that historians (unlike scientists) make value judgments, that they praise and condemn on the basis of certain definite standards Tkachev had yet clearly to express. The sudden popularity of Lavrov's subjective sociology, which Tkachev recognized as neo-Kantian in its demand for moral imperatives, caused the young critic to define his criteria of evaluation in increasingly dogmatic and materialistic terms. He ended by insisting that progress be assessed strictly in terms of the physical standard of living of the working class. In his last years he rejected the utilitarian evaluation of progress, an evaluation he once believed unsurpassed in contemporary thought; the notions of benefit and good were too subjective to admit of mechanical quantitative assessment. Man's benefit must simply be defined in terms of his material possessions.

Tkachev's attitude toward knowledge and scholarship was ambivalent, blurred also by his demand for social reform. Torn between the Western rationalism he respected and the peasant revolution he desired, he forced himself to choose the latter, but his choice was not made without difficulty. He insisted that he disliked intellectualism because he was convinced that intellectuals did not contribute to human progress as he defined it: they seldom concerned themselves with raising the standard of living, and they were congenitally unable to drive themselves to revolutionary activism. Mistrusting laboratory researchers for their remoteness and unconcern, he was not caught up in the excitement about pure science that swept his generation. Yet his attitude toward science was ambivalent too. Like many of his generation, he became fascinated in spite of himself with Spencer's application of Darwinian law to humanity; science was worth while when it applied itself to sociology. Although he was unimpressed by physicists and chemists, he could not help but admire their empirical, objective methods, and he constantly exhorted his contemporaries to adopt the scientific approach. Science, Tkachev concluded, was the wave of the future; it was based on rational investigation while art relied on emotional response. Reason must rule over emotion, except of course where peasant revolution was concerned. Tkachev found himself (along with many Russian revolutionaries) on the horns of a dilemma, the same dilemma he imputed to Lavrov— the choice between intellectual consciousness and revolutionary spontaneity. The best he could do was seek a science of revolution, a science that would divert its practitioners from abstract conclusions and direct them towards the healing of man's ills.

Similarly Tkachev disliked intellectuals because Spencer had convinced him that by nature the *intelligent* must be pitted against the common man. His reading of Spencer had convinced the Russian critic that intelligence was always associated with individualism, and he had never cared for the latter at all. His negative reaction to individualism had separated him from Pisarev's brand of nihilism. Individualism lay at the heart of that bourgeois capitalist morality that he deplored, with its selfishness, competitiveness, and inhumanity.

The sine qua non of individualism was anarchism, in Tkachev's view, and the anarchistic society where each man was left alone to find his own way he regarded as a travesty of justice. In Tkachev's Utopia, a Utopia deplored by most Russian radicals in his generation, the collective must rule over the individual and freedom must take second place.

Only a totally egalitarian pattern of living would bring mankind close to the perfect society. Tkachev solved the Spencerian clash between individual and collective by eliminating the former as a separate force. Absolute egalitarianism must be enforced in the future world; communism had no room for an intellectual elite. Thus, Tkachev was convinced, the perfection of mankind would be achieved.

In these fundamental concepts Tkachev diverged from the men of his times in several important ways. Most apparent is his addiction to mechanistic materialism, which he refused to abandon even when Lavrov's new subjectivism was inspiring the minds of a new generation. His constant battle against the notion that ideas and science should serve as a gauge for the measurement of progress set him against the positivists. He statism was deplored by an almost universally anarchistic generation, and the harshly egalitarian society he idealized would destroy the intelligentsia along with Lavrov's critically thinking men.

In his analysis of contemporary society Tkachev was not so iconoclastic. He moved closer to the Russian radicals of his generation, especially those who became known as populists (*narodniki*) after 1870.

Russian populism has never been clearly defined although scholars have devoted not just articles but books to analysis of its characteristics.[1] Indeed the mood and the principles of *narodnichestvo* were never clearly set forth even by its adherents, who differed one from another in their aims and their analyses of themselves. Richard Pipes in his semantic inquiry has emphasized the differences between the populists and has demonstrated that they thought in varying terms about each other.[2] A Soviet scholar has colorfully described the attempts of Mikhailovskii (a classic populist by most definitions) to set forth a cogent statement of the beliefs held in common by himself and his colleagues on *Fatherland Notes* and the futile efforts of his friends to come to conclusions of their own.[3] Investigating researchers have found definitions equally treacherous. Venturi's massive tome on Russian populism[4] includes studies of Herzen and Chernyshevskii, both of whom are considered prepopulists by most observers on the basis of

---

1. Many efforts have been made by scholars to develop a working definition of populism. Among the most interesting studies in English are the article by Pipes, "*Narodnichestvo:* A Semantic Inquiry," pp. 441-58, and the Marxist-oriented book by Walicki, often cited above.

2. Pipes, passim.

3. Bush, *Ocherki literaturnogo narodnichestva 70-80 gg.*, pp. 11-15.

4. Venturi, *Roots of Revolution*. Venturi's book in the Italian original was entitled *Il populismo russo;* a more accurate title might have included the adjective *revolutionary*.

their beliefs as well as their dates. But Venturi, who includes Tkachev among the *narodniki*, makes little mention of Mikhailovskii, who seemed to many contemporaries to stand at the heart of the populist movement after 1870. Others define populism in terms of its beliefs as well as in terms of its stages of development. Berdiaev insists on a peasant orientation, considering that the *narodniki* had faith in the people,[5] a definition by which Tkachev and certain others would seem to be completely excluded. Pipes believes that the early populists (like Mikhailovskii but not like Chernyshevskii) sought to submerge intellectualism in the uneducated masses; the later populists he regards as united by their conviction that Russia could be saved from capitalism.[6] Walicki defined the *narodniki* in Leninist terms as defenders of small production (particularly by the peasantry) as against industrial capitalism. Yet Walicki calls populism a democratic ideology,[7] a definition that should exclude Tkachev.

The argument rages, but whatever the definition of *narodnichestvo* —and a semantic judgment can hardly be rendered here—it is clear that Tkachev shared many viewpoints with those considered its most typical exponents. In his analysis of society Tkachev like the *narodniki* found Western industrial capitalism to have produced only misery. His vision of the evils of capitalistic society bordered on the hysterical; he described the deadening crush of the labor market place, the degenerative effects of poverty, and the hypocrisy of the bourgeoisie with a passion unmatched even by that of Marx. Tkachev's view of bourgeois progress as a retrogressive phenomenon that was leading the worker away from security and plenty instead of toward them was scorned by the young group of exiled Russians, who by the early 1880s were moving away from populism and leaning toward Marx's views. But even they shared Tkachev's conception of capitalism as brutal and cruel. They, like he, found Western democracy a deceptive sham. This negative attitude toward the European economic, political, and social system was common to many Russians of Tkachev's time.

Common too was a persuasion toward what Walicki calls the "privilege of backwardness"[8]—the conviction that Russia, despite her problems, was better off than the West. For all his awareness of economic need in his native land Tkachev assessed Russian poverty in terms less harsh than those he applied to Europe. Sometimes he exalted

---

5. Berdiaev, *Istoki i smysl russkogo kommunizma*, p. 48.
6. Pipes, p. 458.
7. Walicki, p. 8. Walicki also provides a developmental view of populism and divides its traditions into early, classical, and later periods.
8. Ibid., pp. 107-31.

the socialistic remnants in the Russian economy in the form of peasant communes and worker artels, although he had little faith in the intuitive communism of the Russian peasant in his time. To Engels he bragged about the ease with which revolution might come about in Russia. Like his populist contemporaries he preferred Russia's economy to that of the West even though unlike them he never defended Russian forms as unique. In Lenin's terms he preferred an economy dominated by small producers rather than large industrial enterprises. In Walicki's view he belonged with the sociological romanticizers who preferred to hold Russia to her traditional past rather than see her perverted by industrial revolution.[9]

Yet Tkachev knew capitalism was bound to come. The question of whether capitalism would appear in Russia was hotly debated in the Russian press after 1870. The men of this decade and the next were "preoccupied," to quote one Soviet scholar, by the economic changes that were occurring. They recognized the transitional nature of the times; they were aware of the worker question, of the growing stratification of society, of what they sometimes called the "proletarianization of the old nobility."[10] Tkachev always knew what was happening. He had sensed capitalistic competition creeping even into the *obshchina*, which he had deliberately idealized as the prototype of an egalitarian world. Tkachev did not draw his conclusions from Marx; as has been indicated he did not at first sense Marx's conviction that the economic patterns of the West were bound to spread, and he later rejected the notion that Marxism applied to Russia at all. His own reading told him that capitalism was on the way, and his revolutionary tactics represented his plan to stop it. For in Tkachev's view men could always change history if they so willed.

As to Russian society, Tkachev suffered the tribulations of many of his generation. At first intrigued and challenged by the generation gap, he viewed his own class—that of the radical intelligentsia now enlarged as never before by men of many classes and déclassés—with great hopes and optimistic spirit. But by the 1870s the men of the sixties began to lose faith. Writers of the new decade recognized the symptoms of the doldrums among their own contemporaries; thus a minor poet wrote in the journal *Slovo* (Word) in 1878: "Ailing children of ailing fathers / How pitiful we are, how we are ridiculous."[11] Tkachev 's hopes for his generation were soon dimmed by reality and replaced with pessimism

9. Ibid., pp. 56-79.

10. Bush, pp. 5-10.

11. This poem entitled "Meditation" is by S. Zasimskii and appeared in *Slovo*, no. 1 (1878). It is quoted in Bush, p. 10.

for the future. The men of the sixties had failed to revolutionize Russia and renew the world. By 1875, in spite of his exhortations to revolution published in the *Tocsin*, Tkachev was sharing some of his generation's discouragement.

Tkachev's view of the peasantry too was hardly optimistic; indeed his evaluation of the peasantry's potential was more realistic than that of many populists. Even in his articles idealizing communality and its effects Tkachev admitted that the contemporary peasant had strayed far from pure communism. His revolutionary plans indicated that he did not think the peasant's intuitive communism (of which he bragged in his debate with Engels) was sufficient to guarantee his support of a socialistic society. Nor was the peasant really revolutionary except for the flare of destructive fury Tkachev thought might be kindled under certain carefully constructed circumstances. In Tkachev's *Tocsin* writings the peasant emerged as incompetent to manage revolution or socialism; one of Tkachev's contemporaries who interviewed him in person in 1874 claimed that Tkachev's estimate of the peasantry's potential was even lower than he had indicated in his published works.[12] He actually had no faith in the peasant at all.

Like Lavrov and Bakunin Tkachev based his revolutionary tactics on his analysis of contemporary society. His debt to other revolutionaries—particularly to Buonarroti and Blanqui—is difficult to determine because of the logical sequence in which his plans evolved from his own early convictions. He never acknowledged any obligation to Buonarroti, much less to Nechaev. He himself spoke only of Blanqui. It is worth remarking that his friendship with the Blanquist Communards he met in Geneva was more durable than his association with Blanqui might have been, had the Old Man lived. Many of Blanqui's convictions, extending beyond revolutionary tactics, are reminiscent of the concepts Tkachev so deplored in Lavrov. The similarities in their thought were confined to the tactics for revolutionary action, for which Blanqui was famous. And wherever Tkachev may have drawn his examples, the particular synthesis of revolutionism at which he arrived derived from

---

12. A letter from Alexander Kropotkin, the brother of the anarchist prince, to P. L. Lavrov after Kropotkin had apparently interviewed Tkachev in response to Lavrov's request. This letter is preserved in the Third Section archives and quoted by Martin A. Miller in *The Formative Years of P. A. Kropotkin, 1842-1876* (Ph.D. diss., University of Chicago, 1968), p. 240. The revolutionary tactics of Lavrov, Bakunin, and Tkachev all hinged on their visions of the Russian peasantry, as I have attempted to demonstrate in my article "Consciousness and Spontaneity, 1875: The Peasant Revolution Seen by Tkachev, Lavrov, and Bakunin," *Canadian Slavic Studies* 4, no. 4 (Winter 1970), pp. 699-720.

his own observations of contemporary Russian society, as Blanqui's synthesis derived from his observations of France.

Because he was certain capitalism was creeping into Russia, Tkachev insisted that revolution must be made at once before capitalist competition succeeded in destroying the communal spirit and capitalist industrialization created a powerful bourgeoisie on which the tsar might lean for support. Because the peasant could never initiate successful revolution, revolution must be made without the help of the majority. Because revolution by minority could not hope to succeed in the countryside, the minority must devise a conspiracy with the aim of the seizure of political power, a possibility for which Tkachev had allowed in his theory of "breaking the circle." Most important of all, because the peasantry was really not instinctively communistic, the new society and its new institutions would have to be established by forceful and dictatorial means.

In all these measures Tkachev found himself at odds with many of his radical contemporaries. Lavrov and Marx did not agree that revolution must be made at once. Both of them argued for waiting until the correct historical moment—a moment defined for Marx by the inevitable rising of the proletariat, for Lavrov by the proper development of critically thinking individuals and their propagandizing among the peasantry. Because they were "waiters" Tkachev was less tolerant of the Marxists and Lavrovists than he was of the Bakuninists. But he thoroughly rejected Bakunin's analysis of the peasantry and the call to *bunty* that resulted therefrom. Bakunin was ready to rely on those instincts in which Tkachev never really believed; the old anarchist discarded knowledge out of the prerequisite to revolution. Tkachev could not write knowledge out of the picture any more than Lavrov could. In tactics Tkachev could agree with neither of them. If his dislike of Lavrov was more extreme, it was because of his rejection of Lavrov's elite critical thinkers, his dislike of Lavrov's subjective morality, and his annoyance at the role Lavrov assigned to ideas in history. Although Lavrov's analysis of history had much in common with Tkachev's evaluations, in his determination to contradict willy-nilly every item in Lavrov's world view Tkachev turned polemicist, negating his own ideas to the extent that Lavrov held them too. He was not forced to quite such extremes in his attacks on Bakunin.

In one further aspect of his plans Tkachev antagonized almost the entire revolutionary intelligentsia of the early 1870s. He found no room in his tactics for democratic principles. The secretive, highly disciplined party, the minority revolution, and the dictatorship of the postrevolutionary era were never democratic concepts. Yet the populists for the most part believed in democracy for all their conviction that contemporary Western practices were fraudulent. The common man stood at the heart of their plans. Calling on the intelligentsia to submerge itself in the masses, Mikhailovskii was expressing a key element of the populist creed in Pipes's definition.[13] Lavrov, Bakunin, and Marx anticipated a social revolution made by the broad masses however they might be inspired. Political revolution was regarded with horror even by many of the early People's Will terrorists, who anticipated that assassinations would shock the peasantry into revolutionary action. Among the leading radicals of Tkachev's time only Marx and Blanqui understood the need for a postrevolutionary dictatorship to enforce the revolution's will and to suppress counterrevolutionary elements. Tkachev's rejection of democracy isolated him from the mainstream of the populist cause.

Nevertheless Tkachev had his followers. They were hardly disciples, for few of them acknowledged his influence. Rather they were men who arrived at the same conclusions as he through their own methods and convictions.

First and foremost among them stands the People's Will, the terroristic revolutionary organization of 1878 that espoused not only the Tkachevian idea of political revolution but insisted also on a tightly organized, disciplined, conspiratorial party. Tkachev once claimed credit for the policies of the People's Will although he basically doubted their validity. But the men of the People's Will were not Tkachevists though they harbored Jacobins in their midst. Although they formed a disciplined party dedicated to political rather than social deeds, most of them did so under the pressures of circumstance—the abject failure of classic populism to convert the peasantry to revolution—rather than under the influence of Tkachev. Moreover their aims were not his; the seizure of power was never considered by the terrorists, who confined themselves to assassination in the hopes of fomenting confusion, abdication, and social rebellion. Tkachev never honestly believed they would succeed. He knew that the victorious revolutionary conspiracy would be that which set as its goal the immediate overthrow of the tsarist government. The People's Will did not do so.

The second and greater question revolves around Tkachev's influence on Lenin.[14] Lenin knew and read Tkachev. To V. D. Bonch-

---

13. Pipes, pp. 443-44, 458.
14. American scholars have long been aware of the similarity of Leninism and Tkachevism. It was first pointed out by Karpovich in his article "Forerunner of Lenin," pp. 336-50. It has since provided the title and theme of Weeks, *First Bolshevik*. For a careful analysis see Rolf H. W. Theen's recent work, *Lenin*.

Bruevich in Geneva in 1904 he reported his interest in old revolutionary literature and suggested that his colleagues study the *Tocsin* as well as Bakunin's journals and Nechaev's proclamations.[15] His own statements indicate that he was both intrigued and scornful. He once assessed Tkachev (according to Bonch-Bruevich) as an original writer of rich literature and wrote that Tkachev's schemes had grandeur compared to those of less imaginative men.[16] Yet he referred to his revolutionary forerunner as "Tkachev the Little,"[17] a designation not only scornful but indicating Lenin's feeling that Tkachev himself exaggerated his own importance.

Still Lenin's denigrating view of Tkachev—like his violent attacks on *narodnichestvo* in general—does not at all mean he refused to learn from Russian revolutionary thought and experience. The similarity of Lenin's tactics to those sanctioned by Tkachev was noted in the early Soviet press. In the 1920s an argument extraordinary even in those days of arguments broke out about the relationship of Leninism to Jacobinism, as Tkachev's plans were usually termed in Russia. S. I. Mitskevich began the controversy with a challenging article pointing up the similarities between bolshevism and Tkachevism, not only in terms of their demands for a political seizure of power by a disciplined revolutionary party but in their analysis of Russian society—peasant and proletarian—as well.[18] Immediately he came under fire, primarily from a group of less thoughtful Bolsheviks who insisted upon the differences, as proclaimed polemically by Lenin himself. Mitskevich's opponents generally spoke to the concept that Leninism sprang by necessity from Marxism, with which Tkachev had violently disagreed, and that Leninism could not possibly be associated with Blanquism, against which Marx himself had polemicized. Lenin, they wrote, constantly battled with *narodniki* in his prerevolutionary years. How could he have absconded with Tkachev's populist era plans when he said they were wrong?[19] Among the Mitskevich critics Kozmin is distinguished by his scholarship and

15. V. Bonch-Bruevich, "Biblioteka i arkhiv RSDRP v Zheneve," *Krasnaia letopis*, no. 48 (1932), p. 113. Weeks tends to overstate Lenin's interest in Tkachev when he omits Lenin's reference to other aspects of Russian revolutionary tradition as equally important (Weeks, p. 5).
    16. Bonch-Bruevich, p. 115; Lenin, "What Is to Be Done?" p. 240.
    17. Lenin, "What Is to Be Done?" p. 240.
    18. Mitskevich, "Russkie iakobintsy," pp. 3-26.
    19. See Sineira, "V poriadke diskussii: Eshche o marksizme i blankizme," *Pechat i revoliutsiia*, 2 (1925): 105-14; N. N. Baturin, "O nasledstve russkikh iakobintsev," *Proletarskaia revoliutsiia*, no. 7 (30) (1924), pp. 82-89; and idem, "Eshche o tsvetakh russkogo iakobinstva," *Proletarskaia revoliutsiia*, no. 8 (1925), pp. 97-105. Mitskevich answered his critics in "K voprosu o korniakh bolshevizma," *Katorga i ssylka*, no. 16 (1925), pp. 92-101.

perspective.[20] But the final verdict was clear: Leninism and Tkachevism had no filial ties. The policy became incorporated into official Communist line, and the controversy has not arisen in the Soviet Union again.

Yet the actual kinship remains. Lenin was not consciously a Tkachevist, but he constructed a tightly disciplined, conspiratorial party on the lines that Tkachev and Blanqui had suggested; he achieved his revolution by a political seizure of power not foreseen in the Marxist idea of proletarian revolution; he brought about and enforced social revolution through a taut dictatorship envisaged not only by Marx but by Tkachev. Moreover the Bolshevik revolution became possible when Tkachev's prediction came true: the tsarist government fell and no powerful protector stepped forth to save it. Engels was wrong; at the end the Russian court hung in the air as Tkachev knew it would and collapsed like a punctured balloon, falling from its own weight.

Tkachev remained a prophet without honor in his own land and times. He had to a great extent predicted the future and urged his contemporaries to act accordingly, but no one responded to the peal of his *Tocsin* and no one acknowledged hearing his pleas. Had he lived as long a life as many of his contemporaries he might have worked (if he were permitted) at Lenin's side. He might then one day have claimed a victory approaching his greatest dreams. He anticipated history whether or not he left his personal mark upon it. No other Russian revolutionary writer of his generation earned a more imposing epitaph.

---

20. B. P. Kozmin, "P. N. Tkachev i narodnichestvo," *Katorga i ssylka*, no. 22 (1926), pp. 109-22. In his discussion of this polemic Weeks does not seem to realize that Kozmin had the final and perhaps most telling word (Weeks, pp. 177-83).

Bibliography

The following list does not purport to be all-inclusive, for a complete bibliography on Tkachev and his contemporaries would fill volumes in itself. These are the works to which reference has been made in footnotes and those of greatest value in preparing this book. Similarly, the list of Tkachev's writings includes only major collections and those journal articles (not reprinted in the collections) of special interest for this study. Some were selected for the light they throw on Tkachev's intellectual development, others for their statement of Tkachev's views on substantive issues.

In addition to the sources listed below, the author has consulted several archival collections: namely, the Blanqui papers at the Bibliothèque nationale (Paris), filed under Nouvelle acquisitions françaises, nos. 9578-98; the Archives de la préfecture de police (Paris), particularly file BA 869 on the Blanquists; various files in the Staatsarchiv, Zurich, Switzerland; and the B. Nicolaevsky collection in the archives of the Hoover Institute (Stanford, California), especially Boxes 211 and 221.

The author has made the usual arbitrary decisions in regard to forms of citations (particularly for older periodicals, which lack sequential volume numbers) and problems of Russian orthography. Thus names of persons well known in the West (Herzen, Tolstoy) are spelled as generally accepted in the West with parenthetical references to Russian variants where applicable; Russianized names from other

315

languages (Deich for Deutsch) appear in the text under their original form, but retain the Russian spelling in footnote and bibliographical references.

Certain materials included in this book have found their way into previously published journal articles, always in greatly different form. These articles are cited hereinafter under the author's name.

Akselrod, P. B. *Perezhitoe i peredumannoe*. Berlin, 1923.
Alekseev, V. P. "Revoliutsionnoe i studencheskoe dvizhenie 1869 g. v otsenke tretego otdeleniia." *Katorga i ssylka*, no. 10 (1924), pp. 107-20.
Annenskaia, A. N. "Iz proshlykh let: Vospominaniia o N. F. Annenskom." *Russkoe bogatstvo*, no. 1 (January 1913), pp. 62-81.
Antonov, Vasilii Fedorovich. *Revoliutsionnoe narodnichestvo*. Moscow, 1965.
Ascher, Abraham. *Pavel Axelrod and the Development of Menshevism*. Cambridge, Mass.: Harvard University Press, 1972.
Ashevskii, S. "Russkoe studenchestvo v epokhu 60-kh godov." *Sovremennyi mir*, no. 6 (1907), pp. 8-12.
Bakunin, Michael. *Gosudarstvennost i anarkhii, 1873*. Edited by Arthur Lehning. *Archives Bakounine*, vol. 3. Leiden, 1967.
———. *Michel Bakounine et ses relations avec Sergej Nečaev, 1870-1872: Ecrits et matériaux*. Edited by Arthur Lehning. Leiden, 1971. Vol. 4, *Archives Bakounine*.
———. *The Political Philosophy of Bakunin*. Edited by G. P. Maximoff. London, 1953.
Barghoorn, Frederick C. "The Philosophical Outlook of Chernyshevskii: Materialism and Utilitarianism." *Slavic Review* 6, nos. 18-19 (December 1947): 42-56.
Baron, Samuel H. *Plekhanov: The Father of Russian Marxism*. Stanford: Stanford University Press, 1963.
Baskakov, B. G. *Mirovozzrenie Chernyshevskogo*. Moscow, 1956.
Baturin, N. N. "Esche o tsvetakh russkogo iakobinstva." *Proletarskaia revoliutsiia*, no. 8 (43) (1925), pp. 97-109.
———. "O nasledstve russkikh iakobintsev." *Proletarskaia revoliutsiia*, no. 7 (30) (1924), pp. 82-89.

Belchikov, N. *Nikolai Gavrilovich Chernyshevskii: Kritikobiografi-cheskii ocherk.* Moscow, 1946.
——. "S. G. Nechaev v s. Ivanove v 1860-e gody." *Katorga i ssylka,* no. 14 (1925), pp. 134-56.
——. "Stikhotvornye opyty P. N. Tkacheva." *Russkaia literatura,* no. 4 (1958), pp. 178-87.
Bentham, Jeremy. *An Introduction to the Principles of Morals and Legislation.* Oxford, 1879.
Berdiaev, N. *Istoki i smysl russkogo kommunizma.* Paris, 1955.
Berezina, V. G.; Dementev, A. G.; Esin, B. I.; Zapadov, A. V.; and Sikorskii, N. M. *Istoriia russkoi zhurnalistiki XVIII-XIX vekov.* Moscow, 1963.
Bernstein, Eduard. *Ferdinand Lassalle as a Social Reformer.* London: S. Sonnenschein & Co., 1893.
——. "Karl Marks i russkie revoliutsionery." *Minuvshie gody,* no. 11 (1908), pp. 1-25.
Bernstein, Samuel. *Auguste Blanqui and the Art of Insurrection.* London: Lawrence and Wishart, 1971.
Billington, James H. *Mikhailovsky and Russian Populism.* Oxford: Clarendon Press, 1958.
Blanqui, Jerome Auguste. *Histoire de l'économie politique en Europe depuis les anciens temps jusqu'à nos jours.* Paris, 1837.
Blanqui, Louis Auguste. "Blanquis Anweisungen für den Strassen-kampf." Edited by Georges Bourgin. *Archiv für die Geschichte des Sozialismus und der Arbeiterbewegung* 15 (1930): 270-300.
——. *Critique sociale.* 2 vols. Paris, 1885.
——. *Izbrannye proizvedeniia.* Moscow, 1952.
Boborykin, P. D. "Za polevka." *Minuvshie gody,* nos. 5-6 (1908), pp. 38-58; no. 11 (1908), pp. 111-49; and continued in *Golos minuv-shego,* no. 3 (1913), pp. 172-205.
Bonch-Bruevich, V. "Biblioteka i arkhiv RSDRP v Zheneve." *Krasnaia letopis,* no. 48 (1932), pp. 113-15.
Bourdeau, Jean. *Le socialisme allemand et le nihilisme russe.* Paris, 1892.
Bowman, Herbert E. *Vissarion Belinski, 1811-1848: A Study in the Origins of Social Criticism in Russia.* Cambridge, Mass.: Harvard University Press, 1954.
Briullova-Shaskolskaia, N. V. "Lavrov i Mikhailovskii." In *P. L. Lavrov: Stati, vospominaniia, materialy.* Petrograd, 1922.
Burtsev, Vladimir L. *Za sto let (1800-1896).* London, 1897.

Bush, Vladimir Vladimirovich. *Ocherki literaturnogo narodnichestva 70-80 gg.* Leningrad, 1931.

Cannac, René. *Netchaiev: Du nihilisme au terrorisme.* Paris, 1961.

Carr, E. H. *Michael Bakunin.* London: Macmillan & Co., 1937.

Chernyshevskii, N. G. *Antropologicheskii printsip v filosofii.* Moscow-Leningrad, 1960.

———. *Polnoe sobranie sochinenii.* 16 vols. Moscow: Goslitizdat, 1939-53.

———. *Selected Philosophical Essays.* Moscow: Foreign Languages Publishing House, 1953.

———. *What Is to Be Done?* New York, 1909.

Christoff, Peter K. *The Third Heart: Some Intellectual-Ideological Cross-Currents in Russia.* The Hague: Mouton, 1970.

Cole, G. D. H. *Marxism and Anarchism, 1850-1890.* London and New York: Macmillan, 1961. Vol. 2 of his *History of Socialist Thought.*

Confino, Michael. *Violence dans la violence: Le débat bakounine-nečaev.* Paris: F. Maspero, 1973.

Coquart, Armand. *Dmitri Pisarev, 1840-1868, et l'idéologie du nihilisme russe.* Paris: Université Institut d'études slaves, 1946.

Costa, Charles da. *Les blanquistes.* Paris, 1912.

D——a. "Arest S. G. Nechaeva v Tsiurikhe: Po lichnym vospominaniiam." *Byloe,* no. 7 (1906), pp. 147-50.

Deiateli revoliutsionnogo dvizheniia v Rossii: Biobibliograficheskii slovar. 5 vols. Moscow, 1927-34.

Deich [Deutsch], Lev G. *Russkaia revoliutsionnaia emigratsiia 70-kh godov.* Petrograd, 1920.

———, ed. *Gruppa "Osvobozhdenie truda: Iz arkhivov G. V. Plekhanova, V. I. Zasulich, i L. G. Deicha.* 6 vols. Moscow, 1924-28.

Dobroliubov, Nikolai Aleksandrovich. *Selected Philosophical Essays.* Moscow: Foreign Languages Publishing House, 1956.

———. *Sobranie sochinenii.* 9 vols. Moscow, 1961-64.

Dommanget, Maurice. *Les idées politiques et sociales d'Auguste Blanqui.* Paris: M. Rivière, 1957.

Dostoevsky, Fedor. *Dostoevsky's Occasional Writings.* Edited by David Magarshack. New York: Random House, 1963.

———. *Notes from Underground and the Grand Inquisitor with Relevant Works by Chernyshevskii, Shchedrin, and Dostoevsky.* Edited by Ralph E. Matlaw. New York: Dutton, 1960.

———. *The Possessed.* New York: Random House, Modern Library, 1963.

——. *The Unpublished Dostoevsky: Diaries and Notebooks, 1860-1881.* Ann Arbor: Ardis, c. 1973.

Dragomanov, Michail, ed. *Michail Bakunins sozial-politischer Briefwechsel mit Alexander Iw. Herzen und Ogarjow.* Stuttgart, 1895.

Dzhabadari, I. S. "Protsess 50-ti." *Byloe,* no. 8 (20) (1907), pp. 1-24; no. 9 (21) (1907), pp. 169-92; no. 10 (22) (1907), pp. 168-97.

Dzhanshiev, G. *Epokha velikikh reform.* Moscow, 1900.

Engels, Friedrich. *Fridrik Engels o Rossii.* Geneva, 1894.

——. *Internationales aus dem Volksstaat.* Berlin, 1894.

——. *Soziales aus Russland.* Leipzig, 1875.

Entsiklopedicheskii slovar. 43 vols. St. Petersburg: F. A. Brockhaus and I. A. Efron, 1901-7.

Field, Daniel. "Kavelin and Russian Liberalism." *Slavic Review* 32, no. 1 (March 1973): 59-78.

Florinsky, Michael T. *Russia: A History and an Interpretation.* 2 vols. New York: Macmillan, 1958.

Frolenko, M. "Obshchestvo narodnogo osvobozhdeniia." *Katorga i ssylka,* no. 3 (88) (1932), pp. 81-100.

Galaktionov, Anatolii A., and Nikandrov, P. F. *Ideologi russkogo narodnichestva.* Leningrad, 1966.

Ginsberg, G. "Marks o Tkacheve." In *Gruppa "Osvobozhdenie truda,"* 4: 389-94. Edited by L. G. Deich. Moscow-Leningrad, 1926.

Girardin, Emile de. *Pensées et maximes.* Paris, 1867.

——. *La voix dans le désert.* Paris, 1870.

Goldenberg, L. B. "Vospominaniia L. B. Goldenberg." *Katorga i ssylka,* no. 10 (1924), pp. 88-105.

Gorev, Boris Isaakovich. "K voprosu o blankizme voobshche i russkom blankizme v chastnosti." *Voinstvuiushchii materialist,* bk. 4 (1925), pp. 101-17.

——. *Ogiust Blanki: Ego zhizn, revoliutsionnaia deiatelnost, i rol v istorii sotsializma.* Moscow, 1921.

—— and Kozmin, B. P., eds. *Revoliutsionnoe dvizhenie 1860-kh godov.* Moscow, 1932.

Gorodetskii, B. P.; Lavretskii, A.; and Meilakh, B. S., eds. *Istoriia russkoi kritiki.* Moscow-Leningrad, 1958.

Guillaume, James. *L'internationale: Documents et souvenirs (1864-1878).* 4 vols. Paris, 1905-10.

Hardy, Deborah. "Consciousness and Spontaneity, 1875: The Peasant Revolution Seen by Tkachev, Lavrov, and Bakunin." *Canadian Slavic Studies* 4, no. 4 (Winter 1970): 699-720.

——. "Tkachev and the Marxists." *Slavic Review* 29, no. 1 (March 1970): 22-34.

Herzen, Alexander. *My Past and Thoughts.* 4 vols. New York: Alfred A. Knopf, 1968.

—— [Gertsen, A. I.]. *Sobranie sochinenii v tridtsati tomakh.* 30 vols. Moscow, 1958-63.

Iakovlev, V. Ia. [Bazilevskii, B.; Bogucharskii, B.]. *Aktivnoe narodnichestvo semidesiatykh godov.* Moscow, 1912.

——. *Gosudarstvennye prestupleniia v Rossii v XIX veka: Sbornik.* 2 vols. Stuttgart, 1903-5.

——. *Iz istorii politicheskoi borby v 70- i 80-kh godov.* Moscow, 1912.

——, ed. *Materialy dlia istorii revoliutsionnogo dvizheniia v Rossii v 60-kh gg.* St. Petersburg, 1906.

——, ed. *Revoliutsionnaia zhurnalistika semidesiatykh godov.* Paris, 1905.

Iampolskii, I. G. "P. N. Tkachev kak literaturnyi kritik." *Literatura,* no. 1 (1931), pp. 31-60.

Illeritskii, V. E. *Istoriia Rossii v osveshchenii revoliutsionerov-demokratov.* Moscow, 1963.

Itenberg, Boris Sammilevich. *Dvizhenie revoliutsionnogo narodnichestva.* Moscow, 1966.

——. *Pervyi internatsional i revoliutsionnaia Rossiia.* Moscow, 1964.

Ivanchin-Pisarev, A. I. "Gleb Uspenskii i revoliutsionery 70-kh godov." *Byloe,* no. 10 (1907), pp. 44-58.

Ivanov-Razumnik, V. *Istoriia russkoi obshchestvennoi mysli.* St. Petersburg, 1914.

Karataev, N. K., ed. *Narodnicheskaia ekonomicheskaia literatura: Izbrannye proizvedeniia.* Moscow, 1958.

Karpovich, Michael. "Forerunner of Lenin: P. N. Tkachev." *Review of Politics* 6, no. 3 (July 1944): 336-50.

Kimball, Alan. "The First International and the Russian *Obshchina.*" *Slavic Review* 32, no. 3 (September 1973): 491-514.

——. "The Russian Past and the Socialist Future in the Thought of Peter Lavrov." *Slavic Review* 30, no. 1 (March 1971): 28-44.

Klevenskii, M. M. "P. N. Tkachev kak literaturnyi kritik." *Sovremennyi mir,* nos. 7-8 (1916), pp. 1-27.

Knizhnik, Ivan Sergeevich. *Russkie deiatelnitsy pervogo Internatsionala i Parizhskoi kommuny.* Moscow, 1964.

Kornilov, A. A. *Obshchestvennoe dvizhenie pri Aleksandr II (1855-1881): Istoricheskie ocherki.* Paris, 1905.

Koshovenko, A. E. "K voprosu o londonskoi vstreche N. G. Chernyshevskogo s A. I. Gertsenom v 1859 g. i formule 'Kavelin v kvadrate.' "

In *Revoliutsionnaia situatsiia v Rossii v 1859-1861 gg.* Moscow, 1960.

Kovalevskaia, Sofia Vasilevna. *Literaturnye sochineniia.* St. Petersburg, 1893.

———. *Vospominaniia detstva i avtobiograficheskie ocherki.* Moscow-Leningrad, 1945.

———. *Vospominaniia i pisma.* Moscow, 1951.

Kozmin, B. P. "G. E. Blagosvetlov i *Russkoe Slovo.*" *Sovremennik,* bk. 1 (1922), pp. 192-250.

———. *Iz istorii revoliutsionnoi mysli v Rossii.* Moscow, 1961.

———. "K istorii 'Molodoi Rossii.'" *Katorga i ssylka,* no. 66 (1930), pp. 52-70; no. 67 (1930), pp. 61-76.

———. "K istorii nechaevshchina." *Literaturnoe nasledstvo,* 41-42 (1941): 151-64.

———. "K istorii nechaevskogo protsessa." *Krasnyi arkhiv,* no. 6 (43) (1930), pp. 116-65.

———. "K voprosu otnoshenii P. N. Tkacheva marksizmu." *Literaturnoe nasledstvo,* 7-8 (1933): 117-23.

———. "Okolo nechaevskogo dela: Pamiati A. D. Dementevoi-Tka-chevoi." *Katorga i ssylka,* no. 6 (1923), pp. 55-63.

———. *Ot deviatnadtsatogo fevrialia k pervomu marta: Ocherki po istorii narodnichestva.* Moscow, 1933.

———. "P. N. Tkachev i narodnichestvo." *Katorga i ssylka,* no. 22 (1926), pp. 109-22.

———. *P. N. Tkachev i revoliutsionnoe dvizhenie 1860-kh godov.* Moscow, 1922.

———. *Revoliutsionnoe podpole v epokhu "Belogo terrora."* Moscow, 1929.

———. "S. G. Nechaev i ego protivniki." In *Revoliutsionnoe dvizhenie 1860-kh godov: Sbornik.* Moscow, 1932.

———. *Zhurnal "Sovremennik."* Moscow, 1957.

———, ed. *Nechaev i nechaevtsy: Sbornik materialov.* Moscow-Leningrad, 1931.

Kraineva, N. Ia. *Narodnichestvo v rabotakh sovetskikh issledovatelei za 1953-1970 gg.* Moscow, 1971.

Kravchinskii, S. M. [Stepniak]. *Underground Russia.* New York: Scribner's, 1883.

Kravtsov, N. "P. N. Tkachev: Pervyi kritik-marksist." *Na literaturnom postu,* no. 3 (1927), pp. 22-26.

Kruzhkov, V. S. *Mirovozzrenie N. A. Dobroliubova.* Moscow, 1950.

Kuhn, Alfred. "Dobroliubov's Critique of *Oblomov:* Polemics and Psychology." *Slavic Review* 30, no. 1 (March 1971): 93-109.

Kusheva, E. "Iz istorii 'Obshchestva narodnogo osvobozhdeniia.'"
    Katorga i ssylka, no. 4 (77) (1931), pp. 31-62.
Kuzmin, Dmitrii. *Narodovolcheskaia zhurnalistika*. Moscow, 1930.
Kuznetsov, Feliks. *Publitsisty 1860-kh godov: Krug "Russkogo slova":
    Grigorii Blagosvetlov, Varfolomei Zaitsev, Nikolai Sokolov*. Mos-
    cow, 1969.
Lampert, Evgenii. *Sons against Fathers: Studies in Russian Radicalism
    and Revolution*. Oxford: Clarendon Press, 1965.
――. *Studies in Rebellion*. London: Routledge & Kegan Paul, 1957.
Lavrov, Petr Lavrovich. *Historical Letters*. Translated and edited by
    James P. Scanlan. Berkeley and Los Angeles: University of Califor-
    nia Press, 1967.
――. *Izbrannye sochineniia ne sotsialno-politicheskie temy*. 4 vols.
    Moscow, 1934-35.
――. *Narodniki-propagandisty 1873-1878 gg*. St. Petersburg, 1907.
――. *P. L. Lavrov: Stati, vospominaniia, materialy*. Petrograd, 1922.
――. "Petr Nikitich Tkachev: Nekrolog." *Vestnik narodnoi voli* (Ge-
    neva) 5, pt. 2 (1886): 172-75.
Lehning, Arthur. *From Buonarroti to Bakunin: Studies in International
    Socialism*. Leiden: Brill, 1970.
――, ed. *Michel Bakounine et ses relations avec Sergej Nečaev, 1870-
    1872: Ecrits et matériaux*. Leiden, 1971. Vol. 4, *Archives Ba-
    kounine*.
Lemke, Mikhail. "Materialy dlia biografii P. N. Tkacheva." *Byloe*, no. 8
    (1907), pp. 156-72.
――. *Ocherki osvoboditelnogo dvizheniia "shesti-desiatykh godov."*
    St. Petersburg, 1908.
――. *Politicheskie protsessy v Rossii v 1860-kh godov: Po arkhivnym
    dokumentam*. Moscow-Leningrad, 1923.
Lenin, V. I. *Collected Works*. 4th ed. Moscow: Foreign Languages Pub-
    lishing House, 1960-65.
――. *Selected Works*. 3 vols. New York: International Publishers, 1967.
Livshits, S. "Podpolnye tipografii 60-kh, 70-kh i 80-kh godov." *Katorga
    i ssylka*, no. 41 (1928), pp. 23-33; no. 43 (1928), pp. 60-78; no. 50
    (1929), pp. 64-80; no. 51 (1929), pp. 57-74; no. 54 (1929), pp.
    60-74.
Lothe, Jean. *Gleb Ivanovič Uspensky et le populisme russe: Contribu-
    tion à l'histoire de la pensée et de la littérature populiste en russe,
    1870-1890*. Leiden, 1963.
Malia, Martin. *Alexander Herzen and the Birth of Russian Socialism*.
    New York: Grosset & Dunlap, 1965.
Malinin, Viktor Arsenevich. *Filosofiia revoliutsionnogo narodnichestva*.

Moscow, 1972.

Marx, Karl. *Capital: A Critique of Political Economy*. New York: Random House, n.d.

—— and Engels, Friedrich. *Werke*. 34 vols. Berlin, 1959-64.

Masaryk, Thomas Garrigue. *The Spirit of Russia: Studies in History, Literature, and Philosophy*. 2 vols. London: G. Allen & Unwin, 1961.

Maslin, A. I. *D. I. Pisarev v borbe za materializm i sotsialnyi progress*. Moscow, 1968.

Mathes, William L. "N. I. Pirogov and the Reform of University Government, 1856-1866." *Slavic Review* 31, no. 1 (March 1972): 29-51.

Matlaw, Ralph E., ed. *Belinsky, Chernyshevsky, and Dobrolyubov: Selected Criticism*. New York: Dutton, 1962.

Meijer, J. M. *Knowledge and Revolution: The Russian Colony in Zurich (1870-1873)*. Assen: Van Gorcum, 1955.

Mill, John Stuart. *Auguste Comte and Positivism*. Ann Arbor: University of Michigan Press, 1961.

——. *Principles of Political Economy with Some of Their Applications to Social Philosophy*. London, 1891.

——. *Utilitarianism, Liberty, and Representative Government*. New York, 1910.

Miller, Martin A. "The Formative Years of P. A. Kropotkin, 1842-1876." Ph.D. dissertation, University of Chicago, 1968.

——. "Ideological Conflicts in Russian Populism: The Revolutionary Manifestoes of the Chaikovsky Circle, 1869-1874." *Slavic Review* 29, no. 1 (March 1970): 1-21.

Mitskevich, S. I. "K voprosu o korniakh bolshevizma." *Katorga i ssylka*, no. 16 (1925), pp. 92-101.

——. "Russkie iakobintsy." *Proletarskaia revoliutsiia*, nos. 6-7 (18-19) (1923), pp. 3-26.

Molinier, Sylvain. *Blanqui*. Paris: Presses universitaires de France, 1948.

Morozov, N. A. *Povesti moei zhizni*. 3 vols. Moscow-Leningrad, 1947.

N——n, M. L. "N. V. Shelgunov v Kaluge: Po neizdannym dokumentam." *Golos minuvshego*, no. 11 (1915), pp. 240-73.

Nabat. Eighteen issues published. Geneva and London, 1875-79, 1881.

Nechkina, M. V., ed. *Revoliutsionnaia situatsiia v Rossii v 1859-1861 gg*. Moscow, 1960.

Nettlau, Max. "Bakunin und die russische revolutionäre Bewegung in den Jahren 1868-1873." *Archiv für die Geschichte des Sozialismus und der Arbeiterbewegung* 5 (1915): 357-422.

——. *Bibliographie de l'anarchie*. Brussels, 1897.

——. *Elisée Reclus, Anarchist und Gelehrter, 1830-1905*. Berlin, 1928.

——. *The Life of Michael Bakounine.* 3 vols. in folio. London, 1896-1900.

——. *Zhizn i deiatelnost Mikhaila Bkunina.* Petrograd, 1920.

Ni dieu, ni maître. Paris, 1880-81.

Nikiforov, L. P. "Moi tiurmy." *Golos minuvshego,* no. 5 (1914), pp. 186-88.

Nikitenko, Aleksandr Vasilevich. *Dnevnik.* 3 vols. Moscow, 1955.

——. *Zapiski i dnevnik.* 2 vols. St. Petersburg, 1905.

Nikolaevskii, B. "Materialy i dokumenty: Tkachev i Lavrov." *Na chuzhoi storone,* no. 10 (1925), pp. 187-93.

——. "Pamiati poslednego 'iakobintsa'-semidesiatnika: Gaspar Mikhail Turskii." *Katorga i ssylka,* no. 23 (1926), pp. 211-27.

——. "Varlaam Nikolaevich Cherkezov (1846-1925)." *Katorga i ssylka,* no. 25 (1926), pp. 222-32.

Nomad, Max. *Apostles of Revolution.* Boston: Little, Brown & Co., 1939.

Novikova, Nina Nikolaevna. *Revoliutsionery 1861 goda: "Velikoruss" i ego komitet v revoliutsionnoi borbe 1861 g.* Moscow, 1968.

Novyi entsiklopedicheskii slovar. 29 vols. St. Petersburg: F. A. Brockhaus and I. A. Efron, 1911-16.

Ogarev, N. P. *Izbrannye sotsialno-politicheskie i filosofskie proizvedeniia.* Moscow-Leningrad, 1952-56.

Ostashkina, Vera Spiridovna. *Dalekoe i nedavnee.* Moscow, 1930.

Payne, Robert. *The Fortress.* New York: Simon & Schuster, 1967.

——. *Zero: The Story of Terrorism.* New York: John Day & Co., 1950.

Piksanov, N. K. *Dva veka russkoi literatury.* Moscow-Petrograd, 1923.

Pipes, Richard A. "Narodnichestvo: A Semantic Inquiry." *Slavic Review* 23, no. 3 (September 1964): 441-58.

——. "Russian Marxism and Its Populist Background." *Russian Review* 19, no. 4 (1960): 316-37.

Pisarev, Dmitrii Ivanovich. *Selected Philosophical, Social, and Political Essays.* Moscow: Foreign Languages Publishing House, 1958.

Plekhanov, Georgii Valentinovich. *History of Russian Social Thought.* New York: H. Fertig, 1967.

——. *Sochineniia.* 24 vols. 3rd ed. Moscow, 1923-27.

Plotkin, L. A. *Pisarev i literaturno-obshchestvennoe dvizhenie shestidesiatykh godov.* Moscow-Leningrad, 1945.

Pokrovskii, M. N. *Ocherki russkogo revoliutsionnogo dvizheniia XIX-XX vv.* Moscow, 1924.

Pomper, Philip. "Nechaev and Tsaricide: The Conspiracy within the Conspiracy." *Russian Review* 33, no. 2 (April 1974): 123-38.

——. *Peter Lavrov and the Russian Revolutionary Movement.* Chicago and London: University of Chicago Press, 1972.

Popov, M. R. "Iz moego revoliutsionnogo proshlogo." *Byloe*, no. 5 (1907), pp. 269-305.

Potash, M. A. "Marks i Engels i narodnicheskii sotsializm." *Proletarskaia revoliutsiia*, no. 12 (1929), pp. 36-58.

———. *Narodnicheskii sotsializm*. Moscow, 1930.

Prawdin, Michael. *The Unmentionable Nechaev: A Key to Bolshevism*. New York: Roy, 1963.

Pribylev, A. V. "Neskolko slov o dvukh predstaviteliakh gruppy 'Nabat.' " *Katorga i ssylka*, nos. 84-85 (1931), pp. 105-11.

Prokhorov, G. "P. N. Tkachev ob izdatelskoi i literaturnoi deiatelnosti G. E. Blagosvetlova." In *Shestidesiatye gody: Materialy po istorii literatury i obshchestvennomu dvizheniiu*. Moscow-Leningrad, 1940.

Proudhon, P. J. *La guerre et la paix*. Paris, 1861.

Quételet, Lambert Adolphe Jacques. *Du systeme sociale et des lois qui le régissent*. Paris, 1848.

Quinet, Edgar. *La création*. Paris, 1870.

Ralli-Arbore, Zemfir. "Mikhail Aleksandrovich Bakunin: Iz moikh vospominanii." *Minuvshie gody*, no. 10 (1908), pp. 142-68.

———. "Sergei Gennadevich Nechaev: Iz moikh vospominanii." *Byloe*, no. 7 (1906), pp. 136-46. Also translated and reprinted in *Michel Bakounine et ses relations avec Sergej Nečaev, 1870-1872: Ecrits et matériaux*, edited by Arthur Lehning. Leiden, 1971.

Randall, Frances B. *N. G. Chernyshevskii*. Boston: Twayne Publishing, 1967.

Reclus, Elisée. *L'évolution, la révolution, et l'idéal anarchique*. Paris, 1898.

———. *L'homme et la terre*. Paris, 1905-8.

Reclus, Paul. *Les frères Elie et Elisée Reclus*. Paris, 1964.

Reiser, S. "Peterburgskie pozhary 1862 goda." *Katorga i ssylka*, no. 95 (1932), pp. 79-111.

Resis, Albert. "*Das Kapital* Comes to Russia." *Slavic Review* 29, no. 2 (June 1970): 219-37.

Reuel, A. L. "Ekonomicheskie vzgliady P. N. Tkacheva." *Problemy ekonomiki*, no. 4 (1938), pp. 142-61.

———. "Sotsialno-politicheskie vozzrenie P. N. Tkacheva." Nauchnye zapiski Moskovskogo finansovogo instituta, no. 8. Moscow, 1957.

Rogers, James Allen. "The Russian Populists' Response to Darwin." *Slavic Review* 22, no. 3 (September 1963): 456-69.

Rozental, M. *Filosofskie vzgliady N. G. Chernyshevskogo*. Moscow-Leningrad, 1948.

Russkii biograficheskii slovar. St. Petersburg, 1896-1918.
"S. G. Nechaev v Alekseevskom raveline v 1873-1883 gg." *Byloe*, no. 7 (1906), pp. 151-77.
Sazhin, M. P. [Arman Ross]. "Kratkaia aftobiografiia." *Katorga i ssylka*, no. 6 (1923), pp. 3-5.
——. "Pervoe znakomstvo s M. A. Bakuninym: Iz vospominanii." *Katorga i ssylka*, no. 26 (1926), pp. 9-19.
——. "Russkie v Tsiurike (1870-1873 gg.)." *Katorga i ssylka*, no. 95 (1932), pp. 20-78.
——. *Vospominaniia, 1860-1880 gg.* Moscow, 1925.
Schmidt, Wolf-Heinrich. *Nihilismus und Nihilisten: Untersuchungen zur Typisierung im russischen Roman der zweiten Hälfte des neunzehnten Jahrhunderts.* Munich, 1974.
Sedov, Mikhail Gerasimovich. *Geroicheskii period revoliutsionnogo narodnichestva.* Moscow, 1966.
Senkevich, V. M. "Problema khudozhestvennogo metoda v estetike P. N. Tkacheva." In *Teoriia i istoriia russkoi literatury.* Uchenye zapiski Moskovskogo gosudarstvennogo pedagogicheskogo instituta, vol. 190. Moscow, 1963.
——. "Tipisheskoe v realisticheskom iskusstve: K voprosu o tipicheskom v estetike P. N. Tkacheva." In *Teoriia i istoriia russkoi literatury.* Uchenye zapiski Moskovskogo gosudarstvennogo pedagogicheskogo instituta, vol. 190. Moscow, 1963.
Seth, Ronald. *The Russian Terrorists: The Story of the Narodniki.* London: Barrie & Rockliff, 1966.
Shelgunov, N. V. "Neizdannaia statia N. V. Shelgunova o Dobroliubovtsakh i Pisarevtsakh." *Literaturnoe nasledstvo*, 25-26: 402-3.
——; Shelgunov, L. P.; and Mihailov, M. L. *Vospominaniia.* 2 vols. Moscow-Leningrad, 1967.
Shestidesiatye gody: Materialy po istorii literatury i obshchestvennomu dvizheniiu. Moscow-Leningrad, 1940.
Sineira. "V poriadke diskussii: Eshche o marksizme i blankizme." *Pechat i revoliutsiia* 2 (1925): 105-14.
Skabicherskii, Aleksandr Mikhailovskii. *Belletristy-narodniki: F. Reshetnikov, Gl. Uspenskii, N. Zlatovratskii i pr.* St. Petersburg, 1888.
Sladkevich, N. G. *Ocherki istorii obshchestvennoi mysli Rossii v kontse 50-kh-nachale 60-kh godov XIX veka: Borba obshchestvennykh techenii v gody pervoi revoliutsionnoi situatsii.* Leningrad, 1962.
Smith, Adam. *Adam Smith's Moral and Political Philosophy.* Edited by Herbert W. Schneider. New York: Hafner Publishing Co., 1948.
——. *An Inquiry into the Nature and Causes of the Wealth of Nations.* New York, 1913.

Sokolov, Nikolai Ivanovich. *Russkaia literatura i narodnichestvo: Literaturnoe dvizhenie 70-kh gg. XIX v.* Leningrad, 1968.

Spasovich, V. "Piatidesiatiletie Peterburgskogo universiteta." *Vestnik Evropy* 5 (1870): 312-45.

Spencer, Herbert. *The Evolution of Society: Selections from Herbert Spencer's Principles of Sociology.* Edited by Robert L. Carneiro. Chicago and London: University of Chicago Press, 1967.

Spitzer, Alan B. *The Revolutionary Theories of Louis Auguste Blanqui.* New York: Columbia University Press, 1957.

Steklov, Iu. "Zapiska S. Serebrennikova o Nechaeve." *Katorga i ssylka,* no. 112 (1934), pp. 11-58.

Stewart, Neil. *Blanqui.* London, 1939.

Stukov, Iurii Innokentevich. *Revoliutsionnye narodniki i pervye rabochie-revoliutsionery Rossii serediny 60-kh-80-kh gg. XIX v.* Moscow, 1972.

Suvorov, P. P. "Zapiski o proshlom." *Russkoe obozrenie,* bk. 9 (1893), pp. 132-50.

Svatikov, S. "Studencheskoe dvizhenie 1869 goda: Bakunin i Nechaev." In *Nasha strana: Istoricheskii sbornik.* St. Petersburg, 1907.

Theen, Rolf H. W. *Lenin: Genesis and Development of a Revolutionary.* Philadelphia and New York: Lippincott, 1973.

———. "Nechaev's Auslieferung." *Jahrbuch Geschichte Osteuropas,* no. 4 (1973), pp. 573-83.

———. "Seizure of Political Power as the Prologue to Social Revolution: The Political Ideas of P. N. Tkachev in the Early 1870's." *Canadian Slavic Studies* 4, no. 4 (Winter 1970): 670-98.

Thun, Alphons. *Istoriia revoliutsionnogo dvizhenii v Rossii.* St. Petersburg, 1906.

Tikhomirov, Lev Aleksandrovich. *Russia, Political and Social.* 2 vols. London: S. Sonnenschein, Lowrey & Co., 1892.

———. *Vospominaniia Lva Tikhomirova.* Moscow-Leningrad, 1927.

Tkachev, Petr Nikitich. "Bibliografiia: 'Uchebnik ugolovnogo prava' sostavlennyi V. Spasovichem." *Biblioteka dlia chteniia,* no. 9 (September 1863), pp. 47-64.

———. "Geroi perekhodnoi epokhi." *Biblioteka dlia chteniia,* no. 12 (December 1864), pp. 1-29.

———. *Izbrannye literaturno-kriticheskie stati.* Moscow-Leningrad, 1928.

———. *Izbrannye sochineniia na sotsialno-politicheskie temy.* 6 vols. Edited by B. P. Kozmin. Moscow, 1932-36.

———. "Kladezi mudrosti rossiskikh filosofov." *Delo,* no. 10 (1878), pp. 1-30; no. 11 (1878), pp. 123-66.

———. "Mirovoi sud." *Vremia,* no. 11 (November 1862), pp. 74-87.

———. "Novye knigi." A monthly column of book reviews. *Delo*, no. 4 (April 1867) through no. 3 (March 1869), except no. 10 (October 1867) and no. 12 (December 1868). Reviews of special interest include those of works of Buckle (no. 8 [1867], pp. 76-78), Bentham (no. 12 [1867], pp. 47-72), Hegel (no. 5 [1868], pp. 72-77), Proudhon (no. 5 [1867], pp. 49-63), and Spencer (no. 5 [1867], pp. 63-69).

———. "O mirovykh sudiakh." *Vremia*, no. 7 (July 1862), pp. 83-92.

———. "O polze filosofii." *Delo*, no. 5 (1877), pp. 66-95.

———. "O sude po prestupleniiam protiv zakonov pechati." *Vremia* no. 6 (June 1862), pp. 40-50.

———. *Sochineniia v dvukh tomakh*. Edited by A. A. Galaktionov, V. F. Pustarnakov, and B. M. Shakhmatov. Vol. 1. Moscow, 1975.

———. "Tiurmy vo Frantsii: Ikh istoricheskoe razvitie i sovremennoe polozhenie." *Zhurnal Ministerstva iustitsii* 18, no. 11 (1863): 289-316.

———. "Utilitarnyi printsip nravstvennoi filosofii." Second article. *Delo*, no. 7 (1880), pp. 1-22; no. 8 (1880), pp. 317-41.

———. "Vliianie ekonomicheskogo progressa na polozhenie zhenshchiny i semi." *Zhenskii vestnik*, no. 2 (1866), pp. 67-84.

Troitskii, Nikolai Alekseevich. *Bolshoe obshchestvo propagandy 1871-1874 gg.: Tak nazyvaemye chaikovtsy*. Saratov, 1963.

Turgenev, Ivan. *Fathers and Sons*. New York: Signet Classic, n.d.

———. *Turgenev's Letters*. Edited by Edgar H. Lehrman. New York: Alfred A. Knopf, 1961.

Tursky, K. [Amari, A.]. *Idealizm i materializm v politike*. Geneva, 1877.

Tvardovskaia, V. A. "Istoricheskie kontseptsii revoliutsionnykh demokratov." *Novyi mir* 39, no. 9 (1963): 249-51.

———. "Problema gosudarstva v ideologii narodovolchestva 1879-1883 gg." *Istoricheskie zapiski* 74 (1963): 148-86.

Usakina, T. I. "Statia Gertsena 'Very Dangerous!!!' i polemika vokrug 'oblichitelnoi literatury' v zhurnalistike 1857-1859 gg." In *Revoliutsionnaia situatsiia v Rossii v 1859-1861 gg.*, edited by M. V. Nechkina. Moscow, 1960.

Uspenskaia, A. I. "Vospominaniia shestidesiatnitsy." *Byloe*, no. 18 (1922), pp. 19-45.

Uspenskii, F. "Peterburgskii universitet v 1867-1871 gg." *Dela i dni*, no. 1 (1920).

Valk, S. N., ed. *Arkhiv "Zemli i voli" i "Narodnoi voli."* Moscow, 1932.

———, et al., eds. *Revoliutsionnoe narodnichestvo 70-kh godov XIX veka: Sbornik dokumentov i materialov*. 2 vols. Moscow, 1964-65.

Vengerov, S. A. *Ocherki po istorii russkoi literatury*. 2nd ed. St. Petersburg, 1907.

Venturi, Franco. *Roots of Revolution: A History of the Populist and Socialist Movements in Nineteenth-century Russia*. New York: Alfred A. Knopf, 1960.

Vilenskaia, E. S. *Revoliutsionnoe podpole v Rossii, 60-e gody, XIX v.* Moscow, 1965.

Volk, S. S. *Narodnaia volia, 1879-1882 gg.* Moscow-Leningrad, 1966.

Walicki, Andrzej. *The Controversy over Capitalism: Studies in the Social Philosophy of the Russian Populists*. Oxford: Clarendon Press, 1969.

Weeks, Albert L. *The First Bolshevik: A Political Biography of Peter Tkachev*. New York and London: New York University Press, 1968.

Woehrlin, William F. *Chernyshevskii: The Man and the Journalist*. Cambridge, Mass.: Harvard University Press, 1971.

Wortman, Richard. *The Crisis of Russian Populism*. London: Cambridge University Press, 1967.

Yarmolinsky, Avrahm. *Road to Revolution: A Century of Russian Radicalism*. New York: Macmillan, 1959.

Zakharina, Vera Filippovna. *Golos revoliutsionnoi Rossii: Literatura revoliutsionnogo podpolia 70-kh godov XIX v.* Moscow, 1971.

Zaleski, E. *Mouvements ouvrières et socialistes*. Vol. 1, *La Russie*. Paris, 1956.

Zamiatin, V. N. *Ekonomicheskie vzgliady N. G. Chernyshevskogo*. Moscow, 1951.

Zasulich, Vera I. *Vospominaniia*. Moscow, 1931.

———. "Vospominaniia V. I. Zasulich." *Byloe*, no. 14 (1919), pp. 89-107.

Zevin, V. Ia. *Politicheskie vzgliady i politicheskaia programma N. G. Chernyshevskogo*. Moscow, 1953.

Zimmermann, Wilhelm. *Der grosse deutsche Bauernkrieg*. With an introduction by Friedrich Engels. Berlin, 1953.

Index

INSTITUTE FOR COMPARATIVE AND FOREIGN AREA STUDIES PUBLICATIONS ON RUSSIA AND EASTERN EUROPE

1. Peter F. Sugar and Ivo J. Lederer, eds. *Nationalism in Eastern Europe*. 1969. 487 pp., index.

2. W. A. Douglas Jackson, ed. *Agrarian Policies and Problems in Communist and Non-Communist Countries*. 1971. 485 pp., maps, figures, tables, index.

3. Alexander V. Muller, trans. and ed. *The* Spiritual Regulation *of Peter the Great*. 1972. 150 pp., index.

4. Ben-Cion Pinchuck. *The Octobrists in the Third Duma, 1907-1912*. 1974. 232 pp., bibliog., index.

5. Gale Stokes. *Legitimacy through Liberalism: Vladimir Jovanović and the Transformation of Serbian Politics*. 1975. 280 pp., maps, bibliog., index.

6. Canfield F. Smith. *Vladivostok under Red and White Rule: Revolution and Counterrevolution in the Russian Far East, 1920-1922*. 1975. 304 pp., maps, illus., bibliog., index.

7. Michael Palij. *The Anarchism of Nestor Makhno, 1918-1921: An Aspect of the Ukrainian Revolution*. 1976. 428 pp., map, illus., bibliog., index.

8. Deborah Hardy. *Petr Tkachev, the Critic as Jacobin*. 1977. 339 pp., illus., bibliog., index.